The New England
Transcendentalists
and the *Dial*

The New England Transcendentalists and the *Dial*

A History of the Magazine and Its Contributors

Joel Myerson

Rutherford • Madison • Teaneck
Fairleigh Dickinson University Press
London and Toronto: Associated University Presses

©1980 by Associated University Presses, Inc.

Associated University Presses, Inc.
Cranbury, New Jersey 08512

Associated University Presses
Magdalen House
136-148 Tooley Street
London SE1 2TT, England

Associated University Presses
Toronto M5E 1A7, Canada

Library of Congress Cataloging in Publication Data

Myerson, Joel.
   The New England transcendentalists and the Dial.

   Bibliography: p.
   Includes index.
   1. Dial (Boston) 2. Transcendentalists (New
England) — — Biography. I. Title.
PN4900.D52M9   051   78-66814
ISBN 0-8386-2294-1

PRINTED IN THE UNITED STATES OF AMERICA

To Virginia

Give your good project a fair trial. A year two years. It is of small matter if it should prove on the whole inexpedient. It has done you good if it has not mankind & so has given the state a better citizen for its next occasions.

Emerson's Journal
7 December 1829

Brag, & gasconade & prayer & prophecy, & blasphemy, and preaching, & contention and denunciation; Chardon Street & Bible, & Groton Conventions; Abolition Mobs, & meetings of Non-resistants, & of women; Committees, the Symposeum Club, & the Dial; Fruitlands, Brook Farm, Parkerism, Conversations, and Emerson; these were significant aspects of the time, and elements of the biography of its ruling spirits, looming forth from the canvass bold, & lurid, & serving to illustrate their ideas, endeavours, failures, and experiences.

Bronson Alcott's Journal
17 February 1850

Contents

Acknowledgments

In preparing a book that documents the acitivities of the Transcendentalists and their friends (and enemies) during a period of over four years, I have incurred many debts of gratitude. I would like to thank the many libraries and scholars who have given generously of their resources and time. Unhappily, in this small space I can thank only in a general way the more than 100 librarians who answered my questions about manuscripts and copies of the *Dial* at their libraries.

Most of the research from published sources was done at The Newberry Library, and I am indebted to Richard Colles Johnson, Arthur H. Miller, and James Wells for their help. W. H. Bond, Carolyn Jakeman, Marte Shaw, and the staff of the Houghton Library of Harvard University graciously extended every courtesy to me on my trips there. Marjorie Carpenter of the Northwestern University Library and Beverly Brooks and Claudia Drum of the University of South Carolina Library patiently looked for and found many books that otherwise would have been unavailable to me. I am equally grateful to these other institutions at which I worked and to the people who helped me there: Andover-Harvard Theological School Library (Alan Seaburg); Boston Public Library (James Lawton); Center for Research Libraries; Concord Free Public Library (Marcia Moss); Duke University Library; Fruitlands Museums (William Henry Harrison); Garrett Theological Seminary Library; Henry E. Huntington Library (William Ingoldsby); Massachusetts Historical Society (John D. Cushing); Meadville Theological Seminary Library; New York Public Library (Lola Szladits); Pierpont Morgan Library (Herbert Cahoon); Princeton University Library; Schlesinger Library of Radcliffe College (Mrs. Robert Shenton); Southern Illinois University Library (Thomas J. Jackson); State Historical Society of Wisconsin; Unitarian Universalist Association (Christopher Raible); University of Chicago Library; University of North Carolina Library; University of Wisconsin Library; and Widener Library of Harvard University.

Like all students of Emerson, I owe a great debt to Ralph L. Rusk for his superb edition of Emerson's letters. The late William H. Gilman kindly granted me permission to see the galley proofs for the new edition of Emerson's journals of which he was general editor. Eleanor M. Tilton and Robert N. Hudspeth graciously allowed me free access to the materials they have assembled in preparing their forthcoming editions of, respectively, Emerson's and Fuller's letters. I also wish to thank for their aid Thomas Blanding, Matthew J. Bruccoli, Robert E. Burkholder, Charles R. Crowe, John Olin Eidson, Frederic Faverty, David Hill, Elizabeth Maxfield-Miller, F. DeWolfe Miller, Burton R. Pollin, Ernest Samuels, Merton M. Sealts, G. Thomas Tanselle, Robert L. Volz, and Elizabeth Witherell. Stephen Garrison assisted in reading proofs.

Manuscripts at the Houghton Library are printed by permission of the Harvard College Library. I am equally grateful to the following for permission to quote from manuscripts and printed texts: Andover-Harvard Theological School Library; Bangor Historical Society (deposit collection at the Bangor Public Library); Belknap Press of the Harvard University Press; Billerica Historical Society; Boston Public Library; Brown University Library; Columbia University Press; Cornell University Library; Essex Institute Library; Fruitlands Museums; Henry E. Huntington Library; Isabelle Stuart Gardner Museum; Library of Congress; Louisiana State University Library; Massachusetts Historical Society; Meadville Theological School Library; The Newberry Library; New York Public Library (Astor, Lenox and Tilden Foundations); New York University Library; New York University Press; Pierpont Morgan Library; Ralph Waldo Emerson Memorial Association (David Emerson); Redwood Library and Athenaeum; Schlesinger Library of Radcliffe College; Scripps College Library; Sterling Library of the University of London; University of Chicago Library; University of Texas Library; University of Virginia Library (Clifton Waller Barrett Library); Vassar College Library; Wellesley College Library; and Yale University Library (Beinecke Rare Book and Manuscript Library).

Portions of three chapters have been revised from earlier printed appearances. I am grateful to the following for permission to use material first printed there: *ESQ: A Journal of the American Renaissance*, for "A History of the Transcendental Club" (1977); *Harvard Library Bulletin*, for "Frederic Henry Hedge and the Failure of Transcendentalism" (1975); and *Southwest Review*, for "'A True & High Minded Person': Transcendentalist Sarah Clarke" (1974).

I am grateful to the Woodrow Wilson Foundation for granting me a dissertation year fellowship, and to the American Philosophical Society and the National Endowment for the Humanities for providing research grants that greatly facilitated the completion of my research and the preparation of the manuscript.

Barry V. Qualls read the first draft of this book; his exactness and knowledge of style contributed much toward making the second draft better. Harrison Hayford aided and encouraged me at all stages of this project; his friendship, his example, and his many incisive comments were all needed and appreciated. I am fortunate to work at an institution that actively encourages and aids scholarship. My thanks also go to Bert Dillon, John C. Guilds, William H. Nolte, and the late John R. Welsh for their help and support.

Introduction

The *Dial* was a quarterly journal published in Boston from July 1840 to April 1844 by the Transcendentalists. It was edited by Margaret Fuller, George Ripley, Ralph Waldo Emerson, and — for one issue — Henry David Thoreau. In 1902 George Willis Cooke published a two-volume study of the *Dial*. The length of this study and Cooke's credentials as Emerson's bibliographer and first American biographer apparently discouraged other scholars from undertaking a new study of the same subject. But most of the material in Cooke's work, with the exception of a few personal communications from some of the *Dial*'s contributors, was reprinted from earlier studies of the Transcendentalists. And despite the commonly recognized importance of the *Dial*, neither the many contemporary accounts and comments, by participants and other writers, nor later scholarly studies have given an adequate account of it.

This book, then, is a history of the *Dial* and its contributors. It covers the founding of the magazine, the publication of successive numbers, the shifting editorial policies, the relations of editors and contributors, the varying contemporary reception, and the eventual demise of the magazine. So far as possible the book focuses on the external history of the magazine, which has never been told in detail, rather than on the philosophical or aesthetic views of the editors and contributors, which have already been examined rather thoroughly elsewhere.

The *Dial* has been called "caviare to the general . . . a butt of ridicule for the irreverent, [and] a mystification to the uninitiated" reader.[1] Many of the uninitiated have approached the topic of the *Dial* almost as if it were a folktale and have produced a series of errors about the magazine that this book seeks to correct. For example, the *Dial*'s publication dates have variously been given as 1840-45, 1840-43, 1841-43, and 1841-44. Sometimes it was a monthly magazine, yet it contained fifteen numbers. It was published by Elizabeth Peabody either during all of its existence or only for its last two years. The *Dial* has been described as being started by Ripley and either supported by the members of the Transcendental Club, who took turns in editing it, or functioning as the official organ of Brook Farm, where it was published. An unusually

11

large number of people were erroneously supposed to have been contributors to the *Dial*, including the Reverend William Ellery Channing, Orestes A. Brownson, William Wetmore Story, John Weiss, Horace Greeley, Oliver Wendell Holmes, Nathaniel Hawthorne, Julia Ward Howe and her husband William Page, Thomas Wentworth Higginson, the associationist Charles Sears, Cyrus A. Bartol, Ednah Dow Cheney, and Marston Watson; even a "Miss S. S. Jacobs" of Cambridge was included as a contributor in one account.

A number of the *Dial*'s actual contributors failed to elaborate in later years on their connection with the magazine, and James Russell Lowell even completely forgot that he had written for it. Others had better memories. Bronson Alcott held Conversations on the *Dial*, and Theodore Parker remembered it as the journal established by the "movement party," wherein "their wisdom and folly rode together on the same saddle." John Sullivan Dwight believed that it told "the time of days so far ahead," and George William Curtis, though thinking it "a little crude and excessive," thought that it had had "a profound and humane influence." Frederic Henry Hedge, even though he had at first avoided association with it, prized his set of the *Dial* as among "the choicest treasures" of his library, and to those who scoffed at the magazine he asked: "Would Mammon have the goodness to aid an enterprise whose spirit rebuked his methods and imperilled his assets?" James Freeman Clarke called it "a wild-bugle note, — a reveillé summoning all generous hearts to look toward the coming day," even though Emerson, he added, sometimes had difficulty perceiving that the *Dial*'s eccentric contributors were not always "originalities, but sometimes only poor imitations of himself." For his own part, Emerson was almost totally silent. In 1873 he turned down a request to write an entry on the *Dial* for *Johnson's New Universal Cyclopædia*. Indeed, probably his only published account was a statement that it was "a work of friendship" whose "writers were its chief readers" during its four years of "obscurity."[2]

Emerson should have known better: he was later involved in a number of attempts to reprint writings from the *Dial*. In 1845 John Chapman corresponded with him about publishing in England a volume made up of his poems "scattered in the Dial & elsewhere." In that same year Evert A. Duyckinck, acting on behalf of Wiley & Putnam's Library of Choice Reading, asked Emerson to select a volume of Landor's writings, to be prefaced by his *Dial* essay on him. Duyckinck even suggested making up a volume solely from the more popular papers in the *Dial*. In 1846 Chapman sent Emerson his *Characteristics of Men of Genius*, which reprinted some essays of "high moral and spiritual tone" from the *Dial* and other magazines, and Emerson thanked him for the "unlooked for honour."[3]

Another posthumous honor of sorts for Emerson was the frequent reference to the *Dial* in the published writings of his famous contemporaries. In "Some Words with a Mummy" (1845) Edgar Allan Poe had his narrator attempt to explain "Metaphysics" to that ancient Egyptian personage by reading a few chapters from the *Dial* about "something which is not very clear, but which the

Bostonians call the Great Movement or Progress." The mummy, needless to say, remained wrapped in ignorance. While instructing his readers "How to Write a Blackwood Article" (1845), Poe mentioned that to assume "the tone transcendental" a "little reading of the 'Dial' will carry you a great way." Finally, in giving Hawthorne advice in 1847 on how to improve his writing, Poe suggested that he forgo "Mr. Alcott" and "hang (if possible) the editor of 'The Dial.'" Hawthorne did nothing of the sort; when Miles Coverdale is taken to a sick bed in *The Blithedale Romance* (1852), he passes the time by reading Emerson, Carlyle, and the *Dial*, all of whose utterances, said Hawthorne, were "like the cry of some solitary sentinel, whose station was on the outposts of the advance-guard of human progression." Although it is unlikely that Melville had the *Dial* in mind, as has been suggested, when he referred in *Pierre* (1856) to the "Spinozaist" magazine, which contained "the Ultimate Transcendentals," Louisa May Alcott certainly did when she mentioned *"The Transcendental Tripod"* read by the characters in her "Transcendental Wild Oats" (1873).[4]

In 1882, in the midst of a revival of interest in Margaret Fuller, and probably at Bronson Alcott's suggestion, Roberts Brothers announced that it would, for fifteen dollars, reprint the *Dial* if it could be assured of 200 subscribers; only half that number responded and the project was abandoned. Cooke, who had prepared a "full historical account" of the *Dial* for Roberts Brothers, published his findings instead in the *Journal of Speculative Philosophy* three years later. It was not until 1902 that a book fanciers' club in Cleveland reprinted the complete *Dial* and Cooke's study to accompany it.[5] Until now, no study of the *Dial* has attempted to tell its full history by using both the original manuscript sources that were available to Cooke and those which have come to light since his study.

The New England Transcendentalists and the *Dial*

Part 1 History of the *Dial*

1
The Transcendental Club and the *Dial*

When Harvard University held its bicentennial celebration in September 1836, the oldest graduate present was the Reverend Ezra Ripley of Concord, Massachusetts. Though almost ninety, Ripley spoke with a rich and powerful voice to those at the ceremony. In the audience his relative, Ralph Waldo Emerson, watched as Ripley shared the platform with President Josiah Quincy of Harvard and Governor Edward Everett of Massachusetts. Rather than remaining for the fireworks display, Emerson left after the ceremonies to meet some friends at Willard's Hotel.

Emerson has been anticipating this meeting since June, when his friend Frederic Henry Hedge, a minister at Bangor, Maine, had invited him and two other Unitarian ministers to form a "symposium" to discuss the mood of the times. Hedge had talked with George Putnam, minister at Roxbury, Massachusetts, and George Ripley, Emerson's cousin and minister at Purchase Street in Boston, and they wished to assemble "certain likeminded persons of our acquaintance for the free discussion of theological & moral subjects." The three had recently attended a meeting of the Unitarians where they had been struck by "the lamentable want of courage shown by the members in their discussion of subjects, & the utter neglect of truth for expedients." The proposed "symposium" would be informal: "No constituion, no offices, no formal debates were deemed expedient, conversation alone is contemplated, which an occasional 'reference to the side table' might perhaps render more glib." Emerson agreed with Hedge, and it was decided to use Harvard's bicentennial celebration as the occasion for their first meeting.[1]

Discussion clubs were common in this period; even Concord, where Emerson lived, had its exclusive Social Circle, which, even before Emerson was admitted, had elected a tavern-keeper, a gunsmith, and a farmer. Other clubs were more literary in intent, and one of these, under the guidance of the aspiring Margaret Fuller, had been formed in Cambridge, Massachusetts; besides Hedge, its members included two Harvard Divinity School students, James Freeman Clarke and William Henry Channing, and another well-known bluestocking, Elizabeth Palmer Peabody. When Channing and Clarke were living in Cincinnati, Ohio, in 1835, they had helped to establish a similar group there. Emerson was therefore not surprised, and indeed quite happy, when Hedge asked for his help in forming a new club.[2]

Emerson stood at the beginning of a new career, as the publication that same week of his first book, *Nature*, indicated. Ever since the death of his father in 1811, just two weeks short of his eighth birthday, Emerson's life had borne little resemblance to that which as a minister's son he might have expected. Rather than enter divinity school immediately upon his graduation from Harvard in 1821, Emerson had taught school and continued as a resident graduate until his formal admission four years later. He was officially ordained at the prestigious Second Church in Boston in March 1829, and in September he married Ellen Louisa Tucker. Their happiness was short-lived, for she died in February 1831, and by October of the next year Emerson, torn by doubts about the church and still grieving over his lost wife, resigned his pulpit and went to Europe. Upon his return in October 1834, he embarked upon a new career as a lecturer and settled in Concord. Yet the alternation of sadness and happiness in his life continued: in the same month that he moved to Concord his brother Edward died; in 1835 he became a successful lecturer and married Lydia Jackson; but in the next year he buried his brother Charles. The new club, Emerson hoped, would represent another upward turn.

When they met in Cambridge on 8 September 1836, the four men agreed that the present state of philosophy and theology was very unsatisfactory, and they wished to discuss what, if anything, could be done to protest against the old ideas and to promote the new ones. Specifically, they objected to the sensuous philosophy of John Locke, which was then the prevailing belief. They preferred instead the transcendental or spiritual philosophy of Samuel Coleridge, which had created "a ferment" in their minds, and they wished to see whether and how these new ideas could be given a wider circulation. The discussion was encouraging, and Ripley volunteered his home for another meeting, to which more people were to be invited.[3]

The new participants at the second meeting were all ministers except thirty-six-year-old Bronson Alcott, a self-educated farmer's son who had raised himself from a pedlar to an educator and who was now running the innovative Temple School in Boston.[4] Emerson had sponsored Alcott for membership, and the two were good friends. Orestes A. Brownson, a vigorous reformer, was also added, despite the common knowledge of his egotism and his reluctance to give opposing views a hearing.[5] Clarke, in town during his annual trip from Ohio, was also invited. The last and, at forty-one, the oldest member was Convers Francis, a Unitarian minister at Watertown, Massachusetts, who had known Emerson for many years.[6]

At three o'clock on Monday, 19 September 1836, this group of seven men — Putnam had been unable to come — met at Ripley's house in Boston.

Amos Bronson Alcott.

Collection of Joel Myerson.

Emerson, recalling Hedge's original invitation', dubbed the group the "Symposeum." The tone of dissent that was to become the hallmark of these meetings was quickly established as Emerson described the best talents of the day — Washington Allston and Horatio Greenough in art, William Cullen Bryant in poetry, and the Reverend William Ellery Channing in religion — as having a *"feminine* or receptive" cast of mind, as opposed to a "masculine or creative" one. Francis, who as eldest member had been given the position of moderator, asked the various members for their opinions; and, as Alcott noted, "there was seldom an inclination on the part of any to be silent."

The only steadfast rule adopted by the club was that "no man should be admitted whose presence excluded any one topic." Emerson liked the group's earnestness and felt that the conversation inspired hope. One promising sign was the decision to extend invitations to a number of people whose views the club as a whole opposed. Thus the Reverend Channing, who was wary of the new forces rising up in the Unitarian church, the aristocratic Jonathan Phillips, and James Walker, another conservative Unitarian, were invited. Walker, whose position as editor the *Christian Examiner* made him a major force, was asked after the club had tried, without success, to decide between starting a journal of its own in which to forward its views or working through existing ones. Other ministers, more friendly to the club's aims, were also asked. Alcott volunteered his house for the next meeting, and at seven o'clock, four hours after the conversation had started, they adjourned. Later, at home, Alcott opened his journal and entered: "What good may come to us, and to our *people*, time must unfold."[7]

When the third meeting convened at Alcott's on the afternoon of 3 October 1836, a program of sorts had been planned, and the discussion centered around the topic "American Genius — the causes which hinder its growth, and give us no first rate productions." Again the meeting was a success: Alcott considered the discussion lively and interesting, and Francis thought that many admirable points had been made. Emerson was favorably impressed, especially liking Alcott's statement that every man is a genius. He must have given Alcott support during the discussion, for Alcott thought well of Emerson's contributions, too. Before the company broke up, they decided to meet two weeks later to discuss the "Education of Humanity."[8]

After another meeting in November 1836 the club's activities began to decline. Some members returned to their homes for the winter while others, like Emerson, had their own projects to occupy them. The next major gathering was not until the following spring when Hedge came to Boston for a few weeks. Ripley and Francis then suggested that the club reassemble, and Alcott set about gathering together the old members and inviting new ones. Except for himself, Alcott again limited the company to ministers, hoping that their interaction would be healthful and would "give unity to the action of all." Alcott felt very privileged, for he was in touch with the finest minds of the time. As soon as the date for the meeting had been decided upon, Alcott informed Emerson who would attend and urged him to come "prepared to give us free and bold speech as usual."[9]

When the club met at Ripley's on 29 May 1837, all of the regular members were among the eleven men present. Because Hedge's appearance in Boston had provided the spark for the meeting, others followed Emerson's lead in referring to the group as "Hedge's Club."[10] This meeting was really the first one with important consequences. Earlier discussions had been general, but this time matters that deeply involved all were taken up: "[W]hat is the essence of *religion* as distinct from morality, — what are the features of the present time as to religion." Emerson's answer — that religion was "the emotion of shuddering delight and awe from the perception of the infinite" — pleased many but not all. Disturbed by the general reform-minded tone that the group took, Putnam left and never returned. Brownson, whose personality had proved abrasive, did not disappoint many when he, too, withdrew after this meeting. To him, their philosophy sounded like pantheism, which he feared would eventually lead to infidelity.

Since these were the only losses, Emerson felt that "rivers of encouragement" flowed from the meeting.[11]

Soon, however, bitter foreshadowings of the future opposition to the club's ideas were seen. Alcott had published a book of conversations with his pupils earlier that year, and the Boston press had vigorouly attacked him and his unorthodox ideas. Andrews Norton, the leading conservative Unitarian of the day, said of the book that one-third was absurd, one-third blasphemous, and one-third obscene. Parents began withdrawing their children, and Alcott was forced to close down his Temple School. The city's teachers and preachers continued to revile him for most of the summer, and Alcott remained deeply despondent.

At about the same time, Margaret Fuller had invited Emerson to address the school in Providence, Rhode Island, where she was teaching, and on 17 June 1837 he gave a lecture on education there. Its reception was also indicative of things to come. A correspondent for the *Providence Daily Journal* was very disappointed in the address, saying that while he had admired the "intelligible parts" of Emerson's speech, he could not possibly understand those sections tainted with "Germano-*Sartor-Resartus-ism*." This person was not alone, Fuller told Alcott, and she felt that Emerson's "good words" had fallen on "stony soil."[12]

The Transcendental Club met three times during that summer, which ended with Emerson delivering his address on "The American Scholar" before Harvard's Phi Beta Kappa Society. His oration was not only controversial but poorly timed. Francis Bowen was currently subjecting Emerson's *Nature* to a scathing review in the *Christian Examiner* and in passing was thoroughly condemning the American Transcendentalists. No doubt both liberals and conservatives alike recognized Emerson's careful distinction between "Man Thinking" and the "bookworm" and realized which term was meant to apply to themselves. Although twenty-eight-year-old Oliver Wendell Holmes jokingly considered the address further evidence that "the transcendental nose was one that stretches outward and upward to attain a fore-smell of the Infinite," few others missed its future significance to American literary independence.[13] Both the Transcendentalists and the conservative Unitarians had previously been rather temperate toward each other; then Bowen's review had opened a breach, which Emerson's address widened. The war of words soon began in earnest, and the conservative Unitarians closed the pages of their influential journals to the Transcendentalists. Forced back upon their own resources, the rebellious ministers planned to use the Transcendental Club as their forum.

Emerson's address had brought to a head and out into the open the often heated debate between the conservative Unitarians and the liberal Unitarians, or Transcendentalists, that had been building over the last decade. There were three particular areas of conflict: literature, philosophy, and religion.

In literature the Transcendentalists championed English and continental writers such as Thomas Carlyle and Goethe. Emerson published Carlyle in America, and Ripley introduced continental authors in his series of *Specimens of Foreign Standard Literature*. "The word 'standard' was a deliberate assertion,"

Ralph Waldo Emerson.

Collection of Joel Myerson.

as Perry Miller noted, "as against Norton and Bowen, that what they still regard-ed as the 'new' and suspect literature of Europe had already become, in the capitals of culture, 'standard.'" Yet, dissention existed within the ranks of the Transcendentalists, and Brownson soon complained that American literature should not look toward "great men," as "Mr. Emerson and his friends" propose, but should instead "appeal to the mass, wake up just sentiments, quicken elevated thoughts in them, and direct their attention to great and noble deeds; the literature will follow as a necessary consequence."[14]

In philosophy the Transcendentalists followed Immanuel Kant in believing that man had an innate ability to perceive that his existence transcended mere sensory experience, as opposed to the prevailing belief of Locke that the mind was a blank tablet at birth that later registered only those impressions perceived through the senses and experience. From the writings of Sampson Reed in the 1820s came the idea of correspondence — that every object was a microcosm of the vast spiritual force later named by some the Oversoul — and an early for-mulation of the concept of organic style — that the artist produces his work by giving expression to the forms of nature rather than by imposing an artificial ar-rangement upon nature. The Transcendentalists also took much from the idealism of Victor Cousin.[15]

Finally, in religion the Transcendentalists were on dangerous ground. In 1828 the Reverend Channing had said that "man has a kindred nature with God, and may bear most important and ennobling relations to him." Now, less than a decade later, Channing and his fellow Unitarians were being accused of perpetrating a monstrous duplicity, centering on the question of the accuracy or believability of the miracles that Christ was said to have performed. William Henry Furness proposed in 1836 that, if all nature was truly seen as miraculous, then no specific phenomenon could be more so; hence, to believe in miracles was at once a denial of the miraculous everywhere and a mere skepticism based upon Locke's ideas. In response, Orville Dewey described man as too fallible a creature to discern the truth of Christianity without the evidences provided by miracles.

The conservative Unitarians were now caught in the middle: they had, in denying Calvinism, dedicated themselves to a lofty concept of man, but they refused to glorify him as did the Transcendentalists, who believed that he could attain religion without miracles or supernatural assistance. By placing their elders in this position the Transcendentalists were also accusing them of literally robbing man of his dignity even more shamefully, because more slyly, than the Calvinists had.

The Unitarian response was circumspect: Norton loftily announced that the Transcendentalists, many of whom had taken his courses in the Harvard Divinity School, were simply not competent to speak on such matters, and that their school was characterized by "the most extraordinary assumption, united with great ignorance, and incapacity for reasoning"; Bowen called Transcendentalism an un-American fad, and its adherents arrogant and dogmatic. Ripley led the counterattack by responding to Norton with a plea for intellectual freedom, and by answering Bowen that Harvard itself was so isolated that it failed to see that Transcendentalism was indeed the sentiment of the land. Brownson carried the issue of Harvard's isolation one step further, saying that the battle was social as well as religious, with the aristocratic institutions of the Unitarian church arrayed against the democratic principles of the Transcendentalists; the Unitarians were now themselves accused of being anti-American.

The battle raged, lasting into the 1840s, when Theodore Parker summed up the Transcendentalists' position thus:

> Their [i.e., miracles'] connection with Christianity appears accidental: for if Jesus had taught at Athens, and not at Jerusalem; if he had wrought no miracle, and none but the human nature had ever been ascribed to him; if the Old Testament had forever perished at his birth, — Christianity would still have been the word of God; it would have lost none of its truths. . . . So if it could be proved—as it cannot—in opposition to the greatest amount of historical evidence ever collected on any similar point, that the Gospels were the fabrication of designing and artful men, that Jesus of Nazareth had never lived, still Christianity would stand firm, and fear no evil.

In short, the word and spirit—the teachings—of Christ gave Christianity its validity, and not any mere, and unprovable, "supernatural" actions.[16]

Many weeks before his address at Cambridge, Emerson had planned to give a picnic for the Transcendental Club and many of his own friends in Concord on the following day. The host felt that under such circumstances the "rules" of the club might be let down, and "who knows but the . . . more timid or more gracious may crave the aid of wise & blessed women at their session." Thus when the club met on 1 September 1837, its ranks were temporarily swollen by the addition of Emerson's friends, among whom was twenty-seven-year-old Sarah Margaret Fuller.[17]

From her birth Fuller had been raised to take full advantage of an excellent education.[18] An omnivorous reader, her study of German had brought her to Hedge's attention. She moved with her family to Cambridge in the early 1830s and soon had met most of the people who would become involved with the Transcendental Club and the *Dial*. When her plans for a European trip collapsed after her father's death in 1835, she supported her family by teaching. A brilliant conversationalist, she realized that her position in life would have been different and much higher had she been a man. She therefore set for herself the task of competing with men on purely intellectual terms, hoping that by showing her attainments in that area she would be accepted as an equal. Although she nearly succeeded in her plan, many felt that she had sacrificed the traditional concept of femininity, and Fuller's ego sometimes showed to others "the presence of a rather mountainous ME."[19] Still, at this time she was just becoming known, and she had the full support of Emerson, Alcott, and her old friend Hedge.

Fuller had first been brought to Emerson's attention by Hedge. She had wanted to meet Emerson ever since Hedge had praised him to her in 1834, and in the next year she was pleased to find out that Emerson was also interested in seeing her. The death of her father delayed their meeting, and they did not meet until the summer of 1836 when she stayed with him at Concord for three weeks. At first Emerson had thought the visit would be a failure: "Her extreme plainness, — a trick of incessantly opening and shutting her eyelids, — the nasal tone of her voice, — all repelled; and I said to myself, we shall never get far." But the visit turned out to be a great success, and Emerson decided that she was "a very accomplished & very intelligent person," though he was slightly bothered by her egotism. The following summer Fuller returned and gave him, rather against his will, lessons in German pronunciation. Believing that this visit had placed her on a more equal footing with Emerson, she began writing very breezy and familiar letters to her surprised friend.[20]

Fuller also made a favorable impression on the other members of the Transcendental Club, and she was invited to its next meeting on 5 September 1837. Soon afterward the club again disbanded for the winter. During this period of inactivity the earlier indignant attitude of the public toward Transcendentalism was beginning to be complemented somewhat by an air of ridicule. Whereas previously the public really did not know what Transcendentalism was, except that it was "dreamy, mystical, crazy, and infideleterious to religion," now people such as Almira Barlow described it — "with a wave of her hand" — as *A little beyond.* Everybody had a distinct idea, plan, or project,

Margaret Fuller.

Schlesinger Library.

and no two persons could be found in agreement on any. With so many people pursuing such varied courses of action, it was inevitable that some should go down poorly chosen paths. Alcott, especially, had a singular ability to draw laughter; tramping through the backwoods areas to hand out copies of his and Emerson's writings, he modestly labeled himself a "Missionary of Human Culture."[21]

The end result of all this was that certain aspects of Transcendentalism were slowly becoming objects of public laughter.[22] The Transcendentalists tended to think of themselves as members of a "New School" in literature, philosophy, and religion, inside of which each individual had the right to pursue his own goals. To them, Transcendentalism was the collective name applied to the views of those who opposed existing institutions, especially within the church, which stood in the way of progress. Since each member had different means of approaching his ultimate goal, they rejected any attempt to link their disparate methods under some glib appellation. When the Transcendental Club started meeting again, most of the subjects discussed were topics with which the general public had connected the Transcendentalists; by getting together to discuss public criticisms of their actions the members hoped to be able to defend themselves better in the future.

Consequently, when the Club met on 20 May 1838, one of the subjects it took up was "Is mysticism an element of Christianity?" Most of those present agreed that in the broadest sense Jesus was a mystic who used a "universal tongue" that was understood by all honest men. Yet as the conversation wore on, the participants also agreed that Jesus technically was not a mystic, since he "did not impose his own special views of things on others, by means of special symbols." Alcott was particularly elated by this meeting because his statements were listened to with some degree of respect and not with the public ridicule to which he had become accustomed since the Temple School episode. The young radical preacher Parker was also favorably impressed with this and the "noble" meeting held a week later.[23]

Summer again brought with it a number of events that would prove upsetting to the Transcendental Club. Concerned by his congregation's complaints about his association with the Transcendentalists, Hedge elected to stay in Bangor. Alcott, who usually made arrangements for the club's meetings, was in a depressed state over Emerson's recent decision not to publish his "Psyche," a description of the spiritual development of his young daughters.[24] But the major incident was Emerson's Divinity School Address, delivered on 15 July 1838. As soon as the oration was published in August, the conservative Unitarians, led by Norton, lashed out at it, and, though Emerson himself remained aloof from the resulting controversy, both Parker and Ripley leaped into the fray on behalf of the New School.[25]

One common charge brought against the Transcendentalists was that of pantheism. Not surprisingly then, at the club's meeting in mid-November 1838, this topic was the subject for a discussion — which Alcott at first thought "free, bold, and, sometimes profound" — with himself, Emerson, and John Sullivan Dwight illustrating the "doctrines of the Godhead."[26] The meeting began with Alcott defining three forms of Theism: anthropomorphism ("The affections craving something to rely upon; & create a god like themselves"); pantheism ("The senses, & the verifying reason see identity everywhere"); and deism ("The intellect attempts the problem & makes a god of abstractions"). Most of the company seemed pleased with these statements, but Parker remained unsatisfied, for he could not discern in Alcott's comments the existence of "an objective god" who was both *"intelligent* & *conscious."* When Parker voiced this doubt to him, Alcott replied that *"Justice, Love Truth* &c" were, collectively, God. The company disagreed, saying that these were qualities, but Alcott insisted that they were entities.

As Alcott continued, more objections were raised. His statement that God was always in a state of *"becoming,"* being every day "more perfect than heretofore," drew this derisive comment from Parker: "a progressive god, a triangle becoming a ○ *circle* yet continuing a △ !" Alcott went even further and said that a man who does a good deed *is* God, and "not merely *divine* godlike."

To this the company replied, "[T]he new god means the totality of perfection. You do a just act — are you conscious you are its Totality of Perfection?" Dwight answered that he was, but most remained skeptical, asking, "[W]ill you give us a rule whereof we may verify it ourselves, in the next good act we do?" This question was, Parker noted, "like asking Mahomet for a miracle," and no satisfactory answer was forthcoming.

When the meeting broke up Parker was still worried. He knew that Alcott's concept of the self verifying its own divinity could easily lead to egotism and dogmatism, and he felt that Alcott's general beliefs did indeed resemble pantheism.[27] Alcott, too, was upset and entered into his journal his opinion of his questioners: "Traditions and usages still dominate over the minds of these priests of the modern temples. They fear full, bold, fair, entire statements. The mind is cowed. Men dare not utter what they believe."[28]

The talk on pantheism was carried into the club's next meeting on 5 December 1838, when Alcott revised his position somewhat by proposing that life was "the primary fact" from which "sprang Light, Intellect, and Sense." In making those qualities the manifestations of a central force rather than that force itself, he avoided much of the cross-examination that had been directed at him the previous month.[29]

The meeting of the Transcendental Club the following May took up more concrete subjects: journals, property, and Harvard College. Alcott began the discussion by taking the position that, with the sole exception of William Lloyd Garrison's *Liberator,* contemporary journals were "destitute of life, freshness, independence." Alcott attributed the uniqueness of the *Liberator* to the fact that abolition was "the true Church" and "constituted Christendom," its sympathy with the sentiment of freedom being embraced by "true men of all sects and parties." He also took the lead in discussing property; when he proposed that it be distributed according to the moral worth of each individual, he was pleased by the general assent to his statement.[30] Parker, however, was silently cynical and did not voice his own feeling that the basic concept of property would continue to exist, and that the best that could be hoped for was its distribution in a wiser way. Harvard, the group felt, was not living up to its expectations of it. They thought that the college, as the leading educational institution in the country, should show the way in reform and innovation instead of mocking the independent spirit of the young as it was then doing. The conversation went well, thought Alcott, but Emerson was somewhat disappointed. Rather than the "varied garb" of his own "daily thoughts," he wished to hear "the thoughts of men which differ widely in some important respect." The club's next meeting presented him such an occasion.[31]

The subject proposed when the club met again later in May 1839 was "the Genius and Claims of Jesus," but most of the conversation centered about "the doctrine of Innocence." Francis was not alone in differing with Emerson and Alcott in their denial "of any such thing as a struggle, or combat with sin, in the phenomena of human consciousness." Alcott was disappointed by the adverse reaction of "this circle of men, the freest, the most erudite, truest men of the time," to the "grandeur" of his purpose. But when he found it necessary "to recur quite often to those universal principles, which . . . are intuitive," the more learned members of the club demanded that his propositions be "laboriously demonstrated" before being admitted into discussion. Since many of Alcott's "universal principles" were in fact unique to his own mind, the club's reticence to accept them was understandable; and what resulted was, in Francis's view, merely Alcott's singing "the same monotone" that he always sang, "absolutely ignoring everything but his own view."[32]

Despite his recognition that Alcott tended to monopolize the conversation, Francis had faith in the club and offered his home for its next gathering. The meeting was postponed until Hedge had arrived from Bangor. In early September 1839 Francis sent out invitations for a meeting on the sixteenth. Alcott had proposed "the Esoteric and Exoteric doctrine" for discussion, but the talk soon came around to "whether men shall speak freely, or with reference to the fears & the sleep of others." Parker thought that it was a good meeting, and Alcott considered it "one of our best interviews." He was only sorry that the group lacked the ability to execute works worthy of the position in which "the good Soul" had placed them. Alcott did not know it, but the next meeting of the club would see the beginnings of the solution to that problem.[33]

The club met again two days later, on 18 September 1839, at Cyrus Bartol's house in Boston. Although Emerson did not come, Hedge, Ripley, Francis, Dwight, Alcott, Parker, and Fuller were all there. A letter from the English reformer John Marston was read, thereby launching a discussion of English reform movements. Alcott mentioned his great respect for John A. Heraud's *Monthly Magazine* in England, and soon a topic that many had been discussing privately came out into the open: "the subject of a Journal designed as the organ of views more in accordance with the Soul." Much was said about the possibility of such a journal, but no definite action was taken upon it. Even so, Parker commented privately: "There will be a new journal I doubt not. Emerson Miss Fuller & Hedge alike are confident to the birth." And Alcott even proposed a title for the magazine, "The Dial," named after the heading he had given a collection of thoughts that he had been assembling from his journals and from "Psyche" over the past few years.[34]

When the meeting broke up it was understood by most that the Transcendentalists would soon have their own journal. The Transcendental Club, having provided its members with a body of sorts, was now preparing to supply them with a voice with which to be heard.

The Transcendentalists' decision to start their own journal was not a hasty one; as early as March 1839 Alcott had foreseen the inevitable appearance of a journal that would soon circulate thoughts then only talked about in private circles. Even those not associated with the Transcendentalists felt keen disappointment at the current state of the periodical press in America. Two months before Alcott's statement, Nathaniel Hawthorne had thought it "intolerable that there should not be a single belles-lettres journal in New England." To those who lived in and around Boston—the "New England" of Hawthorne's description—the lack of a solid literary journal was embarrassing in light of their own high claims to greatness. The Boston of this period really believed that "a visible City of God" could be established there by "the forces which it had at command." One such impetus was an apparently insatiable appetite for knowledge. By late 1839 the "rage of Boston" had turned from "parties to lectures": "Emerson and Useful Knowledge, and Lowell Institute and Grammar and Temperance" squeezed "the whole world . . . through the pipe of science," to which all went "to be filled, as the students of old went with their bowl of milk." Another force was New England's cherished heritage of intellectual freedom, which allowed for the claim that it was "the place of places for all sorts of views." The Transcendentalists, with their own firm convictions about the value of dissent, were a product of this attitude. And as Clarence Gohdes has observed, in literature the "closest approximation to connected activity" by the Transcendentalists was "the attempt to bring their views before the public by means of periodicals."[35]

As early as 1832 Emerson had given serious consideration to starting a periodical of his own. He realized that, because of the large number of people that could be reached by the journals,[36] their editors were the "aristocracy" of America, and also that their printer's ink could exorcise "more ghosts & devils than the touch of Holy Water." Accordingly, he planned with the help of his brothers to issue a magazine that would replace the "lean lily-livered aspirant of these undigesting days" with men whose souls spoke out in "eloquence" and "originality." If they could do this, Emerson asked his brother William, would they not "sweep the tables of atheneums & the escritoires of the learned & the fair clean of all the American periodical paper, green yellow olive & gray?"

Unfortunately, an obstinate case of diarrhea had made it impossible for Emerson to accomplish anything, and the project was shelved for a time. The next year, though, he meditated even more seriously the "adventure of a periodical paper which shall speak truth without fear or favor to all who desire to hear it, with such persuasion as shall compel them to speak it also." However,

Emerson's new energy was channeled into his lectures, and his brother Charles, in commenting upon the possibility of Emerson's publishing the journal, said, "I hardly think he will."[37]

Nevertheless, in 1835 Emerson had joined in another attempt to establish a new American magazine. That February Sarah Clarke had told her brother James that the "supernal coterie" were planning a *"Transcendental Journal,"* and, indeed, at the instigation of Henry Hedge, those people who were becoming known as Transcendentalists were approached about starting a periodical "devoted to a spiritual philosophy, and mainly dependent upon translation, to be conducted by . . . leaders in that school of thought." The new magazine, to be called *The Transcendentalist* or *The Spiritual Inquirer*, was to have as its editors Hedge, Emerson, Ephraim Peabody, Clarke, and Ripley. Fuller promised her aid for Hedge's planned journal, although she warned that she was "merely 'Germanico' and not 'transcendental.'" The Reverend Channing, who had lain awake all night with anticipation after hearing of the project, was asked for his assistance by Emerson. But in April Hedge left Boston to settle in Bangor, and the project collapsed.

In a final attempt to secure an editor for the proposed journal, Emerson had written Carlyle that he would do them a great service by becoming editor of the now-transatlantic periodical, and he promised a salaried position should Carlyle accept the offer. But Carlyle's reply, while wishing the unborn journal success, made it clear that he would not consider editing it. A Scotchman named Buove proposed coming to America to edit the journal, and Emerson was glad for his offer of assistance, but he never materialized. Elizabeth Peabody's brief attempt at starting a "manual of Education" in 1836 met with even less support, and the possibility of a Transcendental periodical appeared to be dying away.[38]

Emerson was especially disappointed, for he felt that such a journal was necessary and that it could be made financially successful as well. Boston was not the only city craving knowledge: in 1839 American periodicals were well on their way to the half-million-dollar-a-year business that they had become by 1842, when nearly 3,000,000 numbers were being produced a year, exclusive of newspapers. Some writers went so far as to claim that American periodical literature was the best in the world. Yet Fuller voiced the sentiments of many by declining to contribute to the periodicals because she feared that what she did write would be "mutilated," and she refused to have what she wanted to write "dictated to suit the public taste." And, she would not sell her "soul" for "lucre."[39]

Fuller's comment points to another reason why Emerson believed that a new periodical could succeed: contemporary magazines were filled with complaints about the great quantity of idiocy that was being palmed off on the reading public as good literature. The joyous hosanna of the *Ladies' Repository* that "Verily, New England beats every thing" was a lone cry against the many journals which took up arms against "the enormous quantity of thrice-diluted trash, in the shape of namby-pamby love tales and sketches," which characterized most of the periodical literature of the time. These productions, which catered to "the depraved taste of lovers of light and trashy reading," deluged "every avenue of life" and cheated "millions out of that treasure which gold cannot re-purchase," true art. Too many young men used their money for "the maintainance [sic] of useless and injurious habits," with the result that their "sensual appetites are pampered, but they cannot afford intellectual luxuries!" Consequently, America was overrun with "puerile milk o watery namby-pamby" magazines, whose contributors "cost nothing" and were "worth no more." Even visitors to America quickly realized that the theory behind American periodical literature was that "everything ought to be intelligible to every body, or at least suit every body's taste." The "utter mediocrity" of the magazines, wrote the *Newark (N.J.) Advertiser*, was due to "a very deluge of imbecility — the effusions of myriad idlers and coxcombs" who reported "the judgments of Providence as they would the proceedings of a Police Court." The Reverend Channing sadly told a friend that the merit of a work was no guarantee of public favor, for writings "which amuse, or which pander to the prejudices, passions, party spirit, sectarian spirit, and selfish interests of the day, succeed best." And Alcott, who once calmly wrote that "Vox populi is not vox Dei," finally threw up his hands and cried, "The *Pegasus* of the multitude is a mule." But beyond the complaint that "gilded mediocrity" prevailed, three spheres of interest, and three types of publications that embodied them, could be discerned: moral, literary, and religious.[40]

Family and ladies' magazines tended to attack "light literature" not because of its inherent mediocrity but because of its moral uselessness. Literature that did not preach a lesson was bad literature; it would lead the young into "vain and unsatisfying amusements." Nor, as Samuel Goodrich warned, were just the young suspect: "If parents will take evil companions and counsellors to their own bosoms, will they bring them home also to become the spoilers of their children?" The only solution was to avoid authors like George Lord Byron, who corrupted the "moral feelings," and to build a "rampart" around the Gospel to protect it from invaders. The main audience for this type of reasoning was children and their mothers. Not surprisingly then, magazines for the young consisted of moral tales, articles on manners and taste, and Poor Richard-esque sayings. Mothers were considered to be children of an advanced age, and they were shielded from the real world, too. Copper and steel engravings of the latest fashions were the high points of the women's magazines: the publishers often paid more for one plate than for all the literary contributions. Just as the plates drew attention from the bland contents, the contents themselves drew attention from harsh reality. To "amuse and instruct" was the goal of these magazines, and they did both with a vengeance. Instruction consisted of preparing the woman to fill with perfection that station to which life had assigned her. Reform movements were mostly ignored — they hurt circulation too much. Amusement was provided by maudlin, sentimental verses and stories of love in which the heroine, by following the advice given elsewhere in the magazine, walked along the primrose path of life to a lovely ending of marriage and living happily ever afterward. These magazines were at once much praised and well supported by the public. By 1840 no fewer than fifteen of them covered the country from Boston to Cincinnati to Macon, Georgia. Obviously the Transcendentalists could not hope or want to explain their views in the pages of these magazines.[41]

The prospects for the Transcendentalists were not much brighter in the literary magazines, although these magazines' criticism of the periodicals of "gilded mediocrity" ostensibly gave the Boston group hope: "They injure the intellectual character of their readers; they create a taste for the very weakest and poorest mental aliment; they in fact enfeeble instead of strengthening the mind, and dissipate instead of refreshing or expanding the sensibilities." While most would have agreed with *Arcturus* that literature was treated "not as an Art, but a trade, in which the best workman is the one who can make the most out of the least materials," none saw *Arcturus*'s conclusion as the correct one: "When one school of literature is worn out, another must infallibly take its place." American literature was just entering its hey day, came the reply, and there was no reason to tamper with budding geniuses. No one promoted these geniuses with more enthusiasm than did the *Knickerbocker*, which boasted Washington Irving among its regular contributors. Unquestionably the most influential literary journal in America, the *Knickerbocker* successfully balanced fiction, travel, criticism, poetry, and humor to the point where it honestly believed its tastes to be infallible and its contents, by the writers of the "Knickerbocker school," to be representative of the best American literature of the day. This, combined with its own belief that it was the intellectual guardian of—and dictator to—its readers, resulted in making the *Knickerbocker* a valuable friend and a formidable enemy. Since the *Knickerbocker* and its many imitators and followers continually decried the "foggy compositions" of "Carlyle's small-beer copyists," the Transcendentalists could be assured of no support from their direction. And regional literary magazines were too devoted to developing their own local talent to allow the Transcendentalists to take them over.[42]

The third class of journals—and the most natural for the ministers of the Transcendental Club to look to for an outlet—was the religious magazines. Many of these periodicals also took literature as their province, thus suggesting a forum to the more literary-minded club members, and therefore seeming the ideal place for the Transcendentalists to gain a foothold. Yet, it was only too clear that this was an impossibility. The "New School" was too new for the old guard. The *Christian Examiner* was too "timid and conservative" for the Transcendentalists even had it not been opposed to them.[43] The *Unitarian Review* was such a quiet and respectable production of scholarship that one contributor spoke of his own articles in it as "printed, not published." The editor of the *North American Review*, John Gorham Palfrey, dean of Harvard's Divinity School, had said of Emerson's address there: "That part of it . . . which was not Folly, was downright Atheism." Palfrey and his major contributors called themselves the Mutual Admiration Society, an apt suggestion of how little open to criticism they allowed themselves to be. Nevertheless, most readers agreed with the *New Orleans Daily Picayune* that the *North American Review* stood "higher than any other periodical published in the country," rather than with Emerson, who heard only "the snore of the muses" as he turned its pages. The only religious journal on friendly terms with the Transcendentalists was Brownson's *Boston Quarterly Review*, but it was guided by an egotistical and self-righteous reformer, and was thus too "sectarian and exclusive" to allow the Transcendentalists, who often disagreed with its editor, a free hand in its pages.[44]

The Transcendentalists, then, found all possible existing avenues of expression cut off from them. The ladies' magazines they themselves refused to consider. Literary magazines were not given serious consideration. Religious magazines, especially after Bowen's devastating review of *Nature* and the Norton-Ripley controversy, had shut their pages to the new heretics. What was needed, the Transcendentalists believed, was a new magazine, primarily religious in content but also giving a good amount of space to literary and philosophical matters. In drawing up plans for their new journal they had two models to draw upon.

One such model was an English periodical, the *Monthly Magazine*, edited by John A. Heraud. The magazine, "saturated with the philosophic thought imbibed from Coleridge and from Germany," was brought to the Transcendentalists's attention by Alcott, who called it "the organ of the freest minds in England" and ordered copies to circulate among his friends. He introduced it to Ripley, to Emerson, who read it with interest, and to Fuller, who spoke of it with satisfaction. Alcott thought so highly of Heraud's magazine that he briefly considered sending parts of his own private journal to it, and he even doubted whether the proposed *Dial* could do better.[45] Though the *Monthly Magazine* was friendly toward the Transcendentalists, its actual value to them was limited since it was too far away from the center of action for them to make real use of it.[46] However, as a sign that a journal espousing transcendental philosophy could succeed, it did have a certain encouraging air.

A second and more important model for the *Dial* was the *Western Messenger*, a monthly magazine published first in Louisville, Kentucky, and then in Cincinnati. Since its beginning in June 1835, its editors had included Christopher Pearse Cranch, Clarke, Henry Channing, Samuel Osgood, and Ephraim Peabody. Established "with reference to principles not readers," it was meant to have "a free and unshackled spirit and form." An early statement that "one subject of a western journal [ought to be] to encourage western literature" soon slipped aside, and the *Messenger* kept its readers up-to-date on Emerson, the Norton-Ripley conflict, and other news of New England Transcendentalism. Another stated aim, that the journal would "set forth and defend Unitarian views of Christianity," also changed under the influence of the Transcendentalists, and soon the *Messenger* described itself as "less for Unitarianism, than for those broad and generous views of Christianity" that could be held by "Christians of every shade of opinion." Although nearly half of its contents was religious, the *Messenger* gave considerable space to original creative writing and came very close to attaining a happy balance between the two.

Another major reason why the Boston Transcendentalists looked toward the

Messenger was that the magazine showed outward signs of positive achievement. It had published many of those who would later contribute to the *Dial*, and no public outcry or ridicule had followed. In defending Transcendentalism it had also shown that the public would listen to opposing views and at the same time support them financially. The latest in a line of half a dozen literary periodicals to be published in the Ohio Valley, the *Messenger* was the only one to have lasted more than a few years, a fact which gave it an air of success.

Unfortunately, the Transcendentalists either failed to discover or to take warning from the negative side of the *Messenger*. It had always had trouble in recruiting new subscribers and in making old ones pay, in a much less cluttered marketplace than Boston, and its continued publication had often been assured by cash gifts from the American Unitarian Association or from private backers. Also, the *Messenger's* continuance depended mainly upon editors who were willing to work steadily, and upon contributors who were both willing and able to send in articles on a regular basis. When its main editors finally returned to New England in 1840, the *Messenger* died. But all that the Transcendentalists saw in 1839 was that a magazine supporting Transcendentalism seemed to be succeeding in the Ohio Valley. The inference from this was, of course, that such a journal could easily succeed in Boston, the center of the Transcendental movement. The problems of financial and creative support were never seriously considered by the club's members, who used the example of the *Messenger* solely to give encouragement to their plans and learned nothing from its weak points.[47]

The Transcendentalists, then, had seen the impossibility of breaking into the pages of the established popular, literary, or religious magazines. Since the only journals friendly to them were too far away to be of use, the decision to establish a new periodical in Boston to promote their cause was only natural. But somewhere between agreeing to establish a journal and actually getting an editor and a publisher and soliciting contributors, the Transcendental Club as a driving force dropped from sight, to be replaced by Fuller, Emerson, Ripley, and their — more often than not — nonministerial friends.

2

The Publication of the *Dial*

Theodore Parker had voiced the common consensus that Ralph Waldo Emerson, Margaret Fuller, or Frederic Henry Hedge would do much to "create & keep" the new journal. To Parker Emerson was the obvious first choice since his name would give an immediate public recognition to the *Dial*. But Emerson was adamant: "I will never be editor," he told his brother William. Although he was greatly in sympathy with the plans for a new journal for "the exposition of absolute truth," one which would allow many of his friends the public platform heretofore denied them, personal reasons convinced him that he should restrict his role to that of a contributor only. Both his forthcoming winter lecture series in Boston on "The Present Age" and his plans for publishing a volume of his essays made him doubt that he would be able to spare the time necessary for establishing a new journal. Also, his previous experiences with editing and publishing Thomas Carlyle made him aware of the hardships of the proposed task, and, remembering the lack of voluntary labor five years earlier, he questioned the chances for success this time.[1]

Meanwhile, the prime mover behind that earlier attempt to establish a journal, Hedge, had returned to Bangor for the winter. He had realized that it would now be impossible for him to place all the various Transcendentalists together under his editorial reins; also, as Hedge became estranged from the ideas of the Transcendentalists, the focus had shifted from *his* journal to *their* journal. Consequently, he gave the matter little thought during the following months. Others, correctly assessing Hedge's position, soon dropped him from consideration for a major role on the *Dial*.

In Hedge's place a number of Transcendentalists proposed George Ripley. Bronson Alcott enjoyed an agreeable talk with him in late September 1839, during which Ripley said that he was much impressed by John Heraud's *Monthly Magazine* and would like to establish a similar journal in America. Emerson also proposed Ripley for the editorship.[2] But Ripley was too busy even to consider accepting full responsibility for the *Dial* had it been offered to him. Between editing his *Specimens of Foreign Standard Literature* series and participating in the Unitarian controversy over Transcendentalism, almost all of his time and energies were occupied.

Fuller was also being considered for a major position at this time. She had spent the summer working on a life of Goethe for Ripley's *Specimens* series and was preparing a course of "Conversations" on mythology to begin in November at Elizabeth Peabody's bookstore in Boston. Still, she had been approached by Emerson and others to conduct a journal—a position which would afford her the opportunity and the place for everything she might wish to do. Fuller's own natural desire to be at the center of attention coincided with her wish to help the Transcendentalists, and she gave serious consideration to the possibility of openly declaring herself for the editor's chair. She thought of all the unpublished writings in her journals that she felt were worth printing, and she soon had mentally prepared an "introduction," in which she would point out "the true office of the Critic." When in early October 1839 she hinted to Emerson that she would be available for the editor's job, he invited her to Concord, Massachusetts, to "talk of these things."[3]

Emerson timed his invitation well, for a few days later Orestes Brownson unknowingly set in motion a series of events that resulted in Fuller's being named editor of the *Dial*. In his *Boston Quarterly Review* Brownson had praised Emerson's Divinity School Address and had continuously attacked Andrews Norton and the conservative Unitarians. He had even tried, unsuccessfully, to get Victor Cousin as a contributor to the abortive Transcendental periodical of 1835. Although many Transcendentalists looked somewhat favorably upon Brownson's journal — Ripley later called it the "best indication of the culture of philosophy" in America[4] — it was highly individualistic, and its editor was less than tolerant of dissenting opinions.[5] Many reform-minded people would agree with Alcott that, while the *Boston Quarterly Review* was probably the best American journal, with its favorable "Politico-philosophical" character ("Democratic in politics, and Eclectic in philosophy"), its editorial policies were too exclusively defined to permit the Transendentalists access to the wide and varied audience that they hoped to reach. In short, it fell, as Alcott noted, "far below the Idea of the best minds amongst us."[6]

Therefore, when Brownson visited him in Boston on 19 October 1839 to suggest merging the yet unpublished *Dial* with his own magazine, Alcott listened quietly and made no answer. Brownson suggested that the Transcendentalists contribute to the *Boston Quarterly Review*, and he promised to print even those articles which differed with him in sentiment if they were signed. But after Brownson left, Alcott, feeling that he was "pledged to a party in politics" and that he took "narrow ground both in philosophy and literature," entered into his journal: "No good could come from such seeming union: it would provoke opposition rather." When Fuller left for Concord the next day, Alcott accompanied her, both to convey Brownson's proposal to her and Emerson and to argue for "an organ of our own, wherein we can have entire freedom" to present "the purest thought and tastes."[7]

During their "afternoon and evening of high talk" Emerson, Alcott, and Fuller decided to reject Brownson's offer, and Fuller offered to be the *Dial*'s editor. Emerson, though left with "sleepy eye & flagging spirits" from the visit, felt that it had produced "good tidings" for their literary plans. Alcott, too, had new confidence in Fuller, having found himself even more in agreement with her than before, and he predicted that she would "enrich our literature." And on 4 November Emerson announced to Elizabeth Hoar that Fuller would edit the new journal and that Ripley had "promised to undertake all the business part of it." Even though Fuller considered publishing the first number in April 1840, she preferred waiting until the following autumn. The *Dial* was officially under way, but nearly two months would pass before Fuller set out to marshal her forces and demand that people translate their promises and thoughts into words.[8]

One thing that immediately kept Fuller from working on the *Dial* was her planned Conversations on Greek mythology. The first meeting, attended by about twenty-five women, was held at Elizabeth Peabody's on 6 November 1839. The class met twelve more times, coming together weekly at noon for two hours, and Fuller made about $200 from the series. The Conversations were well received, giving her the confidence to consider instituting another series.[9]

In December, as Fuller settled into the routine of her Conversations, she began making tentative plans for the *Dial*. The new journal was undoubtedly discussed when the Transcendental Club came together at Ripley's on 5 December 1839. This meeting marked the first time that the Reverend William Ellery Channing attended a gathering of the club, his previous absence being due both to his disagreement with the Transcendentalists on many points and to a recent severe winter cold that had limited his activities.[10] Channing was especially interested in hearing about the *Dial*; he had looked favorably upon Hedge's earlier plan and felt a new periodical to be a necessity now that Norton had intensified his attacks on the Transcendentalists. When he discovered that a new journal had definitely been decided upon, he sympathetically cheered on the undertaking.[11]

Fuller also kept interest in the *Dial* alive at the parties that were often held after Emerson's lectures. In fact, it was mainly Emerson whom she at first approached for aid, and he began to write poetry for the *Dial*.[12] He also went to see his own publishers, Charles C. Little and James Brown, to sound them out on the journal, but they were not in when he called. Although he still felt pessimistic about the *Dial*'s chances for success, Emerson promised "honest labor of some sort to each number for a year."[13] Fuller was more optimistic: undaunted by earlier failures to make the Transcendentalists a fairly cohesive group, she rashly took any promise of aid to be a firm commitment. By the end of December her enthusiasm had even touched Emerson, who told his Aunt Mary of the new and "wonderful" journal that already counted Fuller, Ripley, himself, and "twenty more" among its staff.[14] And to brighten its prospects, the *Dial* had received its first literary contribution.

In mid-November 1839 Emerson had received an "Elegy" for the *Dial*'s first number from a fellow Concord resident, twenty-two-year-old Henry David Thoreau. His friendship with Thoreau dated from early 1837 when Emerson had written a comendatory letter about him to President Josiah Quincy of Harvard. After Thoreau's graduation the two spent much time together, and Emerson commented upon the afternoons made "sunny" by "good" Thoreau's "simplicity & clear perception." Thoreau, whose philosophic views were still in the process of being formed, instinctively agreed with much that Emerson believed in, although in later years these points of agreement would become confused with those ideas for which Thoreau was genuinely indebted to Emerson, resulting in the common charge that Thoreau was merely a small-beer imitation of Emerson.[15] The older Emerson, for his part, not only appreciated Thoreau's companionship but also unconsciously allowed him to fill, in some degree, the position in his life left vacant by the death of his brother Charles.[16] Emerson also became the major literary critic and benefactor of Thoreau, commenting upon his poetry to its author and upon the author to others.[17] Thus, when word of the proposed magazine reached him, Thoreau consulted Emerson about contributing to it.

Fuller took Thoreau's poem and Emerson's promise of contributions as signs that those in the Boston area were preparing to help her with the new journal. But many of her friends lived away from Boston, and she began writing to them about the *Dial*. On 1 January 1840 Fuller wrote Henry Channing in Cincinnati

Henry David Thoreau.

Collection of Joel Myerson.

to remind him of his statement to her the previous summer that he had articles already written to give to a new periodical should it arise. She said that the Transcendentalists had begun to tune the intruments for their "grand symphony," and she asked him what part he proposed to take in it. She added that Emerson, Ripley, and John Sullivan Dwight were in earnest and ι ιggested that he approach some of the *Western Messenger*'s contributors for aid. Fuller also wrote Hedge to ask for "solid bullion" from his "sentry-box there in Bangor." By now she was confident enough to tell Hedge that the *Dial* would come out in April, and she not only wanted to know what he would contribute but also how much, since she was "planning out our first No. by the yard." Then she wrote her old friend James Clarke at Louisville, mentioning his earlier dream of participating in a truly free journal and asking for proof of that prophecy by his contribution of an article.[18]

Hedge was the first to reply, and his answer quickly dampened Fuller's enthusiasm. Proclaiming himself frightened by her "sudden" announcement that the *Dial* was finally to appear, Hedge awkwardly tried to disassociate himself from it. "No one can feel a stronger interest in the new journal than myself," he professed, but he said that financial and creative problems compelled him to be only a "reader & subscriber." Mildly promising aid in the future, he added that the *Dial* had his moral support but because of external circumstances, little else. Not until March, after much haggling, did he openly say what Fuller had suspected all along: that he was afraid to be identified with the Transcendentalists, with whom he was now in open and full disagreement. The other replies also did little to cheer the editor. James Clarke wished the *Dial* success, vaguely promising something for it later, and Henry Channing, while telling of his plan for a "religious novelette" to be delivered "piecemeal," confessed that otherwise he intended to be "a listener only" to the "grand concert."[19]

One bright spot was Emerson's search for a publisher. He had finally found James Brown at his office and approached him about publishing the *Dial*. Aware of the fact that many subscribers failed to pay their yearly rates, Brown told Emerson that his firm would not even consider publishing the *Dial* if sales were restricted to subscribers only. Instead, he suggested that they "publish the book for a cash sale of each number," with Little and Brown marketing it as they did all the books they published. When Brown inquired as to the financing of the journal, Emerson replied, as Ripley had told him to do, that Little and Brown should "take all the risk & should give us half the profits," a common enough practice then. Impressed by Emerson's "perfect confidence in the strength & sale-worthiness" of the *Dial*, Brown proposed further discussions, and they decided that Ripley, who thought that the two modes of selling could be combined, should come by. Emerson now radiated confidence, and Fuller told him that his plans for the *Dial*'s publication struck her "very favorably."[20]

Although the news from Emerson about Brown's interest lifted Fuller's spirits, she was still too busy finishing up her Conversations to spend much time actively working on the *Dial*. She kept in touch with Parker, who was busily planning possible works he could do for the new journal, and managed to get an article from him. But the confidence that she had expressed to Hedge earlier about the wealth of material for the first *Dial* soon diminished. By the end of January she seriously considered asking all her friends to send in their thoughts on Shakespeare, which she planned somehow to arrange and print. Clearly, she now knew that an April 1840 publication date was impossible.[21]

As March began, Fuller, now looking to July as a publication date, still felt confident that the first number of the *Dial* would be a good one. She had reworked two four-year-old poems of hers for the magazine[22] and was planning an article on Washington Allston's paintings. She had selected some poems from the portfolio of verses Sam Ward had given her earlier, when their friendship was closer than Ward's romance with Anna Barker now permitted. She already had Thoreau's poem "Sympathy"—the "Elegy" that Emerson had spoken of in November[23]—and the promise of another article from his pen, a criticism of the Roman satirist Aulus Persius Flaccus.[24] Also, Christopher Pearse Cranch had sent two poems directly to Emerson, who told Fuller that they were worth printing. Finally, after negotiations with Little and Brown failed, the Boston firm of Weeks, Jordan & Co., who had previously published many pamphlets by the Transcendentalists, decided to publish the *Dial*.[25] Fuller was encouraged by all this activity but, it was now Emerson who took up the standard and the cause of the *Dial*.

Abandoning his earlier cautious and somewhat pessimistic approach, Emerson now became an earnest champion of the *Dial*. The main reason for this abrupt about-face was his naive—and incorrect—interpretation of the signs of literary activity about him. When Thoreau and Cranch sent their contributions to him, Emerson, unaware that Fuller was herself having little success in getting contributors, supposed that the first number was progressing quite well. Also, he knew that much material was available from his own journals and from Fuller's. Then too, all of the activity associated with publishing the *Dial* forced him to meet with more people; as his friendships increased and deepened, he somewhat dropped his defensive posturing—and sometimes his fondness for his new acquaintances led him to forget his usual carefulness.[26] Partly swayed by this new feeling of cameraderie, Emerson mistakenly assumed that the slow but continuous response for the first number indicated commitments for the prolonged support and continuation of the *Dial*, and he announced its impending birth to all who had ears. He told a New York friend of the "free original & vital paper" that would charm him with "better verses than our American poets have given." To Carlyle he was more subdued, merely promising to send him "some American verses & prose of good intent."[27]

But just as earlier when Fuller had soared with enthusiasm and Emerson had added sober ballast to bring her down, now she restrained him with some doubts of her own. Realizing that "if the first number justify not the magazine, it will not find justification," she began to approach her editorial tasks with a new seriousness. Although the Conversations had ended, she was now preoccupied by new distractions: her health was in a bad state; she began to have doubts about her own work, feeling it not to be "pertinent to the place or time"; and Emerson, whom she had counted on for a good deal of writing, reminded her that his heavy lecture schedule would prohibit any major contributions from his pen.[28] When she wrote to Henry Channing at the end of March 1840 she was as forceful as ever about the aims of the *Dial*[29] but decidedly less happy about its chances for success. "I am not sanguine as to the amount of talent which will be brought to bear on this publication," she said, for she had found "all concerned rather indifferent" and saw "no great promise for the present." Now doubting that they would even show "high culture" or "vigorous thought," she told Channing that she would be happy if the *Dial* only succeeded in providing an outlet for the "free and calm thought . . . of individual minds."[30]

When Emerson, too, received a letter from Fuller expressing similar thoughts and containing with it Hedge's final note of rejection, he was moved to reply forcefully. "I would rather trust for its wit & its verses to the eight or nine persons in whose affections I have a sure place than to eighty or ninety celebrated contributors." Dismissing Hedge's defection as unimportant, Emerson named those who had already promised valuable assistance. Though he warned that his planned book of essays was necessarily first with him, he nevertheless promised to write "as many pages" as Fuller wished.[31]

By now the *Dial* had lost whatever little singleness of purpose had previously existed. The Transcendental Club, which had envisioned a journal for dissenting theological views, had by an almost total lack of unified support made it impossible for the *Dial* to present those views with regularity, as it had no voices with which to utter them. Fuller had acknowledged this in her letter to Channing, but she had not realized — or had not wanted to realize — that the "individual minds" would now have to be, as Emerson had indicated, those persons of her or his close acquaintance who were for the most part not practicing ministers. In short, most of those who were left, as the *Dial* prepared for its first number, neither wished nor were prepared to write on theological subjects, since their writings, like most of Fuller's own private portfolio, were literary rather than theological in character. By being thus forced to fall back upon the only available help, the *Dial* was destined from the beginning to be mainly literary in tone and clannish in supporters.

One other person with a premonition of this new and mostly permanent position that the *Dial* was to take was Alcott. Although he felt that the new journal would be far superior to its contemporaries, he believed that it would fail to take the "noblest and bravest course," and thus would only partially satisfy "the hope of the hopeful" and but partially feed "the hunger of the starving amongst us." What the times needed, Alcott said, were bards and not scholars, prophets and not priests, educators and not politicians, and men, not dilettanti. In place of the many weak-kneed magazines, Alcott wanted the new journal to be one that would "not humour the public but rebuke, and inspire it with a noble theme." Nobler versions of life needed presentation, and "men armed at all points and ready to assault dogmas, usages, institutions" were needed to do it. Clearly Alcott had not been privy to the discussions of Emerson and Fuller over the role and the character of the *Dial*.[32]

Therefore, when in early April 1840 Fuller planned the contents of the *Dial*'s first number, the only ministers she felt that she could count on were Parker, Dwight, and — overoptimistically — Hedge, and even then she was not absolutely certain of their aid. Dwight, Ward, and Thoreau were expected to contribute poems, and Emerson promised to deliver some of his late brother Charles's papers and a poem by his first wife Ellen. As for the rest of the number, Fuller listed herself as providing the "Introduction," articles on Allston's paintings and modern French writers, and a "Chat in Boston Bookstores."[33] Emerson had also promised an article on the poetry of a young friend of Ward's, Ellery Channing, but he did not seem very hopeful about completing it by July. Much needed to be done, and Fuller had not yet decided on the size or length of the journal. Nor had she decided whether the authorship of the contributions was to be, in Emerson's words, "anonymous, or initialed, or blazoned."[34]

In the meantime, word of the *Dial*'s impending debut was circulating. Alcott wrote his friends about the new magazine, through which "we of the sublunary world are to be informed of the time of day in the transcendental regions." When, while visiting Providence, Rhode Island, in early April 1840, Emerson was asked by young men and women there for information about the new journal, he replied that it was to be literary rather than religious, and the tone of their comments plainly showed their disappointment. Another disturbing item was the first notice of the *Dial* to appear in print. On 4 April the *New-Yorker* announced that Weeks, Jordan & Co. would soon publish a new "theological and literary magazine" under "the Editorial direction of Ralph Waldo Emerson and associates," which would reflect the ideas of "the transcendental school of philosophy." Emerson was as unhappy over the misstating of his role as Fuller was over being labeled an "associate." Matters were not helped any when one week later the *New-Yorker* printed a corrected notice, which also appeared three days later in the *New York Evening Post*. Although it did say that the new "Transcendental Magazine" would appear on 1 July 1840, the title was now given as *The Harbinger*, and its editors were now listed as Emerson and "Miss Sophia Margaret Fuller."

When a young Philadelphian read these notices he wrote a poem on the proposed journal, which contained this portrait of a Transcendentalist:

> He's over-grand and sentimental,
> To crush his food by process dental;
> But lives on air, and dainties mental,
> O' purest wit; —
> The foggy — mystic — transcendental! —
> I think they ca' it.

In conclusion the poem's author refused to follow the Transcendentalists' "inner light," saying, "I'd rather buy the farthin' candle / O' common sense!" More seriously, Andrews Norton was so incensed with the heretical position that he thought the *Dial* would take that he unsuccessfully asked the *North American*

Review to print a statement "giving a blow to Transcendentalism, from which it would not recover to work any essential mischief among us."[35]

The unconscious slighting of her by the *New-Yorker* had added to Fuller's depression over the *Dial* and her role on it. "Every body finds fault with me just now," she confided in her journal, and she feared that in exercising her editorial powers she would be exposing herself to enemies on every side. The *New-Yorker* notices gave a validity to her fears that she would also be "stripped for a time of the reputation I have enjoyed for talents and knowledge." And so, when she gave Henry Channing news of her activities in mid-April 1840, she did so with half-hearted enthusiasm. "Things go on pretty well," she told him, but "people will be disappointed, for they seem to be looking for the gospel of transcendentalism." She mentioned her lack of self-confidence, brought about by the discovery that she was far from being the "great original genius" she had considered herself when she had first offered to edit the *Dial*. Nevertheless, Fuller felt that the "experiment" was well worth trying, and she concluded that it was for "dear New England" that she wanted the journal, since "I do not expect to be of much use except to urge on the laggards, and scold the lukewarm."[36]

While Fuller's feelings of self-doubt were real, they were also transitory. Such fits of depression had often occurred earlier in her life and would continue to do so for years to come.[37] The necessities of publication soon forced her out of this state, and she returned to making preparations for the first number, working on the "Introduction," completing some poems, and putting the finishing touches on two long articles. One, an essay on critics, attacked the wholly subjective criticisms and puffs that were so prevalent at the time. Alcott called the essay good, and Emerson found it highly readable, praising its "power & skill." The second piece, on an exhibition of Allston's paintings held the previous summer, was a revision of her journal entries on the subject. Emerson had liked an earlier draft of the article when he had seen it in September 1839, and he "stoutly" admired the revised version, even though Sarah Clarke, one of Allston's pupils, had objected to parts of it. He did ask Fuller to use "I" instead of "we" or "the writer" in the paper, but she rejected his suggestion.[38]

Emerson also went through the papers of his late brothers Edward and Charles and the verse book of his first wife; at the end of April 1840 he gave Fuller some prose selections from Charles's journals and a poem by Edward. From that poem, like the one by Ellen Emerson that he also sent Fuller for the first number, he removed personal references. Emerson also passed on another contribution; on 15 April he had received the article on Flaccus from Thoreau. Having "too mean an opinion" of it to rework the piece himself, Thoreau had said that it could go to the *Dial* if Emerson and Fuller would do the revising, and Emerson, who felt it contained "too much manner" and "too little method," reduced its length and reorganized it. After he had "rewritten" it, Emerson asked Fuller to insert it in the first number, and soon Thoreau found himself reclaiming the manuscript for more revisions prior to its being sent to the printer.[39]

All this activity led Emerson to complain that "the Dial . . . brings me papers to read & judge, which, as I am not editor but only contributor, I like not." Yet, for a self-proclaimed mere contributor Emerson did quite a lot of voluntary work for the *Dial*, and his eager participation no doubt gave others the impression that he was more involved than he thought himself. A mere contributor might tell Parker that he had high hopes for the *Dial* or promise Carlyle that "Margaret Fuller's journal . . . will give you a better knowledge of our young people than any you have had." But Emerson had unconsciously volunteered himself for larger duties as well. When he suggested to Fuller that a section of "Intelligence" be started — "for the communication of foreign & domestic tidings that interest us" — and gave possible sources, including his own correspondence with Carlyle, all in the name of increasing "our possibilities," he should not have been surprised when more demands were made of him than he had expected.[40]

Another factor that caused Emerson to take a larger role on the *Dial* than he had originally planned was that when additional demands were made of him he met them. For example, when Fuller sent him the draft of her "Introduction" in April, he replied at length with his criticisms of it. Though he thought the essay was written with "talent & strength," he enumerated his objections to specific parts and made the general comment: "This paper . . . forestals objection; it bows, though a little haughtily, to all the company; it is not quite confirmed in its own purpose." He particularly disliked "the early preparation for defence & anticipation of enemies" that Fuller's many disclaimers provided, and he told her: "Don't cry before you are hurt." He also called into question Fuller's discussion of the *Dial*'s relation to other journals and asked her to move that section elsewhere, perhaps to her "Essay on Critics," since "the less we say about [it] . . . the less occasion we make for bickering." Finally, though he questioned the need for a "formal Introduction," he rashly concluded: "If you wish me to solve any of my own problems [about the "Introduction"] I would even try to write now an essay on These Men & This Work. I say this as expiation for my petulance."

Fuller replied that she, too, doubted the value of an "Introduction," but that it had been considered "very desirable" by Ripley and the publishers. She promised to show his letter to Ripley, after which the three of them would get together to find "the golden mean." Soon Emerson, who had learned to regret his earlier "capricious offer," put together an introductory sketch from recent journal entries for Fuller. His warning not to tamper with it without first obtaining his consent assured his being consulted again. Apparently he realized this, for he continued to enter thoughts germane to the "Introduction" in his journal. Finally, at the end of the first week in May, he sent off his finished "Introduction" to Fuller with the comment, only partially in jest, that, should his ideas be unsatisfactory, "Introductions" might be requested from everyone, after which they should be collected as a volume of "Rejected Introductions," while the *Dial* itself would be printed without one.[41]

If Emerson's work, albeit reluctant, on the "Introduction" made it appear that he wished to play a larger role on the *Dial*, the part he played in bringing Alcott into its pages surely marked him for a major position on the magazine in the minds of many people. In March Alcott had settled in Concord with his family, where, possibly influenced by Clarke's earlier translation of Goethe's "Orphic Sayings" in the *Western Messenger*, he began composing his own "Orphic Sayings." By April he had copied out the best and had given them to Emerson for the *Dial*. However, Emerson found them unsatisfactory, declaring that Alcott could "never write as well as he talks," and he requested revisions. When he received them in late April 1840, Emerson told Fuller that the "Sayings" were better than he had expected, and, though still laden with Alcott's "inveterate faults" they would "pass muster & even pass for just & great," and he promised to forward them soon.

Yet, as May began Emerson urged the printing of the "Sayings" for different reasons. He again said that he did not like them and predicted that neither Fuller nor Ripley would either. But they should be printed, he argued, even with their "cold vague generalities," and with Alcott's name over them, for "if people are properly acquainted with the prophet himself" they would make the proper allowances, and "the sayings will have a majestical sound." Emerson did not have to repeat this plea for personal privilege, for Alcott and Fuller had a successful meeting in May to discuss the "Sayings." Fuller had read them earlier and had found them "quite grand," though "ofttimes too grandiloquent" and when Alcott promised with "great sweetness" to do more revisions, their publication was assured. Nevertheless, Emerson had asked that they be inserted solely upon his word, and in doing so he had again tacitly admitted his importance in dictating the *Dial*'s policy.[42]

On 4 May 1840 the debut of the new journal was officially announced when a "Prospectus" for "THE DIAL: A Magazine for Literature, Philosophy, and Religion" was sent out. "The purpose of this work," the "Prospectus" stated, "is to furnish a medium for the freest expression of thought on the questions which interest earnest minds in every community." To avoid their being identified with Transcendentalism, or with what the public considered to be Transcendentalism, the contributors were described as people "who possess little in common but the love of intellectual freedom, and the hope of social progress." Similarly, another appeal for a wide audience was made by announcing that the *Dial* would contain "something both for those who read for instruction, and those who search for amusement." The "general design and character" of the *Dial* was described as being, in literature, to "exercise a just and catholic criticism, and to recognize every sincere production of genius"; in philosophy, to "attempt a reconciliation of the universal instincts of humanity with the largest conclusions of reason"; and in religion, to "reverently seek to discover the presence of God in nature, in history and in the soul of man."

Such claims, of course, left little doubt as to the fact that "Emerson and associates" were behind the new journal, as did the rhetoric of the final statement: "The DIAL, as its title indicates, will endeavor to occupy a station on which the light may fall; which is open to the rising sun; and from which it may correctly report the progress of the hour and the day."[43] The "Prospectus" also served as a subscription list, giving the quarterly publication dates and the price—*"Three Dollars per annum"*—for the four numbers, each of "136 octavo pages," which would comprise a volume.[44] As a mark of confidence, the publishers announced that the money need not be paid until the second number had arrived.[45]

May 1840 also saw the Transcendental Club reconvene for three meetings. On 5 May the club met at Caleb Stetson's house in Medford, Massachusetts, to discuss "the doctrine and rites of Worship, and the indications of the new Church and ritual of the present time." Emerson found the meeting agreeable, volunteered his own home for the next gathering, and even sent out letters of invitation. When it met the next week, the club discoursed on "the Inspiration of the Prophet and Bard, the nature of Poetry, and the causes of the sterility of Poetic Inspiration in our age and country."

The last meeting that month, at Cyrus Bartol's in Boston on 27 May, was at once enlivened and upset by the presence of a "hardfeatured, scarred, & wrinkled Methodist," Father Edward Taylor of the Seaman's Bethel. When Taylor entered the discussion on the influence of preaching and the administration of religion, he rebuked the shortcomings of the various religious sects, including his own, with such "sarcastic wit" and "grim but fervent satire" that the members were unable to resume the discussion, for "all other speech seemed so cold and hard after the glowing words they had heard."[46]

The fact that the *Dial* was not a major topic of discussion at any of these club meetings eliminated whatever hopes may have remained for its support by the Transcendental Club as a whole. Still, Fuller used these occasions to visit Emerson, and they did some more work on the magazine, including the final selection of Ellen Hooper's verses to be printed. Fuller was enthusiastic about her rich portfolio of contributions, and Emerson, buoyed by his belief that "American letters" were then "in the optative mood," told Weeks, Jordan & Co. that they may as safely print 1,500 or even 2,000 copies of the first *Dial* as the 1,000 they had decided on earlier. And Clarke, while regretfully announcing that he had nothing to contribute to the July number, longed to see it and promised to canvass for subscribers. The only bad omen was the fact that only thirty subscribers had signed up, but Emerson thought this of no real importance and reiterated to Fuller his belief that the *Dial* would sell.[47]

As June 1840 progressed, Fuller spent much of her time preparing the first number for publication. She was, therefore, unpleasantly surprised when at the end of the month she found herself to be short of the "136 octavo pages" promised by the "Prospectus," and she hurriedly inserted some poems by herself and Sarah Clarke to round the number out. When she told Emerson of this, he exploded against the "established rules of Grub Street" and told her, to no avail, to "leave out all the ballast" and "omit to count pages," for "Every dull sentence vulgarizes the book," and "the sincere & the sensible, will not ask, Are there 110 or 150 pages? but Is there one page?" To lessen Fuller's recurrent, and by now chronic, disappointment with the contents, Emerson again assured her that "It is [good] & shall be." Yet, in telling Carlyle of the *Dial*'s impending publication, he said that it had fallen far short of what it should be, for "puffs and dulness" had crept in "for the sake of the complement of pages." Almost defensively he added:

"but it is better than anything we had."[48] And at the end of June 1840 the first number of the *Dial* was ready to be given to the public.[49]

To friends here, Emerson remained strangely quiet about the *Dial*, seeing it on the whole as a rather bland production. Ripley, fresh from his feud with Norton, obviously had expected something more radical and called it "quite unworthy . . . of its pretensions." Fuller, who had been expressing her disappointment all along, now was pretty much silent, but she did promise a friend that the next number would be better. She also complained about the printer, who, rather than insert her filler material "here and there" throughout the magazine, had "put all her delicate scraps in a cluster at the end," which seemed to her like inviting people to a "stately feast with regular courses and ending with a dish of minced meat." Both she and Emerson were quite vocal over the many typographical errors that the printer had introduced: Thoreau's "Sympathy" contained five misprints and his article on Flaccus even more. Although Fuller had been told by Ripley that Thoreau had failed to correct and return the proofs sent him, she realized that her absence from Boston while the *Dial* was being printed was unfortunate, and she promised to see the next issue completely through the press.[50]

Other people who had been following the progress of the *Dial* with interest and sympathy were less hesitant in expressing their feelings about it. James Russell Lowell, who had eagerly bought a copy just to see Emerson's "Introduction," told Nathan Hale, Jr., that it was a good journal, but Hale found its blood to be "more *blue* than *red*."[51] Clarke, who had attributed Thoreau's "Sympathy" and "Flaccus" to Parker, thought that the last piece was poorly written, though he did like "The Problem"[52] and the "Introduction," both of which he correctly guessed to be by Emerson. On the whole, he believed that the *Dial* promised to be very good.[53] His sister observed that "the spirit of many of the pieces was lonely." Elizabeth Peabody thought the *Dial* "domestic." Sophia Ripley found it "a very charming book" and told Dwight that the next number would be "great."[54]

The mildly favorable reaction of those in the immediate vicinity of Boston was mainly due to the fact that they had known what to expect and were prepared to be sympathetic toward the *Dial*. As the journal traveled farther from Boston, less preconditioned and more mixed responses were registered. At Geneseo, New York, Samuel Treat, Jr., a recent Harvard graduate, called most of the *Dial* "trash." William Emerson liked its sincerity and its "freedom from cant & humbug & party," excepting certain "unintelligibles" of Alcott's. Carlyle read with interest the "pure, ethereal" utterances, but his final conclusion was a negative one: "And yet . . . it is *too* ethereal, speculative, theoretic: all theory becomes more and more confusedly inadequate, untrue, unsatisfactory, almost a kind of mockery to me! I will have all things condense themselves, take shape and body, if they are to have my sympathy." On the other hand, at Newport, Rhode Island, Fanny Appleton told a friend of the "astonishing concentration of thought" in the *Dial* and pronounced it "much more creditable than these patched-up Brobdingnag newspapers." In Providence, Rhoda Newcomb, an aspiring intellectual, found the *Dial* to be "a banquet." She especially liked Alcott's "Orphic Sayings" and the pieces by Dwight, Emerson, Fuller, and Cranch. To those friends of hers who were not pleased with the *Dial* and who thought parts of it sophomoric, she replied: "[T]here is a Spirit through all, which soars to the Empyrean, & carry's you along through Ether whether you will or no."[55]

Probably because many people who liked the *Dial* chose to praise it in such vague terms as Miss Newcomb did, Fuller, Ripley, and Parker all ran it down "unmercifully" to Sophia Ripley.[56] Parker was plainly cynical and expressed disgust with those articles which relied upon intuition rather than the type of careful scholarship he himself practiced. Mostly he held himself to wry or humorous comments in his journal, but when Emerson praised Thoreau's article on Flaccus to him, Parker commented that he considered it to be foolish and highly dependent upon Emerson for its life.[57] Alcott, too, "despaired of the Dial," calling it "a twi-light dial," and he told Parker that he had sent over fifty of his "Orphic Sayings" to Heraud's *Monthly Magazine*, as there was "no place for him" furthermore in the *Dial*.[58] When Alcott sent copies of the *Dial* to his friends in England, he enclosed letters to make sure that they knew of its faults before they even read it. To Heraud Alcott complained that it was "awed somewhat by the bearing of existing orders," and, while it was superior to the other journals, it did not please him at all. J. W. Marston heard that, instead of telling the progress of the sun, the *Dial* reflected neither "the rising or descending divinity." Charles Lane was told that the *Dial* pleased neither the public nor its own supporters, and that Alcott much preferred Heraud's magazine to it. Alcott was no doubt surprised when Lane replied by praising the Boston journal as superior to Heraud's because it was "more pure."[59]

Unfortunately, most reviewers found the *Dial*'s "purity" to be the result of its being uncontaminated by touches of reality. Although eight selections were reprinted elsewhere, the truly important reviewers either heaped ridicule upon the first number or ignored it.[60] The *New-York Review* (October), *Godey's Lady's Book* (November), and the very influential *North American Review* (October) merely noticed it as a new publication. The religious magazines, including the important *Christian Examiner*, did not even mention the *Dial*.

Although the *Boston Courier* (3 July) briefly noted the *Dial* and mentioned Emerson and Ripley as its editors, the *Boston Evening Mercantile Journal* (9 July) gave the *Dial* its first extended review. The *Journal* declared that the metaphysician would be pleased with the "*ideality*" of the *Dial*, while the matter-of-fact man would probably care but little for it, and the reviewer hoped that its writers would not enter "the misty land of error." On the same day the *Providence Daily Journal* briefly noted the "peculiar doctrines" of this "organ of Transcendentalism" and promised a review later. The *Boston Daily Evening Transcript*'s (13 July) review consisted mainly of statements about how the reviewer had endeavored in vain to find out the object of the writers but had been left "perfectly in the dark" after reading the *Dial* through.

The *Boston Morning Post* (14 July) began by complaining about the "dreamy, silly, Carlyle-imitating style of writing" and moved on to a general condemnation of Carlyle. Although the reviewer thought that Ripley's piece on Brownson and William Dexter Wilson's on Théodore Jouffroy were good, he assailed Alcott's "Sayings" as "genuine transcendentalism." In closing, the reviewer sarcastically recommended the *Dial* to those "who like to see a breaking away, once in a while, from the common flow of thought and expression."

The reviewer for the *Boston Times* (17 July), calling the *Dial* "one of the most . . . ridiculous productions of the age," described it as "a grossly compounded mixture of Swedenborgianism, German mysticism . . . infidelity in its higher branches, with some . . . Pantheism; and the mixture is as unintelligible as the confusion of tongues at Babel." In fact, the reviewer concluded, "Duck tracks in the mud convey a more intelligible meaning." Therefore, the reviewer could not criticize the *Dial*'s writers any more than he could "the speeches of Jackdaws or the chattering of monkeys." The reviewer for the *Boston Recorder* (31 July) said that the *Dial* "reflects only the rays of a mock sun" and that "its *religion*, if not all moonshine, is something worse." And the writer for the *Boston Courier* (11 August) complained that "imagination" was "considered more sure and certain than the cool, substantial deduction of ratiocination."

Out-of-town reviews were hardly better; indeed, they were for the most part vicious. The reviewer for the *Philadelphia Gazette* bluntly called the *Dial*'s contributors "considerably madder than the Mormonites" and warned against the "ravings of Alcott, and his fellow-zanies" on "the Incomprehensible and the Indescribable."[61] Similarly, the writer for the *Philadelphia National Gazette and Literary Register* (18 August) stated that if the *Dial* could "promulgate no better axioms" than Alcott's, "the utility of its publication" was doubtful. New Yorkers were warned by the reviewer for the *New World* (8 August) that Transcendentalism was "merely a refined sort of Deism," which struck at "the vital principle of the faith of Christendom." If anyone still had doubts about Transcendentalism, the reviewer printed one of Alcott's "Sayings" and concluded that after reading it one would find Transcendentalism to be "clear as mud." At Cincinnati the reviewer for the *Daily Chronicle* (5 August), long a foe of Brownson's *Boston Quarterly Review*, lashed out at the *Dial* for—in Ripley's review—giving Brownson a favorable hearing, concluding that the *Dial* was a "sickly, fungous literature," a "wild raving, mixed up of German metaphysics and coarse infidelity."

The final blow was dealt by the prestigious *Knickerbocker* (August), whose reviewer dismissed the *Dial* as a lowly species of "*Literary Euphuism*." With both art and malice he alternated sentences from the *Dial*'s "Introduction," proclaiming its lofty aims, with obvious failures to live up to them elsewhere in the text. Grudgingly, the reviewer admitted that there were some "good *thoughts*" in the *Dial*, but he complained that they were smothered in words; or, as the plain-spoken Yankee told the Paris chef, "If your meats are good, what is the use of *disguising* them?" In short, the *Dial* stood little chance to "improve American letters."

Against such shouting, the few whispered words of praise went virtually unheard. The reviewer for the *Western Messenger* (October) briefly said that he regretted the *Cincinnati Daily Chronicle*'s attack on Brownson but deferred any comment on the *Dial* itself until the next number. The reviewer for the *Boston Courier* (8 August) praised Ripley's article on Brownson, and later (11 August), though he complained of occasional vagaries, called the publication a good omen, because it provided a necessary outlet for "inappeasable longings"; when "the fog shall have expanded and vanished, light may appear." The writer for the *New-Yorker* (4 July) was enthusiastic about the "really *new* Magazine" but only gave a quick — and favorable — definition of Transcendentalism. The reviewer, possibly its sympathetic editor Horace Greeley, apologized for his "hasty notice" and promised a longer review later, but that review never came.

The *Providence Daily Journal* (27 July) fulfilled its earlier promise of a review with the most careful and considered notice that the first *Dial* received. It was a mixed one. Before examining the magazine itself, the obviously well-informed reviewer, W. J. Pabodie, described its four major contributors at length. Each vignette started with praise but ended with criticism. He discussed Emerson's high moral character, then regretted his discarding of the understanding and his resulting loss of reason. Fuller he named "a woman of extraordinary application and industry," who yet had "no intuitive perception of either truth or beauty; and . . . no genuine love of knowledge . . . for its own sake, but for the eclat with which it is attended." While the reviewer had read and liked Ripley's letter to Norton, he considered him "[t]ossed about on the vast ocean of metaphysics," unable to find a safe mooring. And he said that Alcott, though "a man of the purest and most elevated character," promoted "absurd" ideas in his "Sayings." In conclusion, though he doubted that it contained anything either new or original as had been promised, the reviewer wished the *Dial* all possible success, for he thought that its influence would be good. Besides, the "absurdities" of the magazine were "so absurd" that they "need but to be clearly perceived to be immediately rejected."[62]

By far the most damaging article in the first *Dial* was Alcott's "Orphic Sayings"; at least three reviewers picked the following "Saying" as illustrating the dubious heights to which Transcendental folly could climb:

GENESIS

The popular genesis is historical. It is written to sense not to the soul. Two principles, diverse and alien, interchange the Godhead and sway the world by turns. God is dual. Spirit is derivative. Identity halts in diversity. Unity is actual merely. The poles of things are not integrated: creation globed and orbed. Yet in the true genesis, nature is globed in the material, souls orbed in the spiritual firmament. Love globes, wisdom orbs, all things. As magnet the steel, so spirit attracts matter, which trembles to traverse the poles of diversity, and rests in the bosom of unity. All genesis is of love. Wisdom is her form; beauty her costume.[63]

Although Fuller felt that these "Sayings" read well and Emerson considered them "quite a necessary ingredient" in the *Dial*, Alcott's own statement that they were "ridiculed by the general Press" was more to the point. The "Sayings" became so notorious in their own way that parodies appeared in many places. The *Knickerbocker* continued to attack Alcott and his work for the next four years in its editorial columns and in its reviews of the *Dial*. As late as April 1843 the *Nantucket Telegraph* parodied Alcott with: "A pound of butter is the sole type of existence in the life actual for cheesedom is but a formula. Firkindom is the sapient recipient. Avoirdupois is the weight, but dont grease your fingers." To Alcott, who genuinely believed his "Sayings" to be wise and farsighted, this reception was a great blow, even though he continued to produce and believe in similar works.[64]

The more tolerant were dismayed by the public flaying that the *Dial* received. Thomas Holley Chivers, in New York, complained to his friend Edgar Allan Poe of the Boston papers' attacks on the *Dial*, and, though he disagreed with some of the *Dial*'s ideas, he also felt that its critics knew "nothing of any thing but what amounts to nothing." Cranch considered the remarks of the reviewers to be vulgar, as did William Emerson, who told his Aunt Mary that the magazine deserved a fairer reading from the public. "Our community begin to stand in some terror of Transcendentalism," Emerson told Carlyle, "and the Dial, poor little thing, whose first number contains scarce anything considerable and even visible, is just now honoured by attacks from almost every newspaper & magazine; which at least betrays the irritability & the instincts of the good public." Still, most out-of-town critics agreed with Sam Ward of New York, who argued that, because all the "Bramanian" and "Emersonian" magazines did was to "proclaim the good works of their fellow citizens and Savants," the *Dial*'s reception was "their own fault," and they had "no right to complain."[65]

Though it was published in a dull brown wrapper and lacked illustrations within and without, the *Dial* did not enter the magazine world quietly. Without embellishments the *Dial* was forced to rely upon its contents for the instruction and amusement its Prospectus promised, and, by the time the reviewers had regurgitated those undigestible segments of its Transcendentalism into print, its chances for success were highly questionable. That only Alcott's "Orphic Sayings" — thirteen of the *Dial*'s 136 pages — were regularly used in representing the contents of the entire magazine ensured public confusion. Although it seemed that after this initial reception the *Dial* could go nowhere but upward, the fact that Transcendentalism had been and would continue to be discredited, and the fact that the *Dial* and the names of its editors were irrevocably linked to that Boston movement, resulted in the *Dial*'s continual fall from serious attention as time went on.

3

The *Dial* Under Margaret Fuller

While the reviewers were examining, often critically, the first number of the new magazine, the *Dial*'s editors were also examining their work. One day after he received a copy of the *Dial* from Bronson Alcott, Ralph Waldo Emerson queried Margaret Fuller about its distribution and design. He wished to give copies to friends and contributors, and he was unsure about what to do. More importantly, he considered the *Dial*'s design to be "cautious," not bold, and made these suggestions: because of the "pale face, lily liver" lettering used on the title page, he wanted the printer to display "the word *Dial* in strong black letters that can be seen in the sunshine"; because the divisions between contributions were not clearly marked, he recommended printing "a strong black line as a landing place to take a breath upon" before going on to the next piece; and he suggested printing the poetry, especially the best poetry, in a "large & glorious" type that betrayed "a slight consciousness" of what it carried. Nevertheless, Emerson reassured Fuller, it was "a good book & the wise public ought to accept it as such."[1]

Fuller responded promptly. Weeks, Jordan & Co. had agreed to supply twelve copies of each number for contributors, with Fuller receiving two, but since she had not informed Emerson of this she agreed that he could have as many numbers of this first issue as he needed for his friends.[2] She also apologized for not having consulted him about the type size; Fuller personally liked poetry better in small type, and, not knowing that Emerson "attached great importance to externals in such matters, as [he did] so little in others," she had proceeded without his advice. However, she felt that having started with a certain design they should continue with it through the first volume. She was glad that Emerson was not totally dissatisfied with the first number, for, still smarting over the "absurdity" of the filler material, she was wont to "suffer" over it herself. Emerson, in turn, was somewhat conciliatory: he apologized for having "pestered" her with "criticism on trifles" when she was in "low spirits and out of health."[3]

Fuller had gone through "a most suffering winter," but her health slowly improved as summer came. Fits of illness, especially headaches, still descended upon her, and she often had to stop working and take to her bed. But as July 1840 wore on and the condition of the *Dial* improved, so did her health. She thought better of the magazine and even sent a copy to her old friend, the well-known author John Neal. Emerson heard that the *Dial* was considered to be "delightful" in Providence, and he jokingly called its editor the "queen of the American Parnassus." Then too, the pages of the October number were almost completely filled, and with submitted manuscripts rather than promises.[4]

Fuller was busily working on a review of the exhibition of painting and sculpture at the Boston Athenæum, and she was happy to find that this and a translation of a poem were all she need contribute to the second number. Since June Emerson had been selecting from a portfolio of verses by Ellen Hooper; at the end of July he sent his choices to Fuller.[5] To Hooper's four poems that Fuller selected for the *Dial* she added ten sent in by Hooper's sister, Caroline Sturgis. Theodore Parker, J. S. Dwight, C. P. Cranch, George Ripley,[6] Henry Hedge, and James Clarke had submitted poems, articles, and reviews. Fuller now felt confident enough to push aside papers on Romaic ballads and on Honoré de Balzac that she had planned to do; she even allowed herself the luxury of putting off her final comment on possible contributions. She did take under consideration an essay on bravery by Henry Thoreau, who had also submitted — and then voluntarily withdrawn — a poem.[7]

Indeed, so fast was Fuller's pace that, when Emerson wrote her at the end of July 1840, he was surprised to find that the printing had already begun, three or four weeks ahead of schedule.[8] At Elizabeth Hoar's suggestion, Emerson allowed Fuller to use a poem that he had sent in earlier, "Woodnotes," even though he was not completely satisfied with it.[9] In April Emerson had volunteered to combine and revise for the second number his two lectures on literature from "The Present Age" series, which he was repeating that month in Concord, Massachusetts. By June he had prepared sixty-three pages and had given them to Fuller, after marking those sections that might be omitted if space limitations made it necessary. Most of the lecture was set in type before Fuller realized that she had miscalculated; thus it was pushed out of the July number. Emerson was not disturbed since he believed that he would have to contribute less to the next number, and he told Thomas Carlyle to watch for its publication then. Indeed, Fuller planned to start the October issue with it, and on 8 July Emerson was sent proof. Another set of proof went to Ripley, who made some suggestions for improving the article before returning it to Fuller, who made her criticisms prior to giving the sheets to Emerson. He was "obliged" to them, Emerson said, and he made a number of the changes that they recommended, although he left some of the "offending words" as they stood because he could not "find better."[10]

This bustle of activity easily led to a new spirit of confidence. Emerson now thought that the *Dial* should not be "a mere literary journal" but ought to contain "the best advice on the topics of Government, Temperance, Abolition, Trade, & Domestic Life."[11] Ripley, while generally disappointed with the *Dial*, was happy that it had made a "decided sensation," which he considered at least an auspicious beginning, and Alcott asked a friend: "What of dialling? do you discern the hour of the universe on our Famous Time Piece?" Fuller was happy, too; not only had she assumed firm editorial control, but interested people were even inquiring about the names of contributors to the mostly anonymous pieces in the first number. Few articles or poems in the July *Dial* were printed over a full signature since many contributors had requested anonymity. Others, such as Fuller's, were signed with a letter or initials that would easily identify the writer to those familiar with the *Dial*'s writers. But most of the poetry, which Fuller had supplied from "the confidential deposits of private friendship in her portfolio," went in anonymously or with misleading initials, and only a small handful of people, pledged to secrecy, knew their authorship.[12]

With most of the work on the October 1840 number either done or nearly completed, the editors began to socialize more. In early August Ripley, Parker, Cranch, Thoreau, and Alcott met in Concord to discuss, among other things, the *Dial*. Parker was disappointed, and felt that his time had been wasted: he found the discussion on the magazine to be poor, and he disliked the way in which Emerson praised Thoreau, who Parker privately hoped would write "for the newspapers more & less for the Dial."[13]

On 2 September 1840 the Transcendental Club met at Parker's to discuss "the organization of a new church." Hedge, Convers Francis, and Caleb Stetson supported the Unitarian Association with vigor, causing Parker to complain that they were wedded to the past. He loved the past, Parker said, but he would "as soon wed [my] grandmother whom [I] love equally well." Together with George Ripley, Parker supported "a new church but a Christian Church," while Emerson, Fuller, and Sophia Ripley proposed "a universal church and creed." Both Parker and Emerson were disappointed in the company's response to their arguments. Emerson felt that their "distrust that the Divine Soul would [not] find its own organs" was "the essence of Atheism," and he complained that important questions went untouched. Only Henry Channing and Cranch seemed to be satisfied with the discussion, for they had wanted to let the matter take care of itself.[14]

Another disappointment to Parker at this meeting was Fuller's attitude. The predicted success of the October 1840 *Dial* must have made her act with an assuredness that appeared to some as mere egotism, as no doubt part of it was. Alcott, who had been turned down by her in an attempt to publish more "Orphic Sayings" in the October number, thought that this certainly was the case and said so to Parker.[15] Earlier, Parker had found "ludicrous" Fuller's "petty jealousies, contemptible lust of power, & falling into freaks of passion"; now he saw them merely as being "melancholy."[16] Alcott and Parker were the lone dissenters, however, and everyone else appeared satisfied with Fuller and her work.

When the club reconvened in late September 1840 for what was probably its last meeting, the church was again discussed. Since Emerson was absent and Fuller mostly silent, the discussion moved toward an exposition of the present conditions of the church rather than toward alternatives to it. Ripley started the meeting by proposing that "the ministers & Church are upheld in order to uphold a society vicious in its foundations." The inherent evil, he went on, was due to the desire of the multitude that the church "should continue in its present conditions." Hedge defended the church by pointing to its past accomplishments, but Ripley finally made him confess that "the Social Principle" had "yet to be educated," and therefore the "Church of Humanity" had "yet to grow." The meeting broke up, as usual, with all sides far apart.[17]

If the Transcendental Club was still less than unified, the *Dial*, on the other hand, was consolidating its resources, and the October 1840 number was almost completed.[18] Emerson, who had hoped to escape providing anything for this number besides his article on "Modern Literature," also contributed an essay on the poetry of Ellery Channing.[19] Sam Ward, a friend of Channing, had given the poems to Emerson at the beginning of the year. Emerson, however, had been unable to get Channing's permission to publish them in time for the July number. He finally received Channing's consent and finished the article in late August; but a protracted discussion over how much Emerson could "correct" delayed the arrival of proof until the end of September, when he gave in to his friends' wishes and published the poetry with few emendations of his own. Possibly because this article went to the printer so late, the new *Dial* was not advertised for sale until 2 October.[20]

The second number of the *Dial* fared better than its predecessor, not only because it was of a higher quality but also because it was less vulnerable to attack. Where the July *Dial* had left itself open for criticisms by defending Orestes Brownson and publishing Alcott, the October 1840 *Dial* began with Emerson's thoughtful article on "Modern Literature" and closed with Ripley's reviews of theological works. A description of the West was provided in pieces by Clarke and Cranch, and the poetry was not so disastrously "Transcendental" in feeling and design as Alcott's "Sayings" had been. Still, Henry Wadsworth Longfellow told his brother that the new *Dial*, which was as "strange" as the first one, would amuse him with its mixture of "wisdom and folly." The inability of the *Dial* to balance successfully the ideal and the practical was also noticed by Clarke's Louisville (Kentucky) friend, George Keats, who was both pleased and intrigued by the magazine but complained that like "other progress works" there was much in it "straining and more than useless." Emerson, too, was aware of this aspect of the *Dial*, but he felt that "one wild line out of a private heart saves the whole book."[21] Carlyle thought that Emerson's "Modern Literature" was the best thing in a magazine that was "very good as a *soul*"; but, alas, it wanted a "body, which want means a great deal!"[22] Yet, that "*soul*" is what made the *Dial* appeal to Caroline Sturgis, who wrote Emerson that "the words of my friends . . . [give] me new love & activity"; in reading the *Dial* "it seemed as if music fell upon my heart."[23] Emerson's brother William and his wife read the new *Dial* with "greater satisfaction" than the previous one. And from British Guiana the utilitarian philosopher, Richard Hildreth, inquired about the new *Dial*, to which he had subscribed.[24]

This time the periodical reviews were kinder, but in general less notice was taken of the *Dial*. Only five selections were reprinted, and four of them were by Horace Greeley's friendly *New-Yorker*. His paper announced (10 October) the *Dial*'s publication, with a short notice praising its "ability," and in a review the next week (17 October) called attention to the "bold originality, manly vigor of thought, [and] lofty conceptions of Man's nature" presented in its pages. Another friend of the *Dial*, John A. Heraud in England, gave the magazine his seal of approval when he told his readers that the views of the *Dial* were the "same as those proposed by ourselves in the *Monthly Magazine*" (October). The

Philadelphia National Gazette and Literary Register (24 October) proved itself no friend of the *Dial* by reprinting some "burlesques" of its "cabalistic contents." The *Dial* was also parodied by the *Providence Daily Journal* (23 October), which this time dismissed it, and in short order, as "the organ of the incomprehensible."

The Boston papers were again less than enthusiastic. In a few sentences the reviewer for the *Evening Mercantile Journal* (8 October) said that, while he had not been able to read the number, he thought that Alcott's "Orphic Sayings" had been wisely discontinued. The reviewer for the *Boston Morning Post* (12 October) recalled that the "tomahawk and the scalping knife" of reviewers had been used in July with "an Indian barbarity," and he praised the number for not "cutting such antic tricks" as the first had. This backhanded compliment was followed by a paragraph on the need for "a true American literature"; no mention was made of any other positive values, if any, that the new *Dial* had.

The reviewer for *Boston Daily Advertiser* (16 October), while feeling that perhaps this number was better than the first, had no qualms about pointing out its seeming errors. Particularly upsetting to the reviewer was Emerson's introduction of Channing's poetry, and he hoped that "a flood of crude versification" would not be showered upon the public because of Emerson's notion that—as the reviewer phrased it—"the failures of genius are better than victories of talent."[25]

Calling the *Dial* a "Queer Book," the reviewer for the *Boston Courier* (6 October) praised its prose but railed against its poetry: "We were petrified, we were confounded, we were taken not *un*-aback . . . by these stupendously stupid 'ejaculations.'" And the reviewer asked, "Are the editors of the Dial ready to receive into their columns any amount of *un*profitable, *un*savory, *un*harmonious, *un*connected, hopeless jargon."

The response from major periodicals was both sparse and unenthusiastic. The writer for the *Western Messenger* (November) started by defending transcendental intuition against its detractors, moved on to a general discussion of the Transcendentalists, and only in the last paragraph gave his own feelings about the *Dial*. Although the *Messenger*'s reviewer wished the *Dial* success and praised its contributors as among "the purest, clearest, and trueist [sic] minds in the land," he also felt that "they have [not] shewn the power they possess."

Brownson's review in his *Boston Quarterly Review* (January 1841), while essentially negative, at least had the virtue of showing Alcott, Emerson, and Fuller how right they were in deciding not to join forces with him earlier. Brownson's general dislike of Transcendentalism was shown in his discussion of Emerson's "Woodnotes"; though he found the poem "better than most notes of the kind," he had no patience with those who actually tried to depict the objects that cast Nature's spell upon the poet. In summation, he described the *Dial* as "a truly remarkable work" whose thought was in general superior to its expression. Like Carlyle, he called its contributors "too vague, evanescent, aerial," and he believed the magazine itself "somewhat injured by its puerile conceits, and childish expressions."

Surprisingly, the best review of the October 1840 *Dial* came from the *Knicker-bocker* (November), which ordained it a decided improvement over the first number. The reviewer praised and quoted much of its contents, although he felt that Emerson's recommendation of Channing's poetry would scarcely be endorsed by the public. Unfortunately, this judicious tone was abandoned in the review's concluding section in favor of another attack, complete with parodies, upon Alcott's "Orphic Sayings."

Because the October number's reception was such a decided improvement over the roasting given its predecessor, Fuller told Emerson that she was becoming more interested in the *Dial*. Even though she was preparing for another series of Conversations to begin in November 1840, she continued to work hard on the magazine. One reason for her confidence was that the *Dial*, having survived its first two numbers, was now fairly well established. Many of her acquaintances looked upon the magazine with a new seriousness, and her old friend in Providence, Albert Gorton Greene, had promised poems, essays, and even humorous sketches on "Pumpkin Monodies" and "Militia musters."

Emerson also had detected signs of acceptance for the new journal. Daniel Parker, a physician in Billerica, Massachusetts, had asked to be sent the first two numbers; after reading them, he declared that, with its excellent contributors, the *Dial* had to succeed, and to that end he promised to circulate it in Billerica. In an unusual and friendly move, Greeley's *New-Yorker* reprinted, almost two months after it had been published in the *Dial*, a selection from Parker's "A Lesson for the Day." This increasing interest made Emerson hopefully predict that the *Dial* would be "better and perhaps next year bigger."[26]

Hedge, Clarke, Dwight, Cranch, and Hooper had all promised articles or poems for January, and Fuller also had available a good deal of material left out of the earlier two numbers. From her portfolio she decided to print Ward's "Letters from Italy." She also had, from Hedge's neighbor in Maine, Thomas Stone, an essay on "Man in the Ages," which had been omitted from the October number because of its length. Caroline Sturgis had sent in some more poetry, and Ellen Emerson's "The Violet," accidentally omitted from the October *Dial*, was also scheduled for insertion. Emerson had forwarded some of James Russell Lowell's sonnets to Fuller who, while complaining that they were imitative of Alfred Tennyson, decided to print them in order not to discourage other "volunteers."[27]

Nevertheless, quite a few "volunteers" were disappointed during the preparations for the January 1841 number. Fuller decided not to print any of Channing's poems that were left over from Emerson's article in October,[28] and Emerson's offer of more of his brother Charles's writings was declined. Emerson himself had turned down Elizabeth Peabody's paper on "Patriarchal Traditions" as being too dry for the *Dial*'s pages, and he also acted as an intermediary when William Wetmore Story sent in a paper for the *Dial*'s consideration. Story had prepared an article on art for the *North American Review*, but it had been returned, Story said, because its views were "too liberal and too aesthetic" for that journal's conservative editorial policy. Rather than see his labors go in vain, Story sent the paper to the *Dial* in care of Emerson, who, in turn, passed it on to Fuller with the comment that it abounded in "common information & trite quotation." A few weeks later Story wrote Emerson that, since he had received no word to the contrary, he assumed that his manuscript had been accepted; then he outlined arrangements to facilitate his proofreading of the article. Fortunately, Fuller had been reading the manuscript; a few days later she returned it to Emerson, saying that because of its "bad faults in style and imagery," as well as its length, it was unacceptable. However, she said, if Story would revise and shorten it, it could be printed in April. Emerson gratefully thanked Fuller for her promptness and returned the manuscript to Story with a letter of explanation, in which, quoting from Fuller's letter, he repeated her strictures and her offer to print a revised version. To give Story comfort, Emerson praised his criticisms on particular works of art, and he hinted that perhaps another reason why the article was being returned was that his own "Thoughts on Art" had been accepted for that number first. Story, however, never resubmitted the article.[29]

Emerson had by now become fully aware that he was chief editorial consultant to the *Dial* and in effect Fuller's second-in-command. In addition to helping with other contributors, he was also involved in his own work for the January 1841 *Dial*. His earlier hope that a single sonnet would suffice for January had by October turned into a promise of "whatever I can muster." In November, as he was preparing a lecture on art to deliver before the Concord Lyceum the next month, Emerson offered Fuller an essay on art for the *Dial*. She gladly accepted his offer, and by mid-November she received his manuscript. After she had made some suggestions, Emerson spent a few weeks revising it, and in late December it went to the printer. In the process of going over the essay Emerson had doubled the length and had become disconcerted with it, but Fuller liked it well enough to print it.[30] Emerson was also unhappy with his poem "The Sphinx," on which he had been working since May, and not even last-minute changes on the proofs succeeded in pleasing him. And as December drew to a close, Emerson was so busy at "writing or collating or compiling" that he was hard pressed to find time even to write letters to his friends.[31]

Emerson's neighbors, Alcott and Thoreau, were also represented in the January 1841 *Dial*. Fuller had purposely left more of Alcott's "Orphic Sayings" out of the October number, but in doing so she had obviously hurt his feelings. Evidently, she felt that by now the furor created by the reviews had died down; partially to soothe Alcott's bruised ego, she told Emerson that it was her "sincere desire" that he should "prithee woo [Alcott] thereto, as you know how." As a result Alcott sent in another fifty "Sayings" and Fuller had them set in type almost at once.

Fuller was not so kind to Thoreau; his essay on bravery, which he had submitted that summer, was finally rejected. Although she said that she had found the paper "rich in thoughts," those thoughts were so disorganized that she could not "read it through without *pain*." She admitted that Emerson had said that other essays "not to be compared" with Thoreau's had found their way into the *Dial*, but while they had been "more unassuming in their tone," his was "so rugged that it ought to be commanding." If he would revise it, Fuller concluded, she would look at it again. She did accept a poem by Thoreau that Emerson had sent her in July with some poems of his own to "fill spaces." Emerson had especially praised the lines "Nature relumes her dawn each day," though he had made suggestions for revisions elsewhere, and he had asked Fuller to give the lines a title. She christened them "Stanzas," and they were duly printed as such.[32]

Fuller was also busily preparing some of her own writings for the next *Dial*. She planned a few reviews, including one of *Grandfather's Chair* by Nathaniel Hawthorne, whom she had always admired,[33] and she took "Meta" from her 1833 notebook. Fuller had also begun in October 1840 working on an essay about the yuca filamentosa plant, but by November she had left it in favor of a similar piece on "The Magnolia of Lake Pontchartrain," which she completed just in time for the January *Dial*.[34] Finishing up her own work and putting the new *Dial* together occupied so much of Fuller's time that as the publication date drew near she found herself, like Emerson, unable to write anything but "business letters" concerning the *Dial*.[35]

Not only were the preparations for the January *Dial* the best so far, but it also looked as if it would receive the best press reception as well. Even before the third number's publication, Greeley's *New-Yorker* (19 December) presented a spirited defense of the *Dial* under the title "Critical Astuteness." Though the writer disagreed with some of the ideas advanced by the *Dial* and found a number of its articles "in bad taste and worthless," he, nevertheless, thought it superior to most popular magazines, whose articles were "merely the fruits of an hour's hasty scribbling by some caterer for the public taste." He rebuked the reviewers who had made themselves merry at the expense of the *Dial* by calling its contributors "owls, asses and other unpopular beasts," merely because such opinions were fashionable. In conclusion, he said that no American magazine contained "as much original and valuable thought" as did the *Dial*, and because of this one should pardon, rather than exaggerate, its "minor faults."

When the *Dial* came out on the first day of the new year, those associated with it saw the magazine in a new and more favorable light. Emerson told Caroline Sturgis that he liked the new *Dial* very much, an opinion he repeated to Fuller. He also praised the editor herself asserting that "the good Public ought to be humbly thankful" to her for keeping the *Dial* together. It was "so irresistable a dainty" to Dwight that the "inward comfort and beautiful thoughts" in the "splendid number clipped the borders" of his sermon.

Alcott was, however, still soured by the public's reaction to his "Orphic Sayings," and he asked his father to look for all "the Dial slanders" that he was sure would be printed. Ellen Sewall also watched for the *Dial* to see if her friend Thoreau's writing was in it.

While fewer readers outside of the Transcendentalists' own circle took the time to write down their thoughts on this number, those who did were not happy. George Keats complained of its "excessive transcendentalism," and Fanny Appleton, who had liked the earlier numbers, now called the *Dial* "'beyond beyond' for absurdity" and cited Emerson's "The Sphinx" as the best example, something which "could only have been written in Bedlam." From Delaware George Allen wrote James Marsh that there was "too much pretension, without power of performance — not one complete backbone to the whole set" of "Dialists." Though William Bellows called the Transcendentalists' doctrine of inspiration "grand, inspiring," he also accused them of "*cant*" and "some little *bigotry* also." His brother Henry, a New York minister, agreed, noting that the *Dial* was sometimes "free, generous, . . . exceedingly original & beautiful," but that at other times, because of "its excessive want of humility & its most offensive irreverence to Christ," it could be "cold, visionary, ignorant, [and] assuming," as in Alcott's "affectation of profundity."[36]

Disappointingly few papers bothered to review the January 1841 *Dial*, even though more of Alcott's "Orphic Sayings" gave the number an easy vulnerability. This portion of the *Dial* was exactly where the *Boston Morning Post* (13 January) struck; over half of its review attacked the "Sayings" as illustrating "the step from the sublime to the ridiculous." Parker's "German Literature" was the only other article discussed; according to the *Post*, because of "its clean style, its manly tone, and able composition," it stood out "in bold relief." But once again, the *Dial* had failed in general to balance "the real and the dreamy" or "the plain and the mystic," and instead remained "rich in the profoundly allegorical and the hopelessly obscure." The *Boston Evening Mercantile Journal* (15 January) also attacked Alcott as one of "a class of philosophers, who seem to bid adieu to the world, and sport in the upper air." The *Journal*'s reviewer, not being of that class, found the *Dial* "the quintessence of folly and extravagance — affected, mystical, bombastic."

In Providence Christopher A. Greene in the reform-minded *Plain Speaker* (30 January) called the *Dial* an "exponent of Literary Liberty; and therefore valuable"; but, he said, it was far from being of the highest value since none of the "Dialists," except Alcott, was "actively engaged in the Great Reforms of the day." The *New-Yorker* (16 January) made brief notice of the *Dial*, calling most of it "comprehensible by the aid of a very moderate capacity." The following week (23 January) it reprinted two pieces and published a long and detailed review. The reviewer, though he found Fuller's works "too fanciful," discussed with favor nearly all the prose pieces and called Emerson's "Thoughts on Art" the best article. Alcott's "Sayings" were mentioned, but the reviewer gently told his readers that "they need not frighten any body."

Another source that was expected to give the *Dial* a favorable review remained silent: the *Western Messenger* (February) did not mention the new number, though it did reprint a poem. Therefore, when a generally favorable review came from an unexpected source, it was all the more pleasant. The reviewer of the *Knickerbocker* (February), which had ridiculed the first *Dial* for printing Alcott's "Sayings," called the third number a better one than either of its predecessors. Nearly everything in this issue the reviewer singled out for praise — everything, that is, but Alcott's contributuion. After printing examples of the "Sayings" of that "second-hand imitator of a second-hand model [Carlyle]" who dressed up "meagre thoughts" in the "garb of a mountebank," the reviewer gave a parody entitled "Putty," which began, "Ever the true Putty fast-sticketh." In conclusion, the *Knickerbocker* writer agreed with Brownson how unfortunate it was that "puerile conceits and childish expressions" had marred the over-all "rich thought" of the magazine.

In much the same way the reviewer for the *Boston Daily Times* (21 January) discussed the two schools of "Transcendentalism." One, led by Brownson and Ripley, was based on French eclecticism; the other, led by Emerson and found in the *Dial*, was influenced by the "wildest and most mystical" of the German metaphysicians. While believing that Transcendentalism could eventually make life "more spiritual," the reviewer said that at present it was too mixed up with "pantheistic notions . . . a great deal of cant, and humbug, and railing against clergymen" to be useful.

The relative calm and thoughtfulness with which the January 1841 *Dial* was received was encouraging to Fuller. She wrote Henry Channing that, as her earlier fears lessened, she was getting more interested in the *Dial*, and she wished that those whom she prized and loved would likewise become more involved. Fuller also began to make preparations for a new series of Conversations on Greek mythology to begin in March. Because the series of ten meetings would bring her nearly $600, she remained silent about the fact that she had not yet received any of the money promised her for her work on the *Dial*. The interest showed in her Conversations pleased Fuller, as did another word of encouragement from the *New-Yorker*. In a discussion of "Our Higher Periodical Literature" (20 February) the magazine commented disparagingly upon the "shallow witticism" of the *Dial*'s detractors and repeated its earlier stand that, despite a "fitful and disconnected" sense of organization, the "frequent glimmerings of high and noble truths" made the *Dial* worthwhile.[37]

As February came to a close, Fuller was also pleased by the state of the April 1841 number. Parker had established himself as a regular contributor with a piece on labor, and three new writers—William D. Wilson, John M. Mackie, John F. Tuckerman—were scheduled to have pieces published. Then too, Fuller had on hand many pages from earlier contributions: Clarke finally finished the poem he had promised for the first number of the *Dial*; the second part of Dwight's "Ideals of Every-Day Life" stood ready for use; and Fuller selected some of Hooper's verses from her portfolio. She also took Channing's poems, which she had held back from the January *Dial*, and a new poem that, after helping Emerson correct, she rather pretentiously titled "Theme for a World-Drama."[38] Thoreau had submitted a poem, "Sic Vita," but Fuller decided not to print it, possibly because Caroline Sturgis had sent in some more verses that she as the editor preferred.[39]

Fuller herself had prepared an autobiographical piece, "Leila,"[40] and had completed a planned "Dialogue" on art.[41] Emerson, who was correcting proof for his first book of *Essays*, offered his lecture on "Man the Reformer." The Mechanics' Institute, where he had delivered the talk in January, wished to print the piece, but he asked whether Fuller would like it for the *Dial*, allowing the institute to sell copies printed from the *Dial*'s plates, or whether she wished to let the institute have the lecture outright, and take a chance on how much material he could then supply her. While Emerson had no real opinion, he did have a slight preference for the *Dial*, wishing to inject something "practical" into their "too spiritual magazine." Fuller rather wisely took the lecture rather than trust him to do something else. But he held up the manuscript for corrections, possibly wishing to use it for his lecture on "Reform" at Concord on 10 March, and it was not sent to the printer until the middle of the month. Fuller, who had listened to an earlier version of it with enjoyment, was happy to have it.[42]

The April 1841 *Dial* was somewhat delayed in reaching the booksellers. Weeks, Jordan & Co. were having financial problems and, as "insolvent debtors," had been forced to place their property in trust with their creditors.[43] As a result the *Dial* was not advertised for sale until 5 April.[44] Fuller, her health once again in a bad state from the strain of both editing a magazine and holding her Conversations, said nothing about the April number, but Emerson was keenly disappointed. He considered most of it to be a "Morgue" and thought the poetry bad; a month later he had still not read it through, and he considered it so dull that he forgot to send a copy to his Aunt Mary. He did send Carlyle a copy, "heartily" wishing that it were better.

James Marsh, former president of the University of Vermont, who had earlier turned down Ripley's invitation to become a contributor, was also disappointed. He considered Transcendentalism itself to be a "superficial affair" and saw its journal as indicating "rather the place of the moon than of the sun." Its writers had much of the "prettinesses of the German writers" but sadly lacked their "manly logic and strong systematizing tendency," a lack resulting in each uttering "the inspiration of the moment, assuming that it all comes from the universal heart, while ten to one it comes only from the stomach of the individual." At least one person in England liked the April number: William Forster told a friend to buy the *Dial* since "[a]lmost every article is worth reading."[45]

A reviewer for the *Dartmouth* (April 1841), an undergraduate literary magazine, did think highly of the articles in the *Dial*, which he found "new," "vigorous," and "heedless of old and withered formalities." In a short paragraph the *Boston Daily Advertiser* (6 April) summarized the *Dial's* contents and commented only that the poetry of the current number fell much below that of former ones. The *Western Messenger* (April), in the last issue it would publish, gave a vacuous puff to the Boston journal, calling it "the wind-flower of a new spring in the western world." Urging its readers to ignore "the Geese, who had hissed their loudest at this new comer," the writer for the *Messenger* asked everyone to subscribe to this new "Era in American Literature." The *New-Yorker* reprinted selections from three articles and a poem, and the reviewer for the New York *Arcturus* (April) told the readers of its favorable essay on "Ralph Waldo Emerson" that Emerson was supposed to be "the spirit of the Dial."

The writer for the *Boston Morning Post* (14 April) gave the *Dial* its shortest — and its best — review yet in that paper. Praising the magazine for not containing any grossly Transcendental writings such as Alcott's, the reviewer said that the *Dial* showed more promise now than at any other time, though it was still not "wholly free from the sin of Transcendental writing." A brief notice in the *Providence Daily Journal* (6 April) also complained of this gap between articles of "great ability" and those of "general nonsense." As the *Dial* was "less dream-like" than usual, the reviewer for the *Boston Evening Mercantile Journal* (10 April) also felt that less Transcendentalism was in this number than in any of its predecessors and gave it a good review. In broadly outlining the articles, the reviewer thought that Wilson's essay on Unitarianism was good — though he disagreed with it — as was Emerson's lecture, although it also was of "little practical" import. On 10 April Greeley began publishing the *New-York Daily Tribune*, where he continued to show his support for the *Dial* by reprinting (15 April) the review from the *New-Yorker* and a selection from Parker's "Thoughts on Labor."[46]

The response to the April 1841 *Dial* was, though favorable, less conspicuous than usual. While Greeley praised it and reprinted selections in two papers, he was hardly considered unbiased and was, besides, not in Boston, where most of the *Dial*'s readers and purchasers were located. Now, one year after its publication had begun, the *Dial* was regularly noticed only by local papers and by friends in New York and Cincinnati — and the latter were to be silent thereafter. No major journal mentioned the April *Dial*, much less reviewed it; even the *Knickerbocker* failed to make fun of it. Its publishers were in financial trouble, and its editor was in bad health. All things considered, the future prospects for the *Dial* were not very bright.

As the second volume of the *Dial* was being prepared for the press, fewer high-sounding declarations of purpose were made while more down-to-earth work was done. Only Alcott continued his obstinate climb to empyrean heights: in June he visited Vermont and passed out, mostly to unlettered farmers, copies of the *Dial* and Emerson's *Essays*. One pleasant item, which indicated the *Dial* did appeal to a variety of tastes, was an American Quaker's letter to the *Monthly Magazine*, in which he praised Heraud's journal and the *Dial* as standing "alone in pointing to the Spirit." Near the end of May Fuller arrived in Concord for a visit of two weeks. She spent much of the time discussing the *Dial* with Emerson; after she left he wished that his next visitor, Caroline Sturgis, would hurry away so that he would have time to work on the matters that Fuller had left with him.[47]

Emerson was trying to write a long poem for the *Dial* — the second part of his "Woodnotes" that had appeared in the October 1840 number — but by 17 June 1841 he had looked into "every cornel bush & buttercup" in Concord for ideas without success. In desperation he set out for Boston, thinking to "explore the Atheneum, nay, even the wharves & the salt water, to pluck up any drowned muse by the locks." His visit was successful, and a few days later he discussed his progress with Fuller and Sturgis. By 22 June the "long bright poem" had grown to eighteen pages, and Emerson personally took it to Boston for the printer. But he arrived two days after the date he had promised the poem, and as a result "the whole number was made up & the last sheet printing," so that he was forced to postpone publishing the poem until the next number.[48] He was, however, represented in the July *Dial* by his favorable review of Jones Very's *Essays and Poems*, which he himself had edited and which he had managed to get in before Fuller's deadline.[49]

One reason why Emerson had found himself pushed out of the July 1841 number was Fuller's success in both attracting new contributions and finding suitable old ones from her portfolio. Henry Channing and Sophia Ripley had contributed articles, and Fuller was able to choose from poems by Cranch, Ellery Channing, Sturgis, and Lowell. She also had verses by Eliza Clapp of Dorchester, Massachusetts, which Emerson had received in October 1840 but, which, because of necessary revisions and because of Clapp's shyness about publishing them, had been unavailable until now. Another new contributor, J. A. Saxton, had sent in a long article on "Prophecy — Transcendentalism — Progress." Parker had finished a long essay on "The Pharisees" and had even given "a couple of little bits of verses" that Fuller decided to print.[50] Thoreau had contributed a poem, just at the time when Fuller was beginning to think better of him as their acquaintance grew.[51] His "Sic Vita" had been with her since January, and, probably at Emerson's urging, she decided to print it.[52]

In fact, the voluntary contributions to this number were so plentiful that Fuller was forced to write a note "To Contributors" on the last page. Explaining that normally any contribution that showed a combination of "individuality of character with vigor and accuracy of style" would have been printed, she apologized to the authors of those many articles "not without merit" that had gone unpublished because the *Dial*'s space was limited. Fuller apparently had kept these pieces for possible future insertion, for she told her readers not to be discouraged if they did not hear from the *Dial*'s editor concerning their contributions. Finally, those who had written demanding answers to "points which interest them" were told to consult instead the pages of the *Dial*, wherein "expressions of sentiment and opinion on those points" could be found, which would be "more satisfactory than any which could be rendered in a private correspondence."

The many contributions to the July 1841 number allowed Fuller to give her full attention to one long article and seven book reviews, including a positive review of Carlyle's *Heroes and Hero-Worship* and a disappointed one of Lowell's *A Year's Life*. The article, "Goethe," took up almost one-third of the number; Fuller made good use of the many notes that she had taken for her planned life of Goethe, and the essay was praised as being one of the finest critiques on him that had yet appeared in the American press.[53]

The July *Dial*, which appeared as promised on the first of the month, was in excellent shape; with a good supply of varied contributions from many pens, it was probably the most balanced issue yet.[54] Unfortunately, the damage of the first experimental year had been done, and the reviews of this issue were few in number and weak in content. The reviewer for the *Boston Morning Post* (10 July) praised the poetry as being for the most part better than that of previous numbers. After calling again on his fellow reviewers to be tolerant of new ideas, the *Post* reviewer pointed to a number of articles—"of much ability"— as exemplifying the new, and more earthbound, character of the latest *Dial*. The writer for the *New-Yorker* (10 July) also approved of the animating spirit behind most of the articles; though it had "no room for a more extended notice," the magazine printed in six other issues six selections from the *Dial* as indicative of its contents. Greeley also reprinted this review and three of the selections in his *New-York Daily Tribune* (13 July). The reviewer in *Godey's Lady's Book* (September) said that he liked some of the articles, although he did have trouble determining exactly what the *Dial* was: "It . . . contains some gems of modern philosophy, but so intermingled with the rubbish of old exploded systems, and so wrapt about with the mysteries of transcendentalism . . . that it is very difficult to estimate its character."

The mildly favorable review of a Boston newspaper, a brief notice by two newspapers known to be sympathetic toward the Transcendentalists, and a baffled response by an influential ladies' magazine: these were not likely to help the *Dial* much in gaining recognition. Surprisingly, the next few months saw an increased, though not wholly favorable, interest in the *Dial*, both by the press and by possible contributors. Yet old contributors either were dropping out or were being troublesome, and other, new contributors were submitting works of uneven quality. And Fuller—who was discovering that she would have to write over half the next number herself—complained that "About our poor little Dial, as often before, it irks me to think."[55]

One favorable public notice was the one in the *Boston Weekly Magazine* (4 September). The writer found the magazine, despite its "occasional absurdities of style and matter," to be "ably conducted" and financially "well supported," and to contain "much useful truth." A comment on the *Dial* from England was less encouraging.[56] In his "Preface" to the English edition of Emerson's *Essays*, Carlyle called the *Dial* a "noteworthy though very unattractive work," which appeared generally to be inbued with Emerson's "way of thinking, and to proceed from the circle that learns of him." The *Presbyterian* was even more blunt: its reviewer said that if the "Transcendentalists of Boston" continued to follow "the doctrine of their quarterly periodical, the *Dial*," they would "sooner or later be cast a helpless wreck upon the rock of Infidelity, alias Reason, alias Pantheism or Transcendentalism."[57] In *Graham's Magazine* (September) Edgar Allan Poe also took a shot at the Transcendentalists. His "Never Bet Your Head,"a satire on Transcendentalism, mentioned the *Dial* twice as the organ of that group and ended on the death of the main character, Toby Dammit, with the narrator sending the "very moderate bill" for the funeral to his friends, the Transcendentalists: the "scoundrels refused to pay it, so I had Mr. Dammit dug up at once, and sold him for dog's meat."[58]

Fortunately, some Transcendentalists and their sympathizers gave a more spirited response to the *Dial*'s need for contributions than Mr. Dammit's friends, although when their writings were of a questionable quality it often fell upon

Emerson to reject them. In April 1841 he had received some verses from a Miss A. D. Woodbridge of Albany, New York, but, feeling that they lacked merit, Emerson had not sent them on to Fuller. When he finally replied in July, he told Miss Woodbridge that her poems, while "uncommonly smooth and eloquent," were too conventional for the *Dial*. He was, as usual, polite in his rejection; the tone of the letter, though clearly indicates that her verses were stilted and uninspired, and when Miss Woodbridge, apparently undeterred by Emerson's kind refusal, wrote again in August, he merely passed the letter on to Fuller, who once again rejected her contributions.[59] Emerson also turned down Daniel Parker's "easy & superficial verses," asking him to keep trying until "the deepest fires of the heart" had revealed to him the "deeper secret" of "the Muse."[60] Some translations of Orpheus were rejected by Emerson after Thoreau had told him that they were inaccurate. When William Henry Orne, a recent Harvard graduate, sent in some poems in August, Emerson forwarded them without comment to Fuller, who rejected them, as she did the poetry and prose of Anthony White, whom Emerson had recommended highly.[61]

The rejected pieces must have truly been poor, for Fuller was not in a position to refuse usable papers. She had been able to take two poems by Caroline Sturgis out of her portfolio, and Elizabeth Peabody had contributed an essay on "A Glimpse of Christ's Idea of Society." Dwight had sent in one of his sermons on "The Religion of Beauty." Alcott, though he had written more "Orphic Sayings,"[62] submitted a poem, "Cupid's Conflict," by the seventeenth-century poet Henry More, "in place," said the *Dial*'s introduction of it, "of the contributuion suggested for himself."[63] Parker was too busy preparing for his course of "Lectures on Religion" in Boston to aid the *Dial*, and a trip to Brook Farm in September by Emerson and Fuller yielded nothing. Thoreau, who had recently moved in with the Emersons for "his board &c for what labor he chooses to do," had under Emerson's sponsorship sent in three poems to Fuller. One, a poem on "The Fisher's Son," which Thoreau had copied from his journal of January 1840, was submitted in August 1841 but apparently was rejected by Fuller at once. A second poem, which Emerson thought very good, described Mount Wachusett. Emerson had requested the poem for the *Dial* in July; the next month Thoreau gave it to him to send to Fuller. She also rejected this poem, but she told Thoreau that the *Dial* might publish it if he would revise it. When Thoreau agreed the poem was returned to him, but he took no further action on it before October. Emerson had read the third poem, on "Friendship," in November 1839; he thought it "grand," and one year later gave it to Fuller to read. Thoreau apparently thought that it had been accepted at that earlier time, and was disappointed not only when it failed to appear in the *Dial* but was returned to him for revision. He omitted the "long lines," and the new version, which Emerson considered "correct & presentable," was sent to the printer in August.[64]

Emerson's interest in Thoreau's poems,[65] his consideration of others' contributions, and his address on "The Method of Nature" at Waterville, Maine, in August all allowed him little time for his own work on material for the *Dial*. Throughout the last part of the summer he was plagued by creative problems. In

July he had worked on the poems "Painting and Sculpture" and "Fate," but when he finally sent them to the printer in August he despaired of their quality. He had also planned to revise "Woodnotes" during this period, but no "angel of regeneration" had stirred him, and when he sent the poem to the printer in August he told Fuller that "all this long waiting" had produced no improvements in the work. Because of the poems he had sent in, Emerson promised nothing in the way of prose. As October 1841 drew closer, though, and Fuller grew almost desperate about finding good material for the *Dial*, Emerson considered writing on Hedge's Phi Beta Kappa Address at Harvard, but nothing came of the notion. Fuller suggested instead that Emerson work up the essay on Walter Savage Landor that he had shown her in June. He agreed to do it, and helped somewhat by Elizabeth Hoar's suggestions, he worked hard on the essay and a week later had sent Fuller the final draft. She needed it so badly that, when Emerson decided that it was not worth the trip to the printer to polish certain parts of it, she sent her brother to Concord to pick up his corrections and return them to her in time to have the essay included.[66]

Fuller was not only pressed for material, she was also physically exhausted. By mid-September 1841 she had written most of her fifty-three-page article on "Lives of the Great Composers," but her review of Bailey's *Festus*, which Emerson had sent her in July, was only half finished. The engagement of Ellery Channing to her sister Ellen had upset her, and she was not certain that she could give full attention to her writing. When Fuller did finish the review, her favorable comments had been stretched to over thirty pages by many selections from the work.[67] Therefore, when Emerson sent her in mid-September two poems he had received from Cranch, she seized them as "a succor of Apollo for her closing pages." But unfortunately, after Fuller had left them off with the printer, he discovered that she had misjudged the length of the issue, and only one of the two poems, which were complementary, was printed, causing Emerson to apologize to Cranch and to promise to print them both together in the next number.[68]

The *Dial*'s publication on 1 October 1841 was different in two respects from that of previous numbers: there was a new publisher and a very different reception by the press.[69] Weeks, Jordan & Co., having assigned their property "in trust for their creditors" in February, had settled their claims on 9 September. It seems that, as part of the settlement, I. H. and William A. Weeks left the company, and Jordan's name stood alone on the cover of the October *Dial*. Jordan obviously was not happy with the *Dial*'s sales, for he continued the policy, begun in July, of making subscribers pay an additional dollar if they waited until after receiving the second number before sending in their three dollars.[70]

The *Dial*'s reception was also different this time. Greeley's *New-Yorker* had ceased publication on 20 September, and both his weekly and daily *New-York Tribunes* failed to review the *Dial*, only selecting one piece, Emerson's article on Landor, to reprint from it. The *New-York Mirror* also reprinted an article from the *Dial*—Fuller's piece on Goethe in July—but failed to give a review of the latest issue. The *Boston Courier* (1 October) and the *Boston Atlas* (4 October) each merely listed the contents of the number, about which the *Courier* writer admitted, "We have read no portion."

Only the *Providence Daily Journal* (14 October) and the *Boston Morning Post* (15 October), among the *Dial*'s regular reviewers, bothered to discuss the new number. The *Journal*'s reviewer mentioned only Sturgis's "Light and Shade," observing that "the muse that would inspire such doggerel, must wear cap and bells." However, in the warmest review in the *Post* yet, the writer praised the "life, soul, freshness, sincerity, [and] originality" of the *Dial* and quoted in its entirety Cranch's "Inworld."

The two other reviews of the October *Dial* were just as favorable. The reviewer for the *Musical Magazine* (6 November) quoted extensively from Fuller's "Lives of the Great Composers" in showing his approval of her article, and the editors of the *Yale Literary Magazine* (November) called the *Dial* "a genial, and most welcome visitor." The *Yale*'s editors had not seen the *Dial* before, but they had been warned by "Fathers in New England Theology" what heresies to expect. Had they seen an earlier number, they would have found such warnings confirmed; this one, however, they said, contained nothing in that vein, and they recommended the *Dial* as "a journal that will meet the wants and wishes of the scholar." And in a satiric "Visit to Hades" "Aeneas, Jr.," writing in the *Dartmouth* (November), described Plato as "busily engaged in writing for the Dial, which lay open before him, and which he looked at occasionally with evident satisfaction."

These words of praise meant comparatively little, though, since no established journal even mentioned the *Dial*; musicians and friends of Yale University and Dartmouth College could hardly be expected to keep the *Dial* afloat by themselves. Parodies were still appearing: the *Christian Advocate and Journal* (10 November) reprinted a definition of Transcendentalism as "the spiritual cognoscence of psychological irrefragibility, connected with concutient ademption of incoluminent spirituality and etherialized contention of subsoltory concretion." In addition, private reactions to the *Dial* were often as distressing as before. Carlyle thought that it was still too "spirit-like, aeriform, aurora-borealis like"; he wanted, instead of an "*angel* body," a "stalwart Yankee *man*." And when one of New York's leading young citizens, George Templeton Strong, entered his local library and saw the *Dial* for the first time, he thought it "a beastly . . . organ of the rankest kind of Deistical New England Socinianism."[71]

The October *Dial* marked not only a high point in the magazine's literary quality but a turning point as well in its publication. Fuller was once again exhausted by her editorial work, and her state of mind was "deeply grave, deeply lonely." Since none of her promised salary as editor had been paid, and since she, like everyone else, received no money for her contributions, Fuller was supporting herself by teaching school and giving private lessons in addition to running the *Dial*.[72] The strain of all this made her even harder to get along with, as Emerson somewhat testily noted.[73] This was the state that Fuller was in when Ripley, her coeditor, resigned and the *Dial*'s publisher was again changed.

As Ripley became more involved with planning his Brook Farm community, his concern for the *Dial* flagged, and while the October 1841 number was being printed he announced his intention to withdraw from "all interest" in it. At the same time, Fuller deemed it "greatly more satisfactory" to all should the *Dial's* publication be shifted to Elizabeth Peabody.[74] Since Ripley was the only one who comprehended how Jordan's muddled financial affairs stood, he went to effect the change. And a month of legal maneuvering passed before accounts were settled and the printing of the next number of the *Dial* could begin.

When Ripley visited Jordan in early October he discovered that the contract for the *Dial* had not been with Weeks, Jordan & Co. but with William and Hubbard Weeks "in their private capacity." Still, upon the bankruptcy of the firm, the *Dial's* subscription list—the only record of its paying subscribers—had been made over to the assignees and was accounted for at a certain price in the settlement of the firm's affairs. Therefore, even though their contract had stipulated that it might be terminated at "the pleasure of either party," the list of subscribers, "according to the book-selling usage," had remained with the publishers, who had sold it to their creditors. Conveniently, the assignee was A. S. Jordan, the publisher's brother, and he proposed these conditions for his giving up the *Dial's* subscription list: the editors would pay all bills that had previously been contracted; Jordan would retain his fifteen percent commission on all numbers previously sold; Jordan would be paid twenty-five cents per name on the subscription list; and Jordan would be allowed a thirty percent discount on any copies he might buy from the future publishers, plus a fifteen percent commission on all of those that he sold. In return, the editors would receive the subscription list. Should the *Dial* remain with Jordan, then he would receive fifty cents for each volume sold and would be responsible for procuring paper and for the printing, with the bills being contracted to Emerson's name. Ripley thought the terms for transferal not very unreasonable and advised Emerson to accept, though he did feel that Jordan had demanded too much for the subscription list. He also proposed waiting until the end of the volume, when matters would be "more simple," before making the change.[75]

Emerson found Jordan's terms unacceptable: it meant paying too much money to make the change in publishers, money that would have to come out of his own pocket, and he therefore engaged the Boston lawyer George Hillard to replace Ripley in the bargaining. But when November came no breakthrough had been made, and Fuller feared that the *Dial* was "likely to fall through entirely." However, during the first week of November 1841, Emerson and Fuller decided to write an advertisement stating the facts of the matter and to move the *Dial* to Elizabeth Peabody's without the list of subscribers and with a new name. Emerson's belief that this would shame Jordan into settling for less than the "Eightynine dollars" that he had proposed was apparently confirmed. Hillard's negotiations suddenly showed progress; by 9 November Fuller announced that the *Dial* would begin printing the following week. Emerson learned from this experience and made sure that when Peabody accepted the *Dial* the contract clearly stated that the title and the subscription list were Fuller's "exclusive property."[76]

The January 1842 *Dial*, despite the delay resulting from the shift in publishers, was in excellent shape. Fuller had on hand long articles by Clarke, Peabody, Parker, and Peabody's friend William Greene, as well as the two poems by Cranch that were to be printed in atonement for the error in the October number. Poems from Hooper, Lowell, and a new contributor, B. F. Presbury, had been obtained by Emerson, who had also gotten Thomas Stone's permission to use his letter to Mary Moody Emerson on Transcendentalism. He included this letter in his own article of the same title, and his "contingent of particolored light infantry" also included three poems, a short discussion of "The Senses and the Soul," and a book review. Alcott had given him selections from his diary, which Emerson considered more readable than his previous contributions. But Fuller already had enough material, and when she offered to print the selections in an abbreviated form Alcott declined. In the meantime, Thoreau revised his lines on Mount Wachusett and sent them in again. Although he had shortened the poem, Fuller still disliked it, complaining of its poor imagery and its detachment of thought, and she suggested that Thoreau try to revise it again and then resubmit it.[77] Thoreau decided against trying the *Dial* yet another time and saved the poem for inclusion in his "A Walk to Wachusett," which was published in the January 1843 *Boston Miscellany*.[78]

Fuller felt confident enough to reject or to shorten Thoreau's and Alcott's contributions because, in addition to the large amount of material already on hand, she had herself written much for the January 1842 number, including a translation from Goethe, six book reviews, and a companion piece to "The Magnolia of Lake Pontchartrain" of the previous January. Called "Yuca Filamentosa," the last was Fuller's recollection of a Boston doctor's description of that flower's blooming at full moon that she had heard two years before,[79] and she prefaced it with some lines by her new brother-in-law Ellery Channing. Her final article was a combined review of both Goethe's correspondence with Bettina, which she had mentioned the previous July, and a translation of Bettina's letters to her friend Günderode.[80] Fuller's choice of this article was fortunate: she had again misjudged the length of the number and, with the help of two of her pupils, she extended the article by using many extracts. Fuller "barely scrambled through" until, when the issue was finally complete, she was left in a state of "extreme fatigue . . . quite unfit to hold a pen"; she planned to do nothing for a few days but bathe and sit in the open air. She might well have heeded Jones Very's warning, which he directed at Emerson, though it applied more aptly to her. Very worried that Emerson might be expending too much strength in his work on the *Dial*, and he cautioned that "[e]nfeeblement of the power is attendant on such mental exertion."[81]

But the tone and quality of the reviews did Fuller little good. Although the Billerica physician Daniel Parker was impressed by the "capital articles" in the number and the "strong and sure" contributors, the *Boston Courier* (6 January) merely gave the contents, and the *Boston Atlas* (3 January) simply announced that it had been published, without even mentioning the contents. *Graham's Magazine* (January) failed to review the *Dial*, but its writer did enveigh against "Orphicism, or Dialism, or Emersonianism, or any other pregnant compound indicative of confusion worse confounded." The writer for both the semiweekly and daily issues of the *Boston Advertiser* (5 January) complimented the *Dial* on being "punctually published," but on little else.[82] He declared that it was unlikely to be read except by those sympathetic to its "mannerisms," since "the 'world's folk'" considered it to be "absurd." Parker's article was good, he said, but it contained *"heresies"*; Fuller's piece on Bettina was "defaced" by the "broken English" of its translation. The reviewer could say little for the poetry, since the *Dial* had "a poetic creed of its own," teaching that "all care of metre and rhyme is useless if not worse."

Greeley, however, helped by reprinting three poems in his *New-York Daily Tribune*, and he described the *Dial* (14 January) as "replete with elevated Thought and profound Spiritualism"; yet the contents were only listed, and no comments of any real value were made. The *Boston Evening Mercantile Journal* (3 January) also passed over the *Dial's* publication, merely noting that it contained several well-written articles on different subjects, some of a "controversial character."

The sole bright spot was the *Boston Morning Post* (19 January), which by now was publishing the most regular and perceptive reviews of the *Dial*. The *Post* reviewer praised the number's "ability and spirit" and went on to describe and point out the virtues of many of the articles. Most important, the reviewer complimented it for showing "Man's soul-nobility" in "letters of vivid light" throughout its pages — the first time that the *Dial's* stated aim had been recognized by an impartial publication. The writer had recognized that Transcendentalism, when stripped of the pejorative connotations associated with its name, was not so bad after all.

William Kelley of Philadelphia felt the same and, when he invited Brownson to preach there, mentioned that his congregation read the *Dial*, which was of great assistance to the members, who lived by listening to their consciences. Carlyle also listened to his conscience, but it spoke in a different tone: the *Dial*, "almost every Number" of which he had read, was still, by reason of its "very high flights about Art, Self-sacrifice, Progress, etc., etc.," too "ghostly" for his taste. It was too "strange" for him to enjoy, and its "shrill, incorporeal, spiritlike" pages were so "hideous" that he sarcastically remarked to a friend, "We live in a most wondrous 'New Era,' do we not?"[83]

A "New Era" was, indeed, about ready to begin for the *Dial*. Even though the April 1842 number was progressing nicely, Fuller had decided to resign as editor. Her already poor health had been further weakened by the effort needed to complete the January number, and she felt that her powers had been "forced to dissipate" as she met "others' mental wants" instead of satisfying her own desires. Then too, Emerson had been unable to give any help at all during the two months since the last *Dial* had been published; his busy lecture schedule and the death in January of his only son had left him with little time or inclination to spend on the magazine. The deciding factor in Fuller's decision, though, was a financial one. Clarke and Peabody had finally been allowed to examine the books of Weeks, Jordan & Co., and they had discovered that the former publishers were "much in debt" to the *Dial* when they had declared bankruptcy. As a result Fuller had never received "a penny" for "her time & toil." Peabody had also found that there were not, as Emerson had supposed, five or six hundred paying subscribers, but only three hundred. If these people continued to take the *Dial*, Peabody said, they would bring in after "deductions for agency" $750 per year. Since Peabody estimated the costs for publishing the *Dial* to be $700 per year, it was clear that even in the future Fuller would not be receiving any payments.[84]

With these thoughts in mind, Fuller wrote Emerson in mid-March about her decision, enclosing a letter from Peabody describing the financial condition of the *Dial* and describing her own deteriorating physical state. For more than three months she had been unable to write anything except letters. The last winter had been especially bad for her, and she felt that she would not fully recover for two or three months more. She was planning another series of Conversations for the next winter, and if she had to continue working at her present pace on the *Dial* she thought that she would "sink under" entirely. A promise of financial remuneration would permit her to devote most of her time to the magazine, but without a salary she needed to earn money elsewhere, and since both her Conversations and the *Dial* were full-time jobs she said that she had had to make a choice. She suggested that either Parker or Emerson take over the *Dial* and promised her aid as a contributor. Her decision was fixed, she told Emerson, and she had written a "little notice with regard to the possibility of suspending the 'Dial' for a time" for Peabody to insert in the April number.[85]

In her letter that accompanied Fuller's, Peabody also recommended that either Emerson or Parker take over and she volunteered herself as assistant editor. Emerson replied to Fuller that, while her decision was both "sad & sudden" to him, he agreed with her reasons completely, and he praised her for being such a "lavish spender of time labor & health for our poor Dial." He was not ready "tonight" to decide the *Dial*'s future, but would let her know his decision very soon. As to the notice about suspending publication, Emerson suggested doing nothing about it now, since they could always insert "a slip of paper" at the last moment.[86]

Three days later Emerson gave Fuller his answer. Despite private misgivings that the *Dial*'s "interior & spiritual life" was "ill fed" and that its "outward & bibliopolic existence" was "worse managed," he agreed to take it over "for a time." Since her friends were also his, there was no reason why they should not aid him as well, though his main resource would be that of "Selection from old or from foreign books," and Chaucer would "speak whenever a dull article is offered and rejected." Saying that he had so little skill in partnerships, Emerson decided against having a coeditor, since he believed that they would make each other "mutually uneasy." He ended by asking Fuller for "folios of information" on the details of running the magazine, and he wished her good luck and improved health.[87]

Emerson accepted the editorship because he was basically unwilling to "disappoint the little company who have really looked to it with a certain religion, tenderness & hope," and because he thought it could be made "greatly better without killing its editor." Since he also valued the *Dial* as "a portfolio which preserves & conveys to distant persons precisely what I should borrow & transcribe to send them if I could," the chance to completely dictate its contents was also appealing. As no other qualified person but Fuller came close to agreeing with him on this last item, he felt himself forced to be the sole editor: the "Humanity & Reform Men" trampled on "letters & poetry," while the "Scholars" were "dead & dry."[88]

Emerson was quite right in his description of the *Dial*'s "company" of followers as both devoted and small. The number of reviews had been falling off, but those which were left were gradually improving. While in New York Emerson had seen a number at Henry James's house, and he had been told, by Thomas Delf, an employee at Wiley & Putnam's who was a "faithful reader" of the magazine, that the *Dial* was highly thought of among the young men in New York. It upset Emerson that fewer people asked about the new and younger writers than they did about such already well-known contributors as Parker, and that occasional pieces still ridiculed the *Dial*. But he did not lose his faith in the magazine's chances for success in the role he had assigned to it as a discoverer and promoter of new talent.[89]

Emerson had no doubts at all about the quantity of material for contributions on which he could depend. Fuller had filled the recent numbers with ease, and the April 1842 issue was already completed. Parker had sent in a long article on theology and seven book reviews; Cranch and Charles Dana of Brook Farm had contributed poems; Alcott's "Days from a Diary" was still set in type from December; and Fuller had translated "Marie Van Oosterwich." Also, more reviews had been forced out of this number by a lack of space. For the future, Emerson had been promised letters of "foreign intelligence" by Charles Stearns Wheeler, who was going to Germany, and by Alcott, who, with Emerson's financial help, was planning to leave for England in May.[90]

Another factor that Emerson did not mention but that had much to do with his decision was his series of eight lectures on "The Times" at Boston in December and January, which had netted him over $300. Although he had received no income from his stocks and his series of five of "The Times" lectures at Providence in February had given him "trivial reward," he took in about $200 in profits when he repeated the entire "Times" course at New York in March.[91] Emerson was, therefore, not in the same financial straits in which Fuller had found herself. His lectures also provided him with available material for use in the *Dial*. Finally, his lectures had kept him away from the *Dial* long

enough—nothing of his was in the April number—for him to forget the problems involved in publishing it. In front of him Emerson saw the *Dial's* acceptance from friends without and promises of continuance from friends within; the
lessons of the past were forgotten. And in view of the fact that the *Dial* was
published at the end of March, four full days ahead of schedule, he cannot be
too much blamed for his hastily-conceived optimism.[92] The only hint of trouble
was Peabody's notice "To the Friends of the Dial" on the back wrapper of the
April number, stating that the expenses of publication and distribution were
"out of proportion to the profits," and asking subscribers to help by paying on
time or in advance.[93] But dunning delinquent subscribers was hardly an unusual
practice, and no mention of financial problems was made by any of the
reviewers.[94]

April 1842 began well enough with a brief essay in the *Magnolia* defending
Transcendentalism against the religious journals that had been attacking it.[95]
Greeley continued his policy of helping the *Dial* with his review of it in the *New-
York Tribune* (2 April). After briefly praising each piece in "this original and excellent work," the reviewer noted with pleasure that Emerson was to become the
editor, and he hoped that Emerson would curb some of the licenses of thought
and expression that had marred the quality of earlier issues. Even so, the
reviewer stated, the *Dial* was still "the best periodical for earnest, large-souled
inquirers yet published in the English tongue." Surprisingly, however, the
Tribune failed to reprint anything from the *Dial*.[96]

The *Boston Morning Post* (5 April) continued its generally favorable attitude.
Parker's article was the best thing in the number, while Alcott's "Days from a
Diary," which contained thoughts ranging from gardening to more "Orphic Sayings," was of uncertain value. As a result, according to the reviewer, the "mixture of the plain and the mystic" was once again noticeable. The *Boston Daily
Times* (6 April), in a review reprinted by the *Quarto Boston Notion* (16 April),
praised the *Dial* for allowing its contributors a free hand in expressing "whatever
they feel impelled to say"; for this reason the review said, "It is therefore always
pleasant reading."

The final review of the April number was one that quite correctly summed up
Fuller's two years as editor. The writer for the *Knickerbocker* (May) spent all but
the last few lines of his page-long review condemning Alcott; by the end there
was only enough space left to briefly mention two other articles. Thus the initial
flurry of ridicule had dwindled to a few, and mostly scanty, reviews. And in
England Carlyle gave away his copy of the new *Dial* to a friend without comment.[97]

The novelty of a Transcendental periodical had worn thin upon the press. As
Emerson began to prepare the *Dial's* third volume, he was faced with the problem of reviving interest in the magazine while at the same time avoiding the
more disastrous sort of reaction that could be brought down by a writer such as
Alcott.

4

The *Dial* Under Emerson

The first thing that Ralph Waldo Emerson did as editor was to ask two of the *Dial*'s best contributors, Margaret Fuller and Theodore Parker, for advice. After the April 1842 *Dial* had been published, Fuller, having worked on the magazine almost daily for six months, went to the country to be in absolute retirement and quiet. When Emerson's letter reached her, she expressed her wish that he would give the *Dial* a full year for "a fair trial." She pointed out what she considered to be the major point of difference between them as regarded the magazine's contents: she had tried to publish a magazine in which "all kinds of people" had the "freedom to say their say, for better, for worse"; he would form the *Dial* after his own tastes. She said this with no bitterness, merely as a statement of fact, and she wished him the best of luck. In response to Emerson's request for "good suggestions for the better conduct of the paper," Parker replied that, while Fuller had done well, he thought that the *Dial* would now "grow up to vigorous manhood" under Emerson's care. He had only one suggestion to make, and he made it forcefully: if Emerson wished to be sure of the *Dial*'s success, then he should *"write a great deal for it himself."*[1]

Even so, Emerson tried to put aside "all thoughts of the Dial until 1 May" in order to concentrate on his own "reading & writing."[2] As usual, he was unable to keep his resolution. Since one of his prime objectives after taking over the *Dial* was to give a greater emphasis to poetry, he soon began assembling verses for the July 1842 number.[3] Eliza Clapp had sent him some of her verses in February, and Emerson chose one, which he titled "Autumn Leaves." He also chose two poems by Jones Very and one by Charles Dana. Ellery Channing had recently asked Fuller to gather up and forward to him at Cincinnati his verses from among his friends, and Emerson added some of these to ones he had left over from his earlier article on "New Poetry," making a total of eight poems by Channing for the next *Dial*. For prose Emerson accepted Fuller's offer to review Nathaniel Hawthorne's *Twice-Told Tales*, and he set Henry Thoreau, whom he had made "private secretary to the President of the Dial," to work on an account of Massachusetts from some books that Emerson had recently read.[4] Although Bronson Alcott was too busy making preparations for his early May departure for England to contribute anything, his brother Junius was represented by a short prayer, which, along with one by Thoreau, Emerson worked into an article he was preparing on the topic of prayer.[5]

THE DIAL:

A

MAGAZINE

FOR

LITERATURE, PHILOSOPHY, AND RELIGION.

TO BE CONTINUED QUARTERLY.

No. IX.

JULY, 1842.

BOSTON:
PUBLISHED BY E. P. PEABODY,
13 WEST STREET.
LONDON:
JOHN GREEN, 121 NEWGATE STREET.
M DCCC XLII.

CAMBRIDGE PRESS:—THURSTON AND TORRY.

Front wrapper of the July 1842 *Dial*, Emerson's first as editor.
Collection of Joel Myerson.

Emerson was busily working on his own contributions all through April 1842. He completed three poems and prepared to publish his introductory lecture from "The Times" series.[6] More good material came from his journal, as Emerson drew upon a conversation with his neighbor Edmund Hosmer and his recent reading in writing an article on the agriculture of Massachusetts. Carrying out his earlier promise to use old authors, he turned to *The Heetopades of Veeshnoo-Sarma*, which he had read the previous July, and made selections.[7] He especially enjoyed doing this, and, helped by Thoreau, he made the "Ethnical Scriptures" a regular feature of the magazine under his editorship.[8] Another regular feature that he planned to introduce was a section on "Intelligence," and he continually scanned the letters of his correspondents and the newspapers for information that he felt would be of interest. He also planned to continue the book reviews and to make them more literary and less theological in character. Accordingly, he went through his journal for the last few months and made over notes from his reading into reviews. One, a review of George Borrow's *The Zincali*, which Thomas Delf had sent him in April, he had decided to prepare only after Fuller had refused to do it herself.[9]

Still, when 1 May 1842 came most of Emerson's own contributions were in "aqueous or gaseous solution, & not yet precipitated." He had been fortunate to get in one month of relatively uninterrupted work; now he was forced to divide his time between his own writings and those of others. Henry Hedge had finally replied to Emerson's request in March for aid by sending a translation of a German poem.[10] Thoreau had looked over the books on Massachusetts that Emerson had recommended; soon Emerson found himself "summoned to a reading" of the nearly sixty-page manuscript that Thoreau had completed on "Natural History of Massachusetts."[11] Parker—despite an exhausting schedule that called for seeing two books through the press and preparing two sermons a week—had sent in some book reviews. Emerson felt confident about the quantity of material for the July 1842 number. Thus when the New York Fourierist Albert Brisbane neglected to return his article on "'Science' &c," which Emerson had asked him to modify in March, he was not upset. All of this activity made him feel "busy & incessant" as a mother hen, "clucking & caring for the little Dial."[12]

One member of the "brood" was Emerson's brief sketch of "Chardon Street and Bible Conventions," which traced the progress since November 1840 of a series of meetings to discuss the "credulity and authority of the Scriptures." Emerson had viewed the proceedings from a good position—he was on the organizational committee—and his report was a colorful one. At his request Nathaniel Whiting of South Marshfield, Massachusetts—who with Alcott had attacked the "divine origin" of the Scriptures at these meetings—drew up a paper on "the subject of miracles and the authority of the Bible," and Emerson printed it with his article.[13]

As the date for publication drew closer, Emerson found even more contributions coming in. Brisbane had finally revised his article, and Emerson printed it in an abbreviated version, with an introduction of his own, as

"Fourierism and the Socialists."[14] He had chosen one of Caroline Sturgis's poems in May but was unable to print it until she visited him in June and gave her permission. Fuller, who had volunteered in April to do an article on "the amusements here this past winter," sent her manuscript to Emerson in June, and he expressed his gratitude for her "fine *manly* . . . deliberate criticism," which was "so flowing too & so readable."[15] One of the last contributions he gave to the printer was a story called "The Two Dolons." Its author, Charles Newcomb, had read it to Emerson in February, and, by constantly encouraging and helping Newcomb both by letters and in person, Emerson had finally obtained the manuscript from him in mid-June. This was to Emerson one of the most personally satisfying contributions, for he knew that Newcomb would have remained unpublished and unknown had it not been for the *Dial*.

By 22 June 1842 Emerson had sent the last of the "sad pile of Dial papers" off to the printer. A few days later he visited Cambridge to check on their progress and to deliver the "Record of the Months." Like Fuller before him, though, Emerson had underestimated the number of printed pages his copy would fill, and he was forced to remove Parker's reviews. Finally, he told Elizabeth Peabody to send free copies to most of the *Dial*'s young poets and also, probably as a suggestion of interest in future contributions from them, to Whiting and Brisbane. Thus, Emerson's first number as editor was published only one day behind schedule.[16]

The publication of the July 1842 number, with its announcement that Emerson was now its editor, was received with a new interest from both its friends and the press. Fuller was able to appreciate the *Dial* more now that the works of her friends were not "indissolubly associated, with proof-reading, post-office, or printer's ink," and she considered the magazine, which she hoped would never perish, to be a "common ground of friendship," the "means of development to us all." Henry Channing liked the number, Alcott read it with the "truest delight," and a young man in Baltimore, Solomon Corner, to whom Emerson had sent an earlier number, wrote to say that he was pleased with what he saw and asked to become a regular paying subscriber. Parker thought that it was a "rich number," but he complained that three of the articles still contained the *"Dialese"* that had marred earlier issues. Thomas Carlyle also had a mixed reaction, telling Emerson that he loved the *Dial* but with "a kind of shudder"; its writers had ignored "the Fact" of the universe, "ugly as it is," to soar into the "perilous altitudes" of Transcendentalism, an ascent which Carlyle believed would lead only to "inanity and mere injuring of the lungs."[17]

The reviews of this number were nearly all favorable. The *New-York Daily Tribune* (6 July) again described and liberally praised the contents in a brief notice and then proceeded to reprint Emerson's entire lecture on "The Times" in four installments.[18] The reviewer for the *Boston Morning Post* (12 July) was generous in his praise and gave many extracts to illustrate positive qualities. He felt compelled, however, to assail Newcomb's "Dolon," which he called "Transcendentalism run to seed," written by a "mind diseased," and—the ultimate snub—"worse than the Orphic Sayings." Even the reviewer for the *Knickerbocker* (August) called the number an excellent one, and he described Emerson's account of the Bible Conventions as "a precious picture of . . . querulous doubters." Most of the articles were praised; apparently—and fortunately—the reviewer had not read "Dolon," for if he had, he would certainly have no doubt attacked Newcomb's obscure style of writing as quickly as previous *Knickerbocker* reviewers had attacked Alcott's. The *Dial* also finally broke into the pages of an established religious periodical when the *Monthly Miscellany of Religion and Letters* (October) reviewed it. Although the reviewer recommended Emerson's lecture, he printed his introduction to the selections from "Veeshnoo Sarma" to show the *Dial*'s unlikely "probable connexion with Christian theology"—"probable" because that introduction stated, in clear opposition to the "divinity" of the Bible, that every race had its own bible. And in England Charles Lane praised the *Dial* in the pages of the *Union* (1 November) as "a beautiful and costly publication, both internally and externally."

Emerson failed to record his thoughts concerning the quality of the first number brought out under his care, but a letter written in July gives an idea about how he felt in general. He had submitted, he wrote Carlyle, to the "necessity of petty literary patriotism" in order to save "our thankless little Dial." Although the magazine had "no penny for editor or contributor" and had received "nothing but abuse in the newspapers, or, at best, silence," he was glad it existed, for it published those "few poems or sentences" that otherwise would have remained in manuscript. Still, editing the *Dial* had taken from him "a great deal of good time, to a small purpose," and he was "ashamed to compute how many hours & days" his chores had consumed when he might have been working on a new book of essays he was planning. To get back to his own work, Emerson resolved "not to meddle with the Dial for the whole month of July." This time he kept to his vow, "meddling" only to the extent of writing a few letters asking for contributions.[19]

Emerson was wise in taking a one-month rest, for during August and into the first week of September he was kept quite busy assembling the October 1842 *Dial*. He wore very impatiently the perplexing and burdensome editorial duties that made the magazine such a "trial" to him.[20] But fortunately contributors rapidly filled up the new *Dial*'s pages, although Newcomb was too ill to send in his sequel to "Dolon." Emerson had received eight poems from Thoreau[21] and two from Ellery Channing.[22] With her permission Emerson chose one of Ellen Hooper's poems from among those he had on hand, and he also planned to use a poem by Christopher Pearse Cranch.[23] Then too, he had been working on his own poetry, and when Fuller told him that she thought "Saadi," his "little poem on poetical ethics," was "lively," he decided to print it.[24] In all, there were so many "poetic contributions" to the October number that Emerson apologized on the verso of the front wrapper "To Correspondents" from Saratoga, New Bedford, West Roxbury, and Billerica (probably Daniel Parker) for omitting their verses.

The prose department also filled up quickly. Emerson planned to print his lecture on "The Conservative" from "The Times" series, and Sam Ward contributed some notes on art. Fuller and Parker kept their earlier promises of articles, and these alone took up almost half the number. As early as April 1842 Parker had planned to do an article defending the Reverend John Pierpont against his dismissal by his congregation, even though Emerson felt the subject too personal and controversial for the *Dial*. In July Emerson had told Parker that he wanted a short notice, but, when Parker's long article arrived at the start of September, all Emerson could do was to send it along to the printer, not even reading it through for fear of discovering more about its "unpoetic unspiritual & un Dialled" contents.[25] A more pleasant promise that Emerson saw kept was Fuller's promise in June to write an article on "Romaic and Rhine Ballads." By July she had done but little work on it, and Emerson, reserving a "desk & inkhorn," invited her to Concord to write it there. When she arrived in late August ᵲ a two-week stay, Emerson gently forced her to start writing immediately; although she feared that she did not do justice to the "richness of material," she finished what he called a "very attractive paper" by 8 September.[26] With all this material on hand, he could easily reject Henry Hedge's "Conservatism and Reform" essay—which he felt sacrificed genuine convictions for a rhetorical flourish—by stating that there was simply no room for it.

All of this activity seemed to give little credence to the *Knickerbocker*'s reprinting in August 1842 of a notice from the *Christian Examiner* that Transcendentalism, being "too absurd and extravagant to last long," was, in a "speedy return to common sense," now ousted from "many a fashionable drawing-room and round many an aesthetic tea-table" in Boston. The *Dial* had been officially deposited in the Concord Athenæum, the joint gift of Emerson and Thoreau, and the Transcendentalists in general had received one of their best notices yet, from the English *Union* (August). The author, Lane, quoted from Emerson, Alcott, and Peabody, greeting their writings with "sincere fraternal affection." Lane had been able to bestow his praise in person as well, for "Orphic" Alcott himself had landed in England that June.[27]

Alcott's trip, mainly financed by Emerson, came at an opportune time since he was still despondent over the failures of his writings and his Temple School. Awaiting him in England was "Alcott House," a community at Ham, Surrey, which used Alcott's precepts as its guide and which published *The Healthian. A Journal of Human Physiology, Diet, and Regimen*, with one of Alcott's "Orphic Sayings" as its motto. Therefore, when Emerson gave him the means to meet his admirers, Alcott was elated, and he sailed in May 1842, just a few weeks before the remaining sheets from his *Conversations with Children on the Gospels* were sold to trunkmakers for wastepaper.[28] Alcott encountered the friendliest reception he had yet received, and he flourished, with his elation turning to a new confidence that soon broke all possible restrictions on his egotism. His truth had prevailed, he felt, and not even a disastrous series of meetings with Carlyle could shake his new-found faith.[29] John Heraud asked him to join in the founding of a new transatlantic journal that would hopefully include John Sterling, Carlyle, Lane, Emerson, Fuller, Parker, Hedge, and George Ripley among its contributors. Alcott even planned to issue his own journal—"wherein my thought shall not be lost amid the confusing discords and witlessnesses of popular letters"—to be called "The Janus, an Ephemeris of the Permanent in Religion, Philosophy, Science, Art, and Letters." But few people rallied to his aid, and Alcott abandoned the plan, complaining that his idea was "obviously too broad and daring for them." As Fuller followed Alcott's account of his trip, she felt increasingly "miserable to see his boyish infatuation and his swelling vanity, already worse than ever."[30]

Fortunately, the *Dial* received some of Alcott's enthusiasm. He went about "facilitating the distribution of the Dial in England." He told his wife that "thirty copies at least will be wanted to supply the demand"; to Emerson he proudly reported that the *Dial* already had six subscribers there, where it was regarded as "quite an Oracle." However, its English distributors, John Green and Wiley & Putnam, had not been receiving the *Dial* regularly, and Alcott suggested spending two or three pounds for advertisements, in order to make the *Dial* "sufficiently famous."[31] He also took part in writing an advertisement for the *Dial* in the August 1842 *Healthian*, which urged the public to join that "superior class of readers" who, "weary of the lifelessness of current literature, philosophy, and religion," had subscribed to the magazine. Throughout the summer he sent parcels of "tracts" and "a MS paper or two" back to Emerson, which, said Alcott, "if worthy may serve the readers of the Dial."[32] From the five manuscript articles that he received, Emerson printed "two & a fraction."[33] The two articles, on "Cromwell" and on the reformer "James Pierrepont Greaves," were by Lane, the *Union*'s reviewer. The "fraction"—reports by Alcott and others about their activities at Alcott House—Emerson used in his own article on "English Reformers."

Alcott's parcels also helped Emerson in preparing his brief section on "Intelligence," which he was continuing as a regular feature in order to provide an "attractive & refreshing" diversion from the *Dial*'s regular fare. Hedge had already sent in an extract from the editor's preface to a new edition of Hegel, and Emerson repeated Alcott's information on Heraud's proposed American lecture tour, as well as Alcott's decision to bring Lane and another reformer—Henry G. Wright, one of the founders of Alcott House—back to America with him.[34] In addition, Emerson already had two of his own reviews and a review of Alfred Tennyson's *Poems* from Fuller, and so he was forced to omit Parker's.[35] At the end of September 1842 he confidently left the last proof of the *Dial* with Thoreau for correction and went off with Hawthorne on a walking tour to the Shaker community at Harvard, Massachusetts.[36]

The *Southern Quarterly Review* (October) greeted the new *Dial*, which was published a few days late,[37] with the longest review it had yet received. In thirty-four pages Daniel Whitaker looked over the first two volumes and pronounced his judgment. He considered most of the poetry to be excellent and even declared that Alcott's "Orphic Sayings," while fairly unintelligible, were not so bad as earlier reviews had made them out to be. The magazine itself, which contained writings by the "choicest and most approved" members of the Transcendental school, was "distinguished by vigor of thought, freedom of opinion, and bold, striking, and often original views of things, disfigured occasionally by an outlandish and affected mode of expression," but "again as often clothed in a style of exceeding beauty, animation, simplicity and elegance." Whitaker was more critical of the Transcendentalists' philosophy, which he described as both pantheistic in its definition of a god and similar to Thomas Paine in its attacks on Christianity. Above all, he disliked the attitude of the Transcendentalists towards "that illustrious metaphysician" John Locke, and most of his review was spent discussing what he felt was the Transcendentalists' incorrect decision to exalt "original instincts" over "rational faculties." Still, the review was mostly complimentary toward the *Dial* itself, and especially its literary department, and contested points were argued with much greater courtesy than had before been accorded the Transcendentalists.

The Transcendentalists were also paid a compliment by Charles Dickens, who had announced in his recently published *American Notes* that despite "occasional vagaries" he liked Transcendentalism, mainly because of its "hearty disgust of Cant, and an aptitude to detect her in all the million varieties of her everlasting wardrobe." Therefore, Dickens said, "if I were a Bostonian, I think I would be a Transcendentalist."[38]

The reviews of the new *Dial* were also mainly complimentary, so much so that James Russell Lowell observed that the October 1842 number was "the most *popular* one ever published." The *New-York Daily Tribune* (11 October) reprinted two selections and gave its usual praise, saying that Emerson's lecture alone was worth the price of the number. The *Boston Post* (15 October) reviewer expressed his approval and praised the "bold, free thoughts," while giving the magazine more space than usual, though much of this was devoted to quotations describing the wild "transcendental musings" from England. Alcott had again, in a smaller way, drawn ridicule down upon the *Dial*, and few read Emerson's account of him and his friends with the genuine interest with which Very did. Even the young Transcendentalist Robert Bartlett saw the English reformers as a group of "crack-brained men" who had welcomed Alcott, no doubt, because all shared in common the ability to produce "monstrosities of unenlivened reason." And the *Knickerbocker* (November), in its "Editor's Table," briefly told its readers of the proceedings at Alcott House and ended by exclaiming: "How *much* room is taken up in this world by ninnies!"[39]

The *Knickerbocker*'s comment came only a few weeks after Alcott arrived home on 20 October with Lane and Wright in tow and with plans for a new community in mind. Emerson greeted Alcott's companions with good cheer; he invited his own friends to meet Alcott and his "captive Englishmen," and he took them as his guests to the Concord Athenæum. Lane repaid Emerson's kindness by giving him a book review and the concluding section to his discussion of

Greaves, prompting Emerson jokingly to tell Hedge that "the faint Radicalism" of the *Dial* would soon become "sansculottism" beyond a doubt if Lane continued to contribute at this rate.[40]

Emerson made his remark in a spirit of good humor since he knew very well that he already had enough material promised for the January 1843 number to avoid printing out of desperation alone any articles that showed too much "sansculottism" for the *Dial*'s pages. Fuller had promised to supply all of the book reviews plus a notice of the Reverend William Ellery Channing's recent death, and Emerson finally had obtained Sturgis's "The Brook." He had on hand Parker's review of a biography of Charles Follen—a former guest at the Transcendental Club meetings who had died in 1840—which had been forced out of the October 1842 *Dial* by a lack of space. Ellery Channing had sent in some more poems from which Emerson chose four. He also printed another lecture from his course on "The Times," and he used a poem that he had written about his first wife in 1830—calling it "To Eva at the South" rather than "To E.T.E. at Philadelphia" to remove the personal connection.[41]

The articles on Follen and Greaves gave good coverage to religion and reform, Emerson's own lecture touched well on philosophy, and he had a good supply of poetry. Therefore, he turned his attention to those features that he had installed as permanent ones: selections from the literature of the past and literary and foreign "intelligence." But Fuller had been unable to do more than one review, one of Jean-Paul Richter, and Emerson found himself writing three reviews and some notices of his own.[42] Because Fuller had felt that her sketch of the Reverend Channing seemed "cold and ungrateful," Emerson had sent her his jottings on Channing. She then deferred the writing of the death notice to him, and he "digested" his disappointment over losing her comments and supplied it himself.

Emerson was, therefore, doubly happy when Charles Stearns Wheeler kept his earlier promise to send the *Dial* news of student life in Germany: October brought his transcription of Friedrich Schelling's first lecture, which Emerson gave Hedge to translate; November saw a "capital report" on German universities; in December Emerson combined the letters that Wheeler had written to him and to Bartlett and used them to preface Hedge's translation. A letter from Wheeler explaining that he had sent similar reports to Lowell for his new periodical, the *Pioneer*, failed to upset Emerson's plans. He went directly to Lowell, explaining that he had asked Wheeler for aid first, and Lowell, who replied that the *Dial* had "clearly a right" to Wheeler's news, promised that Emerson should "publish all & he none."[43]

Thoreau's work for the new number offered Emerson no problems at all: both authors that Thoreau had translated were long dead. Emerson had read "The Laws of Menu" as early as 1836 and had introduced Thoreau to them about five years later. Thoreau was deeply impressed by the universality of ideas shown by these Indian scriptures and soon was even quoting from them in his letters. Emerson probably suggested that Thoreau select some sayings from Menu for the *Dial* and even gave him for reference his own journal, in which he had earlier written his favorites. Thoreau also had been working with "great diligence & consideration" on a translation of Aeschylus's *Prometheus Bound*, which Emerson thought "valuable" when he received it in December.[44]

As the January *Dial* went through the press, Emerson found no last minute writing to do and only a few minor editorial matters to wrap up. Benjamin Apthorp Gould, Jr., the son of his old teacher at the Boston Latin School, had sent in some of his translations from Orpheus. Emerson declined them, mainly because Gould's work possessed "little poetic merit" and "little power," but also because Thoreau's translations took up "quite as much space as the Greeks can claim for this quarter."[45] Finally, in a gesture of goodwill toward Parker, he inserted an "Erratum" notice concerning an error Parker himself had made in his article on Pierpont in October.[46] He also asked Peabody to be sure to send Wheeler, Thoreau, and Lane copies in return for their contributions.[47]

The reviews of the January 1843 *Dial*, published on the sixth, were fewer than the last number's had been. The *New-York Daily Tribune* (17 January) reprinted two pieces and gave its usual accommodating review. In a detailed discussion the *Tribune* reviewer praised the entire contents and called the journal one of "the very best Magazines published in this country." The new *Christian World* (28 January), which James Clarke had helped start, gave brief notice of the *Dial*, stating that it had "much ability" and praising the essays by Emerson and Lane. The only other major periodical that commented upon the new issue was a conservative religious journal, the *New Englander*. In January it introduced its own first number by surveying contemporary periodicals; the *Dial* was included not because of "any influence" that it actually exerted, but because it was "one of the symptoms or manifestations of a morbid influence widely diffused" throughout the era — that of "the infidelity of a self-styled spiritualism." After mentioning the *Dial*'s "baby poetry" and the "solemn fooleries of its misty prose," the *New Englander*'s reviewer not surprisingly condemned it to the "everlasting fog" of its own muddled theories. Hedge considered the January number to be lacking in "good original matter," though the selections from "the treasure-stores of the Past" somewhat made up for this defect.

Emerson, however, was not to be worried by the *Dial*'s reception: as soon as the January 1843 number was published he left for Baltimore, the first stop on a lecture tour that would take him through five cities in two months.[48] He started the new year by delivering a series of lectures on "New England" in Baltimore and Philadelphia; in February he gave nine lectures in New York that were both financially and critically unsuccessful. Although all this activity severely, albeit temporarily, curtailed his activities as editor, he both went about getting new contributors and watched as he and his magazine and its contributors were mentioned by the press.

The *Magnolia*'s oblique reference to the *Dial* (February), when it asked "what mortal man (except the compositor) ever read the 'Orphic Sayings' of Alcott," was the first of two critical mentions of Emerson's friends on the magazine.

Hawthorne, in his "Hall of Fantasy" in the February *Pioneer*, described Emerson as being "surrounded by an admiring crowd of writers and readers of the Dial, and all manner of Transcendentalists and disciples of the Newness," who, Hawthorne felt, betrayed the power of Emerson's intellect by distorting it in their own eccentric productions and actions.

But the *Dial* was defended by *Sargent's New Monthly Magazine* (February) in an imaginary dialogue in "The White Room" about American periodicals. When the conservative "Mr. Sparkle" warned the Editor against using any of the "attenuated transcendentalism" that embraced "ridiculously compounded words that may be found in Carlyle, but not in the dictionary," he received a sharp answer. The Editor said that he admired the Transcendentalists because, even though they were perpetually striving after "they know not what," the "activity and liberality" of their minds was to be preferred to that "inert, slavish, uninquiring spirit, which rests content with the prejudices of the past . . . and shuts its eyes and shakes its head at every new development of truth."

Emerson found the generally good news in the press to be mirrored by the actions of his friends. Arriving for a brief stay in Washington, he had discovered "an intelligent agreeable person" in Giles Waldo who, he exclaimed to his wife, *"takes the Dial."* Parker sent him another book review and even recruited a possible contributor. Emerson's arrival in New York and the poor reception of his lectures there briefly halted his concern with the magazine, as did the sudden attention showered upon him by other reform groups: "Fourierists wish to indoctrinate me . . . Quakers give me printed pamphlets to read . . . [and] separatists wish me to read a few MS. pages that I may 'take their idea.'" Fearing that this "New York dust" would prevent the *Dial* from indicating "the state of the heavens," he wrote Fuller for assistance. Fuller, now living quietly in Cambridge, replied that she could send a long article on the sculptor Antonio Canova and some book reviews.[49] Emerson also managed to obtain an essay for the April 1843 number on "What is Beauty?" from a new contributor, Lydia Maria Child, editor of the *National Anti-Slavery Standard*.

In the meantime, Emerson had left Thoreau in Concord with charge of the *Dial* and with his full authority to send directly to the printer anything that he thought would be acceptable. In early February he wrote to find out what progress, if any, had been made. He was especially eager to know whether Thoreau had received any more "intelligence" from Wheeler, whether Lane had anything to contribute, and whether Thoreau was making any progress on his Greek translations and a review of J. A. Etzler's utopian *The Paradise within the Reach of All Men*. Although Thoreau had heard no news from Wheeler, he replied that he had received a "bulky catalogue" of the books in Alcott's library and a review of Alcott's own writings from Lane. As for himself, Thoreau had borrowed a collection of Greek poetry from Lane, and he promised to "mine there for a scrap or two." But Thoreau had made little progress on the Etzler review and was not hopeful of its completion soon. A few days later he reported that he had reduced the length of Lane's catalogue, and, with Emerson's consent, he would remove the personal references to Emerson from Lane's review. Emerson gave his permission, and when Thoreau wrote again he told of new contributions: Lane had promised to write another review, and more "foreign intelligence" had been received from Wheeler.[50]

Bad news soon intruded upon these preparations when Lowell's coeditor on the *Pioneer*, without his knowledge, printed part of Wheeler's "intelligence" that Lowell had waived for the *Dial's* use in January. Also, at the end of February 1843 Elizabeth Peabody reviewed the *Dial's* accounts and discovered that the "regular income of the Dial does not pay *the cost* of its printing & paper" — a clear indiction of a decrease in the number of paying subscribers — and she suggested that a notice to the "Friends of the Dial," stating these facts, be inserted at the front of the new number. When Emerson heard this he told his wife that he would do something concerning the *Dial's* future that summer; within a week he told a friend that he would soon send him "the last of the Dials, for the book draws nigh to its end, as I think."[51]

When Emerson returned to Concord on 12 March 1843 he discussed the journal's prospects with his friends. Both Alcott and Lane were "zealous for its continuance," but Elizabeth Hoar felt that its contributors would "work just as well, & with some present reward, *out* of the Dial." Emerson was himself uncertain about the magazine's future, being in many moods, depending chiefly upon the person with whom he had last conversed. A cheerless letter from Horace Greeley, who must have heard about the *Dial's* troubles from Emerson while he was in New York, suggested that copies of the magazine on hand be sold at reduced prices, since "$500 in one month would be better than $1,000 scattered through three years."[52]

While debating the *Dial's* survival, Emerson set about completing the number at hand. He was unable to finish his planned review of Parker's *Miscellanies*, and a poem that Giles Waldo had promised failed to come, but the rest of the April 1843 number was in good shape. In addition to what Thoreau had already promised, Emerson had articles and reviews by Fuller, the essay by Lydia Child that he had obtained in New York, an essay by Clarke on George Keats, which would introduce his brother John's annotations in his copy of Milton's poetry, and new verses by Ellery Channing, which Emerson added to those he had failed to print in January. Emerson also made a selection from Chaucer on "Friendship" and from the late Charles Emerson's "A Voyage to Porto Rico," and he suggested to Thoreau that he use Confucius for the next "Ethnical Scriptures." While Thoreau had been unable to complete his review of Etzler's book, he had finished two essays — one, with selections, on the Greek poet Anacreon — and he had also contributed some poetry of his own. Emerson completed the number with his article on "Europe and European Books" and with some more reviews that he had begun in the previous August but had until now been unable to finish.[53]

Emerson was still faced with making a decision about whether to continue the *Dial*. While in New York he had been told by Thomas Delf that the *Dial* should be "the Bible of the Americans," a statement with which he agreed. But, as he complained in his journal, "Here the sceptre is offered us, & we refuse it from poorness of spirit."[54] Deep inside, Emerson still nurtured his hope that the *Dial* would indeed become a leading force in directing American tastes—if not by example, then by inspiration to others. A letter from Carlyle, saying that the first two numbers under Emerson's editorship were "to a marked extent, more like life" than any others he had seen, also buoyed Emerson's spirits and was among the "good reasons" he had for letting the *Dial* live.[55] Thus, he agreed with Thoreau that Peabody's notice to subscribers was not a good idea, and he accepted Lane's proposal to say nothing respecting the possible discontinuance of the *Dial*: "If we please to go on, we can; if not, we can die in silence." He told this to Peabody, and he again planned to send free copies to the *Dial*'s younger poets in the hope that they might contribute again.[56]

When the new *Dial* appeared on 8 April 1843, Peabody had followed Emerson's instructions to make no mention of its possible discontinuance, and she did not even chide delinquent subscribers, as she had done previously. Emerson had also probably told her of Greeley's letter about selling the copies on hand for a quick cash return, for she inserted a notice that back numbers could be obtained for thirty-seven and a half cents each, while a few complete sets of all three volumes were still available from the publisher at five dollars. News of the *Dial*'s financial plight had travelled, though, and William Story felt that the April issue would be its last.[57]

Still, the papers that reviewed this number of the *Dial* did not state similar fears to their readers. The *New-York Daily Tribune* (11 April) gave a long, positive review, recommending that people take advantage of the opportunity to buy back numbers to complete their sets, in order not to be found "deficient in regard to one of the most remarkable phases of American literature." Hoping that the next volume of the *Dial* would see a "liberal increase" in the number of subscribers, the *Tribune*, in its weekly edition, gave the magazine four of the six columns on its front page, printing its review and two selections, and a week later it printed another selection. A reviewer for the *Christian World* (15 April) briefly noted that the present number was "upon the whole, an able one, and interesting," and a reviewer for the *Boston Daily Advertiser* (11 April) mentioned only that the third volume was now completed.

The other review of this number was lukewarm. In a short paragraph the *Boston Post* (15 April) reviewer described as "fine" or "clever" nearly all the *Dial*'s contents, but he still complained of its "curious, strained phraseology" and recommended that it should "eschew Carlyle-ism altogether." And the *Boston Daily Evening Transcript* (13 April) printed a whimsical sketch of Emerson and the "children and dear middle aged people" who listened to him, and who proclaimed, after he had spoken, "beautiful! beautiful! Let us go yonder and dance at the foot of the rainbow."

The personal reactions of Emerson's friends gave little encouragement. Henry James only mentioned Lane's review of Alcott, which he did not wholly like because he felt that Lane had no "divine sanction" with which to go forth from Alcott and "proclaim *him a prophet*." And Hawthorne, when he lay down following his dinner one afternoon, took the *Dial* with him "as a soporific, and had a short nap."[58] Clearly the public and the press alike were not very interested in the *Dial*'s future — subscriptions were lower than before; there were fewer reviews and these were in newspapers, not journals. Therefore, if Emerson wished to find a reason for continuing the *Dial*, it could not be that the public wanted it, or that it was making a profit.

Since Emerson was already an established author, with two books behind him and another in preparation, it was unlikely that he personally needed the *Dial* to keep his own name before the public. As the *Dial* began its fourth volume, then, the sole purpose for Emerson's continuance of the magazine seems to have been that "certain friends are very unwilling it should die." Also, he himself was "unwilling that a book of so good intent & which can avail itself of such costly veins as volunteer to bleed for it, should die." Even though the *Dial*'s finances were in worse shape than ever, he had made plans to correct that fault. Peabody had informed him that the subscription list was now down to 220 subscribers, since people preferred to buy single numbers rather than to subscribe. However, Emerson felt that this attitude should help the *Dial*, which he thought of all the journals had the best "merit in single numbers."

As the public was now purchasing by the copy in preference to subscribing in advance, the *Dial* needed a better distribution setup than Peabody could provide, and Emerson set about looking for a new publisher. Peabody had been unable to get the *Dial* placed on sale by the first of the month, a fact which Emerson felt was "so important to booksellers." And, in an attempt to avoid Peabody's "careless" policy, he turned to James Munroe, who had published both of his books and most of his pamphlets, as well as his editions of Carlyle. In Munroe Emerson rightly expected to find a better distributor and a more experienced publisher than Peabody, and his decision was a good one.[59]

Another factor urging Emerson to continue the *Dial* for one more year was the promise of many contributions, mostly from his friends. He had always vented much "hate" upon the *Dial* when it had to be *"filled up,"* but it was an object of his "love" as soon as "some noble record, some piece of subtle or of honest thought," came to him for its pages. Also, this next *Dial* promised to sell better. Emerson had received an order from England for his *Essays* and *Nature* — and for three sets of the *Dial*. From Birmingham a Mr. Palmer had written that he had seen the first number of the *Dial* and now wished to have them all sent to him. With these signs pointing toward a successful new volume, no one was disturbed when in May Hawthorne published a description of the "Giant Transcendentalist," an "ill-proportioned . . . heap of fog and duskiness," who shouted to the passengers on "The Celestial Railroad" in "so strange a phraseology" that they "knew not what he meant, nor whether to be encouraged or affrighted."[60]

The July 1843 *Dial* would definitely not have to be *"filled up"*; Emerson had received the best response yet from possible contributors. Ellery Channing had sent in a long manuscript of autobiographical letters that Emerson liked and planned to print, in as many installments as Channing could write, as "The Youth of the Poet and the Painter." He was also editing a book of Channing's poetry; from the verses available to him he chose four for the *Dial*. Ward, who had allowed Emerson to print only part of his notes on art in October 1842, now sent him the rest. From Brook Farm Emerson received poems from Dana and George Curtis, and he also planned to print more from his late brother Charles's journals. Because of all this activity, Emerson was able to announce to Fuller that he was going to "accelerate the march of our scanty Immortals and we shall all get ready to print in May."[61]

Emerson made a special point of telling Fuller about the printing date because she had earlier promised to contribute "liberally" to this number as an inducement for him to continue the magazine. By mid-May she had completed nearly fifty printed pages on "The Great Lawsuit," a statement concerning the rights of women, and had forwarded it to Emerson for the *Dial*. This article, expanded and published in 1845 as *Woman in the Nineteenth Century*, was warmly received by the *Dial*'s readers and was probably Fuller's most famous, and best, contribution to the *Dial*.[62] She sent it in early because on 25 May 1843 she planned to leave on a trip of almost four months to Chicago and the West, and this one long article was to serve in effect as her contribution to both the July and October numbers.

Other people were also moving away from Concord. Thoreau left the Emerson household in May to live as a tutor at William Emerson's home on Staten Island, where he would remain until December. A request in late May from Emerson for "something good" for the *Dial* brought some poetry from him. Because he had been "unaccountably" ill with "a cold, bronchitis, acclimation &c" since arriving in New York, Thoreau confessed that his verses were hastily composed, with little correction, and sent only because Emerson was expecting something. Emerson had no chance to give his judgment, for they arrived just as the *Dial* was "making up its last sheets," and he was forced to postpone any serious consideration of them.[63]

Alcott, too, was moving. In late May 1843 Lane had bought a farm at Harvard, Massachusetts, and on 14 June Alcott, his family, Lane, and a few others moved there. Calling his new community "Fruitlands," Alcott set about putting his ideas into action. Such vegetables as carrots, whose roots grew downward, were eschewed in favor of those, such as corn, which showed their higher and more elevated nature by growing ever upward toward heaven. Alcott announced that "the cow should not be robbed of her milk" and that chickens had "the same right to life as human babies."[64] Neighboring farmers said, "They have a lot of crazy fools out there."[65] Even though Emerson felt that Alcott had little chance to succeed,[66] he did print in the *Dial*, after toning it down somewhat, a letter from Alcott and Lane explaining their purpose at Fruitlands.[67]

Emerson had prepared some varied materials for the new *Dial*. In addition to five short book reviews, he wrote a longer essay-review of Carlyle's *Past and Present*. At first he was unhappy with the "mountains of panegyric" he had written, possibly because he was trying to apologize for some of Carlyle's peculiarities, but he finally decided that "Carlyle must write thus or nohow, like a drunken man who can run, but cannot walk," and he finished the review to his satisfaction.[68] Emerson also completed three poems,[69] made selections for the "Ethnical Scriptures," and reprinted a poem by Leigh Hunt.[70]

With all of this material on hand, Emerson was neither disappointed when his requests for aid went to no avail nor was he worried about rejecting other contributions. Letters to Henry James and to Carlyle for articles brought no success, and another attempt to convince Newcomb to send in the sequel to his "Dolon" was equally fruitless. Giles Waldo was now in New York, and he sent Emerson "letters & fragments of journal" and "sonnets &c" for the *Dial*, all of which Emerson rejected. He also sent back the poems of Miss Louise Weston of Augusta, Maine, with "some regret," since they were "a relief from literature, these unhackneyed fresh draughts from the sources of sentiment and thought." Emerson waited too long before giving a decision on the verses of the reformer Mary Gove, and she asked for them back. Thomas Wentworth Higginson sent in a poem, but he was turned down until "a happier hour may add that external perfection which can neither be commanded nor described." In fact, Emerson had received so many contributions that he wrote a notice "To Correspondents" at the end of the number, thanking them for their interest and apologizing for not being able to give each author the reasons why his or her paper had been withheld from publication. He said that he had decided not to print three poems, an article on "The Spirit of Polytheism," and translations of Richter and of "Schiller's Critique of Goethe's Egmont"; the initials of each author were given so that they would not continue to expect to see their papers in the *Dial*.[71]

As June 1843 began, though, Emerson received an account of a "Voyage to Jamaica" from his old pupil, Benjamin Hunt. He was impressed by the "clear good sense" of the piece and decided to print it. To do so, he divided it in half and did the same with Lane's article on "Social Tendencies," thus accommodating both in the same issue. By 15 June the "last sheets" were printing, and Emerson knew that for a change this number would be published on the first of the month.[72]

The July 1843 *Dial* made a favorable impression on its readers, and Emerson reported to Fuller that all of his correspondents were "greatly contented" with it. Caroline Sturgis considered it to be a good number, and Sophia Ripley called it "rich & strong & faithful to its early intentions." Thoreau thought it a "noble number" that "perspires thought and feeling," and he told Emerson that in it he heard "the sober and earnest, the sad and cheery voices of my friends and to me it is like a long letter of encouragement and reproof." Fuller read it with enjoyment, and Parker reported that a friend of his considered the most recent *Dial* the best of all.[73]

The press, though, gave the *Dial* its worst coverage to date. Only the loyal

New-York Daily Tribune (10 July) told its readers about the new number, reprinting four selections and praising the articles by Lane, Fuller, and Emerson; but its short review said little about the rest of the number. Although for Emerson the quality of the personal responses far outweighed the quantity of the public ones, the lack of notices of the new *Dial* did little to help its sales and thus its chances for financial success.

However, Emerson was unruffled by the lack of public attention and soon turned to preparing the next number. In the previous November Christopher A. Greene, formerly coeditor of the now-defunct Providence *Plain Speaker*, had sent a lecture on reform. Not until the end of July, though, when Greene had become a resident at Fruitlands, did Emerson find time to reply. He praised Greene's "generosity & insight" and the "clearness of the method," but he decided not to publish the piece. Reform, said Emerson, "is a word which spoken once too often sounds very hollow, & in the Dial & in the circles of the Dial we have conjugated & declined it through all numbers & modes & tenses." Besides, he felt that he would have no trouble in finding other contributions to fill the pages of the October 1843 *Dial*. He already had the concluding parts of Lane's and Hunt's papers and the second installment of Channing's letters ready to print, as he did an old poem by Hooper. Dana, Channing, and William Tappan of New York, whom Emerson knew slightly but thought highly of, had all sent in poems. Parker had forwarded a review of Charles Hennell's *Inquiry Concerning the Origin of Christianity*—after Henry Channing had failed to do it as he had promised the previous May—and Lane contributed an essay on the Shakers. And when two men arrived at Concord asking for money for the Anti-Slavery Office and the Oberlin Institute, Emerson happily sent them on their way instead with copies of the *Dial*.[74]

Yet as summer passed, the *Dial*'s prospects began to look less cheerful. By August Emerson had looked over the poetical contributions and, though not completely happy with them, decided to print them all—they were all he had. A letter to Newcomb asking for a "morsel of criticism on poet or novelist" brought nothing in reply. A request on behalf of "that modest mendicant magazine" to Fuller also failed to obtain a contribution. By September Emerson was complaining that "The Dial is in great straits of spiritual poverty."[75]

Emerson had good reason to be unhappy; Fuller was still out in the West, and his other reliable contributor, Parker, was sailing for Europe on 9 September 1843. He, therefore, turned to Thoreau, whose "A Winter Walk" he had fortunately kept out of the last *Dial* when it had arrived too late for publication. Thoreau, who had found it hard to "finish an account of a winter's walk in Concord in the midst of a Staten Island summer," had in July said that he would be happy to wait until October, but he asked for Emerson's help in revising it. Emerson was not happy with the paper, especially because of Thoreau's "trick" of "substituting for the obvious word and thought its diametrical antagonist," as in his description of "wild mountains" possessing a "domestic air." Even though Ellery Channing liked the piece as it was, Emerson made "pretty free omissions" to remove his "principal objections," and with Thoreau's approval, sent it to the printer in mid-September.[76] Although Thoreau had also been working on translations from Pindar and Aeschylus, he had not attempted to complete them by October, since he had thought there would be no room for them. He did, however, help Emerson in assembling the "Ethnical Scriptures" for that issue.[77]

As the *Dial*'s publication date drew near, Emerson found it necessary to fill up the remaining space himself. He therefore put the finishing touches on two poems,[78] an essay on "The Comic,"[79] three reviews, and an essay-review of German writers.[80] Fuller arrived in Concord on 16 September, too late to help, as was the case when Sturgis's "shining verses" arrived at the end of the month.[81]

After the *Dial* was published on 3 October 1843, it met with a mostly positive reception from readers and high praise from reviewers. In England Sterling discovered it to be pleasant reading; Sturgis called this issue "a better mine of gems than the last," but Parker's only comment was an expression of disgust at Thoreau's piece.[82] The *New-York Daily Tribune* (19 October) gave the *Dial* another favorable review, composed after an hour's ramble "among its fair pages," and reprinted two poems in order to flesh out its discussion. The *Ladies' Companion* (November) briefly mentioned the *Dial* when, in an announcement that Henry Channing's reform-minded *Present* had just been published, it noticed that "the field" was already "pretty well occupied by The Dial." The best review was the *Knickerbocker*'s (November); in two highly comendatory pages the reviewer gave many extracts to show that this *Dial* was a "very excellent and lifeful number of that greatly-improved journal." Just as this number had fewer "verbal affectations" than its predecessors, it was "in this proportion the more readable and attractive."

Other encouraging signs appeared elsewhere. Although Parker had left for Europe, he had promised to do what he could for the *Dial* while abroad. Carlyle wrote to say that Richard Monckton Milnes had donated anonymously a subscription to the *Dial* to the London Library. Emerson was even more pleased that the *Dial* went to "Cincinnati & Nashville," where he said, its chances for doing good for American letters were much better. In his *Present* Henry Channing praised the *Dial* for "opening unexplored mines of purest thought, brilliant with wit, rich with beauty." Newspapers arrived from Genoa, Paris, and New York asking to exchange with the *Dial*, and many domestic journals, poets, and novelists sent their works in for review; Emerson called their actions "very wonderful, seeing how small notice they get from us." The October 1843 *New Englander*, in "A Plain Discussion with a Transcendentalist," refused to "consider the writers of the Dial on a par with Christ," causing Emerson to tell Thoreau that he was not at all upset because the *Dial* was not, as the *New Englander* "angrily affirms," as "good as the Bible." Yet, while all these instances indicated to Emerson that "we make some figure in the literary world," the *Dial* was not "encouraged by a swollen publication list."[83]

Perhaps to Emerson the last bit of news was fortunate, for it strengthened his resolve to halt "[t]he felon Dial" at the end of the current volume.[84] He was being placed in debt by the magazine, he told Ward, and if it were wanted for another year, then perhaps "its particular friends might add to their contribution of writing some contribution of money for the Editor."[85] Emerson clearly did not want to continue on as editor himself, and he even thought of giving Ellery Channing the editorship—"if it could pay him anything"—should the *Dial*'s life be extended. The *Dial* was indeed costing Emerson money: Peabody had received seventy-five dollars "on account of *Dial*" in October, and Emerson's own desire to help his ofttimes impecunious friends led him to break all rules and pay Thoreau ten dollars and Channing twenty "for papers for Dial." He also had other personal reasons for wanting to disassociate himself from "that unattractive journal"; his second book of essays was "impatient to be done," booksellers were asking him to complete a volume of his poems, and he had nearly two dozen lecture engagements scheduled for the first three months of the coming year.[86] Even with all this in mind, Emerson decided to finish out the *Dial*'s last volume because he wished to try, to the very end, to use the *Dial* for the promotion of his friends' writings.

And he was still receiving contributions. Moses George Thomas of Concord, New Hampshire, a friend of Emerson's first wife, had sent an article that was critical of Parker and his review of Hennell. Emerson replied that he did not care to have Parker "pointedly & by name lectured in the Dial," but since he liked the "honesty & plain force" of Thomas's arguments, Emerson would be glad to print it if Thomas would agree to the "substitution of abstract x & y & z for 'you and 'I.'" The suggested revisions were made, but Emerson held the manuscript—either from absentmindedness or on purpose—until it was too late to be used in the January 1844 number. Thomas finally asked for it back and published it himself as a pamphlet.[87]

Emerson could afford to allow Thomas's article to slip away, for the new issue was progressing quite well. His own contributions included a little over a page of critical notices, two poems, and "Tantalus," an essay on "the impossibility of drinking the waters of thought which are always gleaming & waving within sight of the soul." Lane had sent him two essays, and Dana had forwarded his poetic obituary of Robert Bartlett, a former Transcendental Club member who had died earlier that year. In addition to the third installment of his letters, Channing had written a poem and a dramatic sketch, which Emerson, though acknowledging its "dulness," had thought "full of warm life" and fit for publication.[88] And there was an article by Ward on Dante, plus Sturgis's poem left over from the previous number. But over half of the January 1844 *Dial* was supplied by two of its steady contributors, Fuller and Thoreau.

Fuller, who was planning a book about her recent visit to the West—to be called *Summer on the Lakes*—had volunteered to do, instead of an account of her trip, an article on "The Modern Drama," based upon Sterling's *Strafford* and two other plays that he had sent Emerson in October. Fuller was ill during the time she was writing and thought poorly of the article, but when it arrived very late in December Emerson could hardly refuse it, for it would take up a third of the number.[89] Fuller also contributed a review. Thoreau, in addition to selecting the "Ethnical Scriptures," also made selections from "The Preaching of Buddha" at Emerson's urging. And he agreed to condense for publication his lecture on "The Ancient Poets," which he had given at the Concord Lyceum in late November. Furthermore, he sent along translations of Pindar's writings, which Emerson had, at Newcomb's suggestion, requested in July.[90] Still, mainly because Fuller's article had arrived quite late, the *Dial* was published behind schedule on 8 January 1844.[91]

The delay in publication was hardly noticed: only the faithful *New-York Daily Tribune* (25 January) reviewed the magazine. Again calling it one of the best journals in the country, the *Tribune* gave nearly two columns of quotations, mostly from Thoreau's lecture, to show the high quality of the number. The review concluded by berating the American public, with its self-proclaimed "hundred thousand liberally educated men, ten thousand professed scholars, and over one hundred colleges and 'universities,'" for failing to support the *Dial*, which had only "*three hundred* subscribers," and for turning instead to "Popular Literature."

There were, however, notices, less kind, about the Transcendentalists. Oliver Wendell Holmes published in *Graham's Magazine* (January) "Terpsichore," a pungent satire on Transcendentalism that obviously used the *Dial* as an object of its humor:

> "Ever" "The Ages" in their page appear,
> "Alway" the bedlamite is called a "Seer,"
> On every leaf the "earnest" sage may scan,
> Pretentious bore! their "many-sided" man, —
>
> . . . .
>
> Blind as a mole and curious as a lynx,
> Who rides a beetle which he calls a "Sphinx,"
> And O what questions asked in club-foot rhyme
> Of Earth the tongueless and the deaf mute time!
> Here babbling "Insight" shouts in Nature's ears
> His last conundrum on the orbs and spheres,
> There Self-inspection sucks its little thumb,
> With "Whence am I?" and "Wherefore did I come?"
> Deluded infants! . . .

The reviewer for the *Knickerbocker* (January) immediately recognized this as a "palpable hit at the small-beer imitators of CARLYLE . . . who have occasionally shown themselves up in the pages of 'The Dial,' a work which formerly 'indicated rather the place of the moon than the sun.'" After printing an extract from Holmes's poem, the *Knickerbocker* writer slyly commented: "We should exceedingly like to hear Mr. A. BRONSON ALCOTT'S opinion as touching the *faithfulness* of the foregoing." And the reviewer for the *Boston Post* (16 January)

described a "Mr. *Dial*" as being "more ardent than ever in the cause of the elevation of the masses, being himself elevated on high-heeled boots."

Between his lectures in January and February 1844 Emerson took the time to
prepare the next—and final—number of the *Dial* for its publication in April. A
poem on "Childhood" by Lydia Child was rejected because it did not have the
"finish" that Emerson's eye demanded. A prose obituary of Bartlett by a friend
of Dana's was also returned. And Emerson was not disappointed when Dana, in
a letter accompanying the notice, expressed his regret that he would not supply
his promised translation of Aeschylus's *Agamemnon*. Emerson already planned
to print four of Channing's poems and the last part of his letters, an article on
"Fourierism" by Peabody, an essay on Immanuel Kant by a Harvard law student
James Elliot Cabot, and two papers by Lane. In response to a request for aid,
Fuller sent in a "Dialogue" on literature. Emerson's old friends, Benjamin Hunt
and Charles Brooks of Newport, Rhode Island, contributed, respectively, a
sketch of the Creoles and two translations of German poems. The *Dial* also
received poems from Ward. And Thoreau, besides submitting more translations
from Pindar, had reviewed the *Herald of Freedom*, an abolitionist newspaper.
Emerson himself decided to write a short book review, a poem, and more
"Ethnical Scriptures." He was definitely approaching this last issue merely as
something to get out: one part of his "Ethnical Scriptures" was not even selected,
but instead was a verbatim reprint, including notes, from an eighteenth-century
periodical. He quickly revised and printed "The Tragic," a selection from his
lecture on tragedy from his 1838-39 lecture series, and he planned to print his
lecture on "The Young American," or "another thing nearly as long," just so the
issue would be completed. Emerson, apologizing to Fuller for being "the spoiled
child of luxury" because he found himself constantly thinking of how "gay" the
prospect of "liberation from the Dial" would be, was greatly anticipating centering all his attention on his own writings.[92]

The *Knickerbocker*'s "What is Transcendentalism? By a Thinking Man"
(March) offered him no encouragement in "the grinding out of Dials," even the
last one. After discussing, in a mock-serious tone, the various types of
Transcendentalism, including that which consisted in "believing nothing except
the spiritual existence of the unbeliever himself, and hardly that," the author,
James Kennard, declared that one might as well call the Boston philosophy "*In-
comprehensibilityosityivityalityationmentnessism*" and be done with it. Emerson
pressed on, rushing the "extreme unction" of the *Dial* and becoming in the process "nervous & peaked." Finally, on 1 April 1844 he wrote his brother William:
"I have sent away the last proof sheets, and will edit no more Dials."[93]

The *New-York Daily Tribune* (27 April) was apparently the sole
reviewer—and published mourner—of the *Dial*, which came out on 8 April.[94]
However, Greeley's paper could not give a full review, since some "pilfering
friend" had stolen the *Tribune*'s only copy, and the *Dial*'s New York agent had
no second copy "for love nor money." So the reviewer recounted the contents
from memory, and the *Tribune*, over a period of six days, reprinted Emerson's
lecture, which fortunately had been torn out and sent to the printer before the

theft had taken place. The *Tribune* also mentioned with regret that the *Dial* would not be continued, advised its readers to purchase any back numbers that they might be missing, and even offered to act as the agent for any sales. The proceeds would form, according to a statement made to the *Tribune*, "the first modicum of recompense accruing to the Editor."

The *Herald of Freedom* (10 May), though not actually reviewing the *Dial*, did reprint the *Dial*'s review of the *Herald*, and the *Herald*'s editor, Nathaniel P. Rogers, said in introducing the review that he was agreeably surprised to see his own "little outcast sheet getting at all the eye of so respectable a periodical" as the *Dial*.

On 25 May the *New-York Weekly Tribune* officially announced the *Dial*'s passing. The "most original and thoughtful periodical ever published in this country," the notice said, had "suspended its issues for the present." Even the "free-will contributions" by the "deepest thinkers and most advanced minds in our country" could not help increase its "very limited" list of subscribers. The *Tribune* mentioned that there were only two complete sets of the *Dial* for sale in New York and suggested that "they ought to be promptly secured for our best Libraries."

George William Curtis said that he felt that the *Dial*'s end was like "the going out of a star," and he lamented the fact that it would no longer report "the progress of the day." The loss of the "Good service" the *Dial* had performed by using "high and true standards" in judging art and literature was bemoaned by the New York writer, Cornelius Mathews. Emerson himself wrote:

> I have just done with the Dial. Its last number is printed; & having lived four years, which is a Presidential term in America, it may respectably end. I have continued it for some time against my own judgment to please other people, and though it has now some standing & increasing favour in England, it makes a very slow gain at home, and it is for home that it is designed. It is time that each of the principal contributors to it, should write in their own names, and go to their proper readers. In New England its whole quadrennium will be a pretty historiette in literary annals. I have been impatient to dismiss it as I am a very *un*able editor, and only lose good time in my choosing & refusing & patching, that I want for more grateful work.

Throughout the rest of 1844 little was said about the late *Dial*. In June the *Columbian Magazine*, while reviewing Cranch's *Poems*, noted that "much of what is written by the Alcotts and others of the Dial family, not excepting Mr. Emerson himself, rather vexes and baffles us by its obscurity than instructs by its truth or pleases by its originality." And the September *Democratic Review* told its readers that the *Dial*, which had contained "some of the choicest morceaus [morsels] of Emerson and kindred minds," had "lately stopped," and speculated on why the "refined community" of Boston could not support a literary magazine. The Transcendentalists, now widely spread and nearly all in new or settled careers, were silent.[95]

Part II Contributors to the *Dial*

5

Charles Timothy Brooks

Charles Timothy Brooks, who contributed two German translations to the last number of the *Dial*, was born in Salem, Massachusetts, on 20 June 1813. The next important event in his life was his graduation from Harvard in 1832. He had entered at the age of fifteen, and among his classmates were Samuel Osgood and John Sullivan Dwight. Brooks joined the Hasty Pudding Club and served as its secretary. His record was impressive enough to convince Charles Follen to ask him stay on as Greek tutor and proctor, but Brooks refused when a cash gift allowed him to prepare for the ministry. He entered the Harvard Divinity School with Dwight, and they joined Cyrus Bartol and Christopher Pearse Cranch in the class that graduated in 1835. Brooks also became a friend of Theodore Parker, whom he called his "quondam fellow-student, hall-mate, brother-linguist, punster, [and] German scholar."[1]

After his graduation in the summer of 1835, Brooks continued his study of German and supplied various pulpits for two years. On 14 May 1837 he was ordained at Newport, Rhode Island, by the Reverend William Ellery Channing. He was married in October, and a son was born the following July. Brooks's decision to settle in Newport at an early stage of his life restricted his activities among the Transcendentalists. This, and the fact that he was busily working on his own German translations, limited his contact with the *Dial*.[2]

Although Brooks remained at Newport as a permanent resident, he was not completely cut off from the Boston literati. He was introduced to James and Sarah Clarke, and to the Sturgis sisters, went north to exchange pulpits with Hedge, and began a correspondence that included James T. Fields, Charles Eliot Norton, and George Bancroft. Apparently Brooks made little effort to keep in touch with Cranch, but his best friend, Dwight, wrote often about the German translations in which they were both engaged.

Brooks's first verse publication was a translation of Friedrich Schiller's *William Tell*, published anonymously at Providence in 1838 and favorably reviewed by Dwight in the January 1839 *Christian Examiner*. Soon afterward Brooks began to translate Jean-Paul Richter's *Titan*. When Charles Newcomb, recuperating at Newport from an illness in the summer of 1840, read Brooks's

Charles Timothy Brooks.

Collection of Joel Myerson.

translation in manuscript, he praised its "glorious descriptions" and copied passages into his notebook that became the basis for his "The Two Dolons" in the *Dial*.[3]

Also in manuscript by the summer of 1840 were Brooks's translations of Schiller's *Maid of Orleans* and *Mary Stuart*. When Ralph Waldo Emerson visited Providence that March, he looked over the *Mary Stuart* translation and reported to his wife that he found Brooks a "very agreeable companion."[4] He also recommended Brooks to Margaret Fuller as a possible contributor to the *Dial*. It was undoubtedly Emerson, then, who asked Brooks for his translations for the April 1844 number. These were Brooks's only contributions to the magazine. His few attempts at theological writings were too moderate, and the majority of his translations too full of sentiment and piety, to be appropriate for the *Dial*.[5]

6

James Elliot Cabot

James Elliot Cabot was born in Boston on 18 June 1821. The son of a wealthy merchant, he passed a normal childhood for a member of a well-to-do Boston family, with an excellent education and summers at Nahant, Massachusetts. Cabot entered Harvard in the summer of 1836 and joined the Hasty Pudding Club. Reading Thomas Carlyle's *Sartor Resartus* turned him into "something of a 'Transcendentalist,' " and he studied the German philosophers. Later he recalled that, being "without enticement of ambition or the sting of poverty" to spur him on, he thus "very much wasted" his time at college.[1]

Inspired by Henry Wadsworth Longfellow's *Hyperion* to obtain a foreign education, and admitting somewhat of "a contempt of the working day world," Cabot set sail for Europe immediately after his graduation in 1840. He went directly to Switzerland, joined his brother on a tour of that country and Italy, and returned to Paris, where he planned to attend courses in literature and natural history. Instead, he left Paris to join J. F. Heath and two other former classmates in Heidelberg, Germany. After a brief stay there, Cabot and Heath went to Berlin, arriving in October 1841, in time for the lectures by Friedrich Schelling which were reported in the January 1843 *Dial*. Here Cabot continued in earnest his study of Immanuel Kant, and following a summer walking tour he returned to Heidelberg for the winter. The next winter he attended classes at the University of Göttingen with Heath and Charles Stearns Wheeler. Cabot stayed for only a short time and went to England before returning to the United States in the early summer of 1843. Although he had spent three years traveling and studying in Europe, Cabot felt that he was still little more than a dabbler, for what struck him most about this period was "the waste of time and energy from having had no settled purpose."[2]

Upon his return Cabot enrolled in the Harvard Law School, where he stayed until his graduation in 1845. He met James Russell Lowell there but apparently remained outside of the Transcendentalist circle. A relative, Lydia Dodge

Cabot, married Theodore Parker, but Cabot seems not to have known Parker until much later. In fact, until his work on the *Massachusetts Quarterly Review* in 1847 the only other *Dial* contributors Cabot probably knew well were Wheeler, Jones Very, Henry David Thoreau, and Ralph Waldo Emerson, who provided Cabot's real link with the *Dial*.[3]

Although Emerson recorded in his journal that "J. E. C." had been to Concord in April 1843, it is unlikely that this was Cabot.[4] The two apparently did not meet until after the *Dial*'s collapse, for when Emerson received Cabot's paper on "Immanuel Kant" on 26 February 1844 he wrote Margaret Fuller that it came from "an unknown hand." The article impressed Emerson, and he planned to print it in the next issue of the *Dial*.[5] He could not notify the anonymous author of this, and Cabot had to wait until the April *Dial* reached Cambridge to discover that his piece was the lead article.

Emboldened by his first success, Cabot wrote directly to Emerson. He enclosed a "fragmentary essay" on Baruch Spinoza and a copy of Charles Wilkins's translation of the *Bhagavat Gita*, a hard-to-find book that he thought Emerson very likely had not seen. Cabot said that he would be happy if any part of the Spinoza critique was acceptable and offered the Wilkins book as suitable for the "Ethnical Scriptures" series. Neither plan was realized because no more issues of the *Dial* appeared. Although this time Cabot had identified himself, he received no immediate response; Emerson must have been too busy preparing his second volume of essays for publication to be bothered with old *Dial* business. In December Emerson remembered Cabot's essay and asked his friends about its author. He wrote to Samuel Gray Ward about the "admirable paper on Spinoza" by "a master in the abstruse science of psychology," whom he had "just discovered" to be a law student at Cambridge, and asked whether Ward knew him. Three months later Emrson finally wrote directly to Cabot and expressed his regret that the *Dial* had not lasted long enough to print the Spinoza piece, since he was unaware of any other journal in which it seemed "rightly to belong." Emerson added that, unless Cabot had any special plans for the article, he would keep it himself until a new "liberal journal" could be established. Emerson also appreciated the gift of Wilkins's book, and in May he asked his English publisher, John Chapman, to obtain another copy of it for him.[6]

Although Cabot came along too late to play a major role in the *Dial*, it whetted his appetite for journalism, and eventually he took a brief, though important, role in the *Massachusetts Quarterly Review*. The *Dial* also served to introduce Emerson and the man who would later become editor, literary executor, and biographer.

7

William Ellery Channing

William Ellery Channing contributed more pieces to the *Dial* than anyone except Margaret Fuller and Ralph Waldo Emerson. Born in Boston on 29 November 1817, Ellery had many of the illustrious family connections of his older cousin, Henry Channing. He was related to the Danas and the Higginsons, and his uncles included the Reverend William Ellery Channing, Washington Allston, and Edward Tyrell Channing, Boylston Professor at Harvard. His family prospered, and by the time Ellery was five his father had become dean of the Harvard Medical School. Ellery's childhood was then shattered by the death of his mother in 1822, and he was sent to live with relatives. Two years later he joined his cousin John Murray Forbes in attending the progressive Round Hill school at Northampton, Massachusetts. From there he returned to Boston and went to a number of schools while preparing for college.

Channing entered Harvard in September 1834, and from the beginning he had problems. Family tradition said that he was so unhappy with compulsory chapel, memorization, and recitations that he submitted his own curriculum instead. Unable to force himself into a routine for which he was intellectually and temperamentally unsuited, Channing quietly left Cambridge in December, going to Newbury, Massachusetts, where he stayed with his friends the Curzons at their mill on the Artichoke River. He refused Harvard's offer to take him back and spent the next five years alternating between Newbury, where he enjoyed the company of Caroline and Ellen Sturgis, and Boston, where he halfheartedly studied medicine. He also attended Emerson's lectures and went to the Reverend Channing's discussions, where he met Fuller.[1] In the fall of 1838 he contemplated migrating to the Ohio Valley, where his uncle James Perkins was editing the *Western Messenger* and his cousin Henry was preaching. One year later he journeyed to McHenry County in Illinois to take up farming.

Channing planned a life close to nature in an attempt to support, both financially and imaginatively, his poetic endeavors. He had already left behind him a brief but mildly successful record of publications. In 1835 he had contributed, under the name Hal Menge, a number of pieces, ranging from "rhapsody to clowning," to the Boston *Mercantile Journal*. Also that year his poem "The Spider" had been sent without his knowledge to the prestigious *New England Magazine*, which had printed it.

Channing continued to write poetry, though he failed to publish anything, and before he left for the West he gave some fifty of his poems to his old Round Hill classmate Sam Ward. Ward thought them good enough to show Emerson,

William Ellery Channing.

Courtesy Judith C. Marriner and The Thoreau Lyceum.

and he, too, liked Channing's verses very much. He told Ward of their high "poetical temperament" and "sunny sweetness of thought & feeling"—although he noted that the poet had gone "to the very end of the poetic license" and had defied "a little too disdainfully his dictionary & logic"—and he expressed a desire to meet Channing. Ward, meanwhile, without waiting for Emerson's reply, had sent him some more verses and told him of Channing's trip westward. Emerson wrote back, again praised the poems, and expressed his sorrow that he had not met Channing before his departure.

Channing's poetry was in Emerson's mind when preparations for the *Dial's* first number began in January 1840, and he was among the first to be asked for contributions. Praising the "inward music" and "authentic inspiration" of Channing's poems, Emerson requested his permission to publish them, along with a prose commentary to be supplied by Emerson, but by April Channing had not replied. Although Emerson had already begun writing his paper, Channing's lack of response and Emerson's other contributions to the *Dial's* first number caused him, regretfully, to put the project aside at the end of the month.[2]

In June Channing, freed from winter's snows but not wishing to face spring plowing, returned to Boston for a brief visit. Unaccountably, he neither told Emerson of his visit nor made any attempt to see him. Despite his growing awareness of Channing's "eccentricity" that seemed "so decided & so persisted in," Emerson immediately wrote Ward upon hearing of Channing's arrival and asked his advice about the best way to reach the poet. But Channing managed to leave without seeing Emerson, though he did grant the latter permission to print his poems on the condition that their author remain anonymous. Emerson joyfully reported this news to Fuller—"They are what I wanted the Journal for"—and he added: "They shall save the next number." When Fuller promised a place in the October 1840 issue, Emerson immediately set about finishing his commentary while selecting the best of the poetry for inclusion. Three weeks later he had copied fifteen pages of poetry and added seven or eight pages of his own comments.[3]

As Emerson often did when he edited other people's poems, he made a few emendations in Channing's verses before sending them to the printer. He was surprised when his suggestions came back "dishonoured" by Ward and Fuller, who both wished to retain the original readings. Emerson complained to Elizabeth Hoar that they had excused Channing's "bad grammar & his nonsense" as being "all consecrated by his true *afflatus*," and he asked her opinion. Hoar, however, sided with Ward and Fuller. Emerson then protested somewhat humorously to Caroline Sturgis—who had also felt that Channing's poems should have been left alone—that he, "a Laureate Critic & Dictator on Rhymes," was "unable to hint that this slip of a boy had misspelled a word or omitted a semicolon" without arousing their indignation. As a result, when Emerson set about correcting some miscopying in the proofs, he merely promised to "consider" the "other *errata*." Channing—or more accurately his friends—had won.[4]

The October 1840 *Dial* carried Emerson's introduction of Channing under the

title "New Poetry." Emerson drew upon his earlier journal entries to praise the
new poet's "fineness of perception" and "absence of all conventional imagery,"
but at the same time he admitted that the very symbol that the "moment's
mood" had "made sacred" to the poet, who was "quite careless that it could be
sacred to no other," might appear "slightly ludicrous" to the reader.[5] Channing's
poetry was "more purely intellectual than any American verse" he had yet seen.
Emerson, believing that here was genius and not talent, inspiration and not imitation, recognized the unevenness of the poems but attributed it to the fact that
they were "*Verses of the Portfolio*" and, not having been written for publication,
therefore lacked the finish that the "conventions of literature" required. They
were "proper Manuscript inspirations, honest, great, but crude," which had not
been "filed or decorated for the eye that studies surface."[6]

Channing must have been pleased when he saw this article, and the praise
came at a most welcome time. After returning to Illinois he had half heartedly
farmed for a time before selling his land in October. When he returned to
Massachusetts he found both the *Dial* and the censure from his uncle, the
Reverend Channing, waiting for him.[7] Unimpressed by the sixty-dollar profit he
had made, his uncle upbraided him for again failing to complete a project.
Somewhat chastened, he remained around Lenox, Massachusetts, for a few
months; he was finally introduced to Emerson by Ward and Caroline Sturgis in
December; and, after a hurried and unsuccessful attempt at a romance, he left
to try his luck again in the West.[8] This time he went to Cincinnati to join his uncle, James Perkins. Arriving too late to play a part in the dying *Western
Messenger*, Channing submitted new poems to the *Dial*, which in April 1841
printed some of the poems not selected earlier by Emerson for his article.

Another good omen for Channing came when he met and fell in love with
Ellen Fuller, Margaret's sister, who had opened a school with Perkins. The
romance continued through the summer, and at its end Channing happily wrote
Mrs. Fuller that he had found what he had "longed for these twenty years — a
home." He told of their plans for marriage and asked the family's blessing.
Margaret answered for her mother and wished them happiness, keeping hidden
her own misgivings about the match. They were married in September, and
Channing settled down as an editor of the *Cincinnati Gazette* at a promised
salary of $400 a year, with a prospect for $700.[9]

Although Channing had assumed the role of a model husband — as his
mother-in-law reported when she visited them — he was beginning to get restless
again. Another uncomfortable winter had passed, and when spring came Channing found himself "chiefly busy with idling," writing Ward that he had been "so
long habitua[ted] to rusty coats, rusty caps, & rusty appearances" that he
thought himself "rust-proof." Somewhat defensively, he proclaimed poverty a
privilege and expressed doubts whether he would ever grow intellectually or
materially richer. In March he wrote Margaret Fuller, requesting that she gather
up the manuscripts of verses he had given to friends and return them to him, not for
future publication but for "curiosity & comparison." As he told her, "they are all

the evidence I have, upon which to rest my claims not only as a poet, but as a person of industry."[10]

When summer came Channing found himself in difficult financial straits, when his *Gazette* salary, none of which he had seen, appeared unlikely ever to be paid him. Leaving Ellen in Cincinnati, he returned to the East and stayed with Emerson while looking for a home in Concord. Fuller asked her friend Nathaniel Hawthorne to take the Channings in as boarders, but the newly-married Hawthorne gracefully declined.[11] Channing soon abandoned his search for a home of his own, and after Ellen arrived in September the two stayed the winter with Margaret Fuller at Cambridge. The following April, with Thoreau's help, they rented a house next to Emerson's.[12]

Channing's first residence in Concord, though it lasted little more than a year, presented him with immediate friendships and future possibilities. He quickly joined in the life of the town and made friends. Channing liked Bronson Alcott and called him in jest "Thou bee without a sting, / Thou ball that will not roll, / Thou rose without a thorn," a veritable "Don Quixote of the soul."[13] Hoar described Channing as "a wood-elf which one of the maids in a story fell in love with; & then grew uneasy, desiring that he might be baptised." However, George William Curtis, who spent some of 1844 in Concord, thought that Channing was a "selfish, indolent person," though he "certainly [did] write good Poetry."[14]

The more perceptive of Channing's companions had mixed feelings about him. They saw his potential but also realized that his vagaries would always keep him from realizing it. As Fuller put it, "he reminded one of a great genius with a little wretched boy trotting beside him." Her first impression that Channing's views were "as spiritual as Mr. Alcott's," having "a far finer sense of beauty, without priggishness or cant," gave way to this description when she became better acquainted with him: "hobogoblin nature and full of indirections." As if in response, Channing soon said that he thought Fuller "too ideal," making everybody restless by always "wanting to grow forward," while he liked to "grow backward too."[15]

To Channing Henry Thoreau was "the man to be with in the woods," even though the former thought the latter somewhat "oakum-brained."[16] Thoreau used Channing to partially fill the void left by the death in January 1842 of his brother John. On their walks through the woods, Thoreau noted, Channing confined himself to the ideal, leaving the facts for his companion. Thoreau thought that Channing should write his verses in Latin: it would be good discipline for his "sublimo-slipshod" style.[17] Hawthorne saw Channing as a "gnome" with "some originality and self-inspiration in his character, but none, or very little, in his intellect";[18] altogether "a poor substitute for Mr. Thoreau." He classed him as "one of those queer and clever young men whom Mr. Emerson (that everlasting rejector of all that is, and seeker for he knows not what) is continually picking up by way of a genius."[19]

Emerson also had mixed feelings about Channing.[20] A month before his arrival in Concord, Emerson wistfully told Fuller that Channing "ought to write every month for the Dial which ought to have fifty thousand subscribers & ought to yield him house, diet, clothes, power & fame." Emerson found him a good companion but realized that one had to make allowance for his "petulances." In a less charitable mood, he complained that "Ellery has freaks which are entitled to no more charity than the dulness & madness of others which he despises."[21]

As time went on, Emerson began to realize that the "crude" quality of Channing's poems was not so much due to their being "Portfolio Verses" as it was to the poet's "negligent impatient way of writing."[22] He thought that Channing continually used a license that would have been acceptable in oral improvisations but was unpardonable in written verses. He was "a very imperfect artist" who would never finish anything because he lacked the "artistic executive power of completing a design."[23] Although Emerson called Channing's verses "poetry for poets,"[24] he understood that Channing could not achieve artistic success unless his muse found "an aim . . . any kind of string on which all these wild & sometimes brilliant beads can be strung." Emerson was also upset that when he pointed out "a rude expression, a feeble line, [or] a wrong word" and asked Channing to alter them, "the hardened bard" replied: "Not one letter."[25] At last realizing that Channing would never gain the discipline needed to turn loosely organized thoughts into polished forms,[26] Emerson somewhat disgustedly entered into his journal: "No man deserves a patron until first he has been his own. What do you bring us slipshod verses for? no occasional delicacy of expression or music of rhythm can atone for stupidities."[27]

Channing, who felt Emerson never realized that he was "the child of impulse, the creature of imagination," was as unwilling to conform to the rules of poetry as he had been unwilling to conform to the rules of Harvard. He, therefore, resented somewhat Emerson's attempts at forcing upon him the "conventions of literature." As he complained to Hoar, "To Emerson, I have sacrificed one half my life, one good half . . . Born with an ardent nature, framed for affection, for gaiety, the creature of impulse, and the child of passion, under the unsparing hand of this terrible master, I have become like a statue, a machine, in which no part of myself is left. . . . I have paid a fearful price."

He later called Emerson "a terrible man to deal with . . . he cannot establish a personal relation with any one, while he can get on agreeably with everybody." While Channing always cherished Emerson's friendship, he nevertheless felt that Emerson's characteristic reserve and taskmasterlike attitude forbade the closer, more personal relationship that he himself desired. Emerson obviously thought that his walks and talks with Channing and his well-meaning criticisms of his verses were sufficient evidence of his own feelings: he gave no friend more. He also thought that his active promotion of Channing's poetry should have made the younger man happy—over half of his poems in the *Dial* were printed while Emerson was editor.[28]

Channing's contributions to the *Dial* were often autobiographical. "Boat Song" recalled the days at Curzon's Mill when he floated down the Artichoke River with Caroline Sturgis.[29] Most of his poems were well liked by his friends, who were often their subject.[30] "Dirge," which was Channing's own favorite, impressed Fuller with its "exquisite music," and it grew "more & more beautiful" to her and Ward as they reread it together.[31] Channing addressed at least one poem each to Emerson, Hoar, Caroline Sturgis, and Anna Ward.[32] Emerson thought the poem "Death" was "really good" and contained "great beauties" and he recommended it, along with the lines addressed to Hoar, to Charles Stearns Wheeler. Others thought highly of "Death," too. From England, Thomas Carlyle called it "the utterance of a valiant noble heart," and the *New-York Daily Tribune* reprinted both it and "Life." Thoreau especially liked "Autumn" because, he said, it rang true. Fuller read "The Earth" while visiting Brook Farm, where, as she told a friend, thoughts of its lines kept coming to her all night.[33]

Channing's best received piece was "The Youth of the Poet and the Painter," a collection of autobiographical letters that was the *Dial*'s longest-running serial contribution. Emerson told Fuller that the letters were "greatly liked & loved," and he described them as "very agreeable reading, their wisdom lightened by a vivacity very rare" for the *Dial*. Sophia Ripley, who at first thought they were the youthful letters of Channing and Ward, wondered at the "extreme manliness of the boys." When told that they were the sole creation of Channing, she began to wonder "still more at the boyishness of the man." Thoreau, eagerly awaiting further installments while he was staying with William Emerson on Staten Island, found the letters "full of life" and enjoyed "their wit highly." Caroline Sturgis also wished that she could have "all Ellery's story to read" as it was "so very fine."[34]

Channing was not so fond of the *Dial* as it was of him. As the magazine neared its end, he told Emerson that he saw "the expiring Nestor . . . charm with its bright surface, the expectant world, without watches"; the thing for him was a "magazine written by professed drunkards, gentlemen who ate nothing but beefstakes [sic], and believers in Original Sin." And to Fuller he described the *Dial* as an object that "flounders, & flickers" like a "keepsake in an empty purse."[35]

At the same time that he was promoting Channing in the *Dial*, Emerson was helping him publish a volume of his poetry. By February 1843 Ward had agreed to finance the book, with Emerson making the selections, including twenty-five pieces from the *Dial*, and Channing's *Poems* was published in May.[36] Emerson sent copies to Carlyle and John Sterling,[37] to whom he described Channing as "the best poet we have." Sterling replied that the volume seemed to show "abundant receptivity, but of productivity little," since everything in it could "too easily be referred to some other parent." Hawthorne thought that while some of the poems had a certain richness, they seemed "carelessly wrought,"[38] but *Poems* gave Fuller the "greatest pleasure."[39] Hoar considered the volume an unqualified success: after staying up most of the night in order to finish the book, she told a friend that no other verses had "ever so haunted" her "by their music" and "the subtle life both perceptive & affectionate" that inspired them.[40]

Reviews of *Poems* by Edgar Allan Poe and Emerson appeared in major magazines. In the August *Graham's Magazine* Poe scathingly criticized the things "which [Channing] calls poems." After complaining that "[w]ere we to quote specimens under the general head of 'utter and irredeemable nonsense,' we should quote nine tenths of the book," Poe proceeded to demolish the poems by pointing out metrical errors, verbal irregularities, and what he called "affectations." But their main mistake, he said, was "that of their having been printed at all." The next month, in an anonymous piece in the *Democratic Review*, Emerson started by quoting freely from the poems to show them as "the simplest expressions of a gentle and thoughtful mind." Not until the end of the review did he express his reservations, many of which were copied directly from his journal. By giving himself up to "the delight of improvising," he said, Channing had fallen victim to a "certain want of intellectual integrity" by which the poems lost "unity of character and impression." Moreover, Emerson regretted "many inferior blemishes, such as some quite needless licenses or negligences of speech and imperfect sentences, some unnecessary irregularities of metre, and redundant or defective lines."[41]

Poems had a slow sale[42] and despite Emerson's placing some of Channing's poems in the *Gift* for 1844[43] and doing him an almost unheard-of honor by paying him for *Dial* contributions, Channing's financial worries increased.[44] Ellen started a school in July, but it attracted only four pupils, including Emerson's daughter Ellen, and since she charged only three dollars a week, including board, per student — and less if they could not afford that — this money was not enough.[45] Emerson even briefly considered the desperate expedient of turning over the editorship of the *Dial* to Channing,[46] but he decided instead to help him out by paying him for chopping wood.[47] The birth of Margaret Fuller Channing on her namesake's birthday in 1844 further drained Ellen's strength and their finances. When Fuller pursuaded Horace Greeley to offer Channing a job in November, he left for New York, leaving Ellen behind in Concord.

Channing's impulsive and capricious actions continued as he grew older, and their ramifications grew even greater. His marriage disintegrated, and he became estranged from his friends, while those who remained friends were slowly dying off. His reputation was made not as a poet but as Thoreau's first American biographer. A lonely old man, he lived his last years as the guest of F. B. Sanborn. Through him Channing told others the story of his youth, a story ultimately of opportunities missed, of momentary pleasures and impulses that resulted in extended failure and misery. Ellery Channing gave his own epitaph: "I am a poet, or of a poetical temper or mood, with a very limited income both of brains and of moneys."[48]

8

William Henry Channing

When William Henry Channing was born in Boston on 25 May 1810, it was understood that great things were expected from a child whose family ties were to the Danas, Allstons, Cabots, and Lowells; whose father was a member of the Anthology Club; and whose uncle, the Reverend William Ellery Channing, was quickly becoming the most famous preacher of the day. These external influences on his life became stronger when, only five months after his birth, his father died. In the years that followed, the family was guided by the Reverend Channing, who looked upon William as his favorite nephew.[1] Young Channing went to the Boston Latin School in preparation for Harvard, which he entered in 1825 with Oliver Wendell Holmes.

At Harvard Channing stayed well within the family sphere: he lived with the Danas, visited Washington Allston, and took classes from his uncle, Edward Tyrell Channing. Among his new acquaintances were James Clarke, who became his "most intimate friend," and his sister Sarah. And by his graduation in 1829, as his connections with the coming intellectual generation deepened, Channing had met Margaret Fuller and Frederic Henry Hedge. Undoubtedly influenced by their conversation, he joined with them in questioning the established order both of society and of the church, to which he himself had close ties. But these doubts remained in check as William, who still looked upon the Reverend Channing as his spiritual father, entered Harvard Divinity School in 1830. Settling in Cambridge after his graduation in 1833, he joined Charles Timothy Brooks and Hedge in the antislavery society there, preached occasionally, and pondered his future.[2]

In 1834, probably at the suggestion of Clarke, who had moved to Louisville the previous year, Channing started toward the Ohio Valley. First he stopped at Meadville, Pennsylvania, where he met Harm Jan Huidekoper and accepted his invitation to stay for a while. Although some thought Channing a "mystic" and "somewhat erratic in his course," his devotion to "every sort of philanthropy and reform" made him "much beloved" by most of those who knew him in Meadville. Channing was still wondering about his future when he continued on to Cincinnati, but he decided on the ministry as a career and was ordained there in 1835. Later that year he travelled to Europe, and three months after his return in September 1836 he was married. Hoping to find his elusive spiritual happiness, Channing settled in New York City with his new bride and earnestly began a ministerial career. However, the old spiritual doubts soon rose again, and these, combined with a growing fear of his own ineffectiveness as a minister, made him resign his pastorate one year later. Unwilling to commit himself to anything else

William Henry Channing.

Collection of Joel Myerson.

so soon, Channing took his wife and infant daughter back to Boston, where he paused in his wanderings.[3]

By this time Channing had become convinced that sermons and social visits might be acceptable for most of his churchgoers but were in themselves not enough to meet the needs of all his parishioners. New York had exposed another, seamier side of life to Channing, bringing out the social reformer in him. The Reverend Channing's solution of "self-culture," the education of the masses as the means by which they could raise themselves up, offered no help to his nephew, who felt that ossified institutions and ideas must be questioned and reforms undertaken. Behind all this lay the younger Channing's deepening belief in the intrinsic worth of man, and he soon found himself allied with the Transcendentalists.

Channing's friends followed with interest his gradual shift to Transcendentalism. Clarke remembered him as an undergraduate who had an "expression of serious thought, earnest purpose, and noble aspiration." Just as the years following divinity school showed Channing that he was unsure of his purpose, his experiences in New York made him aware that the ministry, as an end in itself, was not his goal. During 1838 Channing saw his friends and told them of his plight.

A visit to Ralph Waldo Emerson in Concord in late July seemed to be a turning point for him. Channing probably approached the meeting with trepidation, believing that he had disappointed Emerson by failing to keep his earlier promise to obtain subscribers for Emerson's American edition of Thomas Carlyle's *French Revolution*. But after passing the night in Concord, he joyfully wrote his mother that the "icy pinnacle" that Emerson had previously appeared as had melted, and in its place Channing now found "verdure of sweet affections." Besides feeling that he now communicated with Emerson on a more personal level, Channing told his mother of the *"seed thoughts"* that Emerson had scattered. These were to grow in Channing's mind throughout the summer.

In August he stayed for a few days with Theodore Parker, who observed that Channing's good tendencies and noble aspirations gave him "an eye to see the evils of society, a heart to feel them, a soul to hope better things; a willingness to endure all self-denial to accomplish the end whereto he is sent." Although Channing now understood what he wanted to change and had confidence in his powers to do so, he still lacked the means, the office through which to work. Parker realized this: "But alas poor-fellow he cannot get settled."[4]

The chance to put his new ideas into action came early in 1839 when the First Unitarian Church of Cincinnati asked Channing to come and serve as its pastor.[5] Even before officially taking up his duties there in March, Channing began to make up for his earlier inaction. In Louisville Clarke was editing the *Western Messenger*, a periodical espousing Transcendental causes, and Channing soon became a member of its staff. When told of this by Clarke, Emerson wrote back that he was glad to see Channing as one of Clarke's "coadjutors," instinctively realizing that this new outlet for Channing's energies would do him good.[6] The timing did indeed seem right, for Channing was helping James Perkins coedit the magazine by May, when they transferred it to Cincinnati, where both men edited it until its collapse in April 1841. His work on the *Messenger* was satisfying to Channing, and in February 1840 he wrote to Fuller that his chief pleasure was the opening of his "whole soul" to his hearers, hoping to give them the best of truth and life. But old doubts remained: "I confess to you I am restless, and not energetic enough to make for myself the sphere I crave. I walk in a consciousness of unemployed force, and see not the when nor the how to make a world out of my chaos."[7]

By June of the following year, with the *Messenger* gone, Channing was directing his "unemployed force" into antislavery and Fourierist activities. He signed the petition for the Chardon Street Convention and had a run-in with his church over whether to allow the local antislavery society to meet there. It was apparently at this time that he renounced the ministry. Elizabeth Peabody, who had known Channing since 1820, told John Sullvian Dwight that Channing was being reviled; that some of his friends were saying that he was mad and others that he was wicked. In a pique she added that Dwight was fortunate not to have a wife and children so that if he, too, decided to leave the ministry he would be accused "not of murdering innocents &c but only of suicide." Shortly after resigning, Channing went back to New York and with his new friend Horace Greeley began to campaign for associationism.[8]

Although Channing's new cause brought him closer to Charles Dana, Dwight, Ripley, and the others at Brook Farm who were also caught up in associationism, it soon estranged him from Emerson and Henry Thoreau. Emerson now saw that Channing believed that the answer to society's problems would be found "not in solitude but in love, in the actual society of beloved persons." To Emerson, who had just been arguing the same society versus solitude question with Fuller and Caroline Sturgis, Channing's solution sounded like "shallow verbs & nouns; for in closest society a man is by thought rapt into remotest isolation."

Thoreau, while staying at William Emerson's house on Staten Island, was closer to Channing and more particular in his comments. In June 1843 Thoreau wrote Emerson that he had seen Channing, who, filled with "sad doubts," was retreating both from himself and from others. Thoreau met Channing again in July and spent a few pleasant hours with him talking about "the all absorbing question—What to do for the race." By this time the retreat that Thoreau had noticed earlier was an actuality, for Channing told him that he was going to "rusticate" for six weeks and return to issue a new reform journal, to be called the *Present*, in September. Although his rustication did result in the *Present*, it did not produce the inner calm he also desired. When Channing returned to New York in September, his unsettled condition was obvious to one friend, who interpreted it this way: "He is catholic in heart, protestant in head. If once he gets his head, heart, and hands in unison, in harmony, what beauty, what music would come forth." Thoreau, writing Lidian Emerson in October, said that while he liked Channing the better he liked his schemes the less. He was upset by Channing's "confessions," for, as Thoreau pointed out, "Faith never makes a confession." Thoreau also did not like the *Present* and "all that fraternity," for he said, they lacked "faith and mistake their private ail for an infected atmosphere."[9]

Even Lydia Maria Child, who greatly liked Channing, confessed that she had little faith in his plans because she felt that he had no fixed goal to steer by. While Channing was "in a state to sympathise. . .with the *spirit* of all reforms," she told a friend that "he would not work in their *machinery* for a week."[10] What would have happened had Channing continued his search will never be known, for he gave up the *Present* in 1844 to write a biography of the Reverend Channing, who had died in 1842. Thus, he came back full circle to his uncle's Unitarianism, if only as an observer.

When Fuller moved to New York in 1844, one of the first persons she looked up was Channing, who had earlier led her on mercy missions to the women's prisons there, and who was to prove a valuable contact with his friend and her new employer, Greeley. Although he had known her since his graduation in 1829, Channing dated the beginning of their real friendship from the summer of 1839. This must be so, for on New Year's Day 1840 Fuller, whom Channing called "The Friend," wrote him at Cincinnati and asked him to be part of the "grand concert" for the *Dial*. He replied that he intended to be a "listener" only, but would help as much as he could. Expressing his fear that the *Western Messenger* would soon die, he added that if it did fail he would for "a better prospect" unite with the *Dial*.

He also told Fuller of his plans for an article that had been "coming in glimpses and vanishing in shadows" in his mind during the last year or two: a "religious novelette" following a young man on his search for truth through various sects, showing him absorbing the best each has to offer, and then "guiding him to a love of Jesus in himself, thence to his own soul as the temple of the Spirit, and thence to life and society as the true sphere for his own development." The hero would be called "Ernest (True, or) the Seeker," and the story's success, would depend upon the amount and worth of Channing's own experiences. Stating that he did not feel "wholly fitted" to begin at that time, Channing suggested sending the story "piecemeal" as it developed, if that would be acceptable to Fuller.[11] In order to make sure that he would finish in time, Channing turned down her suggestion in March that he contribute some short pieces. "Ernest the Seeker" appeared in the July and October 1840 *Dial*s, and Clarke correctly guessed that Ernest was a fictional portrait of Channing himself. As only these two chapters appeared, Channing must have stopped his fictional hero's search at about the same time that he resumed his own.[12]

Channing's only other contributions to the *Dial* were two short pieces in the July 1841 issue. Having the *Present* to fill unquestionably made it impractical for him to write for the *Dial*, too. Besides, anything that was left over from the *Present* was more suited to Fourierist journals than to Emerson's *Dial*. Another factor was that Channing was not as close to Emerson as he was to Fuller. Still, by June 1842 Emerson had extracted from him a promise to review Parker's *Discourse of Matters Pertaining to Religion* for the October 1842 *Dial* in place of

Charles C. Hennell's *An Inquiry Concerning the Origin of Christianity*, which Channing had earlier agreed to do. This change must have been a quick decision by Channing, because in May, when Emerson, acting upon Parker's suggestion, had written to him about the possibility of his contributing an article, Channing had replied with a "good letter" but apparently made no mention of a contribution. As he had with Carlyle's book earlier, though, Channing again disappointed Emerson, who regretfully told Parker to expect neither the review of his book nor the piece on Hennell. Undisturbed, Parker himself wrote the Hennell review.[13]

Channing seemed to like the *Dial* even though he contributed little to it. He wrote Fuller that he considered the July 1842 *Dial*—Emerson's first number as editor—very good. While he never reviewed the *Dial* in his *Present*, Channing praised other publications by the *Dial*'s contributors and printed a number of Bronson Alcott's "Orphic Sayings." Writing on "Unity" in November 1843, Channing lamented the fact that "the Dial, opening unexplored mines of purest thought, brilliant with wit, rich with beauty, and pervaded by a tone of serene, cheerful, manly piety and wisdom as it is, has only a circulation of a few hundred," while cheap novels sold in the "tens of thousands." This was probably more of an attack on the public's reading tastes than a stand for the *Dial*, for in the previous number Channing had called the *Boston Quarterly Review* the "best journal this country has ever produced."[14]

In his later years Channing became disillusioned with the enthusiasms of his youth. In 1848 he tried to recapture his earlier zeal and started the reform-minded *Spirit of the Age*. Two years later he gave up the attempt, flatly declaring: "The paper is discontinued because, in brief, I am brain-sick—and it does not pay." His *Dial* writings, especially "Ernest the Seeker," which chronicled his inner search for peace, were also put away with his unhappy memories of the past. In 1850 Channing wrote that if he died before writing the book he had "so long meditated," on "The Laws of Life," he wished that someone would gather the best of his contributions from the *Present*, the *Harbinger*, and the *Spirit of the Age* as an expression of his "Credo" and "Spero"; no mention was made of the *Dial*. Years later, when he was spending more time in England than in America, Channing summed up his feelings about the Transcendental period when he commented on Brook Farm to Caroline Dall: "Had I understood human nature then, I should never have believed its success possible."[15] The seeker had not found what he wanted to find, and he knew it.

9

Lydia Maria Child

Of the better-known contributors to the *Dial*, Lydia Maria (Francis) Child probably had the most tenuous connections to Transcendentalism when the magazine was being published. She was born on 11 February 1802 at Medford, Massachusetts, the youngest of six children. At twelve her mother died, and she was sent to live with her married sister in Maine. She remained there until 1824, when her brother Convers Francis was married, and she then joined his household at Watertown, Massachusetts. He took a personal hand in her education and began introducing her into the circle of friends — which included Ralph Waldo Emerson — that came to his house for discussions. Lydia Francis's most important and lasting friendships among the Transcendentalists were formed with Theodore Parker and Margaret Fuller.

Convers Francis was Parker's earliest and possibly his most important supporter. Beginning in 1832 Parker spent much time at Watertown talking with Francis and using his personal library. As a fellow student, Lydia studied and talked with him and gave him much needed and appreciated encouragement; Parker later told her that he would always remember her "cheering words" to him and "much more" when he was at Watertown. He left an equally favorable impression upon her, for years later she told a friend that he was "the greatest man, morally and intellectually," that America had ever produced.[1]

Fuller also visited the Francis home when she was in Watertown and, though eight years younger than Lydia, struck up an immediate friendship with her. They began reading John Locke together, and Fuller was soon referring to her friend as "a most interesting woman," a "natural person, — a most rare thing in this age of cant and pretension," whose conversation was "charming." Years later Mrs. Child remembered that Fuller's egotism had marred "the nobleness of her views and of her expression," but she blamed her strict upbringing by her father for it.[2]

This sisterly relationship was interrupted when David Lee Child began to court Lydia. Child, an active reformer who would soon be a founding member of the New England Anti-Slavery Society, quickly had all of her time, and the two were married in October 1828. Soon after moving to the Boston area, Mrs. Child found herself the mainstay of the family's finances as her husband remained an unemployed reformer, with an occasional unsuccessful foray into agriculture.[3] Starting with *Hobomok; A Tale of Early Times* in 1824, Mrs. Child had authored five books by the time of her marriage and had edited the *Juvenile Miscellany* since 1826. *The Frugal Housewife*, a compendium of household hints, was a great success in 1830 and was followed by *The Mother's Book* and

Lydia Maria Child.

Collection of Joel Myerson.

The Girl's Own Book in the next year. Stirred to action by her husband's words, she joined the antislavery cause and in 1833 published *An Appeal in Favor of That Class of Americans called Africans.* The Reverend William Ellery Channing personally congratulated her for discussing the subject, but the general public responded by boycotting her works. More antislavery pieces and books dealing with the exploitation of the Indian also earned her more animosity than money. Partly as a result of the declining sales of her books, and partly because of David's perpetual unemployment, she agreed in May 1841 to go to New York to take over the editorship of the *National Anti-Slavery Standard* for the Anti-Slavery Society.

As Mrs. Child settled into her new role, she found herself opposed to William Lloyd Garrison's belief that the antislavery movement should not, and could not work through normal governmental channels. To her, it was obvious that "a vast amount of *political* power" was left untouched by this policy. Garrison's *Liberator* was abhorrent to her, and she tried to avoid "inter-abolitionist controversy" by aiming the *Standard* at the uncommitted general public. She angrily wrote to a friend about her feelings: "I am willing to do hard work, but no *dirty* work, for any cause." The friction between her and Garrison's supporters in the Anti-Slavery Society proved too much, and she resigned in May 1843. Her husband, who was her associate on the paper, took over the editorship, and Mrs. Child returned to writing and editing her own books.[4]

It was in the mid-1830s that Lydia Child began making new friends among the Transcendentalists. Described as a "most kindly looking and motherly woman . . . garbed simply as a Quakeress," she was brought into contact with the younger people around her by such humanitarian statements as, "If God pleases to give me a degree of strength to break any of the shackles that bind human souls, or human bodies, it will be by the voice of conscience uttered in all simplicity."

In 1837 the Childs moved to Northampton, Massachusetts, where David would raise beets. There Mrs. Child later met John Sullivan Dwight, a young minister who kept her abreast of the current intellectual movements. He provided her "intellectual nature" with more "excitement" than the previous minister had and, Mrs. Child added, "I dont [sic] know but he does me as much spiritual good." Their friendship was a close and lasting one, and Mrs. Child jokingly remarked to a friend that Dwight had ministered to her soul so much that "the parish are paying for a missionary to me." At other times she could be more serious, as when she told her brother in 1840 that Dwight had saved her from "a disastrous state of feeling, in which God seemed a tyrant, and this life a dungeon." And she wrote Dwight: "You are one of the few whom I want to go into heaven with, and stay near forever."[5]

Although settling in New York had removed her from the Transcendentalists, she still wrote to them and read the copies of the *Dial* that the *Standard* received in exchange. Mrs. Child appreciated Caroline Sturgis not only for the "sweet images" in the poems she wrote for the *Dial* but even more "for her own sake." She also made the acquaintance of another person who was moving away, though more purposefully, from the Boston movement. In August 1840 Maria White had loaned her fiancé, James Russell Lowell, Mrs. Child's *Philothea*, and he thought the novel so good that he recommended it to a friend.[6] Lowell met her soon afterward, and in April 1842 he told Emelyn Eldredge to be sure to visit Mrs. Child when she was in New York because, of all the American women writers, he thought that she had shown "the most of what can truly be called genius." As Lowell himself gravitated toward the abolitionist movement, he saw her more frequently. In 1843 he publicly referred to her as "a woman of genius, who lives with humble content in the intellectual Coventry to which her conscientiousness has banished her—a fate the hardest for genius to bear."[7]

One thing that drew Lydia Child to the *Dial* was her increasing correspondence with the Brook Farmers. She felt an "affectionate respect" for George Ripley, being in "great sympathy with his advance-guard in the settlement of social freedom," and she also knew Mrs. Ripley and Charles Dana. Dwight tried to convince her to join the West Roxbury (Massachusetts) community, but she replied that, while she had a "strong faith in *principles*," she had a "troublesome distrust of *men*." She said that if she could find a band that was clear-sighted yet mystical, and ideal yet actual, she would be severely tempted to join a phalanx, but she felt that experience had taught her to be cautious, "to avoid the blinding excitement of conventions and meetings, and examine the subject in stillness."[8]

Fortunately for Emerson, Mrs. Child's split from the antislavery movement came when he was editing the *Dial* and eagerly seeking contributors. They had kept in touch following the days at Watertown, and, although she did not attend any meetings of the Transcendental Club, her brother was a member and had kept her informed of Emerson's activities. Both she and Emerson were in correspondence with Thomas Carlyle, and in 1835, when her planned trip to England was canceled, Emerson had regretfully informed Carlyle that the "little lady with a mighty heart" would not be able to visit him as planned.[9]

She was close enough to Lidian Emerson to tell her, before her marriage, that the gossips were saying that Emerson was about to marry "a Swedenborgian lady, who, the first time she heard him lecture, received a very strong impression that they were spiritual partners; insomuch that . . . she said to a friend, 'That man is certainly my pre-destined husband.'" Emerson was familiar with her writings: he recommended *Philothea* as a "divine book," and he copied passages from her biographies of Madame de Staël and Madame Roland into his journal.[10]

On her side, even though she thought that Emerson's works were occasionally "full of deep and original sayings," she complained to a friend: "What is the use of telling us . . . that nothing is real, that everything eludes us?"[11] She had thought so highly of Emerson's "Man the Reformer" that she reprinted it in the *Standard*.[12] Emerson asked Mrs. Child for her help during his 1843 lecture trip to New York, and on 26 February he wrote his wife that he had a paper from her.[13] This paper—"What is Beauty?"—quickly appeared over her name in the April 1843 *Dial*.

It is doubtful that Mrs. Child could have contributed more to the *Dial* than she did.[14] Her abolitionist writings did not fit into the "literature, philosophy, and religion" categories of the *Dial*'s title, and editing the *Standard* and the *Anti-Slavery Alamanac* occupied all of her time. After her resignation in 1843, the success of her *Letters from New-York* led her to write a sequel to it.[15] The chance of finding the long-elusive financial security, and her basically non-Transcendental interests, made more contributions to the *Dial* from Mrs. Child unlikely.

10
Eliza Thayer Clapp

Eliza Thayer Clapp, who contributed six poems to the *Dial*, was born at Dorchester, Massachusetts, on 13 November 1818. She was adopted at an early age by Isaac Clapp, a successful merchant whose marriage had been childless.[1] Though Clapp led a quiet existence at Dorchester all of her life, she nonetheless was aware of the prevailing intellectual trends.

Clapp thought Transcendentalism "the protest of a cramped, oppressed, and slandered natural order of thought, feeling, and activity against the externalism of the Christian Church, its unmeaning formalism . . . [and] its doctrinal statements that had become such dead formulas as to be rather statements of falsehood than truth." With such feelings she was easily swept up by the "iconoclastic zeal" of Theodore Parker, and she soon met other Transcendentalists, becoming good friends with Henry Channing and Elizabeth Peabody. When Frederic Henry Hedge met her, he was struck by her "profound spiritual insight." Clapp looked toward Ralph Waldo Emerson as the culmination of "the pure and helpful side of Transcendentalism" and thought him a "man of genius," although she felt that he said many things that "he had not the rationality to develop." She was also an enthusiastic reader of the *Dial* from its inception.[2]

In the fall of 1840 a friend of Clapp sent some of her poems to Emerson, who found them so "pleasing & even beautiful" that he wrote her a letter of appreciation and encouragement. Emerson was surprised by the quality of her verses, for he had been unimpressed by her when they had met on an earlier occasion. Praising the "simplicity & elegance" of the poems, Emerson explained why he liked them so much. Their "objectiveness" was due to her ability to recognize that nature contained universal symbols. Too many young poets, he said, wrote only about themselves and could not see beyond the particular to the universal. Her verses, on the other hand, contained "honest experience," as opposed to mere "poetic diction." He returned the verses, after marking a few words or lines which struck him as "imperfect," and asked her to send along to him anything else she might write.[3]

Clapp was given enough encouragement by Emerson's letter to mail some of her poems to Margaret Fuller for possible inclusion in the *Dial*. Fuller, aware that Emerson had been in correspondence with Clapp about her poetry, offered to send these new poems to him for his criticisms.[4] After Emerson had kept the poems for over two months, Clapp began to have second thoughts about her work and apparently wrote him to express her reservations about their quality in regard to his own standards for publication.

Emerson's reply in February was calculated to brush aside whatever doubts she may have had. He thought that the second of her two "Hymns" was probably the best poem, though the first "Hymn" and "Clouds" were "more agreeable" to him. After praising the poems for having "simple & genuine . . . sentiment & reflection," Emerson asked her if she would not, after looking them over herself, allow him to print them in the *Dial* "for the enjoyment of many who can read but cannot write." Clapp took some time to consider this proposal, and, though they missed the April number, four of her poems did appear in the July 1841 *Dial*.[5]

The reception that her works received was gratifying to Clapp. Many people thought that her "The Future is better than the Past" was written by Emerson, and both the *New-Yorker* and the *New-York Daily Tribune* reprinted it.[6] She planned to spend the rest of the year working on her poetry, but her duties as a Sunday school teacher led to the writing and publication of *Words in a Sunday School*, a collection of her class lessons, and it was not until the following year that she was able to submit more poetry to the *Dial*.

By February 1842 Emerson had received at least three more poems from Clapp. One, "a very amusing *jeu d'esprit*," was about Emerson himself, which made its publication in the *Dial* impossible. Even so, Emerson did not like it as much as "The Leaves," which he found "a true poem," new in "matter & form." Emerson retitled the poem "Autumn Leaves," and, as Clapp voiced no objection to the new title, it appeared that way in the July 1842 *Dial*. He also made sure that a free *Dial* was sent to her for her labors.[7] Surprisingly, though Emerson and Clapp kept in touch with one another after July, and though she did continue to write poetry, no more of her work appeared in the *Dial*.

11

James Freeman Clarke

James Freeman Clarke was born at Hanover, New Hampshire, on 4 April 1810. His parents, following a number of business failures, left him with his grandparents at Newton, Massachusetts, thus allowing the youth to enjoy the advantages of a Boston education. He entered the Boston Latin School in 1821 and there met Charles Sumner and Henry Channing.

Clarke entered Harvard in 1825, a time when most of the men who were to be involved in the intellectual and religious upheavals of the next two decades were there: George Ripley, Caleb Stetson, G. P. Bradford, Frederic Henry Hedge, and Ralph Waldo Emerson were in the divinity school; Cornelius Felton and Charles Emerson were undergraduates; Clarke's own classmates included Henry Channing, Oliver Wendell Holmes, and Chandler Robbins. Clarke and Holmes served jointly as poet and secretary of the Hasty Pudding Club, and Clarke won second place in the Bowdoin Prize competition in his senior year. Upon graduation he entered the divinity school, and during his four years there he added Charles Timothy Brooks, Christopher Pearse Cranch, John Sullivan Dwight, Samuel Osgood, and Cyrus Bartol to his circle of acquaintances.

Clarke also became a friend of Elizabeth Peabody and Margaret Fuller. Peabody had met Clarke at his mother's boarding house, where she had occasionally stayed. The two never quite hit it off, and the brash Peabody once told Clarke that he would never amount to much. They saw each other infrequently, and Clarke considered Fuller a much more agreeable companion.[1]

Fuller was Clarke's distant cousin, and their occasional meetings grew more and more frequent by the spring of 1830. That summer Fuller helped him find a teaching job. Although he always remained "puzzled" by her, he recognized that she was "the most remarkable of women," never "at a loss to explain what to others is inscrutable, never blinded by appearances." They took up the study of German together, influenced alike by "the wild-bugle call of Thomas Carlyle," and had many talks on literary matters. Clarke best described their relationship when he thanked Fuller for "the high intellectual culture and excitement" of which she had been the source.[2] Though Clarke's father feared that Fuller would "marry James—and make him miserable," it is clear that romance was never a part of their relationship;[3] in fact, Clarke rather idolized Fuller and playfully asked her to edit his "posthumous works." Once he told her that she would become "the founder of an American literature," and that he would be the first to join her "*school*" when that time came.[4]

After graduating from the divinity school in 1832, Clarke remained at Harvard as a proctor, staying near old friends and making new ones. One new friend

James Freeman Clarke.

Collection of Joel Myerson.

was Emerson. The two were initially drawn together by a mutual interest in Carlyle, and it was Clarke who first told Emerson of Carlyle's authorship of the articles in the *Foreign Quarterly Review* that they both read so eagerly. Soon they were having discussions of Carlyle, Goethe, and German literature, and Clarke was invited to Concord to continue the talks, which he reported on to Fuller.[5]

Clarke's Cambridge period was brought to an end when a congregation in Louisville, Kentucky, offered him a position. His intellectual life of the past seven years gave him the confidence to accept, and he planned to carry the message of change to the West. Three days after his ordination on 21 July 1833 Clarke left for Louisville, taking with him for his journal a richly bound album, a present from Fuller, who had adorned the first page with inspirational mottoes. Clarke needed this inspiration; his first year at Louisville was a hard one because of the resistance aroused by his efforts to put into practice the ideas he had absorbed in Boston.[6]

By November 1834 he was trying to reach a larger audience than just his own congregation. An attack by Andrews Norton upon Carlyle and his writings caused Clarke to take up his pen in Carlyle's defense. Believing that his piece would have been unsuitable for the local press, Clarke sent it east to his sister Sarah, who showed it to Charles Emerson. Peabody obtained it and passed it on to Emerson, who wrote Clarke that he had read it with great pleasure and with a regret that it was not published. Although Emerson encouraged him to revise and publish it, Clarke never did.[7] However, this recognition of his writing abilities by others greatly improved his self-confidence, and when prominent men from Cincinnati and Louisville proposed to start a new periodical, Clarke volunteered his aid.

The publication of the *Western Messenger* fulfilled Clarke's earlier desire to help establish a magazine conducted by "a band of illuminati with reference to principles not readers." As Clarke wrote Fuller, they planned a "first rate affair . . . a free and unshackled spirit and form." He asked Hedge for a contribution and also Fuller, whom he told: "Be as transcendental as you please; if you express transcendentalism distinctly there is no objection to it drawn from its logical inconsistence with a domineering philosophy. Even thorough going . . . Unitarians have their minds open enough to receive all sorts of religious supernaturalism — only not under that name." In April 1836 Clarke began a three-year editorship of the *Western Messenger*, acting as "publisher, editor, contributor, proof-reader, and boy to pack up the copies and carry them to the post-office." He rapidly matured in his new position, and soon the man who had earlier felt "a very decided feeling of inferiority" in Fuller's presence began to warn her that her writing was "too Latinized" and lacked "condensation and point."[8]

Clarke's success in the West drew him even closer to New England. On his annual trips to Boston he regularly attended meetings of the Transcendental Club, and when he returned to Louisville he defended Bronson Alcott, Emerson, and Jones Very in the pages of the *Western Messenger* against attacks on them by the Boston papers. He accepted contributions from Emerson, Cranch, Henry Channing, Very, and Fuller for his magazine, and Cranch and Channing also helped him edit it. Clarke corresponded with Dwight and contributed to his volume in Ripley's *Specimens of Foreign Standard Literature* series. He also canvassed for Emerson's edition of Carlyle's *French Revolution*. All these activities made him acutely aware of what he was missing by not being near Boston.[9]

This period of extreme intellectual activity in his life reached a peak in 1838 when he read Emerson's Phi Beta Kappa address on "The American Scholar." Clarke was struck by its "relation to life" and was happy to see that it had totally confounded those who thought Emerson "a mere dreamer." Stimulated by Emerson's encouragement of both God-reliance and self-reliance, Clarke firmly placed himself on the side of a "small but determined minority" who took Emerson as their guide. Peabody reported to Emerson that Clarke had "swallowed the whole address & felt it digest as strong food for men."[10]

Clarke also praised Emerson's "holiness" and "heroism" to Anna Huidekoper, a young woman in his congregation whom he married a year later, on 15 August 1839. By this time Clarke had definitely decided to return to Boston. For personal reasons, his ministry was turning out to be unsuccessful, and his annual trips to Boston, which gave him a welcome respite, would have to cease when he had a wife to care for. When Henry Channing took the *Western Messenger* to Cincinnati that April, Clarke used the move as an excuse to sever his editorial connections with it. In June 1840 he took his pregnant wife to her family's home at Meadville, Pennsylvania.[11]

Before leaving Louisville, though, Clarke had received a letter from his sister announcing that Fuller had asked for his help with her new periodical. He replied to Sarah that he wished Fuller success and would be glad to help if he could, and in April Sarah received two poems from him for Fuller's new journal. Clarke explained that both poems would need to have the "prosaic lines poetized & the rough ones smoothed," and because he was too accustomed to them to "feel these blemishes" he asked for Fuller's advice on how to finish them. Clarke then heard nothing about the "new Margaret-Waldo-Ripley review," not even the name it was to take, until Henry Channing told him in May that things were progressing well and that the name would be the *Dial*. Soon afterward he wrote directly to Fuller, enclosed a poem called "The Dream," and offered to canvass Louisville for subscribers. Fuller apparently returned the poem to him for revision, along with the ones he had sent to Sarah earlier. By June he was still unable to prepare them for publication, explaining to Fuller that the poems were written to relieve his mind during "the most unhappy hours of the last ten years," and that they required more work.[12]

Clarke was not without comment on the new journal. He told Sarah that he especially liked the "excellent poetry" and that, overall, the *Dial* showed promise, for as it continues, "it will acquire more directness & concentration . . . one does not plunge with much earnestness into the conversation on first entering the room." Also at this time he was defending Transcendentalism in general from its accusers, as when he wrote a friend: "[I]t seems to me that though there may be much that is crude extravagant & mystical, it is better to see free thought & earnest enquiry than the smooth & stagnant surface of mental indifference & lethargy."[13]

The Clarkes stayed at Meadville after the birth of their son. While adjusting to parenthood and an enforced idleness from work, Clarke's attention turned toward poetry. He finally polished "The Dream" enough to secure its publication in the April 1841 *Dial*; Emerson thought it one of the finest poems in that number, and Sarah Clarke considered it one of the best things her brother had done. The *New-Yorker* reprinted "The Genuine Portrait," which, along with its companion piece "The Real and the Ideal," Clarke had revived from his 1833 letter-journal.[14] Most of Clarke's six poems in the *Dial*'s first volume were the product of the leisurely pruning of his more youthful endeavors.

By 1841 he was getting restless and was looking about for a new pulpit. After unsuccessfully negotiating for the pulpit that Ripley had vacated when he moved to Brook Farm, Clarke decided to assemble his own congregation, one which would hold the same liberal beliefs as he did. He found forty-six such people, and that April they established the Church of the Disciples in Boston.[15] Within the next two years Clarke began a translation of Wilhelm De Wette's *Theodore; or, the Skeptic's Conversion* for Ripley's *Specimens of Foreign Standard Literature* series, became an editor of the *Christian World*, and contributed to other Boston papers. These activities limited Clarke's connection with the *Dial*; his only other contributions were a book review and an article on George Keats, which introduced a transcription of his brother John Keats's comments in the latter's volume of Milton.[16]

Many years later Clarke looked back and remembered the *Dial*'s influence on his generation in much the same language as he had earlier decribed Carlyle's influence on him: "By the elders it was cordially declared to be unintelligible mysticism; and so, no doubt, much of it was. Those inside, its own friends, often made as much fun of it as those outside. Yet it opened the door for many new and noble thoughts, and was a wild-bugle note,—a reveillé calling on all generous hearts to look toward the coming day."[17]

12

Sarah Clarke

Sarah Clarke stayed on the periphery of the *Dial*: beyond contributing one poem and keeping her brother James informed about the magazine, she was merely a reader of it. She was born at Dorchester, Massachusetts, on 21 January 1808. When James was left with his grandparents at Newton, she stayed with the family. A promising young artist, she soon became Washington Allston's pupil and later she taught art at Bronson Alcott's Temple School until financial reasons forced her to leave for a salaried position elsewhere.

During most of the 1830s Miss Clarke stayed in and around Boston, visiting friends and painting. Most of James's friends were also hers, and she acted as his link between Louisville and Boston. After she returned from visiting him in the summer of 1837, she reported on his activities in Kentucky at the Transcendental Club meeting on 6 September. She was well liked by everyone, and because she was so friendly and complimentary to all her friends called her "the perpetual peace-offering." When Alcott was pilloried by the press in 1837 for his *Conversations on the Gospels,* she staunchly defended him, just as she later praised his "Orphic Sayings" in the *Dial.*[1] She strongly recommended her friend Elizabeth Peabody as a teacher and was one of the few nonfamily members present at Sophia Peabody's marriage to Nathaniel Hawthorne. Caught up by the interest in German literature at the time, Miss Clarke appreciated Frederic Henry Hedge's use of Goethe in his sermons and was pleased by Lydia Jackson's admiration of Thomas Carlyle and Goethe.[2]

Miss Clarke's friendship with Miss Jackson, whom she favorably called "a real Transcendentalist," continued after her marriage to Ralph Waldo Emerson, and the three became close friends. Miss Clarke thought that Emerson's Divinity School Address was "a strain of high music rising from sweet melody to awful grandeur," and she often gave the Emersons her paintings. Emerson always appreciated these "good enchantments," for he liked the way Miss Clarke "fixed" nature upon her canvas. He thought her a "true & high minded person," and when Margaret Fuller began the *Dial* he recommended Miss Clarke as a possible contributor.[3]

Fuller, who was an old friend of both James and Sarah, probably broached the subject to her at a meeting of the Transcendental Club at Emerson's in May. Soon she had received a poem on Dante, which she liked well enough to have set in type, to be used in case filler material was necessary. When the first number of the *Dial* unexpectedly ran two pages short, Miss Clarke's poem was inserted with a number of Fuller's poems and epigrams to fill out the issue.[4]

James Clarke thought "Dante" was by Fuller. At the same time, because Sarah was studying under Allston, Clarke assumed that Fuller's unsigned article on the Allston exhibition was by his sister, and he praised her for trusting her own, often critical judgments in discussing her teacher. In deference to her abilities, Clarke added that he had "no doubt" that her criticisms were correct. Normally Miss Clarke would have been happy to have her work confused with Fuller's but, unfortunately for James, she had disagreed with much in her friend's article, even to the extent of writing a letter of protest to Emerson.[5] She was "mortified" by his error and told James: "I certainly cannot survive having such a piece of dogmatism attributed to me." James immediately wrote back to remedy his "blunder." This time, after saying that he had read the article more carefully and in a different light, he scolded Fuller for having the "audacity" to accuse Allston of "want of 'force'" and for calling his work "unsatisfactory."[6]

As for herself, Miss Clarke left but one comment on the *Dial,* saying of the first number that "its spirit was lonely."[7] She contributed nothing else to the magazine because her talent was for art, not for literature. As she once explained to her brother in declining to contribute to his *Western Messenger,* even if she had possessed the style of an Addison she had "nothing to say, and the most elegant and tasteful dress is useless if there is no one to wear it."[8]

13
Christopher Pearse Cranch

Christopher Pearse Cranch was unique among the *Dial*'s contributors in that he was a Southerner, being born at Alexandria, then in the District of Columbia, on 8 March 1813. His father was a judge and a lifelong friend of John Quincy Adams, whose niece he had married. Cranch counted Noah Webster among his uncles and W. H. Furness as his cousin. After his graduation from Columbian College in 1832, Cranch followed the example of his brother Edward, who had gone to Cincinnati, by seeking his fortune elsewhere. Then planning to be a minister, he entered the Harvard Divinity School, where he became a friend of Theodore Parker, a model student whom Cranch remembered as always coming back from the library to his room with "huge, venerable tomes" in Greek and Latin, which he proceeded to devour just as "a boarding-school girl would go into a novel."[1]

Cranch graduated in 1835 and left to preach in Providence, Rhode Island. That fall he was in Andover, Maine, where he stayed the winter. To pass the time he wrote a parody of "The Ancient Mariner," called "Childe Christophe," with himself as the title character. When the snow melted, Cranch returned to Boston where he met and fell in love with Sarah Bigelow of Peoria, Illinois. He also saw many of his old friends. John Sullivan Dwight invited him to join the musical society at Harvard and in August asked him for German translations for his volume in George Ripley's *Specimens of Foreign Standard Literature* series. That summer, perhaps while returning from a trip to Illinois, he found himself at Cincinnati visiting his brother Edward and at the threshold of a new career.[2]

Cranch had always shown a talent for writing, and in November 1836 the prestigious *Knickerbocker* had published one of his poems. At Cincinnati the youthful *Western Messenger* was carrying the call of Transcendentalism to the West, and Cranch joined its staff. His work appealed to the editors, and because James Clarke, then in charge of the magazine in Louisville, was preparing for his annual trip to New England, Cranch was approached to supply both Clarke's pulpit and his editorial chair during his absence.[3] Cranch agreed at once and moved to Louisville, where he coedited the October *Western Messenger*. He was

Christopher Pearse Cranch.

Collection of Joel Myerson.

happy in his work, and not even the sole responsibility for the November issue prevented him from joking with his sister about his hectic pace: humorously he complained that the "child" Clarke had left behind was continually crying for food, adding, "Clarke just lets his offspring go to the dickens."[4]

Cranch stayed in the Ohio Valley during 1838, writing for the *Messenger*, coediting two more issues, and substituting again for Clarke. When Clarke returned in January 1839, he stayed with Cranch for three weeks and passed on to him information about Ralph Waldo Emerson's activities and the latest Boston news. During 1839 Cranch produced two of the best works of his life. A talented man with little discipline, Cranch was a dabbler in music, art, and literature who tried each before he finally became an artist. In 1839 music held out little promise as a career, and Cranch's lack of haste to be ordained implies that he was seriously considering either literature or art for his possible vocation. He was more serious about poetry than art at the time, and by March one tangible result of Emerson's growing influence was Cranch's fine poem "Correspondences."[5] Equally fine, though in a different vein, was his "New Philosophy Scrapbook," which contained caricatures based on lines from Emerson's writings, the most famous of which was the long-legged, barefoot, dinner-coat-clad transparent eyeball.[6]

Cranch left Cincinnati and the West to return to New England, settling at Quincy, Massachusetts, where he renewed his friendship with Parker. Although the two had not been in correspondence since their divinity school days, each knew of the other's activities through their mutual contact with Dwight. Cranch was soon invited to West Roxbury, Massachusetts, where Parker found him "full of spontaneous fellowship," though, more critically, he recognized that Cranch's dilettantish attitude would not make him "a man who the world will use well." Cranch considered Parker a "congenial friend" who was "fresh, strong and original as well as learned," and in no danger of exemplifying Emerson's saying that "[I]nstead of Man Thinking we have the Bookworm." One day he overheard three men talking about one of Parker's sermons that Cranch had thought "fine" and "sound withal"; the first called it "strange preaching," the second mentioned its "new doctrine," and the third shrieked "Emersonianism!"[7]

"Emersonianism" was quickly taking hold of Cranch himself. On 5 December 1839 he attended a Transcendental Club meeting at Ripley's, and he moved into Boston that month to be closer to the center of activity. Though Boston was "overrun with lectures" that winter, Cranch significantly went only to Emerson's series on "The Present Age," which he found "a treat whose worth I can find no words to express." Cranch had first read *Nature* during the winter of 1836 and had greatly admired it. The book set him "athinking," and he surely carried out his earlier promise to his brother to read it again. He was even more impressed by Emerson's Divinity School Address, calling it "the utterance of a seer and a prophet, a word of profound truth." Cranch had also praised Emerson's address on "The American Scholar" in the pages of the *Western Messenger*. Since his cousin Furness was an old friend of Emerson, and since Emerson had known Cranch's brother John when they were both in Rome in 1833, Cranch must have felt that he would not be considered forward if he wrote directly to Emerson to express his thoughts.[8]

On 2 March 1840 Cranch copied "Enosis" and "To the Aurora Borealis" and sent them off with a letter to Emerson. "Enosis," which he sent untitled, had been written in Cranch's Boston hotel room during the period he attended Emerson's lectures.[9] While asking Emerson to be the poems' "godfather" by placing them in the *Dial* if he found them worthy, Cranch at the same time expressed his "deep gratitude" for Emerson's thoughts and his pleasure in Emerson's works, concluding: "I utter no hollow compliments or vain imaginings when I say that I have owed to you more quickening influences and more elevating views in shaping my faith, than I can ever possibly express to you."[10] Emerson thought well of the poems and the next day wrote Fuller that "Aurora Borealis" was "worthy of its subject" while "Enosis" was perhaps even better.[11] Holding them for Fuller, Emerson thanked Cranch for the "beautiful verses" and especially praised lines that appeared to him as "Miltonic" or "true and descriptive." Emerson assured Cranch that they would be acceptable for the "yet unsunned journal" and praised him for his "decided poetic taste." In answer to Cranch's compliments, Emerson modestly replied that if such thoughts "have interested you, it only shows how much they were already yours," and he invited Cranch to Concord to see Walden Pond and "our Concord poet," Henry Thoreau.[12]

However, Cranch was too busy to accept this invitation, having promised to preach in Portland, Maine, for a month. After stopping on the way to supply Parker's pulpit, he arrived there in the middle of April and found to his dismay that the Boston movements were looked down upon. On one occasion he was reluctantly drawn into a "tea-table" discussion of Transcendentalism, and after listening to Fuller's Conversations described as Transcendental because "they 'transcended common sense,'" Cranch quickly, though quietly, replied in her defense. But a decided fervor built in him as he pondered over his response, and he wrote Dwight that he was nursing his wrath for "some fit occasion to blaze out on them in righteous zeal for the good cause. Pray for me that I may be bold, that I may cry aloud and spare not." In preparation for that day Cranch was writing poetry and, although he still contributed to the *Western Messenger*, he saved his best pieces for the *Dial*. By May he had sent a draft of "Correspondences" to Clarke with the comment that he was getting to be "somewhat of a Swedenborgian." His drawn-out affair with Sarah Bigelow came to an unsuccessful conclusion, though he told Dwight that he had used it in his poetry. He also sent copies of the poems that were to appear in the *Dial* to Parker, who copied them into his journal.[13]

The summer of 1840 was a happy one for Cranch. The first number of the *Dial* carried the two poems he had sent Emerson, and the *New-Yorker* reprinted "To the Aurora Borealis," which Clarke thought to be excellent. The first week in August was marked by a visit with Emerson in Concord where Emerson read his poetry and that of his "anonymous young lady correspondents," and Cranch found him "more of a brother than [he] had thought him." Parker was also present, and they adjourned to West Roxbury to attend a meeting of the

Transcendental Club on the questions of whether any hope existed for the Unitarian Association and if not, did a new Christian church need to be established or was a new universal church and creed called for. Cranch joined Henry Channing in suggesting that they let the matter take care of itself. The next week the club met in Boston, but Cranch did not come, for he was off to supply the pulpit in Barnstable, Massachusetts.[14]

Being linked with the Transcendentalists was a source of pride for Cranch, but it was also a danger. Writing to his father in July 1840 concerning the rumors that he was intimately involved with Emerson and his circle, Cranch disavowed the "Transcendental philosophy" and described it as a "cold, barren system of Idealism." He also complained that "Transcendentalism" was a label fixed upon all who professed to be on "the movement side" even though they may differ among themselves. He preferred the term "New School," which included "all free seekers after truth, however their opinions differ." Cranch thus neatly sidestepped his affiliation with the Transcendentalists, but his deeds revealed his true feelings. After watching him preach at Quincy in August, his father's old friend John Quincy Adams wrote in his journal that Cranch "gave out quite a stream of transcendentalism, quite unexpectedly." And a few months later Lydia Child complained, after hearing Cranch preach at Northampton, Massachusetts, that he was "unconscious of the evil that lies under his very whiskers!"[15]

The publication of two of his contributions in the October 1840 *Dial*[16] ended Cranch's summer on a happy note, but by November his affairs looked bleaker. At that time Cranch wrote Dwight that he had not had a preaching engagement for pay in the past two months and was barely surviving. He surmised that this might be due to rumors that he was financially independent but thought it more likely to be the fault of the "sapient owls" of the Unitarian Association who had "expunged" his name from "the list of *safe* men." He continued: "I am of the goats and not the evangelical sheep. It is your quick non-commital man who receives the sweet plaudits and puddings of ecclesiastical patronage. I have the misfortune to have associated with Emerson, Ripley & those corrupters of youth, and have written for the Dial, and these are unpardonable offences." Fortunately Dwight came to Boston and allowed Cranch to supply for him. A visit to Parker on his return also encouraged Cranch somewhat.[17]

Cranch's prospects looked brighter as 1841 began. The January *Dial* contained eight of his poems; the *New-Yorker* reprinted "The Riddle," and Clarke must have told Cranch of his friend George Keats's favorable reaction to "Glimmerings."[18] In February Cranch supplied the pulpit in Bangor, Maine, at Hedge's request, but his affairs had not otherwise improved much by that summer, when he decided to visit his brother Edward and his new bride in Washington, D.C.

While in Washington, Cranch began to take stock of his future. Although he read Emerson's *Essays* ("a living fountain to me"), he had not bothered to have the July 1841 *Dial*, which contained his "The Blind Seer," sent on to him. He wrote Dwight that he had "no plans; no prospects, save of the vaguest sort," but that he planned to inquire about Brook Farm when he returned. The last point was an indication of Cranch's uncertainty, for he had earlier doubted that Ripley's colony would be a "panacea" or "pitch plaster for the healing of the nations." At the end of the summer an offer came from a small society in Fishkill-on-the-Hudson, New York, and Cranch went there as minister.[19]

While in upstate New York, Cranch still kept in touch with his friends. Elizabeth Peabody gave him a copy of Parker's *A Discourse on the Transient and Permanent in Christianity*, and Henry Channing came up to visit him. Cranch sent Emerson some verses in September, mentioning that they had been written during the previous winter, "since which time an affection of the head has indisposed me almost entirely to any inspirational of mental labor." Emerson copied the poems and sent them to Margaret Fuller, who was looking for something to fill out the October 1841 number as "Inworld" and "Outworld" arrived. She quickly gave them to Metcalf, the *Dial*'s printer. But after she had left, he discovered that the poems were too long to be printed together, and he ran off proof just for "Inworld." Since Fuller was out of town, the proof was sent to Emerson, but it did not reach him until 1 October, shortly before Fuller arrived to announce that the *Dial* would appear that very day and that Metcalf had informed her that any correction would be impossible. Emerson informed Cranch of this, promised him that the two would appear together in the next number, and entreated him not to "cease to give us good-will and verses" because of the error.[20]

Cranch left Fishkill-on-the-Hudson to winter in Boston. He supplied the pulpit in Burlington, Vermont, the next summer and then returned to Boston for another winter, still unsettled about his future. During this period he sent in two more contributions to the *Dial*[21] and returned to his caricatures again, this time drawing upon the *Dial* as his subject. The best of these that have survived shows a man lying on a couch, sipping wine while his wife glowers at him as she polishes his boots. A copy of the *Dial* is under the couch and the caption is a stanza from Caroline Sturgis's "Life":

> Why for work art thou striving,
> Why seek'st thou for aught?
> To the soul that is living
> All things shall be brought.[22]

Julia Ward Howe remembered another drawing of Fuller driving a winged chariot inscribed with "The Dial" across the sky as the conservative Unitarian Andrews Norton "regarded her with holy horror." Cranch showed these drawings with "great glee" to Parker and Ripley and even gave one to Peabody.[23] The only other work Cranch did during this period was two translations from Goethe for Charles Brooks's *Songs and Ballads*, which was published in 1842.

During this time Cranch was also tutoring his cousin Elizabeth de Windt in German. They soon fell in love and he proposed to her. As a last chance to gain a financial windfall, and probably to promote a paying magazine market for his future writings, Cranch turned his attention toward producing a volume of his poetry. When Rufus Griswold solicited biographical information from him for the second edition of his *Poets and Poetry of America*, Cranch responded that he wanted some of his poems from the *Dial* to be substituted for those Griswold had printed in the first edition. In April 1843 Cranch asked Emerson's help in finding a publisher for his poems, and Emerson responded with the names of Horace Greeley, Griswold, and John L. O'Sullivan. However, Cranch turned to the Philadelphia firm of Carey and Hart, whose *Gift* for 1844 had contained two of his poems, and with whom his cousin Furness was involved, and they published his *Poems* in May 1844. Cranch reprinted all of his *Dial* contributions except for "The True in Dreams" and dedicated the volume to Emerson, who wrote Cranch that he was "glad to find my old friends in the book . . . and, throughout, the same sweetness and elegance of versification which I admired in the pieces which adorned our first 'Dials.' "[24]

The publication of his poems was Cranch's last real contact with the *Dial* group. Just as preparing his volume of poetry had stopped him from contributing more to the *Dial*, his growing interest in landscape painting and his settling in New York City after his marriage in October 1843 drew him away from the interests of men like Emerson and Parker.[25] Backed with financial support from his wife's father, Cranch finally abandoned the ministry and devoted his full attention to painting, leaving for a European tour in August 1846. The month before he left, Edgar Allan Poe portrayed him in his "Literati of New York City." After noting that Cranch had been "one of the least absurd contributors" to the *Dial*, Poe approvingly said that he had since then "reformed his habits of thought and speech."[26] Later, Henry James left this description of him: "Christopher Pearse Cranch, painter, poet, musician, mild and melancholy humourist, produced pictures that the American traveller sometimes acquired and left verses that the American compiler sometimes includes."[27]

14
George William Curtis

George William Curtis was brought into touch with the *Dial* by his friends at Brook Farm. He was born at Providence, Rhode Island, on 24 February 1824. After the death of his mother when he was two, George and his older brother Burrill were brought up by their father. When they were old enough for schooling, the elder Curtis sent his sons to Jamaica Plain, near Boston, and they stayed there for five years. In 1835 their father remarried, and the boys returned to Providence, where they went to school and planned to attend Brown University. However, when George took the entrance examination in 1838, he

George William Curtis.

Collection of Joel Myerson.

failed two of the four subjects, including English, and received Ds in the others; Brown turned down his application.

This rejection quickly faded into the background when, in the next year, the family moved to New York City. There Curtis worked as a clerk in an importing house but soon tired of it. What he really wanted to try was literature, a wish that was furthered when the *New-York American* printed some poems that he had submitted anonymously before leaving Providence. Following a brief attempt at resuming his studies, Curtis looked toward Brook Farm as holding out the best hope for his future; there he planned both to earn a living and to pursue his literary interests. He and Burrill arrived at West Roxbury, Massachusetts, in May 1842, and George Ripley welcomed the arrival of the "two wonderfully charming young men" by announcing to the Brook Farmers: "Now we're going to have two young Greek gods among us."[1]

Providence, Boston, and New York were all major centers of literary activity at this period, and all had connections to either the Transcendental or Fourierist movements. Curtis himself remembered that the period was like "the time of witchcraft," when the "air magnified and multiplied every appearance, and exceptions and idiosyncracies and ludicrous follies were regarded as the rule, not as the logical masquerade of this foul fiend Transcendentalism, which was evidently unappeasable, and was about to devour manners, morals, religion, and common-sense." Curtis had earlier come into touch with the "foul fiend Transcendentalism" in the person of Ralph Waldo Emerson and was not to be put off by the ridicule of other, secondhand reports. In 1835 the Curtis brothers had heard Emerson lecture on the Oversoul at their school, and Burrill's memories of the occasion leave no doubt that both were attracted by the man more than by the movement he represented. By moving to Brook Farm, the eighteen-year-old George Curtis not only had a greater degree of freedom but was also closer to Emerson.[2]

To be close to Emerson was also to know Emerson's friends. Curtis soon made the acquaintance of John Sullivan Dwight and Charles King Newcomb. The "picturesquely handsome aspect" of Christopher Pearse Cranch drew Curtis toward him, and they formed a close and lasting friendship. Charles Dana liked Curtis and paid him a compliment once by mistakenly thinking one of Curtis's poems to be by Emerson. However, Curtis, prompted by "sympathy for Emerson's reputation," confessed it to be his. He also became a friend of the "droll" Theodore Parker and was delighted to find that he was "as humorous as he was learned."[3]

Curtis was more critical of his female acquaintances. He thought Elizabeth Peabody noble and respected her, but he later wrote his fiancée that she was "very fat and funny." Even though Margaret Fuller was "always kind and very full of fun" toward Curtis, he described her as dressing "simply, but dowdily, and never handsomely." Like Fuller's later biographers, Curtis explained her annoying facial expressions and movements as the result of illness. Her main trouble, Curtis felt, was that she knew "so much more than all women and most of the men she met that she could not disguise her superiority, from a consciousness already full of self-esteem."[4]

Curtis's sole contribution to the *Dial*, a poem called "A Song of Death," was sent in anonymously, and, while the Ripleys apparently knew of Curtis's authorship of it, Emerson did not. He derived a "singular pleasure" from having his earlier works published anonymously, seeing himself as "addressing the world not as Geo. Curtis, but as some distinguished messenger, the mystery of whom is a charm, if nothing more." The fact that Curtis quickly realized that his best work was in prose rather than in verse must also have made his anonymity a pleasant cloak to be wrapped in. When Emerson selected his poem for publication in the July 1843 *Dial*, Curtis was pleased, for he felt that Emerson knew the difference between the "power of the poet" and the "force of talented imitation," and Emerson's personal, though indirect acceptance of him was a great honor. Sophia Ripley had mixed feelings about the poem: it was "very graceful," she told Emerson, but she felt it also showed the poet's refusal of "deep experience" in favor of sentiment.[5]

Soon after his poem was published in the *Dial*, Curtis became restless among the Brook Farmers. He felt that there was "a selfish and an unheroic aspect" about their lives and believed that they were destined to failure for not recognizing that "our evils are entirely individual, not social." The "protestants against the sin of flesh-eating," who belived that to "purloin milk from the udder was to injure the maternal affections of the cow," that to "eat eggs was Feejee canabalism," and that to "swallow an oyster was to mask murder," began to irk rather than to amuse him. He soon lost respect for such ardent associationists as Henry Channing, whose fanaticism, Curtis believed, was caused by his perceiving "by the heart and not the head." In an attempt to get his own life in order, Curtis left Brook Farm in October 1843 for New York. As his letters to Dwight show, Curtis enjoyed the city life, but when spring came he joined his brother Burrill in settling in Concord, Massachusetts; he was too late, however, to do anything more for the *Dial*, the last number of which coincided with his arrival.[6]

15

Charles Anderson Dana

Charles Anderson Dana was one of the *Dial*'s contributors whose basic allegiances and ties were to West Roxbury, Massachusetts, and Brook Farm rather than to Concord, Massachusetts, and Ralph Waldo Emerson. He was born at Hinsdale, New Hampshire, on 8 August 1819. His mother died when he was nine and, after staying three years with relatives in Vermont, Dana went to Buffalo, New York, to work as a clerk in his uncle's store. There he taught himself the Seneca Indian language and Latin and independently pursued literary studies. These stood him in good stead when his uncle's business fell victim to the financial panic of 1837 and he was forced to look elsewhere for a living. With the eventual goal of attending Harvard, Dana founded a literary society in Buffalo, and within two years he had saved $200 from it. With this money and high hopes he set off for Cambridge, Massachusetts.

Entering Harvard in 1839, Dana worked hard to stay in school. Though he ranked safely in the top fifth of his class, his money slowly gave out, and he was forced to spend two winter terms teaching. His exhausting pace caught up with him in his sophomore year when he stayed up all night to read a cheaply printed edition of *Oliver Twist* by candlelight, severely impairing his eyesight. The damage was bad enough to force his withdrawal from Harvard in June 1841.

While waiting to recover full use of his vision, Dana took a job teaching at Scituate, Massachusetts, but he soon became restless. In July Dana, who had earlier confessed to a " 'supersublimated transcendentalism' . . . though I stumble sadly at some notions," wrote to George Ripley concerning the community at Brook Farm.[1] Though he basically sympathized with Ripley and his followers, Dana disagreed with their religious beliefs and even doubted the eventual success of their project.[2] Nevertheless, Dana put one-third down on three five-hundred-dollar shares and joined Ripley's group in September. Although he thought their theology "nothing more nor less than Pantheism," he felt that he could make a place for himself there and, maintaining his individuality by refusing to curl his hair or to affect a plain tunic, he settled into a happy routine. He soon became the community's secretary and taught Greek and German in the school, where he was given the honorary title of "Professor."[3] Dana's involvement in a lecture series with Horace Greeley, however, led to a growing interest in the New York literary and social scene, and he left Brook Farm for that city in 1846.[4]

Although Dana had been in Cambridge during the time that preparations for the *Dial*'s publication were being made, he did not know about the magazine until its first issue appeared.[5] By then he was in Scituate, and it was not until he joined Brook Farm that he became informed, through the Ripleys, of the circumstances of the *Dial*. Ripley, who thought Dana "a prince among men by his character & feelings," and Margaret Fuller both accepted his first few poems for the *Dial*. When Emerson took over as editor, Dana dealt directly with him.[6] After Emerson had accepted one of Dana's poems, the younger man asked permission to send him another, which he hoped would "seem fit to stand as a minute-mark in the Dial." The death of the promising young Transcendentalist Robert Bartlett provided Dana with his subject, and in October 1843 he sent a poetic "obituary" of him to Emerson. Dana was unsure of the poem's quality, and he told Emerson to return it if he felt it to be poor, so that Dana could submit it to "some journal of less excellence." Emerson, who also mourned Barlett's loss, printed "To R.B." in the January 1844 number.[7]

Charles Anderson Dana.

Collection of Joel Myerson.

Although Dana later described his connection with the *Dial* as that of "an outside sympathizer and spectator," he had, in all, five poems published in the magazine. One, "Manhood," was reprinted by the *New-York Daily Tribune*, and Sophia Ripley told her friends of its "organ tone."[8] Still, Dana felt that literature was not his strongest point and instead devoted himself to Fourierist and other reform activities.[9] As a result, he became too involved in these movements to work on other, nonrelated activities, and the *Dial* certainly was not a Fourierist forum.[10]

16
John Sullivan Dwight

John Sullivan Dwight was another *Dial* contributor who was also a Brook Farm resident. Dwight was born in Boston on 13 May 1813, the son of a Harvard-educated man who counted Lemuel Shaw and Washington Allston among his friends. He was given the usual fine education of a proper Bostonian, and from the Boston Latin School he entered Harvard.

Dwight had a good record at the college, where his classmates included LeBarron Russell, Charles Timothy Brooks, and Samuel Osgood. They were also his fellow members in the Hasty Pudding Club, of which Dwight was vice-president and poet. He was also class poet at his graduation in 1832. Following a short stay at the divinity school, Dwight left Cambridge, Massachusetts, for Meadville, Pennsylvania, where he served as tutor to the Huidekoper family. He obviously had his doubts about pursuing the ministry as a career but soon realized that this was the only course open to him, especially since his musical talents seemed unlikely to provide him with a living.[1] Not surprisingly then, he returned to the divinity school in August 1834 and settled down to the task of getting his degree. Brooks and Osgood were still at Harvard, and Theodore Parker and Christopher Pearse Cranch also became his friends.[2] In Cranch, Dwight discovered a fellow musician, and Divinity Hall often echoed with their flute duets, which on one occasion drove Parker to sawing wood in an attempt to drown them out. Dwight's pastime was incorporated into his senior thesis, "The Proper Character of Poetry and Music for Public Worship," which the *Christian Examiner* published soon after his graduation in August 1836.

As the title of Dwight's paper indicates, he was more interested in connecting religion to everyday life than he was in attacking weighty theological problems. The way to learn about life, he felt, was to experience it, and he therefore spent the next three years as an itinerant preacher. The fact that he made no attempt to hide his sympathies for the Transcendental movement no doubt added to his mobility. One benefit of such an unsettled life was meeting people, by supplying pulpits or by attending Bronson Alcott's Conversations and Transcendental Club meetings, and soon Dwight had met most of those who would become contributors to the *Dial*.

John Sullivan Dwight.

Collection of Joel Myerson.

Dwight put these friendships to good use in 1838, when the one tangible product of these years of wandering was produced. This was his edition of *Select Minor Poems of Goethe and Schiller* for George Ripley's *Specimens of Foreign Standard Literature* series. Dwight had asked his friends, as early as mid-1837, for aid, and eventually Brooks, Margaret Fuller, Frederic Henry Hedge, Henry Channing, James Clarke, and Cranch contributed to the volume. Ralph Waldo Emerson, who found Dwight a "very accurate mind active & genial with fine moral qualities though not of great reading or variously cultivated," suggested that he write Thomas Carlyle for permission to dedicate the volume to him. Carlyle gave his consent, though he asked Emerson: "What are they or he?"[3] When the volume came out in December 1838,[4] Dwight sent Carlyle a copy and was pleased by his reply, which praised Dwight's understanding of the original. Emerson also liked the volume and praised it to Carlyle, who again expressed his delight by telling Emerson that no Englishman, to his own knowledge, had yet "uttered as much sense about Goethe and German things" as Dwight had.[5] Henry Wadsworth Longfellow complained that there were too many poems and that the translations were too loose, and Hedge warned that it was "impossible to english [sic]" Goethe without "degrading" him, but they were definitely in the minority.[6] Ripley pronounced Dwight's translation "singularly accurate," and Parker, while objecting to a few lines, also praised the volume. Clarke, in the February 1839 *Western Messenger*, spoke highly of the "beautiful" volume and of its editor, who had done his work "admirably" and had embellished it with excellent notes.[7]

While Dwight's literary career was drawing praise, his ministerial career was also progressing. At Emerson's suggestion, he had been supplying the pulpit at East Lexington, Massachusetts, for over a year and had by 1839 become more or less the regular pastor. He pleased the congregation by his attempts to integrate music into the service and by his genuine concern about their lives.[8] Still, his sermons were sketchy and poorly prepared, and, although he was invited to the dedication of the new church in January 1840, no attempt was made to secure his services on a permanent basis.[9] His Transcendental leanings were also a detraction. Yet it was this side of Dwight that led Lydia Child to introduce him to her friends at Northampton, Massachusetts, who soon extended a position to him.

Dwight was ordained on 20 May 1840 with Ripley giving the sermon and Osgood the right hand of fellowship.[10] The Reverend William Ellery Channing gave the charge, and Dwight was installed at Northampton in an auspicious manner. He was happy with his first permanent assignment, but it was soon obvious that it would be his last.[11] On the day of his ordination Elizabeth Peabody had written Dwight to warn him about his "want of fluency in prayer," which she called the result of his "idea of being *spontaneous*."[12] While he continued to be "spontaneous," his congregation began to think that he was merely unprepared. The next year they failed to renew his contract, and Dwight joined Ripley at Brook Farm.[13] There he was joined by his two sisters and settled down for a three-year stay.

Ripley brought Dwight into touch with the *Dial* as well as with Brook Farm: all three of Dwight's contributions to the magazine went through him. For the first number Dwight had sent three pieces to Ripley. One, a "Homily" on the church at work, was incomplete and was not printed. Ripley thought that Dwight's article on "The Concerts of the Past Winter" was an "atoning offering for the many sins" of the first *Dial*, and Clarke correctly guessed Dwight's authorship. His other contribution, "The Religion of Beauty," was one of his sermons. For this Dwight had sat down and carefully gone over his work for publication, but Ripley still complained that it was unfinished: "almost every sentence promises something better than we get; and the sum total is a feeling of disappointment." Clark also guessed Dwight to be the author of this piece, and Emerson considered it very good. At the end of the article was an untitled poem that even Ripley praised, calling it "an exquisite expression of a noble & true thought," and that Parker liked well enough to copy into his journal some three months before the *Dial* published it. For many years the poem, under the title "Rest," was reprinted as being by Goethe. Dwight himself called the first number of the *Dial* well done.[14]

Soon after the July 1840 *Dial* was published, Ripley asked Dwight to contribute to the next number. He also warned: "Your beautiful improvisations are a sin against your own soul; and unless you repent & amend your ways, you will be damned, when the day of judgment comes." Dwight apparently took Ripley's warning to heart and diligently worked over what was on hand rather than contributing anything immediately. After dropping his idea for an article on the church at work, Dwight turned to another of his sermons, "Ideals of Every-Day Life," which appeared in the January and April 1841 *Dial*s. This piece, like Dwight's others, was reprinted in many papers and drew the praise of friends. A New York acquaintance told him that, if these articles were his "esoteric confession," he heartily wished that Dwight had more disciples and volunteered himself to be among their number. Dwight's old classmate Osgood also wrote him in praise of the pieces.[15]

Dwight tried to help the *Dial* by canvassing Northampton and neighboring Greenfield for subscribers, but he met with little success. Personally, he liked the *Dial*, especially the January 1841 issue, which he called "a splendid number," and he confessed to his sister that it even "clipped the borders of my sermon some, it was so irresistible a dainty." Yet, as the *Dial* continued, Dwight lost interest in it, even forgetting to obtain copies of some of the later numbers. There were two reasons for this neglect. First, after the initial volume of the *Dial* Dwight was at Brook Farm and spent most of his time on his activities there. Second, what little he did produce he was able to sell to various musical magazines, and even James Russell Lowell had promised him ten dollars an article (more if "the magazine succeeds") for contributions to the *Pioneer*.[16]

Dwight always remembered with pleasure the *Dial* and his contributions to it. In 1845 he planned to collect his articles, including the *Dial* pieces, into a single volume. A publisher's agent, probably Evert A. Duyckinck, editor of the Wiley and Putnam's Library of Choice Reading, wrote Dwight that if he would expand

"Ideals of Every-Day Life" to "fifty or seventy-five printed pages of a 12mo" and add a "few choice things" from among his other articles, the result would be a nice and publishable volume.[17] But Dwight, who always had trouble preparing copy for the press and meeting deadlines, never acted upon the suggestion. Although he never did reprint his *Dial* contributions, he always retained his high opinion of the magazine. Writing nearly thirty years after its last number, Dwight praised the *Dial* to the readers of the *Atlantic Monthly* for telling "the time of days so far ahead."[18]

17

Edward Bliss Emerson, Charles Chauncy Emerson, and Ellen Louisa Tucker Emerson

Three of the *Dial*'s contributors had a total of three articles and three poems published posthumously. They were Ralph Waldo Emerson's brothers, Charles and Edward, and his first wife, Ellen. Emerson placed the poems of Edward and Ellen in the *Dial* because he was genuinely convinced of their worth. While he also thought Charles's articles were good, another motive, a long unfulfilled promise, helped him in his decision to publish them.

Edward Bliss Emerson was born in 1805, two years after his brother Waldo. Considered the best scholar in his class at the Boston Latin School, Edward entered Harvard in 1820 and roomed with Waldo at Number 9, Hollis Hall. He joined the Hasty Pudding Club, serving both as its president and poet, and he gave the commencement oration on "The Advancement of the Age" at his graduation in 1824.

Afterward Edward taught school at Roxbury, Massachusetts. But the following year the strain of simultaneously teaching and studying law accentuated a tubercular condition, and he was forced to give up both. He went to Europe for eleven months in an attempt to regain his health, but upon his return, even though he admitted that the trip had taxed his strength, he took positions with both the Boston Athenæum and Daniel Webster's law firm.

In early 1828 Edward suffered a complete mental and physical breakdown in Concord but recovered with Waldo's help. The doctor prescribed an enforced

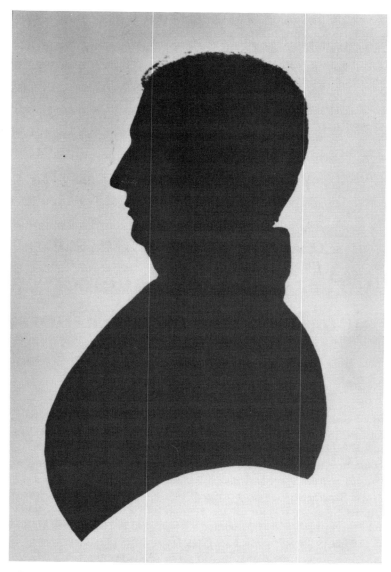

Edward Bliss Emerson.

From Emerson's *Journals*.

rest, advising him not even to touch a book for a year, but Edward failed to follow this advice. In June he became violently deranged and was committed to the McLean asylum in Charlestown, Massachusetts. Although he was soon released, his tuberculosis remained unchecked.

Edward was admitted to the bar in 1829 and went to New York with his brother William to practice, but his health grew progressively worse and he was forced to try a change of climate. That fall he shipped to Santa Cruz in the West Indies, where he stayed, his health seemingly improving, until the fall of 1832, when he returned to Boston for a brief visit. He also purchased supplies and merchandise, for he was now employed in San Juan, Puerto Rico, both as a clerk and as an assistant to the American consul there. His trip to Boston was the last time his family saw him alive: his chronic illness worsened in August 1834, and on 1 October of that year he died.

Edward's poem in the *Dial*, titled "The Last Farewell," was written on board ship when he left Boston for, as he himself probably assumed, the last time. By April 1840 Waldo had decided to print the poem, but after "two or three considerings" he decided to omit the fifth stanza, dealing with a lost love of Edward's. Although Margaret Fuller thought the omission greatly hurt the poem, she understood and agreed with Emerson's feelings on the matter.[1]

Of the *Dial*'s other contributors only George Ripley and Frederic Henry Hedge seem to have known Edward well. Ripley was in the class ahead of him at Harvard, and Hedge was in the one behind him. Hedge was impressed by Edward and later recalled that Waldo's promise had seemed "faint in comparison." Fuller, as she told Hedge when informed of Edward's death, did not know him but said that he was to her, when she was very young, a "living type of noble ambition and refinement." Perhaps, she continued, "this opinion of him was a mistaken one. Fate forbad its being tested." Waldo Emerson compared himself with his brother in this manner: "My brother lived & acted & spoke with preternatural energy. My own manner is sluggish; my speech sometimes flippant, sometimes embarrassed & ragged; my actions (if I may say so) are of a passive kind. Edward had always great power of face. I have none. I laugh; I blush; I look ill tempered; against my will & against my interest."[2]

Emerson was not as close to Edward as to his other brother, Charles Chauncy Emerson, who was born in 1808. Like Edward, Charles promised to be a brilliant scholar, and he entered Harvard in 1824. During his stay there he also joined the Hasty Pudding Club, serving both as its president and orator. Charles did better as an undergraduate than either Edward or Waldo had, winning the Bowdoin Prize and giving the valedictory oration at his commencement. Unfortunately, he also had tuberculosis, and after his graduation he left for the West Indies hoping that the different climate would help.

When he returned in 1832, Charles went to work as an attorney in Boston. He soon fell in love with Elizabeth Hoar, the daughter of a fellow lawyer, and they were engaged in August 1833.[3] Elizabeth thought highly of her fiancé's promise and convinced him that after their marriage he should come into her father's Concord (Massachusetts) law practice.[4] However, in the spring of 1836 the

Charles Chauncy Emerson.

From Emerson's *Journals*.

symptoms of Charles's tuberculosis reappeared, and on 9 May of that year he died while staying in New York with his brother William, just a few hours before Waldo and Elizabeth could reach his side.

Charles's death shocked everyone who knew him. Hoar, whom Waldo Emerson subsequently treated as a sister, still wore black for him twenty years later. Oliver Wendell Holmes, in a poem before the Harvard Phi Beta Kappa chapter in the following year, called him a "calm, chaste scholar" who was "[t]oo bright to live, — but oh, too fair to die!" Fuller, too, wrote a poem in his memory. Bronson Alcott also mourned his passing, for he had found Charles, like his brother Waldo, "scholarlike," but Charles, thought Alcott, did not lose the man in the scholar.

But it was Waldo Emerson who grieved the most; while walking away after Charles's funeral, he was heard to say absently, "When one has never had but little society — and *all that society* is taken away — what is there worth living for?"

Waldo had greatly treasured Charles's companionship, for the latter often acted as a sounding board for many of his own ideas. As Emerson told Thomas Carlyle, "we made but one man together." And Emerson entered into his journal, "Now commences a new & gloomy epoch of my life."[5]

A few months after Charles's death some of his friends asked Emerson to prepare a memoir of him together with a collection of his writings. A week later, though, Emerson replied that Charles had left very little in "a fit state for publication," and the project was abandoned. The following March Emerson briefly revived the plan, but nothing came of it. When the *Dial* was established, Emerson again returned to Charles's manuscripts, and in April 1840 he sent copies of Charles's comments on Homer, Shakespeare, and Edmund Burke, under the title of "Notes from the Journal of a Scholar," to Fuller, who planned to include them in the *Dial*'s first number. James Clarke thought the whole piece "very fine" when it appeared in July, and the section on Shakespeare was reprinted by the *New-Yorker*. Emerson volunteered more of Charles's material for the *Dial* in November, but there was no room to print it. It was not until April 1843 that Emerson, now the *Dial*'s editor, printed Charles's impressions on his voyage to Puerto Rico. In the next issue Emerson printed more "Notes from the Journal of a Scholar" and was again pleased to see them well received. Fuller, who had previously read the selections in Charles's journal, told Emerson that "it is good to have it in my own possession," and Henry Thoreau asked him to print more from Charles's writings. However, Emerson did not, and that was Charles's last piece to be printed in the *Dial*.[6]

Ellen Louisa Tucker Emerson was sixteen when Waldo Emerson first met her on Christmas Day 1827 while preaching at Concord, New Hampshire. A beautiful and sensitive young girl, Ellen made a deep impression on the twenty-four-year-old Waldo, and when he returned there nearly a year later, he waited only ten days before asking her to marry him. The engagement was announced on 17 December, and the following September they were married.[7]

Emerson deeply loved his "Ellinelli," and she provided him with an admiring and rewarding love of her own. Her letters show her to be a kind and gentle girl, and when the two were together, or wrote to one another, they looked like and acted the parts of young lovers, having pet names and private jokes. Emerson even gave her one of the saccharine giftbooks so popular with young lovers of that time, called *Forget Me Not*.

Yet their happiness was short-lived. Ellen had never been healthy, a fact that Emerson and others had already noticed.[8] Early in their marriage she had coughed up blood, and her tuberculosis became progressively worse. She died on 8 February 1831 with Waldo by her side; they had been married for only a little over sixteen months and she had not yet reached her twentieth birthday. Emerson was greatly affected by her death: not until his return from Europe two years later was he able to pick up his life where he had left it.

When the *Dial* was formed, Emerson looked over those poems written by Ellen that he had copied into a versebook and sent an untitled one to Fuller, who liked it well enough to place it in the first number. Emerson made several changes in

Ellen Louisa Tucker Emerson.

Collection of Joel Myerson.

the poem, including two different lines at the end in order to remove a reference to himself, before it was published as "Lines."[9] The *Boston Morning Post* reprinted it, and, knowing that others appreciated Ellen's poetry, Emerson sent another poem, "The Violet," off to Fuller. This poem was omitted from the next *Dial* through "some blunder" but was printed in the January number.[10] This was Ellen's last piece in the *Dial*.

Emerson acted with great restraint in placing the works of his late brothers and wife in the *Dial*. No one commented adversely on his selections, and many praised them. Ellen's poems were as good as most published in the magazine, and Edward's poem, while having a personal meaning to Emerson, was the type that would affect anyone who had ever left behind a loved one or a favorite place. Emerson wisely selected the best of Charles's critical writings, and the *Dial* published other pieces of travel literature besides his. In fact, an examination of the manuscripts available to him shows that Emerson chose the best pieces of writing from those available and stopped at the point where his own sentiment would have been a greater reason for publishing them than their inherent quality or worth.

18
William Batchelder Greene

William Batchelder Greene was one of the *Dial*'s contributors who was brought to Ralph Waldo Emerson's attention by Elizabeth Peabody. Greene was born at Haverhill, Massachusetts, on 4 April 1819. His father was active in literary matters, being a newspaper editor and having published many of his own German translations. At first the son seemed unlikely to follow in his father's footsteps: he enrolled in the West Point Military Academy in 1835. Ill health forced him to leave before graduation, and in 1837 he joined the Army's campaign against the Indians in Florida. He was made a second lieutenant two years later, but, again plagued by illness, Greene returned to New England and resigned his commission in 1841.

Although the doctors apparently gave him little chance to recover, Greene quickly regained his health after settling near Boston. He stayed at Brook Farm for a while and then attended the Baptist Seminary at Newton, Massachusetts. For a time he was influenced by Orestes Brownson, but he gradually found himself drifting toward the group that regularly met at the West Street bookstore of Elizabeth Peabody.[1]

Greene first met Peabody in the winter of 1841, when he entered her bookstore in search of an English translation of Immanuel Kant. They struck up a conversation, and Peabody soon found herself very impressed by him.[2] It was indeed rare for her to find anyone as outspoken and opinionated as herself. She would have agreed with T. W. Higginson's later comment that Greene was "strikingly handsome and mercilessly opinionated," and with Ednah Dow Cheney that Greene "almost rivalled Socrates in winding an adversary up into a complete snarl." Peabody brought her new acquaintance to see the Reverend

William Ellery Channing and told her other friends about him. Word reached Concord, Massachusetts, and Greene traveled there in November 1841 to meet Emerson.[3]

Greene liked many aspects of Emerson and his writings. Of all the "Transcendentalists of Boston," he said, only Emerson saw "the transcendental objective," which he called the Oversoul; the others incorrectly thought that it was they themselves who had transcended. When Margaret Fuller heard of the visit, she wrote Emerson: "How did you like the military-spiritual-heroico-vivacious phoenix of the day." She had heard that he was "delighted," but since she "never knew that word made use of in [Emerson's] vocabulary," she thought that she would ask him to confirm the story. Fuller's source was indeed correct, for Emerson printed Greene's "First Principles" as the opening article in the next number of the *Dial*.[4]

At the same time, Greene entered the intellectual life of Boston by attending some of the many Conversations then in progress. Mrs. Cheney was present during a conversation at which Bronson Alcott described the "demonic man" as one whose qualities exactly matched Greene's. This point was not lost on the audience, and Greene soon replied, "But has not the demonic man his value?" Alcott responded: "Oh, yes, the demonic man is good in his place, very good, — he is good to build railroads; but I do not like to see him in pulpits, begging Mr. Greene's pardon." Greene, who was in the ministry at this time, took the remark silently but soon began to ask Alcott a string of questions, which, if Alcott had continued to answer them, would have driven him, as Mrs. Cheney recalled, "to the wall." However, Alcott's answers "soared higher and higher," and Greene was reduced to watching helplessly as "his opponent was borne away in a cloud far out of sight."[5]

As his interest in Transcendentalism grew, Greene entered the Harvard Divinity School. He submitted a sequel to his "First Principles" to the *Dial*, but Emerson did not print it.[6] This action of Emerson's did not jeopardize their friendship;[7] Greene's marriage,[8] his attending school, and his other publications were the reasons why his first contribution to the *Dial* was also his only one.[9]

19

Frederic Henry Hedge

Frederic Henry Hedge was the *Dial*'s most disappointing contributor. That he contributed only one article, one poem, and two translations was not as surprising as was his general lack of support for the journal. To those who had known him for many years it appeared that Hedge was passing up his chance to forward in print causes that he had been supporting in conversation for some time.

Hedge was born at Cambridge, Massachusetts, on 12 December 1805. His father, Levi Hedge, became a professor at Harvard and gave his talented son the best education available. He was tutored by the brilliant young George Bancroft and accompanied him in 1818 to Germany, where Hedge attended the *gymnasia*. Upon his return in 1822 he was given junior standing in the next year's class at Harvard. There, Hedge quickly became a friend of Horatio Greenough, Caleb Stetson, Edward Emerson, G. P. Bradford, and George Ripley. He served both as vice-president and poet of the Hasty Pudding Club and was elected class poet in his senior year. Although he considered poetry and medicine as possible careers, Hedge followed his father's wishes and entered Harvard Divinity School in 1825. After his graduation in 1829, he was ordained pastor at West Cambridge. He married a girl from his congregation in 1830, and they had two children by 1834.

His love for Germany and his location kept Hedge from becoming a quiet parish preacher who rarely left home except for the yearly ministerial conferences. As one of the few people who at that time had actually studied in Germany, his conversation was much in demand. His old friends were near Cambridge, and he quickly made new friends among the brighter Harvard students that had arrived since his own days there. Following the publication of his important and favorable article on Samuel Taylor Coleridge and German philosophy in the March 1833 *Christian Examiner*, he was firmly established in his position as a popular and wanted member of any conversational group. In February 1835 Hedge proposed a new journal "devoted to a spiritual philosophy, and mainly dependent upon translations, to be conducted by . . . leaders in that school of thought," such as himself, Ralph Waldo Emerson, and Ripley. Yet in May 1835 Hedge left Cambridge to become the minister to the Unitarian society at Bangor, Maine, and the project collapsed.[1]

The move to Bangor was not hastily conceived and was made partially through the efforts of Hedge's old friend from divinity school days, Waldo Emerson.[2] In 1833 the Bangor congregation had approached Hedge about the possibility of his moving there, but the immensity of this step, which, after having been taken, he thought "may be impossible to retrace," kept Hedge from giving it serious consideration. However, the next year Emerson went to preach in Bangor and wrote a glowing letter back to Hedge. In it he praised the "shrewd liberal men who are sanguine in their expectation of the great future importance of this place" and who were so "very anxious to have a minister of ability settled here" that they saw no difficulty in giving him "an ample support." Hedge preached in Bangor that fall and agreed with Emerson's high estimate of the situation. When the congregation tendered their offer of a position at $1,500 a year, nearly twice Hedge's Cambridge salary, he accepted.[3]

Hedge did not allow his new position to isolate him from his old friends. On 14 June 1836 he wrote Emerson about the possibility of gathering "certain

Frederic Henry Hedge.

Collection of Joel Myerson.

likeminded persons of our acquaintance for the free discussion of theological & moral subjects." Emerson agreed with Hedge's plan for a "symposium," and on 8 September 1836 the two met with George Putnam and Ripley in what was the first meeting of the Transcendental Club.[4]

Hedge continued to attend Transcendental Club meetings and to correspond with old friends. Bronson Alcott liked Hedge, even though he often found his own Socratic ideas of education at odds with Hedge's inclination toward "scholastic instruction." Alcott was disappointed when Hedge failed to review his *Conversations with Children on the Gospels* for the *Christian Examiner* as he had promised to do.[5] Even so, Alcott wished to know Hedge better[6] and thought that he and Emerson showed more promise "than others amongst us." When Parker began an intensive reading program in German philosophy, he wrote Hedge for advice because, as he told him, Hedge knew more than any man of his acquaintance about the subject.[7]

When the idea for the *Dial* was brought up at the 18 September 1839 meeting of the Transcendental Club, it was assumed that Hedge would want to be a leader of the magazine. Emerson, Margaret Fuller, and Hedge all expressed confidence in it, and Parker proposed Hedge as one of its editors.[8] Hedge, however, probably realized that, unlike his earlier plan, it would be impossible for him to place all the various Transcendentalists together under his editorial reins. Also, Hedge was becoming estranged from the ideas of the Transcendentalists, and the focus was shifting from *his* journal to *their* journal. Consequently, when he returned to Bangor for the winter months, he gave the matter little thought. Others, correctly assessing Hedge's position, dropped him from consideration for a major role on the *Dial*, and in November Fuller was named editor.

Heavy snows kept Hedge in Bangor, and not until January did he hear again of the planned journal, when Fuller wrote to ask for his help. They had first met in 1823 when Hedge had been "simply astonished" at her intellectual powers. She had been excited by his "periodical plan" of 1835 and had offered her assistance. Therefore, Hedge was one of the first to whom she wrote for help with the *Dial*. She wished him "all happiness" for the coming year and said that she anticipated with "greatest pleasure" the prospect of working with him. The first number was to come out in April, and she asked for "solid bullion" from his pen, wishing to know directly whether he would contribute "poems or philosophy or criticism," and how much, since they were planning the first number "by the yard."[9]

Hedge expressed surpise at Fuller's "sudden announcement," for he confessed that he had scarcely thought of the project since he was last in Boston. His letter of reply was a well-constructed, if transparent, "no" to her request. After stating that no one could feel a stronger interest in the new journal than himself, Hedge recounted his past efforts at establishing a periodical. Yet, since that time he had grown less "enterprising" and more "diffident." He finally announced that he wanted to be a "reader & subscriber" and not a contributor. As reasons he gave the "most unproductive state" of his mind, his "very imperfect health," and his "pecuniary embarrassment," reminding her of the four children depending upon his efforts. Probably realizing that both Emerson and Fuller had overcome these obstacles in their own lives, Hedge then retreated somewhat. These reasons were not "a preamble to withdrawing from our joint concern," he said, but an explanation of his present inability to help her. A visit from the Reverend Mr. Upham of Salem and a lyceum lecture would probably prevent him from making any contributions to the planned April number, but he proposed these possibilities for the following one: "perhaps a word on *Hegel*," sermons, translations of German literature, a series on "the relation of modern philosophy to Christianity," or a course on "Metaphysics proper." But whatever he did write, Hedge wanted to remain anonymous. He ended by telling Fuller that his "whole heart" was with her and that all he had "of intellectual energy & of literary resource" was at her command.[10]

Fuller took Hedge at his word and optimistically left his name in her notebook at a possible contributor to the *Dial*'s first number. When it became obvious that the magazine would not come out until July, she again wrote to Hedge and called upon him, "in the name of all the Genii, Muses, Pegasus, [and] Apollo," to send "something good for this journal before the 1st May." She sympathized with his inability to write but impressed upon him the necessity of having a successful first number.

Finding himself unable to get out by diplomatic means, Hedge wrote back and frankly confessed that, by identifying himself publicly with the Transcendentalists, he feared that he would stand forth as "an atheist in disguise." And he clearly expressed his disagreement with the ideas of Emerson and Alcott. His position was at last clear, and Emerson and Fuller were disappointed not only by his stance, but by his failure to say so at the start. Emerson told Fuller that he was "sorry" for Hedge and that Hedge's reply would make a sad page in his biography. He wrote Fuller not to worry: "It is much for him, but it is not important to the book. The book would be glad of his aid, but it will do as well without." And so the first number of the *Dial* appeared without anything from Hedge.[11]

Hedge managed to contribute an article on "The Art of Life, — The Scholar's Calling," to the October 1840 *Dial*. When, from Louisville, George Keats wrote James Clarke about the piece, he correctly recalled from memory "passages to the effect that a student desiring progress, and the highest self culture, should altogether disregard fame, and the means of living; but be satisfied with the Hermit's fare, and retirement, and live the life of an anchorite." Keats's comment was: "Now what sort of man would be produced, never mind how lofty his genius or how great his acquirements . . . Only think of how the world would laugh at a flock of students seeking out solitary places, and dotting our forests with hermitages."[12] Hedge's only other original contribution to the *Dial*, the poem "Questionings," was written one sleepless night while watching the stars as he took the mail coach back to Bangor. Emerson was "very proud" of these verses and always treasured them.[13]

Problems with his congregation and a natural reluctance to become further involved with the Transcendentalists kept Hedge away from the *Dial* until July 1842, when he sent in a translation from Johann Ludwig Uhland for that issue. He was prompted to do so by a new appeal from Emerson, who had replaced Fuller as editor. In March Emerson had asked if Hedge had "any word to print on these Times? fact or thought; history, poem, or exhortation?" By May Emerson told Parker that Hedge had promised "good aid," and the Uhland poem was the first tangible result. Hedge also sent along a copy of his 1841 Harvard Phi Beta Kappa oration on "Conservatism and Reform," but Emerson was not as enthusiastic about this piece. He had heard Hedge deliver it and was upset that he had failed to value "any position or any principal" but had thought only of "the tactics or method of the fight." Emerson felt that "[i]ntellectual play" was Hedge's only interest, while he was actually indifferent to the question itself. Upon returning home from the oration, Emerson had written in his journal: "It was the profoundest of superficiality . . . The sentence which began with an attack on the conservatives ended with a blow at the reformers: the first clause was applauded by one party & the other party had their revenge & gave their applause before the period was closed." Not surprisingly then, Emerson declined to print it in the *Dial*. However, being a diplomatic editor, Emerson returned the manuscript to Hedge with the comment that a separate publication would be "juster & better" for it. Besides, his own lecture "The Conservative" was too similar, and, along with a long article by Fuller, took up too many pages for the varied magazine he wanted. Still, Emerson thanked Hedge for considering the *Dial* and promised instead to print a seciton on Friedrich Schelling from the preface to a new edition of Georg Hegel's works, which Hedge had copied and sent to Emerson.[14] The latter appeared as the final item in the October "Editor's Table."

Hedge's last work for the *Dial* was another translation. In October Charles Stearns Wheeler had sent a copy of Schelling's introductory lecture given to his classes at Berlin in November 1841 to Emerson, who had asked Hedge to translate it. Hedge worked steadily and in three weeks gave his completed translation to Emerson. It was printed in the January 1843 *Dial*, a number that Hedge considered deficient in "good, original matter," the only satisfactory articles being Emerson's selections from Menu, Thoreau's translation of Prometheus, and the catalogue of the library at Fruitlands.[15]

Hedge's choice of the best pieces from that number of the *Dial* indirectly points to one of his major objections to the magazine. He was essentially conservative and preferred solid studies of more established literature, or even reprints of that literature, to the experimental flights of the younger Transcendentalists. To challenge such stalwart publications as the *Christian Examiner* and the *North American Review* on their own ground, rather than to break new paths, was Hedge's goal. The fact that he opposed most of the Transcendentalists, especially their concept of the validity of divine inspiration belonging to the individual soul, made this an easy position for him to take.

Hedge's growing conservatism was not only the result of his convictions but also of his immediate circumstances. His congregation had always been troublesome, and in July 1840 Hedge had threatened to resign if his original salary, previously reneged on, was not produced. It was met, and the society grew successfully until 1842, when some of the *"ultra* conservative" members, "frightened about Transcendentalism," tried to get him dismissed. Hedge again almost resigned before the society voted down his detractors. He surely realized that a permanent role on the *Dial* would only exacerbate the situation, and this, too, explains why he did not participate any more than he did in the *Dial*.[16]

Another factor that kept Hedge away from the *Dial* was probably his own egotism and a resulting feeling of bitterness.[17] He had been at the center of the intellectual life at Cambridge before his move to Maine — the Transcendental Club was sometimes called "Hedge's Club" because it often used his visits to Boston as the occasion for a meeting — and Hedge felt that nothing could "compensate for the sacrifice" he had made in going to Bangor.[18] Unable by reason of distance to play a major role in the running of the *Dial*, and unable by temperament to shape the journal's ideology, he retreated into himself. The knowledge that he had had a chance five years earlier to do exactly what he had wanted to, and had seen it slip away, also hurt. And when some of the very same people for whom he had left Boston complained of his loose connections with the Transcendentalists, the sense of frustration and bitterness must have been great.

Although Elizabeth Peabody felt that Hedge "might have introduced Transcendentalism in such a way that it would not have become identified with the extreme Individualism which is now perhaps indelibly associated with it in America," no one else really missed Hedge's participation once the initial surprise over his refusal has passed. Fuller, who genuinely tried to include all views while she edited the *Dial*, was hurt by Hedge's refusal to participate. Emerson, who felt that Hedge missed the heart of important questions in an attempt to discuss them with an intellectual flourish, thought Hedge's reasons for and manner of disavowing the *Dial* were ignoble. And Theodore Parker, certainly a driving force of the period, had earlier marked Hedge as a man who was tied too firmly to the past.[19] When these opinions were compared with recollections of the younger Hedge, the disciple of German culture and philosophy who had proposed his own journal five years before the *Dial*, many thought that he had betrayed his earlier convictions and promise. A number of the *Dial's* other contributors had left the ministry when their own deep convictions were in opposition to the prevailing ones; they thought that Hedge had accommodated himself to the church and saw his development as regressive. Because of this feeling, none of the Transcendentalists associated with the *Dial* really regretted the loss of Hedge once his true reasons for not wanting to participate became known.

20

Elizabeth Hoar

Elizabeth Hoar's contributions to the *Dial* extended beyond her one article, a translation of "Discoveries in the Nubian Pyramids," which appeared in the January 1843 issue. As a resident of Concord, Massachusetts, and as an "adopted" sister of the Emersons, she served in many editorial capacities for the *Dial*, especially by furnishing printer's copy from the cramped manuscripts often submitted, and she gave Ralph Waldo Emerson much comfort and advice.[1] Yet, despite the success of her brothers Ebeneezer Rockwood and George Frisbie Hoar, little is known of her beyond what her friends have recorded.

Elizabeth was born in 1814 and lived most of her life in Concord. Her association with the Transcendental movement began when she became engaged to Charles Emerson. After he died in 1836, she stayed close to the Emerson family, both physically and spiritually. Her devotion to Emerson's dead brother — twenty years later she was still wearing black for Charles — kept her close to him, and the two always maintained a sympathetic relationship. Her reverence for the dead and respect for the living gave Emerson spiritual comfort, and her part in their many conversations provided him with material for his published writings. He in turn provided a visible link to that part of the past that was so dear to her.[2]

When Charles Emerson died, one of his legacies to Elizabeth was his friends, and she actively pursued their company. Along with Fuller and Sarah Ripley, Hoar was the only other woman invited to the Transcendental Club meeting on 1 September 1837, and she was in constant attendance at Fuller's Conversations. A certain physical frailness combined with her pious and sublime sayings to surround her with a very spiritual, almost holy, air. Charles Newcomb, always in search of religious answers, was pleased with her, and even George William Curtis, who at this time worshipped music more than the Bible, called her "the calm star that matches the hills in sturdy strength." Nathaniel Hawthorne felt that she was "more at home among spirits than among fleshy bodies," and once, after she had not been to see the Hawthornes in some time, he thought that she might have "vanished into some other region of the infinite space." Charles Lane was so taken by her spirituality that he personally carried her a copy of *An Introduction to a Devout Life*.[3] Caroline Sturgis said that Hoar infused her with "such a respect for usefulness" that, immediately after a talk with her, she had helped a boy lift some heavy bags of corn from his cart.[4] Sturgis was one of Hoar's best friends; they attended Fuller's and Bronson Alcott's Conversations together, and Hoar and Lidian Emerson were, along with Emerson himself and Fuller, the only ones who knew for certain Sturgis's authorship of her poems in the *Dial*.[5]

Hoar made even closer friends than Sturgis among her neighbors in Concord.

Elizabeth Hoar.

From Emerson's *Journals*.

She thought Ellery Channing was a "wood-elf" and stayed up most of the night reading his first volume of poems when it appeared.[6] She had known Henry Thoreau since the days they had attended the Concord Academy together.[7] The association of both Hoar and Thoreau with the *Dial* brought them closer together, and she was saddened when Thoreau, carrying her gift to him of an ink-stand, left to live at William Emerson's on Staten Island. Still, Hoar differentiated between the brilliant mind and the cantankerous man, and she once shrewdly commented on Thoreau, "I love H., but do not like him."[8]

Fuller, a very good friend of Hoar, said that she loved no woman more, and she praised her "pleasing and dignified" conversation and her "real refinement *both* of character and intellect." Still, they were both capable of seeing each other's weaknesses. Hoar felt that Fuller considered her friends to be a "necklace of diamonds about her neck," and that her impatience with complacency acted to gain herself enemies. Fuller believed that Hoar was sometimes too secure in her adopted spiritual role, and once, when Emerson mentioned Hoar's "expression of unbroken purity," Fuller replied, "Yes, but she knows."[9]

Hoar's deepest friendship was with Ralph Waldo Emerson. Her brother felt, with good reason, that she was Emerson's most intimate friend during the period of the *Dial*. They had first met in 1821 when she was left in his charge for a day, and she remembered having listened to him as if "an angel spoke." After Charles's death, Waldo accepted her as a sister. When he brought Lidian to Concord to meet his family before their marriage, she liked Hoar above all. Emerson greatly valued the friendship and conversation of this woman he called a "lovely nun" and "Elizabeth the Wise." That she agreed with his philosophic and moral positions endeared her to him all the more. It is not surprising to find, for instance, that these two people who had both lost their first and deepest loves would agree that "the presence or absence of friends is [not] material to our highest states of minds." Ellery Channing, who always complained of Emerson's coldness in personal relations, bitterly admitted that Hoar had "got more from him than anybody else had."[10]

When Emerson was deciding the future of the *Dial* in early 1843, he turned to Hoar for advice. She believed that its contributors would "work just as well, & with some present reward," in other journals or in books. No doubt Emerson was reminded of this in 1844 when so many of the *Dial*'s contributors had made names for themselves elsewhere. Emerson never pressed Hoar for original contributions to the *Dial*, both because he knew her limitations as a writer and because he felt "her holiness is substantive & must be felt, like the heat of a stove."[11]

21

Ellen Sturgis Hooper

Ellen Sturgis Hooper was one of the young women introduced to Ralph Waldo Emerson and the *Dial* by Margaret Fuller. Her sister, Caroline Sturgis, was one of Fuller's best friends, and Ellen also gained easy access to the other Transcendentalists through them.

Ellen Sturgis was born in 1812, the second child of a wealthy Boston merchant who had, by 1825, control over half of the shipping done to China. She showed considerable poetic talent and was given an excellent education. While in her twenties she met Robert William Hooper, a Harvard graduate recently returned from studying medicine in Paris. After receiving his M.D. degree in 1836, Hooper established his practice in Boston, and they were married on 25 September 1837. Two children were born within two years, but Mrs. Hooper continued to write poetry and to expand her circle of acquaintances.[1]

In the early 1830s Hooper had asked Elizabeth Peabody to conduct "Reading Parties" for her and her friends, and she was later a regular attender at Fuller's Conversations at Peabody's bookstore. Fuller described her as being a "most beautiful" person, and some years later she wrote from Europe that she had not found any woman there more naturally gifted than Ellen Hooper. James Clarke greatly admired her, and T. W. Higginson thought her "a woman of genius." James Russell Lowell liked her, even though they sometimes came together under unusual circumstances. Once when he was returning from Salem, Massachusetts, fortified by some "devilish good wine," he met Hooper on the ferryboat. Lowell, who had, under the influence of a "winegiven independence," just started to chew tobacco, managed to survive this interview and confessed to a friend the rather "strange sensation produced by the awkwardness" of the situation. Emerson liked her well enough to make her one of the privileged few who were privy to the identity of some of the *Dial*'s anonymous contributors.[2]

Hooper contributed eleven poems to the *Dial*, most of them through Emerson.[3] Emerson seemed to like her verses, referring to them as "sincere & great & still harmonious" poems, which would "enrich & ensoul" the *Dial*. "Ellen's sweet though pale buds of early life" also appealed to Fuller.[4] Henry Thoreau, from Staten Island, told Emerson that Hooper's "Sweep Ho!" was well done, and he later reprinted her "The Wood-Fire" in *Walden*. Christopher Pearse Cranch thought that "The Poet" was good, and Rufus Griswold incorrectly attributed it to Clarke in the first edition of his *Poets and Poetry of America*.[5] Two of Hooper's other poems suffered similar misattributions. Her "I slept and dreamed that life was Beauty," which Clarke had thought "very pretty," was translated into Italian and attributed to Immanuel Kant; and Sam

Ward was often thought to be the author of her "The Poor Rich Man."[6]

Since she was not a writer in any professional sense, Mrs. Hooper did not contribute more to the *Dial*. She was a devoted wife who wrote only for her own enjoyment and that of her close friends. Once when Emerson asked her for contributions to an upcoming issue of the *Dial*, she refused to write anything special for that number, telling Emerson instead to look through an old portfolio of her pieces to see if anything there seemed to him worth printing. She was associated with the Transcendentalists only peripherally and because her friends were, not because she agreed with their views.[7] She felt that her intimate friends were her most important readers and had no interest in reaching a wider public through the pages of the *Dial*.

22
Benjamin Peter Hunt

Benjamin Peter Hunt, who was one of the *Dial*'s foreign correspondents, contributed two articles on the West Indies to its last volume. Hunt was born at Chelmsford, Massachusetts, on 18 May 1808. He received part of his education in Ralph Waldo Emerson's school there in 1825 and entered Harvard three years later. However, Hunt soon left for Philadelphia, teaching science and the classics for a living, and in March 1840 he sailed to Kingston, Jamaica, in the pursuit of a business career.[1]

At Chelmsford Hunt was the oldest of Emerson's pupils, only five years younger than his teacher, and the two had become friends. Emerson remembered Hunt as a "philosopher whose conversation made all the social comfort" he had at Chelmsford, and after Emerson closed his school they kept in touch with each other. When Hunt left Harvard for Philadelphia, he made sure that Emerson was informed of his new address. Although the two met infrequently, Emerson always remembered Hunt as the excellent conversationalist of his school-teaching days and, when he prepared to return home from England in 1833, he recorded in his journal the names of the literary figures he had met — Walter Savage Landor, Samuel Taylor Coleridge, Thomas Carlyle, William Wordsworth — and then added: "Peter Hunt is as wise a talker as either of these men. Don't laugh."[2]

Emerson was always disappointed that Hunt could never express himself in writing as well as he did in conversation. Hunt's increased involvement with his mercantile business in Philadelphia led Emerson to complain that he was losing sight of "the dreams of his youth." Whatever talents Hunt possessed were sharply affected by Emerson, and he reverted to the brilliant pupil of old whenever he was with Emerson. In 1837 he visited Emerson at Concord, Massachusetts, and "seemed suddenly" to "reverence" again those youthful dreams, but his return to Philadelphia prevented any literary accomplishments.[3]

The promise that Emerson had seen in Hunt was finally realized when they met again six years later. Hunt had moved from Jamaica to Haiti in 1842 and in the next year he returned to Philadelphia to pick up stocks for his mercantile business on the island. When Emerson passed through Philadelphia at the end of January, he looked up his old friend and was pleased to find him as "refreshing" as ever. Hunt told Emerson about his plans and recommended some books on Haiti, possibly for review in the *Dial*. No doubt infected by the literary activity Emerson was engaged in, Hunt recorded his impressions of his return voyage and sent them back to Emerson.[4]

Emerson was happy with Hunt's account. He informed Henry Thoreau of the "valuable manuscript" and told him that he might push aside some of Charles Lane's "graver sheets" from the next number of the *Dial* in order to make room for Hunt's "honest story." To Hunt Emerson appreciatively wrote about what seemed to him "the best of all sea voyages," and he expressed his delight in "its directness & veracity," and in "its capital art of compression & of omission." The piece also made Emerson happy, in that it realized for him "the promise of the large wise boy who made my school days at Chelmsford so glad."[5] Nathaniel Hawthorne set a very high value on the account, Emerson told Hunt, as "a solitary example of facts which had not lost their vigour by passing through the mind of a thinker." Emerson also reported that he had many other testimonies to its "rare merit": Sophia Ripley thought the piece so good that for her it threw *Two Years Before the Mast* into the background; Thoreau felt that it was quite possibly the best piece in the July number; and Maragret Fuller called it excellent.[6]

All of these favorable comments and Emerson's own high opinion made him urge Hunt to continue his travel narrative. He even offered to help find a publisher, adding that the *Dial*, being in "happy obscurity," would be a "very harmless rehearsal to a very small private audience" for any future pieces.[7] Hunt was "very much surprised" at Emerson's high opinion of the article and promised to send him an account of "Saturday and Sunday among the Creoles," which was published in the *Dial*'s last number.[8]

As his business career prospered, Hunt found that the time he had available for literary pursuits diminished. Nevertheless, the early influences of Emerson and the success of his pieces in the *Dial* were lasting. Hunt continued to write at intervals over the following years, although he never finished any of the three books on the West Indies he worked on, and they remained in manuscript at his death.

23

Charles Lane

Charles Lane, born on 31 March 1800 in England, was the only foreign-born contributor to the *Dial*. Little is known of his early life except that his marriage was an unhappy one and that his wife divorced him in the late 1830s. At that time he was editing and managing the *London Mercantile Price-Current*. He also had become a disciple of the reformer James Pierrepont Greaves and was involved in various health and associationist movements.

Lane probably would have remained in England wandering from one cause to another had he not begun a correspondence with Bronson Alcott. He had read and appreciated Alcott's educational works, and in October 1839 he wrote Alcott a letter of "love & encou[r]agement." Few people had bothered to praise Alcott in this way, and the latter immediately responded, launching a warm, friendly correspondence. When the *Dial* was published, Lane was one of the select few in England to whom Alcott sent a copy. And naturally, when Alcott sailed for England in May 1842, he counted on meeting Lane. They had a "cordial chat" on 7 June at Lane's newspaper office, and Alcott wrote his wife that Lane's was "the deepest, sharpest, intellect" he had encountered. Alcott, whose ego had been greatly bolstered by the disciples he had found in England and especially at Alcott House, began to think of establishing a "New Eden" in America. To this end he brought Lane, Lane's ten-year-old son William, and the English reformer Henry G. Wright back with him to America. After they landed in October 1842, Alcott happily wrote to his brother Junius that Lane was the best substitute for Junius himself at his fireside.[1]

Lane and Alcott became good friends because they had similar interests and ideas. Both were idealists, intent upon reforming society, and both were vegetarians who had tried most of the health cures of the day. Lane also had some money saved from his newspaper work and seemed to Alcott just the person to underwrite his new Eden. Accordingly, an arrangement was agreed upon whereby Lane paid off Alcott's debts and purchased a farm in Harvard, Massachusetts. Alcott named it "Fruitlands" and the following May moved there with his family, Lane, and some friends. The communal experiment was a failure: neither man was practical enough to be a farmer, and both were away too often on reform missions to work the place properly. Lane, whose own unsuccessful marriage had soured him on that institution in general, created friction between Mr. and Mrs. Alcott when he tried to convert Alcott to his position. When both men officially gave up on Fruitlands in January 1844, Lane and his son went to live with the Shaker community at Harvard, where they stayed until May of that year.[2]

Charles Lane.

Collection of Joel Myerson.

During the seven months that Lane had been in Concord, Massachusetts, he became well acquainted with the people there. Even though he spent the following seven months at Fruitlands, his frequent trips to various reform meetings made him other acquaintances. These people had mixed feelings about him. Everyone expected a zealous and, because of his association with Alcott, a somewhat eccentric reformer. Anne Lynch, in Providence, Rhose Island, heard of the "lions of the North" and asked Orestes Brownson whether he thought that they would "revolutionize the country." Theodore Parker said that he would not be rushed into a judgment; he thought that Lane had a "singular elevation of character" but worried about his "greenness." He told Caroline Dall that, while Lane and Alcott had an abundance of "new notions" for Fruitlands, "at present they do nothing but *abstain from eating flesh*." Parker's old teacher, Convers Francis, was less restrained and, after meeting Lane, had thought him "a straightforward sort of man, of high philosophy, but no flummery, apparently, & with considerable literature." Sophia Hawthorne found Lane "very genial" and "full of sense."[3]

Margaret Fuller also liked Lane, noting with favor his asceticism, his "depth of experience," and his "gentle and reverent spirit."[4] While thinking Lane an excellent public speaker, James Russell Lowell said of him and of Henry Wright: "the earth has bubbles, as the water has; and these [two] are of them." Lydia Child did not like Lane's "countenance," saying it looked as if "the washwomen had . . . rubbed it on a wash-board," and she declared that his "expression" would "make me slow to put myself in his powers." Even Mrs. Child's husband, a reformer himself, told his wife after he had listened to Lane talk for a while, "I'll be cursed if I knew whether I *had* any mind at all." And of Lane and Alcott, Mrs. Child could only say that there was "no prank so mad" that it would surprise her "in these insane, well-meaning egotists."[5]

Another person on whom Lane made a strong first impression was Ralph Waldo Emerson. He had liked Lane's letters to Alcott and, upon seeing him, discovered "a man of fine powers and of an elevated character of good manners and of a religious life." After a few months with Lane as a neighbor, however, Emerson began to have reservations. Although he thought Lane a "very superior person" and a "masterful debater with a tyrannous logic," Emerson found him "very provoking & warlike in his manner." He also realized that Lane, rather than complementing the visionary Alcott by being in firm touch with reality, only gave Alcott added and, in Emerson's view, unneeded support: "He is not precisely that man whom Alcott wants, for he is not a pair of hands, & does not see how the all-shining city of God is to pass out of heart & brain into brick & mortar." Emerson, who never appreciated monomaniacal reformers, soon felt that Lane was little better than those he attacked, only that he possessed "sharper beak & talons." He recognized that Lane's "nature & influence" did not invite his own response; rather, they froze him up. In the final analysis, although Emerson found it "hard," "tedious," and almost "insupportable" to talk with Lane, he nevertheless found his company valuable for, as Emerson put it, he "accuses & arouses me." Emerson also found Lane bearable because he became a mainstay of the last two volumes of the *Dial* and contributed about one-eighth of their total number of pages.[6]

When Alcott sent him a copy of the first number of the *Dial*, Lane considered it superior to the *Monthly Magazine*, being "more pure, more one in its character" than Heraud's journal. He responded to meeting Alcott by writing an article on "Transatlantic Transcendentalism" for the English *Union*, in which he quoted from Emerson's *Essays*, from Alcott, and from Elizabeth Peabody's *Record of a School* to show the "sincere fraternal affection" of the New England Transcendentalists. Alcott in turn reacted to their meeting by telling Emerson of Lane, and Emerson mentioned Lane in his piece on "English Reformers" in the *Dial*. Alcott also sent along five manuscript articles for the *Dial*, from which Emerson selected two by Lane—on Greaves and on Oliver Cromwell—and the material for the "English Reformers" sketch.[7] Emerson received the article on Cromwell in early September and immediately sent it to the printer, not knowing that Lane was the author.[8] Lane was engaged in editing the late Greaves's manuscripts, and, when Alcott informed Emerson of this in July, it was probably suggested to Lane that he produce something for the *Dial* from them. Lane hurried and the article arrived, as Emerson said in his introduction to it in the *Dial*, just as the magazine was preparing for the press.[9]

In November 1842 Lane reviewed the *Dial* for the *Union*. He called it "a beautiful and costly publication, both internally and externally," which put forth "some of the purest and advanced sentiments which the age has witnessed." The *Dial*, Lane declared, "steadily announces the presence of the sun, the coming day." In early December he gave Emerson another section on Greaves for the January 1843 *Dial* and a book review, and Emerson happily declared that Lane was "the best new contributor we have." Emerson also told Peabody to make sure that Lane received the free copy of the *Dial* due to him as a contributor.[10]

Emerson found himself out of town when the April 1843 *Dial* was being prepared for the press and he left Henry Thoreau to edit it. Emerson instructed Thoreau to approach Lane for a contribution, which, if Thoreau considered it good enough, could be printed without its first being sent to Emerson. On 15 February Thoreau called on Lane to ask for aid, and Lane responded with a catalogue of the library at Fruitlands and a review article on Alcott and his works. Lane became genuinely enthusiastic about the number and promised to help Thoreau sell it at the bookstores.[11] He even asked for extra copies, or offprints, of both of his pieces for private distribution.[12] When Alcott received John Heraud's new book on Savonarola in late February, Lane quickly wrote a review of it for the April 1843 *Dial*.[13] Lane became so involved with this number that when Emerson told him that he doubted whether to keep the *Dial* alive, Lane replied that he was "zealous for its continuance" and asked Emerson to let it live a little longer to see if it would gain support.[14]

The article on "A. Bronson Alcott's Works" was Lane's attempt to vindicate the man and his philosophy. Thoreau thought it good enough to print without first letting Emerson read it, although he did suggest to Emerson that the *Dial* omit any personal references to its editor.[15] Emerson took Thoreau's advice and authorized him to print the piece, after first deleting the references to himself and making certain "verbal corrections" that Thoreau had proposed earlier. Thoreau found the published article to be better than any notice Alcott had yet received. The *Liberator* favorably reviewed the pamphlet publication of the article and explained that Alcott had been "widely misapprehended" because his "mode of reasoning" was "somewhat peculiar to himself." However, the skeptical remained skeptical. Nathaniel Hawthorne thought the piece unsatisfactory and felt that it had not said much. Ellery Channing did not even bother to read it. As he told Emerson: "Me also, with tired breast, does all thoughts ejected from the Alcottian syringe, drive into dejection. Such work for nothing, such fine-drawn gauze safety-lamps, by which all the carburetted hydrogen of society is forever rendered harmless, such supposed interest in what concerns only some retired gentleman who is making cucumbers of moonshine."[16]

Lane's "Catalogue of Books" from the Fruitlands library was composed mainly of the books Alcott had brought back from England, which Emerson had considered "a cabalistic collection" of "rare & valuable mystical" titles when he saw them. In early December Lane and Alcott began to prepare the catalogue for the *Dial*, and the following February Thoreau picked up the manuscript, which had been completed by Lane alone. Thoreau described it to Emerson as "a bulky catalogue" of some 800 books that would probably run ten or a dozen printed pages. However, after he had looked more closely, Thoreau realized that the catalogue now included *every* book Alcott owned, even the Bible. Thoreau wanted something more specialized, something that would "tell Mr. [Henry] Hedge and Parker" and other learned people what titles were needed for a truly superior library, and he used his editorial scissors to reduce the piece to four printed pages. When Hedge read the catalogue in Bangor, he wished that the books mentioned in it could be reprinted for mass circulation.[17]

Lane was settling down as a regular contributor to the *Dial* even while he was publishing in other reform journals materials too controversial — by Emerson's standards — to print in the *Dial* itself. In May 1843 he gave the *Dial* a long article on "Social Tendencies"; but when Hunt's article on Jamaica arrived, Emerson was forced to divide Lane's in half for the July and October numbers. Fuller thought it was a "pity" to do so because the division destroyed some of the article's unity. Thoreau, who was put off by the "straight and solid" but dull style, placed the article aside unread "to a future day — which," he confessed to Emerson, "may never come."[18] Lane's other piece in the July 1843 *Dial* was a letter to the editor on his and Alcott's prospects at Fruitlands.[19] Although it was signed by both men, Lane probably wrote most of it. They had asked Emerson to print the letter as if it had been written by the editor of the *Dial*, and they used the editorial "we" throughout. Emerson, as editor, was not about to have such a piece attributed to him, and he clearly labeled it as the joint product of Lane and Alcott. He also rearranged and shortened it and omitted some of the more flowery prose.[20]

Along with the second half of "Social Tendencies," the October 1843 *Dial* had Lane's favorable account of "A Day with the Shakers." Lane, whose own antipathy toward marriage found kinship with Shaker marital customs, impressed Emerson as being "very much engaged with the Shakers," and a month after his visit to them in August he sent the piece to the *Dial*. The previous year Emerson had visited the same community with Hawthorne, where both had found them "less stupid, more honest" than they had expected, and he now gladly printed Lane's impressions.[21]

In January 1844 Lane contributed a book review and reported on his visit to Brook Farm to the *Dial*. Lane himself thought these pieces "dull," and the next month he sent a review of "The Millennial Church" and a reflective piece, "Life in the Woods," to make up for them. Emerson printed both pieces, thus making unnecessary Lane's wish for him to send them to Henry Channing for his *Present* if there was not enough room in the *Dial*.[22]

Lane would have written more for the *Dial* had it survived. He continued publishing in reform papers until his return to England in 1846. Emerson especially liked Lane as a contributor because of the variety of work—reflective pieces, descriptive pieces, and foreign information—he offered. All appealed to the catholic tastes Emerson hoped for in the *Dial*'s readers. That Lane respected, or at least was aware of Emerson's wish to avoid hotly contested local issues also endeared him to the *Dial*'s editor.

24

James Russell Lowell

James Russell Lowell was born on 22 February 1819, the youngest child of the distinguished Cambridge (Massachusetts) Lowells. Young James became the petted favorite of the family and grew up among friends who were to serve him well throughout his life. He went to school with T. W. Higginson, played with Richard Henry Dana, and took lessons from Miss Sophia Dana, who was later to become George Ripley's wife.[1]

As befitted a person of his station and promise, Lowell entered Harvard in 1834. Academically, his first year was his best, but his standing dropped as he turned his attention to new fields. Elected to the Hasty Pudding Club in 1836, Lowell shared the secretary's position with John Weiss, and the next year he became both secretary and poet. He also joined Alpha Delta Phi, a forbidden society.

In 1837 Lowell became an editor of *Harvardiana*, the undergraduate literary magazine that had some 250 subscribers, most of them Lowell's fellow students. His contributions were undistinguished, and many years later, when asked for his permission to reprint some of them, Lowell replied that they were "wretched

James Russell Lowell.

Collection of Joel Myerson.

stuff" written when he was "as great an ass as ever brayed and thought it singing," and he hoped that the editor would be "too charitable to exhume" them. His classmates thought better of Lowell's abilities then, and they elected him to deliver the class poem.[2]

This steady progression of successes was broken when, on 25 June 1838, Lowell was rusticated to Concord, Massachusetts, for what the Harvard officials termed "continued neglect of his college duties." There he was to study John Locke's *Essay on the Human Understanding* and James Mackintosh's *Review of Ethical Philosophy* under the Reverend Barzillai Frost. To someone who was "boyish, frolicsome, very immature in expression, and disposed, in a fitful fashion, to assert an independence of authority," the rustication stung bitterly. Before his first week in Concord was out, Lowell had written to a friend that he damned the town, and later he complained that he doubted whether they would find "ten decent people" there "to save the place."[3] Lowell thought Frost dense and continually mocked him to his face and in his letters.[4] The only person he liked was Ralph Waldo Emerson, and even then Lowell took more pleasure in humorously depicting him to his friends than from the meetings themselves. Of Henry Thoreau he reported: "[I]t is exquisitely amusing to see how he imitates Emerson's tone & manner. With my eyes shut I shouldn't kn[ow] them apart."[5]

Lowell liked Emerson the man and orator more than he liked Emerson the Transcendentalist and philosopher.[6] He had heard Emerson lecture in Boston and had been impressed with the Phi Beta Kappa address, which he had attended in his junior year. Soon after arriving in Concord he had sought Emerson out, and though he found him "a very pleasant man in private conversation," he reported to Nathan Hale, Jr., that after "all I'd heard of him, as an Eagle soaring in pride of place, I was surprised to see a poor little hawk stooping at flies or at best sparrows & groundlings." Soon afterward, Lowell attacked Emerson's Divinity School Address, which he had not seen or heard, and told Hale that as people say "that man sees himself in everything around him, if E. could see *him*self & it didn't drive him crazy (if indeed in that respect he isn't past mending) why—amen." He added: "I've talked more about the man than he deserves—but I never can help it." Emerson, unaware of the *enfant terrible* pose that Lowell had adopted when writing to his friends, continued his congenial relations with the young student. After he brought a book to Lowell that had inadvertently been sent to his own house, Lowell confessed that Emerson was a "good natured man" but added, "in spite of his doctrines."[7]

Lowell worked diligently on the class poem during his two months in Concord. When it finally appeared, it held Emerson up in a distorted light that showed Lowell's lack of understanding of Emerson and his doctrines. The knifelike humor of Lowell's *A Fable for Critics* was whetted here, but the truth of its aim was lacking. Lowell himself saw the whole poem as being in good taste and fun, and, when some classmates expressed surprise that he would apparently thus turn on his Concord host, Lowell wrote Emerson that he would have written the same of his own brother. He enclosed a copy of the poem for Emerson to read, hoping that it would show that Lowell would not "willfully malign" a man who had invited him to share his table and whose "little child I had danced on my knee." The ever-gracious Emerson thanked Lowell for his letter and the poem, which he said that he enjoyed, having found nothing on himself that "the license of the occasion" did not more than excuse. With this point dismissed, he invited Lowell back for a walk and sent him a copy of his Dartmouth oration. The incident was quickly forgotten, though in later years Lowell remembered it with embarrassment.[8]

Lowell left Concord with an interest in Walter Savage Landor and a desire to write poetry, neither of which was self-supporting. Therefore, he began to study law and to sharpen his poetic talents during whatever free time was available. One product of this effort was his lecture on "Modern Poetry" before the Concord Lyceum in March 1839. In December 1838 Lowell had met "a very pleasant & pleasing young lady" named Maria White. As the new year dawned, Lowell found himself in love and, inspired by Maria, he turned in earnest to both law and poetry.[9]

Although he received his law degree in August 1840, Lowell waited two years before being admitted to the bar, a period during which he turned his full attention toward a literary career. The *Southern Literary Messenger* had been publishing his poems, and in March 1840 he sent off his "Callirhoe" to Burton's *Gentleman's Magazine* in competition for a $100 prize. Hearing nothing from Burton by June, Lowell planned to send a revised version of the poem to Margaret Fuller for the *Dial* but apparently nothing came of this idea.[10]

In November 1840 Lowell became formally engaged to Maria White, Her influence had been so great that Lowell was then in the process of preparing a volume of his poems for publication, and from these he chose a "sheet of sonnets," which he mailed to Emerson in December for possible use in the *Dial*. Emerson read them "slightly" and forwarded them without Lowell's name to Fuller, saying that he was unimpressed and adding that the author considered the last sonnet, "To a Voice Heard in Mount Auburn," to be "a good one." Fuller soon replied that, while the sonnets seemed imitative of Alfred Tennyson, she would print the last one because she did not wish to "discourage these volunteers who are much wanted to vary the manoeuvres of the regular platoon" of contributors. Emerson then thanked Lowell for his "gay verses" and announced that the *Dial* would print the last one unless Lowell forbade its separation from the others, which would have to "take their chance for future insertion with other sylphs & gnomes now imprisoned or hereafter to be imprisoned" in the "vast editorial Drawer." Lowell pronounced this plan acceptable, and the sonnet appeared, over the initials "M.L.O.," in the January 1841 *Dial*.[11]

Lowell's *A Year's Life* was published in January, and, although the book was generally well received, Lowell was somewhat upset at the friendly but vacuous puffs by friends such as Hale, Charles Stearns Wheeler, and William Story.[12] Lowell soon heard that "the Dial Clique" seemed "sufficiently well pleased" and would probably review his book favorably in the next number.[13] The review, when it appeared in July 1841, was hardly what he would have wished for. Fuller started her review by noting that the book spoke of "noble feelings" and "a genuine love of beauty," but soon she reaffirmed in print her earlier opinion that neither "the imagery nor the music" was original. The proper critic of this book, she said, would be "some youthful friend to whom it has been of real value as a stimulus." Lowell, whose youthful friends had indeed unabashedly and uncritically praised the book, had his ruffled feathers smoothed somewhat by the rest of the review, which told how most youthful poems were below the caliber of later efforts. At any rate Lowell apparently made no mention of the review when he saw Emerson at the beach at Nantasket, Massachusetts, a few weeks later.[14]

That November Lowell was prompted by Emerson's present of his "The Method of Nature" address to write him. Buoyed by his happy engagement and mild literary successes, Lowell was no longer the brash youth of three years before. He told Emerson of his respect and love for him, praised the address and "Woodnotes" in the *Dial*, and added: "I do not write this expecting any reply—but only because it makes me privately happy to say it." He also enclosed a sonnet, "When in a book . . . ," written in April,[15] which Maria thought that Emerson would like. Emerson thanked Lowell for his kind words and "in a sort of selfish way" begged the sonnet for the next *Dial*. Lowell gave his permission, saying that Maria would be especially happy "for everything I write is more than half her's [sic]," and he also enclosed two more sonnets, "the first ["Only as thou herein . . . "] because Maria loves it, and the next ["To Irene on Her Birthday"] because I do." Lowell asked if the *Dial* would print them, since his friend Hale might want the poems for his own *Boston Miscellany*. Quickly Emerson responded in the affirmative and promised to have the printer send Lowell a copy of the number in which they would appear. These poems, Lowell's last in the *Dial*, were published in the January 1842 issue over his own initials.[16]

By October 1842 Lowell had joined Robert Carter in proposing a new literary magazine to be called the *Pioneer*. Invitations were sent to his friends and other writers to join "a *free* magazine" that was "to take as high an aim in Art as may be." His promise to give contributors "carte blanche as to what they say," in order to offer "a rational substitute for the enormous quantity of thrice-diluted trash, in the shape of namby-pamby love tales and sketches" of the other monthlies, appealed to many. John Neal, Edgar Allan Poe, Jones Very, Story, Wheeler, Elizabeth Peabody, Nathaniel Hawthorne, John Sullivan Dwight, Elizabeth Barrett, and Carter joined Lowell in carrying the magazine through three monthly issues before its collapse, as Lowell said, from lack of its publisher's support, in March. Lowell's confinement in New York for an eye operation helped lessen the *Pioneer*'s chances for success, too. It also resulted in an awkward situation with Emerson over Wheeler's "Letters from Germany" in the *Pioneer*. Wheeler had earlier sent copies of his "intelligence" to both Emerson and Lowell and had explained the situation to them both. Lowell then met with Emerson and told him that Wheeler's articles were properly the *Dial*'s by right of Emerson's having asked first. But while Lowell was recuperating in New York, Carter set Wheeler's letter in type and published it. To make things worse, Carter prefaced the letter by mentioning that parts of it had appeared earlier in a "contemporary quarterly magazine of limited circulation." Emerson, who considered Lowell to be quite blameless in this matter, apparently said nothing.[17]

With the *Pioneer*'s collapse, Lowell was saddled with nearly $750 in debts to pay and lengthy litigations to endure. His approaching marriage made his earn-ing cash all the more important, and he turned his attention to those periodicals and papers that paid the highest sums to contributors. At the same time his interest shifted to the antislavery movement. The *Dial*, and the poetry that had characterized *A Year's Life*, most of which was not reprinted by Lowell in later editions of his works, faded into the background. Over forty years later, when he saw an article on the *Dial*, Lowell was moved to write its author: "Till you reminded me of it I had forgotten that I had written for the *Dial* at all."[18]

25

John Milton Mackie

John Milton Mackie, who contributed an article on Percy Bysshe Shelley to the April 1841 *Dial*, was born in 19 December 1813 at Wareham, Massachusetts. After his graduation from Brown University in 1832 he attended Andover Theological Seminary. In 1833 he went to study at the University of Berlin, and the next year he returned to Brown as a tutor. He also studied law but apparently never opened a practice.

Mackie made New York his permanent home and became a regular contributor to the *North American Review* and the *American Whig Review*, writing articles on history and German literature. He admired Theodore Parker and Ralph Waldo Emerson but never became identified with the Transcendental movement.

Mackie probably sent his essay for the *Dial* to Emerson, though Emerson classed it in the "Morgue" of that number, which he confessed too dull to read, and by 1846 he had even forgotten the author of the piece.[1] Mackie's distance from Boston and his lack of interest in the Transcendentalists made further contributions from him unlikely.

26

Charles King Newcomb

Charles King Newcomb's "The Two Dolons," like Bronson Alcott's "Orphic Sayings," was often used to ridicule the "Transcendental" aspects of the *Dial*. Not only his contribution to the *Dial* but his whole way of life made Newcomb a convenient figure for those wishing to make fun of New England Transcendentalism.

Newcomb was born in 1820. His early childhood was uneventful, but when he was five his father died, leaving his mother with six children to raise. Young Charles and a brother were sent to school in Connecticut until he was ready to enter Andover Academy in 1832. Newcomb's mother, a Providence (Rhode Island) bluestocking who was a member of Sarah Helen Whitman's coterie, wanted her son to continue on to Brown University, and in 1833 Newcomb entered that school.

Newcomb began to drift away from the well-planned life set out for him soon after his graduation from Brown in 1837. Despite his plans to attend an Episcopal seminary, he showed strong leanings toward Catholicism. When his mother asked her friend Margaret Fuller to talk to Newcomb about his feelings for "the Superstition of Romanism," he "ridiculed the idea" to his family. But by January of the next year Newcomb had decided that, even if he were not a true Catholic at heart, he surely was not an Episcopalian, and at the end of the term he left the seminary.[1]

During the next three years Newcomb divided his time between Providence and Boston. In Boston he visited Fuller much and soon saw her in a light that was, in her opinion, too romantic. Although she accepted his confidences, Newcomb must have allowed his true feelings to show too often, and soon by mutual agreement their correspondence ceased. Newcomb's family added to his discomfort by encouraging him in the affair. As late as July 1840, when Newcomb passed some time with Fuller at Jamaica Plain near Boston, one of his sisters archly told him: "& then you *know* the great charm of what comes from that Plain!!"[2]

Newcomb soon began to look for a more settled place in life. When he stayed in Providence, his mother continually pushed him toward literary efforts he was in no haste to attempt. At Jamaica Plain Fuller could not help him, for even she doubted his ability to make a place for himself in the world; she thanked heaven that she was made of "firmer fibre and more resolute mind."[3] When George Ripley announced his plans for a community at West Roxbury, Massachusetts, Newcomb gladly accepted the chance to be in a new location, and on 20 May 1841 he arrived at Brook Farm. His four years there were to be the happiest in

Charles King Newcomb.

From Emerson's *Journals*.

Newcomb's life: his odd behavior was accepted, his circle of friends widened and improved, and he produced his only published work—the article in the *Dial*.

The Brook Farmers remembered Newcomb as a shy introvert, "in every way. . . eccentric," and "never taken very seriously by anybody." At twenty-one he was "slight in body, uncertain in carriage, with eyes of a peculiar expression . . . and long, dark, rather unkempt hair." He "carried an air of mystery about him" and "held up contemplation as a cult." Newcomb continued to be a "sentimental devotee of unattached Catholicism," drawn more by the Church's mystical elements than by its dogma or theology. The walls of his room were covered with crosses and pictures of saints, and visitors there were often less disturbed by the Catholic artifacts than they were at seeing between pictures of Jesus and Loyola one of the dancer Fanny Ellsler.[4]

While at Brook Farm, Newcomb met many visitors and boarders who were involved with the *Dial*. He told Fuller of the pleasant visits from Elizabeth Hoar, and he happily accepted gifts of pictures from Caroline Sturgis. In Sturgis, Newcomb formed a passing romantic interest; they took walks in the woods and often read Greek together in the haymow. When news of this reached Providence, Mrs. Newcomb wrote to ask her son if the couple had had "a romantic time in the woods" and pointedly inquired: "*is she engaged?*" His sisters were just as blunt, especially Charlotte: "So your *beloved Caroline* is coming to see you . . . Don't be *too* excited Charley." Because Sturgis recognized that Newcomb's genius was "mystical, not creative," and because she felt that his ideas usually surpassed his ability to actualize them, there was no danger of any serious involvement. When Sturgis soon began to spend an increasing amount of time at Newburyport, Massachusetts, their meetings became less frequent, and nothing ever came of the matter.[5]

George William Curtis remembered Newcomb as a "solitary self-involved youth, preferring to associate with children," who had a "feminine temperament." Nathaniel Hawthorne, whom Newcomb often visited at Concord, Massachusetts, saw him as "involved in a deep mist of metaphysical fantasies." Henry Thoreau considered him a good walking companion, though he lacked a "a firm enough hold on this world." But the most lasting and important friendship that Newcomb made during his Brook Farm days was with Ralph Waldo Emerson.[6]

Fuller had mentioned Newcomb and his problems to Emerson in her letters, and, when the first number of the *Dial* came out, Emerson told her that he hoped that it would "cure our young Catholic Fra Carlo." When Newcomb bought a copybook in 1840, among his first entries were passages from Emerson's writings, which he copied from Fuller's journal. The two finally met at Providence in February 1842, and Emerson was impressed by the "young genius" as he listened to Newcomb read from his manuscripts, including a piece he called "Dolon." Thus began four months of intense work for both men in preparing "Dolon" for the *Dial*.[7]

Newcomb began his copybook and his journals in emulation of the literary figures of the time, and, guided by a vague literary inclination and a strong desire to fulfill his mother's hopes for him, he quickly began to fill them. During the summer of 1840, while recuperating at Newport, Rhode Island, from an illness, he became friendly with Charles Timothy Brooks. There he read in manuscript Brooks's translation of Jean-Paul Richter's *Titan* and copied out passages of "glorious descriptions" into his journal. These lines served as an inspiration for Newcomb's own work, and by the following September the first draft of the section of "Dolon" that eventually appeared in the *Dial* was finished. "Dolon" may have been one of the pieces Newcomb sent Fuller in October for her comments. Fuller hedged—"Let me be your audience, but not your judge"—and declined to give a critical opinion because it would "chill" him. Still, she praised his pleasing "poetical reveries" and told him to continue writing, but with "a view to finish [sic] pieces." Judging from Emerson's pleased reaction to Newcomb's work in February, he must have taken her advice.[8]

In March Newcomb visited Fuller in Boston, and she reported to Emerson that, given "courage" by Emerson's "sympathy," he had promised "Dolon" for the *Dial*. Emerson thought this "excellent," and he invited Newcomb to bring all of "Dolon" to Concord, where he especially wanted Hoar to hear it. Newcomb was apparently unprepared for such a quick and positive response, and not even another letter from Emerson could succeed in making the writer or the manuscript appear. Finally, on 7 May 1842 Emerson wrote again, asking that "no dreams, hallucinations 'delays of genius,' & the like" hold up Newcomb further. If he was still writing, Emerson offered to take the parts already finished off his hands and to have someone begin transcribing them. Newcomb responded that he was still working and preferred to copy it all himself. But he promised to deliver the finished manuscript by the end of the month, although he warned: "Do not run any risk on account of it." Emerson, thinking that Newcomb was worried at the prospect of being published, replied that, while perhaps he would never print "Dolon" he did wish to read what he called "every rich word of the Imagination spoken in solitude & long unintelligible except to hermits."[9]

Newcomb finally sent the first part of "Dolon" to Emerson on 5 June 1842 but said that its unfinished state made publication in July impossible, and he suggested leaving it for the October number. Since Newcomb had found no time to "punctuate or orthographise" it, and because he spelled words as they sounded ("I am apt to forget my spelling while I am writing"), he told Emerson to "*do as you please about it.*" After reading the manuscript, Emerson enthusiastically wrote Newcomb that he "must print it," though more work did need to be done. He invited Newcomb to Concord for a visit and an editorial conference, and, when the latter arrived a week later, the meeting was a success. Newcomb read to Emerson from his journals, and Emerson reread "Dolon" in "the armchair of the upturned root of a pinetree" and "felt for the first time since [his son] Waldo's death some efficient faith again in the . . . Universe." Apprently, they spent too little time on the *Dial*'s affairs; for when Newcomb left, Emerson, who had been so "foolish [sic] good natured" as to promise to make no corrections without Newcomb's consent, had to write another letter. Emerson's comments upon new words that Newcomb had coined and upon his chronically bad grammar ended with his chiding the author: "Does Apollo cherish his warts? Must the Muse babble?" Since Hoar was making a fair copy for the printer, Emerson required an immediate answer. Newcomb replied at once that Emerson could make the changes he suggested. Emerson made the corrections on the proof, and "Dolon" was finally published.[10]

When "The First Dolon" (described as from "The Two Dolons," which in turn was from the manuscript "symphony of Dolon") came out in the July 1842 *Dial*, some felt that it excited more mirth than sentiment from readers.[11] Fuller told Newcomb that its "redundant and involved style displeases, and hides, not drapes the thought." He must "prune as well as water" his vine, she warned. Henry Channing, while pleased with the story's "truth and beauty," complained that its song had "no key-note for earthly instruments." The piece was in Robert Bartlett's mind when he contemptuously referred to Alcott and his English friends as "restive Dolons." Emerson thought "Dolon" had "more native gold" than anything else since the Swedenborgian Sampson Reed's *Observations on the Growth of the Mind*, and he told Fuller, "There are sentences in Dolon worth the printing the Dial [sic] that they may go forth." While he admitted to Parker that it was the "maddest piece in the number," whose "license of composition" was "odious" to him, Emerson still thought that on some accounts it was the "best & most valued" article. He also made sure that Newcomb received a free copy of the July 1842 number.[12]

One reason for Emerson's enthusiasm was the resemblance of the title character of "Dolon" to Emerson's own son Waldo, who had died in January. Newcomb had earlier borrowed family letters touching on Waldo, and it is likely that his "beautiful boy, with long auburn-brown hair," was modeled on him. Newcomb's desire to see more letters dealing with what he called "the assumption of the hero-boy," in order to add an "angel-human's voice to the choir of the Second Dolon," made Emerson equally eager to see the sequel.[13]

Newcomb was at work on the second part of "Dolon" when the first went to press, but by the end of July he had started another piece called "Edith," which Caroline Sturgis thought "far more beautiful than Dolon." But she also noticed that Newcomb was tired and ill during the whole time she had visited him. When Emerson wrote on 16 August to inquire about his progress, Newcomb replied that he had been sick for three weeks and that there was "little chance of the 2d Dolon or any writing (if I publish more) being ready [for] October."[14]

Newcomb's illness continued through the winter, and in January 1843, thinking that new surroundings might help him, Fuller asked Hawthorne if he would take Newcomb on as a boarder and handyman. Hawthorne politely declined, "for a reason at present undeveloped, but which," he trusted, time would "bring to light." Having thus delicately alluded to Sophia's pregnancy, Hawthorne went on to say that he would be happy to help Newcomb find another place to stay and that he looked forward to "long days with him on the river and in the woods." Yet, when he next discussed Newcomb, Hawthorne found him "silent, inexpressive . . . and . . . without response except a sardonic laugh." Some of

Newcomb's friends, Hawthorne agreed with Emerson, thought that he was "passing into permanent eclipse."[15]

Hawthorne and Emerson were right. In May Newcomb told Emerson that he had thought about copying the second "Dolon" for the *Dial* but did not have enough energy to do it. Emerson, attempting to check Newcomb's dissipation, pleaded: "Where are all the fine stories I was to have from your imaginative pen which so took my love, & excited so many hopes? Where all the criticism [sic] on your various reading, which I was to share?" In June Emerson saw him in "solitude & obscurity" at Brook Farm, and his letter in September asking for a contribution to the *Dial* failed to get a positive response. Newcomb tried the following year to write some "new stories" but failed, and the first part of "The Two Dolons" in the *Dial* remains his sole published work.[16]

27

Theodore Parker

Theodore Parker's participation in the *Dial* was important both to the journal and to its contributor. The magazine provided Parker a platform for his own often controversial views, and he in turn gave the *Dial* his name and articles of much contemporary interest, both of which greatly boosted the magazine's sales.

Parker was born at Lexington, Massachusetts, on 24 August 1810, the last child in a family of eleven. The harsh life of a farmer's son matured Parker early; by the time he reached his teens, two sisters and his mother had died, and most of the other children had married, leaving Parker and his father to run the farm. Not surprisingly then, Parker's formal schooling was slight and short-lived. His early promise—at ten he could repeat a thousand-line poem from memory after only one reading—led him to enter the local academy when he was sixteen, but, despite his success there, he was financially strapped and had to leave after only one quarter. However, he did not surrender his hopes for an education.

Parker had the intelligence but not the money to pursue his studies, and he therefore began his own program of reading. Recognition of his success came during the next four years, as every winter he taught in local schools. Even then, however, most of his salary went toward hiring a substitute for himself to help his father with the farm work. The rest of the money, less a small amount for bare necessities, went for books, the raw material for his education.[1] In 1830 he went to Cambridge, Massachusetts, and passed the entrance examination for Har-

Theodore Parker.

Collection of Joel Myerson.

vard. Lacking the money to enroll officially and without the time to attend classes, Parker kept up his studies at home and returned to Cambridge only to take and pass his final examinations. That March he took a position in a private school in Boston that allowed him to hire a permanent substitute for himself on the farm, and at the end of 1831 he left for a similar position at Watertown, Massachusetts.

The move to Watertown was the turning point in Parker's life. There he met Convers Francis, a young clergyman with a large library and, borrowing freely from both Francis's books and his knowledge, Parker soon reached full intellectual maturity. Francis recognized the quality of his student and helped Parker to enter Harvard Divinity School in April 1834. Parker quickly became a friend of Christopher Pearse Cranch, John Sullivan Dwight, and Charles Timothy Brooks and made a reputation for himself as an avid reader and student. Classmates remembered one occasion when, while reading one of the great armful of books he was carrying back from the library, the distracted Parker ran "smack into a tree and fell unconscious." James Clarke once asked Parker if he had actually read all the books he had accumulated and was surprised by Parker's reply that he had not only read them all but could give "a table of contents for each book."[2]

To support himself, Parker helped to translate Lafayette's letters for Jared Sparks, but after one term a scholarship considerably eased his financial difficulties, though one vacation found him with money enough only for dry bread and water. He was made instructor in Hebrew in 1835 and coedited the school's *Scriptural Interpreter* during its final year of publication. His forty articles there also made him its leading contributor.

After his graduation in 1836, Parker returned to Watertown, where he continued his reading and resumed his courtship of Lydia Cabot, who had taught Sunday school with him. Miss Cabot was a warm and kind woman whom Parker affectionately called "Bearsie," and she offered him encouragement and understanding at a time of need.[3] They were married on 20 April 1837, and the next month Parker was ordained. Caleb Stetson, George Ripley, and Dwight participated, with Francis proudly giving the sermon. The Parkers then left for his first parish assignment at West Roxbury, Massachusetts.

Just as Parker's ambition had refused to let him remain an unlettered farmboy, it now refused to allow him to be content as a parish minister.[4] Only a few months after taking up his ministerial duties, Parker felt that he was "well-nigh wasting" his talents. At West Roxbury, he believed, he was only "preaching to an audience of seventy to a hundred and twenty souls; going about talking tattle with old women; giving good advice to hypocrites; and scattering here and there, I hope, a corn that will one day germinate and bear fruit."[5] Moved by his desire to carry his word to a larger audience, Parker renewed his friendships with the reform-minded Boston ministers and literati, and, through a constant attendance at Transcendental Club meetings, he soon became a solid figure among the people who were to form the *Dial*.

While the story that Parker "thanked God in his prayers for the sun, moon, and Emerson" is probably apocryphal, he did admire Ralph Waldo Emerson greatly. Emerson in turn respected Parker's vast learning and the way he had obtained it, and when Parker lectured in Concord, Massachusetts, in 1836, the two dined together. Parker, who had read and liked Emerson's *Nature*, though he criticized its excess of idealism, found Emerson "truly a most delightful man." Two years later Parker heard Emerson's Divinity School Address and was roused by his "so true, & terribly sublime" picture of the "faults of the Church."[6] Though younger than Emerson, Parker was not awed by him. He greatly admired him for saying things that he felt needed to be said, but he was never able to accept Emerson's idealism or his faith in the writers of the Transcendental school. Like Margaret Fuller, Parker respected Emerson the writer, but, even more than her, he always approached Emerson the man on equal footing.

Parker's relationship to Fuller was at best distant. Although Fuller and Mrs. Hemans were the only "learned women" whose books occupied Parker's shelves, he thought Fuller "a critic, not a creator," who put herself "upon her genius rather too much."[7] They had first been attracted to each other by an intellectual kinship and similar attitudes toward questioning the times.[8] Parker, actually a warm man at heart, presented the ferocious exterior typical of many zealous reformers.[9] Fuller was not a woman likely to be cowed by anyone, and these two rather large egos soon met head on. Caroline Dall quite perceptively observed that both required "a sort of personal submission before new-comers could be admitted to a cordial understanding." As neither Parker nor Fuller would submit, they soon developed a genuine dislike for each other. It seemed to Mrs. Dall that they even shared a mutual hatred, probably because "in their *faults*, they resemble each other." Fuller realized their basic conflicts, and, when the *Dial* was started, she put Parker down as a "very valuable aid" but emphatically added: "He cannot be the leader of my journal."[10]

When the *Dial* was proposed at the Transcendental Club meeting of 18 September 1839, Parker reacted enthusiastically. He thought it would "certainly go" and proposed Emerson as its head to give the new magazine "a name forthwith," with Fuller and Henry Hedge as coeditors. The new magazine appealed to him, for he felt that it would "open a free press for valuable articles on every subject of general interest," wherein each article would be judged not by party philosophy, or by fear of the public's reaction to it, but by "merit in the article, such in its *view*, or *being*."[11]

The founding of the *Dial* coincided with a period of greatly increased activity in Parker's own life. In May 1840 he had attended the Berry Street Conference of the Unitarian Association, where he had heard discussed: "Ought differences of opinion on the value & authority of miracles to exclude men from fellowship & sympathy with one another?" Parker was shocked that such a proposal would even have been brought up, and he wrote in his journal: "This is the 19 [sic] century! This is Boston!! This among the Unitarians!!!" Parker's own reaction to their stand was a promise to personally let out "all the force of Transcendentalism," come what may, and to let off "truth fast as it comes." Toward that end he worked on articles for the *Dial* about inspiration, about the relation of the Bible to other religions, and about Sunday parables. He also planned articles on Plato, on Aristotle, and on the mythology of the Old and New Testaments.[12]

Despite his good and wide-ranging intentions, Parker only contributed one article—an old sermon on "The Divine Presence in Nature and in the Soul"—to the July 1840 *Dial*, a number that did not much please him.[13] He had expected a journal more concerned with the issues of the day than the literary magazine that appeared. Writing as a "matter of fact-man," Parker addressed a mock letter to "Miss Dial" in his journal. He praised her poetry as better than her prose—except for Emerson's "Introduction," which was "graceful & exquisitely well done"—and added, "Your young men good maiden should be sent to the dancing school for a few quarters, at least, & a little literary culture would improve some of them." Cranch's "Aurora Borealis" had merit but was somewhat imitative. But, Parker went on: "We would not for a moment suggest that it is an imitation for young poets never *imitate*. Not they! *Shame* on the thought. *Servile pieces imitations*. What give up originality! . . . & write like Byron, Milton, Shakespeare or Pindar or Hermes! not we."[14]

Parker began to hit his stride with the October 1840 *Dial*. He contributed a parable—copied with slight changes from a two-year-old journal entry—called "Truth Against the World," a review, and an article, called simply, "A Lesson for the Day." The last was a sermon, heavily indebted to Thomas Carlyle's "Signs of the Times," that Parker had successfully preached a number of times in Boston. Brownson charged that Parker had seemingly incorporated bodily many of his own ideas into the article, but otherwise it was successful. Sarah Helen Whitman thought it the best piece in the number. Bronson Alcott declared that he had never "enjoyed a written or spoken word so much." And both William Emerson and his wife were much pleased by it. In Billerica, Massachusetts, Daniel Parker, who later called the article "admirable, as are all [Parker's] writings," at first believed that the work was Emerson's and when told otherwise still thought highly of it.[15]

To the January 1841 *Dial* Parker contributed a lengthy article on "German Literature." Francis wrote Parker that his learning was "far outdone by the riches of profoundly significant thought," and that exactly such pieces were needed to make the *Dial* equal to or better than any American or English journal, adding that, according to a friend of his, if Parker's article had appeared in the first number, "it would have at the outset placed the 'Dial' triumphantly high, above all cavil."[16] "Thoughts on Labor," in the April 1841 *Dial*, was also well received. A friend of Orestes Brownson in Philadelphia told him that, together with Brownson's own writings, Parker's article was so highly thought of that it had "constituted the Sunday morning readings at the 'Hall of the Friends of Human Progress' for some time past."[17]

Parker contributed seven short reviews, one essay review, two articles, and two poems to the *Dial*'s second volume. The latter, printed as "Protean Wishes," he had sent Fuller with the confession that he did not think that he was "made for a poet, least of all for an *amatory poet*," and said that he would not be "grieved, vexed, or ruffled" should they not appear.[18] By April 1842 Parker stood at a high point in his career: his famous *A Discourse on the Transient and Perma-nent in Chritianity* had been delivered, and he was a preacher of great con-troversy and reknown. The fledgling "amatory poet" was becoming a crusader, and the *Dial* was to be his next platform.

When the *Dial*'s second volume was completed, Fuller resigned as editor. She had never given Parker any trouble over his contributions to the magazine; the worst she had done was to warn him that his writing was impossible to read.[19] When she quit, Parker told Emerson that she had done truly well, but that under Emerson the magazine would "grow up to vigorous manhood."[20] Parker's proposed article on John Pierpont and the Hollis Street Council was going to be his contribution to the *Dial*'s growth.

The Reverend John Pierpont had been dismissed by his parish for calling them hypocrites. Pierpont could not see, for instance, how members of his congrega-tion could piously inveigh against drinking when they themselves made money from selling liquor. When Pierpont's case was reviewed by a council of the Unitarian Association meeting at Hollis Street, the ministers upheld Pierpont's dismissal. Parker was outraged and wrote Pierpont that nothing had happened for years "so reflecting disgrace on the Boston clergy" as the association's action. Parker then wrote Emerson, calling the case one of "the signs of the times" that demanded attention, and proposed a piece on the council for the *Dial*. Emerson, who had his reservations about turning the *Dial* into a pulpit for ecclesiastical debate, replied that he would rather have the article on David Friedrich Strauss's *Dogmatick* that Parker was already working on. He preferred to avoid the Pier-pont article for the reason that, "although the injury done to Mr Pierpont in that controversy may be indefensible *in the forms*, yet there probably existed in this case that *general objection* to the pastor which could not get stated, yet which is felt in the mind of each parishoner as the highest reason for displacing a pastor." Also, he took the position that a minister had no right to force his ideas on his parishoners—ten years earlier Emerson had himself resigned rather than press upon his congregation his personal objections to administering the Lord's Sup-per. But this case did not turn on a highly complex theological issue: Parker saw the question as whether a minister had the right to tell the truth or whether he should only tell his congregation what they wanted to hear, and, in his mind, principle had been sacrificed to expediency. He answered that, if Emerson did not like the article, he was under no obligation to use it, and when Emerson ap-parently procrastinated on the issue Parker wrote again: "If you don't like it, don't insert it. I am not a *baby* to be vexed with you, either because you *delay* or *reject* my writings." Parker's position was clear: Emerson could take the article or leave it, but he could not shake Parker's convictions. Emerson replied in a compromising tone and agreed to a short notice.[21] He was, therefore, upset when a long article—twenty-one pages when set in type—arrived, telling Parker that his "heart sank" upon seeing the "most unpoetic unspiritual & un Dialled" piece on Pierpont.[22] However, Emerson felt that he would probably be "more in-disposed to the matter" if he "looked into the details," and he decided to print the entire article without even reading it, "purely out of honor to the contributor." Parker would receive the proof directly, for Emerson wished to avoid even that much involvement with it.[23]

The "Hollis Street Council" was duly printed in the October 1842 issue and became one of the most controversial and sensational articles the *Dial* ever published. Fuller liked the piece and told Emerson that "the sneer is mild, almost courtly."[24] The article forced Parker's long feud with the Unitarian ministers to a head, and immediately after its publication they met and in effect prohibited him from supplying any pulpit in Boston.[25]

Parker's subsequent relations with Emerson and the *Dial* were smoother, though he must have been somewhat perturbed by Emerson's failure to print all his reviews.[26] When the Reverend Charles Follen died, Parker offered to review his life and works, but he did prefer that someone else would do it, since he feared he could not "do justice to so noble a man." When no one else volunteered, Parker completed the article for the January 1843 *Dial*, though he did not much like it. Parker's final contribution, "Hennell on the Origin of Christianity," arose from Henry Channing's failure to review Parker's own *Discourse of Matters Pertaining to Religion* for the July 1843 number. Channing's piece was planned to replace a review of Charles Hennell, but he never wrote it. Emerson was reminded of this when he received from London a translation of a German magazine's review of Hennell's book. Since the translation was far too long for the *Dial*, Emerson turned to Parker, who by August had the article written. He suggested that Emerson send it "to press *directly*," for, if he could not read proof before he sailed to Europe in September, the task — "which is no light one" — would fall on Emerson. Thus the article was published in October 1843, when Parker was abroad.[27]

Before he left, Parker had volunteered to do something for the *Dial* while on his trip, and Emerson asked for "some good news" for the "Foreign Intelligence" section.[28] Since Parker had gone specifically for his health, however, no more contributions to the *Dial* appeared from his pen. Besides, Emerson already had an excellent foreign correspondent in Charles Stearns Wheeler. By the time Wheeler died in 1843, the *Dial* was coming to an end, and Emerson never had to ask Parker for another contribution.

Parker and Emerson were, to the public, the *Dial*'s most important contributors. Both gave the magazine the notoriety of their names. Their styles and subjects were too distinctive to allow them to preserve the anonymity that unsigned articles furnished other contributors. Parker saw the *Dial* as a journal that, being outside of any established order, should do more to print articles on important contemporary subjects that would otherwise remain unpublished. Fuller and later Emerson both saw it primarily as a literary magazine designed to promote the "New School" in literature, philosophy, and religion. Emerson, especially, would let more temporal magazines deal with subjects like the "Hollis Street Council"; the *Dial* could simply report particulars without necessarily taking a position on them.

Parker was also able to see the *Dial* with a greater detachment than some of those more closely involved with the magazine. While mulling over a pamphlet on "the Supernatural in literary composition," he told Emerson that he was sorely tempted to collect "a whole ship-load of 'parallel passages' out of the Dial alone." He disliked the highly "Transcendental" side of the *Dial* and was willing and able to carry his complaints to its editor, as when he mentioned that it contained a *"substance"* found nowhere else but in John Heraud's *Monthly Magazine* and "the 'aesthetic circles' of 'transcendental' men & maidens," a substance he called *"Dialese"* after "the place where it is concentered." He had supposed that it was the "smoke of the torches of young genius" but had since found it too many times where "there was no *flame.*" Parker's most memorable description of the *Dial* was in a letter to Francis. After only two issues had been published, he was quite ready to pass — and to illustrate — his judgment:

> Apropos of the Dial. To mind [sic] it bears about the same relation to the Boston Quarterly [Review], that Antimachus does to Hercules, Alcott to Brownson, or a band of men & maidens, daintily arrayed in finery . . . to a body of stout men, in blue frocks, with great arms, & hard hands & legs — like the Pillars of Hercules. If I was going to do the thing in paint, it should be thus. I would represent a body of minute Philosophers — men & maidens elegantly dressed, bearing a banner, inscribed with "The Dial," a Baby & a Pap Spoon, & a cradle should be the accompaniment thereof. The whole body should have "rings on their fingers, & bells on their toes," & go "mincing as they walk," forced by a body of fiddlers . . . & repeating "New Poetry." This body of the excellent should come out of a canvass city of Jerusalem, set upon a hill, on the other hand should come up a small body of warriors, looking like the seven chiefs before Thebes, and swearing as they did . . . They should be men who looked battles, with organs of combativeness big as your fist. They should be covered with sweat & blood & dust, with an earnest look, & confident tread. "Sonorous metal blowing martial sounds" should encourage them, at their head should stand "Orestes Augustus Brownson," dressed like David; with Goliath's sword in one hand, & that giant's head in the other. Would not this make a picture?[29]

28
Elizabeth Palmer Peabody

Elizabeth Palmer Peabody not only wrote for the *Dial* but was its publisher during the third year of its existence. She was a well-known figure of the time, but, like Bronson Alcott's, her eccentricities are included among the less serious aspects of Transcendentalism.[1]

Elizabeth Peabody was born on 16 May 1804 at Billerica, Massachusetts, and she moved with her family to Salem in 1815. She was a bright girl who showed

Elizabeth Palmer Peabody.

Collection of Joel Myerson.

promise, but college was out of the question because of her sex, and she turned to the only course open to her, teaching. In 1820 she moved to Lancaster, Massachusetts, and taught in the Boy's Academy run there by Jared Sparks. Two years later she became dissatisfied and decided to move to Boston, where she felt more opportunities would await her.

While teaching school in Boston, Peabody also took Greek lessons from nineteen-year-old Waldo Emerson. A beautiful young girl, she was also shy, as was Emerson, even though he was teaching a young ladies' school.[2] The two never lifted their eyes from their books and were "too much afraid of each other to venture any other conversation" beyond the lesson. When the lessons were over, Emerson refused to take any money because, she said, "he found he could teach me nothing." George B. Emerson was present at their last interview and, Peabody noted, Waldo, "protected by his cousin's presence," had a long conversation with her on Edward Everett's oratory.[3] Although she did not meet Emerson again for another ten years, this occasion was the beginning of their long friendship.

Peabody gave up her Greek lessons and ended her Boston school to be governess to a family of English Unitarians in Kennebec, Maine. She made the most of the two years she spent there by freely drawing upon the magnificent library that the family had assembled. But she could not forget the excitement of Boston life, and she returned to Brookline, Massachusetts, where friends helped her and her sister Mary to gather a class. By 1826 Peabody felt that she was finally beginning to realize her potential, and she called this "the first year of my *intellectual* life properly speaking." Recognition of her abilities came from all sides. The Reverend William Ellery Channing, whose daughter was a student at her school, asked Peabody to become his amanuensis, and she copied his sermons and prepared his manuscripts for the printer.[4] Her series of discussions on the "Historical School" in 1827 were among the earliest of the Conversations later made famous by Alcott and Margaret Fuller, and they were certainly the first to be given by a woman.

The next decade began on an auspicious note. While walking by King's Chapel on 23 May 1830, Peabody stopped to watch a wedding that was in progress and met the bridegroom, Bronson Alcott. As he saw more of Peabody, he discovered her to be "interesting," though he thought that by aiming too hard at being "original" she sometimes became "offensively assertive"; there was "too much of the man and too little of the woman in her familiarity and freedom, her affected indifference of manner." Alcott voiced a common complaint when he mentioned Peabody's manner. The words "tact" and "sensitivity" were absent from her vocabulary, and not everyone agreed that her sharp and pointed suggestions were always in the recipient's best interest, as she herself always professed them to be. She and Charles Emerson, for example, were "nearly entirely strangers" because her lack of "fine taste & delicate manners" put him off.[5] Mrs. Clarke, who ran the boarding house where Peabody was staying, almost refused her at first because she found her "so queer."[6] Known as the "talkative" one, Peabody sometimes drove her fellow boarders from the table with her incessant chatter. Very few people, then or later, were as charitable about this as was the landlady's daughter, Sarah Clarke: "Not always sane in her enthusiasms, or wise or prudent, but such sweet insanity."[7]

During 1832 and 1833 the two Peabody sisters continued their school, renting a section of Mrs. Clarke's house to hold classes in. Emerson passed through Boston on his way to Europe after his first wife's death and renewed his friendship with Elizabeth.[8] She was soon able to put some money aside when twenty young women, including the Sturgis sisters, paid five dollars apiece to attend her "reading parties" on such people as Harriet Martineau.

In 1834 Alcott came to Peabody and asked for her help in his new Temple School. Volunteering to teach two and a half hours a day for whatever Alcott could afford to pay, she spent afternoons going over Latin and geography with his pupils. Things went so well that by the following spring she was boarding with Alcott's family, but it did not take long for these two egos to come into combat. Both Peabody and Alcott had opinions on everything and freely expressed them, and they soon found themselves arguing over even the most ridiculous matters. Once, when Peabody said that she had no desire to live for two hundred years, Alcott snapped back that she had a "suicidal temperament." Soon she was resolving to "take more pains to be silent" about subjects on which Alcott could possibly differ with her, but she admitted: "I think I shall find it quite a trial to my patience." The breaking point was reached when the *Record of a School*, her transcription of Alcott's conversations with his pupils, was published in 1836. Sex and religion were among the subjects covered, and since Alcott was embarrassingly honest in telling the truth about the first and in expressing his doubts about the second, Peabody feared the possible reaction of the public. She expressed her reservations to Alcott and asked him to delete some of the more questionable passages, but Alcott thought that she had turned on him, and, although she defended both the book and him in print against their many critics, he never really forgave her.[9]

Peabody spent the next three years developing various projects and friendships. She published articles in the *Boston Observer* and the *Christian Register* for which she received about $100. She thought of using this money to start a journal and solicited John Sullivan Dwight for an article on music, telling him that Emerson had already promised to contribute. Alcott, who had been unable to pay Peabody anything for her work at his school, put aside his animosity toward her and wished her luck, for he felt that a new periodical was "extensively wanted." However, nothing ever came of this plan.[10]

One side result of Peabody's periodical plan was that she championed her friends in person when she found that she was unable to do so in print. She arranged for Fuller to visit Emerson in Concord, Massachusetts, by convincing him that his first feelings of a strong but unfounded prejudice against Fuller would, like her own, disappear when he got to know her better.[11] She introduced Jones Very to Emerson and promoted him among her friends.[12] Emerson, who sometimes stayed with the Peabody family when he was in Salem, returned the favor by inviting Elizabeth to Concord, and she went back to Boston with "an ocean of gladsome feelings."[13] She frequently attended the Transcendental Club meetings, where Parker found her to be "a woman of rare qualities of head & heart," whose "office" was to be the "*Boswell*" of the day.[14]

With so many friends and with her desire to help them all she could—one person called her "a lion everywhere"—Peabody decided that she needed a place for them to meet and a means for them to be heard.[15] Accordingly, she began planning to open a bookstore in Boston and to set up a printing press in it. In July 1840 she officially opened her shop at 13 West Street, selling books and art supplies charged through the generosity of the Reverend Channing and Washington Allston to their accounts. The store soon became a meeting place for the Transcendentalists: Fuller held her Conversations there, and Peabody distributed the *Western Messenger*.[16]

Yet with all her promise Peabody was not at first asked to become a contributor to the *Dial*. There were two main reasons for this: her topics and her style. Soon after the first number had been published, she sent Emerson a paper on "Patriarchal Traditions." Emerson patiently read through the fifty-odd manuscript pages and told her that, though he had liked the article, "our ancient and honorable acquaintances Abraham & Isaac & Jacob & Esau have a certin air of unseasonableness, like octogenarians at a young party, and one would willingly spare such valued friends the shadow of a disrespect." Saying that the piece was "too good to be lost," he proposed one of the theological journals or a separate publication for it. But he also suggested that, if she would revise the first nine or ten pages into a "short chapter," he would see if Fuller would print it. Then he told Fuller of the paper, which he called "a little too venerable for our slight modern purpose."[17] The article was, in plain English, too staid for the *Dial*, and Peabody never resubmitted it.

Peabody's style suggests a manful attempt to match the abstractness of the subjects upon which she usually wrote. As Fuller put it: "I never saw anything like her for impossibility of being clear and accurate in a brief space"; and she warned Emerson, when he took over the *Dial*, against "trusting E.P.P. to write the slightest notice or advertisement."[18] Emerson felt that Peabody's "superlative of grammar" was "suicidal" and defeated its ends. He complained of such phrases as "most perfect," "most exquisite," and "most masculine," and told her that "the positive degree is the sinew of speech, the superlative is the fat."[19] Whether Peabody would have actually accepted these suggestions is doubtful, but fortunately she turned to more temporal subjects and soon found herself published in the *Dial*.

Peabody's three articles in the *Dial* were all concerned with Brook Farm. The first, "A Glimpse of Christ's Idea of Society" in the October 1841 number, was a general discussion of Christian life that had originally been sent as a letter to Harriet Martineau at George Ripley's request. In the next issue she discussed Brook Farm as the embodiment of this type of society. Very found the first a "good statement," and, when a magazine correspondent later visited the community, she reported to her readers that it "more than answers the expectation" held out by Peabody's account of it.[20] But one skeptical reader said that

Peabody's description of Brook Farm interested him less "than would at the end of the year the page of Mr. Ripley's ledger in which the accounts" were kept. Her final contribution, an article on "Fourierism," was accepted at once by Emerson when he received the manuscript in February 1844 and was published in the last number of the *Dial*. From her side, Peabody told Sophia Ripley this about the *Dial*: "[I]t is domestic, giving the every day state of feeling & thought of the writers, there is no effort about it, & much strength behind."[21]

It is unlikely that Peabody could have played a larger part in the *Dial* than she did.[22] Most of her writings, on theology and education, were simply unacceptable for that magazine. Her brief role as the publisher of the *Dial* did not have happy results for those concerned. Then too, as her sisters married and left her, Peabody slipped into spinsterhood. Her attention then turned toward education, and she was instrumental in introducing the kindergarten to America. Even as the *Dial* was drawing to a close, she began to resemble Henry James's Miss Birdseye, a woman "consumed by the passion of sympathy; it had crumpled her into as many pieces as an old glazed, distended glove. She had been laughed at, but she never knew it; she was treated as a bore, but she never cared."[23]

29
Benjamin Franklin Presbury

Benjamin Franklin Presbury, who contributed two poems to the *Dial*, was born on 23 October 1810 at Taunton, Massachusetts. His father was a sea captain and, after a brief time at the Bristol Academy, the young man was taken to sea in preparation for a shipboard career. However, a "want of robustness, and his distaste for a sea-faring life" decided Presbury against such a course of action, and he returned to Taunton where he became apprenticed to a tailor.[1] There he stayed until 1849, when he joined the California gold rush.

When Ralph Waldo Emerson first received some verses from Presbury, whom he did not know, in November 1841, he told Margaret Fuller that one was printable but that "the others must wait." He then wrote Presbury that he had sent one of the sonnets to Fuller for the January *Dial* after making a few corrections, which he mentioned. Another poem, "Music," needed more work as it was not quite correct enough to satisfy Emerson and he suggested revisions, for he had found the poem of sufficient quality to justify Presbury's pains. Presbury responded at once and enclosed revised copies of his "Sonnet. To Mary on Her Birthday" and "Music. To Martha." Thanking Emerson for his "kind words," which had done him "Yeoman's service," he mentioned that he had incorporated Emerson's earlier suggestions into the new drafts of his poems. Presbury was still not certain that they would satisfy Emerson, but he had been rewarded by "the pleasure of reconstruction."[2] The "Sonnet" appeared in the January 1842 *Dial* with few changes, but Emerson either sent "Music" back for further work or altered it himself, for it appeared in the same issue with many variants from Presbury's original copy.[3] Presbury apparently sent more poems to the *Dial*, but none were printed there.[4]

30
George Ripley

George Ripley was managing editor of the *Dial* during its first year. His activities at Brook Farm took precedence, however, and he contributed only two articles and some brief reviews to the magazine.

Ripley was born on 3 October 1802 at Greenfield, Massachusetts. His mother's side of the family was related to Benjamin Franklin, and another relative was Ezra Ripley of Concord, Massachusetts, whose nephew, Waldo Emerson, was George Ripley's cousin. The latter two had met as young boys, and their friendship grew after Ripley entered Harvard in 1819, where he also made the acquaintance of Edward Emerson.[1]

Ripley, who made up for average intelligence by methodically feeding his "voracious intellectual appetite," did well on the drills and routine exercises that characterized education at that time, and he joined the Hasty Pudding Club.[2] After spending the winter of his senior year teaching at Fitchburg, Massachusetts, he returned and won the Bowdoin Prize with a mathematical thesis on the shape of the earth. At his commencement Ripley gave the English oration on "Genius as Affected by Moral Feeling."

When Ripley was graduated in 1823, he wanted to study in Germany, but lack of funds forced him to enter Harvard Divinity School. Caleb Stetson and George Bradford were also there, and Ripley's thirst for German philosophy was partially quenched by his fellow student Henry Hedge, who had been to Germany. In his senior year Ripley's income was supplemented by an appointment as tutor in mathematics and natural philosophy.

Although he had contributed an article to the *Christian Examiner* the year before, upon his graduation in 1826 Ripley decided to find himself a settled position before he devoted more time to literary pursuits. He also wished to provide a home for his fiancée Sophia Dana, and the year after he was ordained at his new pastorate at Purchase Street in Boston they were married.

Ripley soon settled into the learned and placid life that he thought all ministers led. By 1833 he was a coeditor of the *Christian Register*. He was well

George Ripley.

Collection of Joel Myerson

liked and participated in the ordinations of Orestes Brownson, John Sullivan Dwight, and Theodore Parker. Yet he soon became restless and dissatisfied. Following the celebration of Harvard's bicentennial on 8 September 1836, Ripley joined Emerson, Hedge, and George Putnam in a talk, which resulted in the first real meeting of the Transcendental Club at Ripley's house on 19 September. Through this group Ripley became friends with others who would later be instrumental in founding the *Dial*.

Emerson, who thought Ripley a "very able" man, continued as his friend even as he made new ones. Despite the fact that Ripley classified his beliefs as "Atheism," Bronson Alcott became his friend and called Ripley one of the best people in the "liberal church."[3] Margaret Fuller thought well of Ripley but, like Alcott, realized that his intelligence was the product of much hard work rather than of inspiration or genius.[4] The most lasting friendship Ripley made from this circle was with Parker, and the two men, fellow battlers against conservative Unitarianism, remained close friends until Parker's death. Ripley thought Parker "a true man" in the midst of "dwarfs, mountebanks . . . and monkeys," all of whom made "modern society so mean and false and hollow and repulsive."[5]

The three years following the founding of the Transcendental Club saw Ripley plunged into the intellectual and social movements of the time. His interest in German literature led to a correspondence with Thomas Carlyle.[6] Ripley also decided on a plan aimed at bringing the writings of foreign philosophers into America; as he informed James Marsh, an early exponent of Samuel Taylor Coleridge in America, he planned a series of translations under the general title of *Specimens of Foreign Standard Literature*, which would lay before the "literary public some of the most celebrated writings in philosophy, history and theology which admit of naturalisation on American soil." In 1838 Ripley personally initiated the series with two volumes of his translations of Victor Cousin, Theodore Jouffroy, and Benjamin Constant.[7] The Unitarian press favorably reviewed the volumes, and, despite their transcendental message, Ripley still seemed to hold a safe position within the church. This picture of calm was shattered in 1839 when Andrews Norton, Boston's leading conservative Unitarian, attacked Emerson's Divinity School Address and Ripley leaped to the defense.

In late 1839, just as his controversy with Norton was getting under way, the seed of a new career was put into Ripley's mind. James Clarke's mother had met the socialist reformer Albert Brisbane in the West, and she soon introduced Ripley to his ideas. Ripley began reading all he could on associationism, and in May 1840 a fellow minister, Ezra Stiles Gannett, noticed that Ripley had become "uncomfortable in his present situation" and "dissatisfied with the present religious and social institutions." When Gannett told him this, Ripley answered that he contemplated "a change of his own mode of action." By September other friends were commenting on how he was "fermenting and effervescing" with his new ideas.[8] The next month Ripley announced to his parish that he wished to resign, and in January 1841 he preached his farewell sermon. He and his followers settled at West Roxbury, Massachusetts, in April and called their experiment Brook Farm.

Before leaving for Brook Farm, Ripley had taken an active part in the founding of the *Dial*. Like Alcott, he had thought highly of John Heraud's *Monthly Magazine* and wanted a "free Journal" like it in America. When the *Dial* was formally established, he offered his aid as a contributor and managing or business editor, and he probably wrote the "Prospectus." To the first number Ripley contributed a favorable review of "Brownson's Writings," which Clarke immediately recognized as his by its style and ideas. Although he had promised a review of James Martineau's works for the second number,[9] Ripley instead sent Fuller a number of shorter reviews[10] and a "Letter to a Theological Student" that he had written in December 1836. The letter, telling a student about the opportunities for reform and change within the church, appeared at an ironic time, for Ripley himself had just left the ministry. He hunted up possible contributors and approached Marsh without success for an article.[11] He also directed many of the young writers at Brook Farm to send their products to the *Dial*, and in this way a new source of talent was found.

Ripley's initial enthusiasm toward the *Dial* lessened when he saw the finished product. He thought the first number "quite unworthy . . . of its pretensions" and was afraid it would be passed over unnoticed by the public. Ripley's fears were quickly dispelled, for, when he glanced through the papers, he saw that "People seem to look on with wonder, while the Philistines who dare show out are wrathy as fighting cocks." He told a friend that he "could not have prayed for a more auspicious beginning," and that he hoped the *Dial* would help overthrow those men who bowed down to "the huge shapeless idols of brass & clay which are set up in the holiest-spots." Still, Ripley had expected "hoofs & horns," and he felt that in reality the *Dial* had proved "gentle as any sucking dove." He trusted that the next number would "make amends."[12]

Subsequent numbers, however, proved to be too "Transcendental" for Ripley, and his support soon became negligible. While Brook Farm did take up almost all of his time, the "naive subjectivity and Orphic mysticism" that he felt surrounded the *Dial* no doubt strengthened his resolve to stay at West Roxbury as much as possible. Aside from briefly returning to straighten out the *Dial*'s finances after Weeks, Jordan & Co. went bankrupt, Ripley had nothing more to do with the magazine.[13] His disagreements with Emerson at this time over the general philosophy behind the Brook Farm venture also helped to make the separation a more permanent one.[14]

31
Sophia Ripley

Sophia Ripley was born on 16 July 1803 into the prosperous Dana family of Boston. Not content to follow the usual simple domestic life, Sophia Dana did much reading and in 1823 opened a school in Cambridge, Massachusetts, with her mother and younger sister. The school prospered and counted among its pupils the Reverend William Ellery Channing's daughter and the children of the Parkmans and the Higginsons. James Russell Lowell, who was also one of her students, remembered Sophia Dana as a "very learned and accomplished woman."

Miss Dana quickly moved into the social and intellectual life of the city: her sister married Washington Allston, thus joining two famous families, and her own store of knowledge, which included a facility for Greek and Italian, made her a favorite with the Harvard people. In 1825 she met George Ripley, then in the divinity school, and by the next year they were unofficially engaged. After their marriage on 22 August 1837 they settled in Boston, where Ripley was a minister.[1]

Sophia Ripley's marriage was to all outward appearances a happy one. She followed her husband to Brook Farm and there gave him all the help she could. Yet a recent biographer of Ripley's, after examining the surviving letters of the years of his marriage, has commented upon the absence of any suggestion of "physical attraction, great emotional warmth, or the mutual dependence that men and women often fell into even in Ripley's reticent day."[2]

An independent woman, Mrs. Ripley was noticed by her husband's friends and soon had made them her own. Those who met her commented upon the "elegant manners and perfect self-control" of this "graceful" and "vivacious" woman. O. B. Frothingham recalled her "burning enthusiasm, warm feeling, and passonate will."[3] She became a good friend of Theodore Parker and attended Transcendental Club meetings and various Conversations.[4] Convers Francis thought her "superior to the other female *distinguées*, Miss Fuller, Miss Peabody &c,"[5] and Margaret Fuller asked for her advice before proceeding with her Conversations at Elizabeth Peabody's bookstore. Fuller liked Mrs. Ripley better than she did her husband and noted that she "goes higher and sees clearer" than Ripley. And Ralph Waldo Emerson, though he found her nature "somewhat hard," also formed a closer friendship with her than with her husband. One reason for this was the time she spent in Concord, Massachusetts, reading proof and aiding in other routine literary tasks connected with Emerson's writings and the *Dial*.[6]

Mrs. Ripley's first contribution to the *Dial* was an article on the rights of "Woman" in the January 1841 number. Anne Lyman of Northampton, Massachusetts, found it one of the few pieces she could understand and told a friend that it gave her much pleasure. William Bellows wrote his newly-married brother that, if his bride ever despaired of housekeeping, she should read Mrs. Ripley's article for moral support. In reply, Henry Bellows said that both he and his wife admired Mrs. Ripley's article "exceedingly."

To the second volume of the *Dial* Mrs. Ripley contributed an article on "Painting and Sculpture" and a "Letter" written from the socialist community in Zoar, Ohio, when she and her husband had visited it in 1838. Emerson thought highly of the last piece and recommended it to his brother William.[7]

Unlike her husband, Mrs. Ripley was pleased with the *Dial*, and, even though her contributions to the magazine ended in July 1841, she always gave it her support. She had found the first number "very charming" and had defended it against her husband, Fuller, and Parker, who, she said, ran it down "unmercifully." As late as 1843 she told Emerson that she still found the *Dial* "rich & strong & faithful to its early intentions," and said it "takes possession of one, haunts one's dreams & is the first thing we think of when waking."[8] Even though she thought highly of the magazine, Mrs. Ripley's own lack of literary ambition and the work involved in running Brook Farm prevented her from taking a more active role in it.

32
Jonathan Ashley Saxton

Jonathan Ashley Saxton contributed only one article to the *Dial*, a forty-page essay titled "Prophecy — Transcendentalism — Progress." The oldest contributor to the *Dial*, Saxton was born at Greenfield, Massachusetts, on 12 January 1795. He started his college career at Yale but was graduated from Harvard in 1813, after which he took a degree in law and was admitted to the bar four years later. Law did not appeal to him as a career, however, and by 1823 he had turned to journalism as the coeditor of the *Franklin (Massachusetts) Herald*. Two years later he established the *Franklin Post and Christian Examiner* in his home town and through it spread the interests of the Unitarians. The paper failed to do well, and in 1827 it failed. He then unsuccessfully tried his hand at editing a paper at Troy, New York.

Saxton's failure as an editor did not discourage him from continuing in the world of letters. Unable to have his own periodical, he began writing books and contributing to other journals. In 1835 he published his *Child's Book of the Atmosphere* and soon became a frequent contributor to the *Boston Quarterly Review* and the *Democratic Reivew*. He also contributed a paper to the *Dial* in which he traced the evolution of Transcendentalism. Saxton knew George Ripley and admired Theodore Parker, and he no doubt correctly felt that the *Dial* was the perfect place in which to have his piece printed. It came out in the July 1841 issue, and, although Ralph Waldo Emerson felt "contempt" for it, others liked it. The *New-Yorker* reprinted extracts from the article, and in 1842 a book on contemporary philosophy quoted from it to explain the philosophic system of Victor Cousin.[1]

Saxton probably contributed no more than this one article to the *Dial* because, as a professional journalist, he expected money in return for his work.[2] He also had returned to Greenfield and needed to support his wife and six children. Although he sympathized with the Transcendentalists, he was not close enough to them to be willing to sacrifice an income for a place in the pages of the *Dial*.[3]

33

Thomas Treadwell Stone

Thomas Treadwell Stone was born on 9 February 1801, the second of a Water-
ford, Maine, farmer and church deacon. He prepared for college at the
Bridgton (Maine) Academy and went to Bowdoin College in 1816, sharing a
room with Jacob Abbott, who later gained fame as the creator of the "Rollo
Books." After his graduation in 1820, Stone served as a missionary in Oxford
County, Maine, while continuing his theological studies at Augusta. In 1824 he
accepted an offer from the Orthodox Congregational Church at Andover,
Maine, to become their pastor, and the following year he was married.

By 1830, though, Stone had become a Unitarian, and, because his new beliefs
were not suited to his present pulpit, he left Andover. Stone settled with his wife
and three children at Bridgton, became the principal of the academy he himself
had attended, and, putting his earlier missionary experiences to use, published
Sketches of Oxford County in 1830. Through his correspondence with Mary
Moody Emerson, Stone became acquainted with her nephew Waldo and promised to send him an account of James Mackintosh's *Ethics*. The addition of
another child to his family and his growing interest in reform movements led
him to move to East Machias, Maine, in 1832 to become the pastor there.[1]

Both Stone's family and his public life blossomed during the fourteen years he
stayed in East Machias. Seven more children arrived, and in 1837 Stone publicly
committed himself to the antislavery movement. Soon afterward he probably attended a few of the Transcendental Club meetings, and in 1839 he met John
Greenleaf Whittier and William Lloyd Garrison while attending the National
Anti-Slavery Convention in New York. Even though this involvement and his
liberal preaching record caused him to be officially expelled from the main body
of the church, his parishoners gave him a vote of confidence by asking him to remain, which he did.[2]

When the *Dial*'s first number was being planned, Stone found himself approached for a contribution. In January 1840 Henry Hedge, Stone's neighbor
and friend, promised Margaret Fuller to request Stone's permission to print a
letter he had written to Mary Moody Emerson the year before. Fuller must have
told Ralph Waldo Emerson of this, for in April 1840 he wrote about the letter to
Stone, who replied that he felt himself privileged to be considered for the new
journal, and that he rejoiced in this chance for "the advancement of American
thought." He authorized the *Dial*'s use of the letter and permitted Emerson to
make any necessary corrections, but he asked that it be printed with his initials
rather than his full name. Stone apparently sent the letter directly to Fuller, for
Emerson asked that she bring it with her to the meeting of the Transcendental

Club on 20 May 1840. At that time, she and Emerson discussed the letter and decided not to print it.[3]

Fuller also brought with her to the meeting another paper by Stone about which Hedge had told Emerson. She gave it to Emerson for comment, but when he remained silent for ten days she wrote a reminder. He briefly replied that the article seemed a "high statement" to him, though "a little verbose, & careless sometimes in expression," but he did not feel like correcting it, since "the writing was so close & the page so long."[4]

Either the article did need revision or Fuller just did not have enough room, for it was absent from the July 1840 number. Emerson complained about this omission and asked Fuller to make sure that Stone's article was in the next number. Although she definitely planned for its insertion in October, when she discovered that Emerson's "New Poetry" and "Thoughts on Modern Literature," Henry Channing's "Ernest the Seeker," and lengthy reviews by George Ripley left little room for more than scattered poems, it was again left out.[5] At any rate, "Man in the Ages" appeared in the January 1841 *Dial* where, possibly to assuage Emerson's and Stone's feelings, it began the number.

The month after the publication of his article, Stone went to Bangor, Maine, where he stopped and visited Christopher Pearse Cranch, who was substituting for Hedge. Cranch remembered Stone's article favorably and wrote John Sullivan Dwight that Stone was "fragrant with the very warmest bloom of the true transcendentalism — a true Christian Pantheist," a man who represented all "the best things" of Emerson and the *Dial*.[6]

In June Stone wrote to Mary Moody Emerson concerning his reservations about the Transcendentalists. While strongly in sympathy with them, he noted that he differed with them as to means. Like the Transcendentalists, Stone saw God in all, but, while they believed that men could approach God by perfecting their infinite goodness, he felt that the consummation was obtained through a redemption of original sin. The Transcendentalists' lack of faith in the Scriptures and their corresponding faith in post lapsarian man had made their overall faith "too dim of sight, too feeble of grasp, too wanting in certainty." Aunt Mary passed the letter on to Emerson, who, perhaps seeing that "practical" Transcendentalism was going awry at Brook Farm and elsewhere, replied that he thought that nothing could be "better in the way of general statement on the subject," though he himself "should not say the same things," and added that Stone, who was working in the Calvinist tradition, should. Emerson copied the section on Transcendentalism to show his friends and printed it in the January 1842 *Dial*.[7]

This was Stone's last contribution to the *Dial*, though Emerson later urged Hedge to ask Stone for another piece.[8] Stone was willing to become involved in controversial issues, but the abstract Transcendentalism of many of the *Dial*'s contributors did not interest him as much as the more positive social actions taken by other reform papers, and Stone channeled his future energies in that other direction.

34
Caroline Sturgis

Caroline Sturgis contributed twenty-six poems to the *Dial*. She was Margaret Fuller's best friend, and, although she also enjoyed a close friendship with Ralph Waldo Emerson, her devotion to Fuller was deeper, and all but three of her poems appeared while the latter was editor.

Caroline was born in August 1819, the third girl of the four children of a wealthy Boston merchant. She and her sister Ellen both showed early promise and were given an excellent education. After she met Fuller, Caroline's circle of acquaintances quickly grew, and she joined the fringe of the Transcendental movement, more interested in its participants than in their philosophy.

Sturgis's beauty, charm, and wit appealed to all who met her.[1] She became a friend of Lydia Child,[2] Sarah Clarke,[3] and Henry Thoreau, though she was rather bemused by the latter.[4] Bronson Alcott was impressed by her deep interest in "the spiritual philosophy," and their friendship was firmly established when she asked to read the manuscript of Alcott's "Psyche."[5]

As Sturgis was young, single, and beautiful, she was romantically linked with many young men, including some of the *Dial*'s contributors. Charles Newcomb took a friendly, though not romantic, interest in her when he was at Brook Farm. Although they spent many hours together there, the combination of Newcomb's parents—who continually reminded him that she was marriageable—and Sturgis's own ability to draw out of Newcomb more than he wanted to give inhibited their relationship.[6] She was deeply enamored of Ellery Channing, whom she had first met along with Sam Ward at Curzon's Mill in Newbury, Massachusetts, in 1837. Her family felt that Channing was "in his queer way rather in love with her," and she clung to the rosy image of him that she had from this time for years afterward, becoming deeply disappointed when he married Ellen Fuller.[7] Her most important male friend, though, was Emerson.

Sturgis had originally met Emerson briefly in 1836, but the occasion for their first real meeting came in the summer of 1838, when he invited Fuller and her to visit him in Concord. They arrived in June, and Sturgis had a pleasant time, including many long talks with Emerson. After she had left Emerson vowed to "see her hereafter as an old acquaintance," and he wrote Fuller: "For a hermit I begin to think I now know several very fine people." The activities of the next few years kept them apart, but when the *Dial* began Sturgis again came into contact with Emerson, and soon they were exchanging "golden epistles" as if between "brother & sister."

After an initial period of bantering, however, Sturgis soon became more serious and joined with Fuller in trying to force Emerson out of his shell. She aligned herself spiritually with Emerson and told him that "Where we differ in nature from Margaret & others, is that we unfold from within, while they seek without, & having accumulated much treasure, look within for a treasure house that can contain it all, — we have to bring forth our gold and coin it for use." She complained to him that "With all your faith in Man you have but little faith in men."[8]

When her male friends, such as Ward and Channing, started to drift away, Sturgis became a lonely, romantic young girl, and Emerson became embarrassed by her cries for help.[9] After a brief cooling-off period, their correspondence continued, and Sturgis, like Fuller, accepted Emerson on his own terms. Emerson subtly tried to interest her in other men, and by 1843 he had succeeded in introducing her to William Tappan, the man she would marry four years later.[10]

When Fuller was named editor of the *Dial*, she naturally thought of Sturgis for one of her contributors. Fuller gathered up Sturgis's verses from among her friends and sat down to select some for the first number. Unfortunately, she was unable to decide among them and chose them all. Would she help, Fuller wrote Sturgis, by choosing the ones she herself thought best to print? Emerson, too, was soon asked to help choose "ethically or lyrically" those poems that he wished to see published.

Emerson received the verses in April but was unable to make his selections before the deadline for the July 1840 *Dial*. By the end of July Emerson had fulfilled his promise to "elect & edit" some of Sturgis's verses to "enrich & ensoul" the *Dial*, and he returned nearly a dozen poems, with his "slight corrections," to her. In his letter accompanying them Emerson praised her verses for "their courage, their perception, their rude strength, their magnanimity, [and] their religion," adding that she was at liberty to accept or reject his "few and insignificant alterations" as she pleased. Finally, not wanting to jeopardize her "incognito," Emerson suggested "putting names to the poems only as a protection to their privacy." Fuller soon followed this up with a letter of her own, urging Sturgis to send the poems to her as soon as possible, for Fuller wished "very much to make this no. of the Dial really good." Sturgis complied, and eleven of her poems appeared in the October 1840 *Dial*.[11]

Soon after that number was published, Emerson thanked Sturgis for her "poesies," which added a "joyful note" to the magazine that contained them. Emerson's letter was Sturgis's first notice that her verses had been published in the *Dial*, and, while she appreciated his praise, she was "a *little* in doubt" of his ability "to keep a secret," and she made him promise to tell "no person whether man, woman, or child" that she was the author. Emerson's reply assured her to "Rest in peace," her secret was safe with him, and, though Elizabeth Hoar and his wife knew of her authorship, both held "the trust sacred," knowing that she genuinely valued her anonymity. Emerson added that he himself would "shrink a little if in these days of newspapers, the Courier or Morning Post should print your verses & discuss you by name." Sturgis was satisfied by this and accepted

Emerson's designation of "Z." for the author of her poems, although she once impishly asked him: "What does my signature of Z. mean[?] Zeal? Zephyr? or is it that I am the last of the Mohicans, or Zacharias he [sic], who climbed a tree, the lord to see?"[12]

Sturgis was enthusiastic about the publication of her poems, and in November 1840 she sent some more in to the *Dial*. However, as her friends married or moved away, Sturgis, who wrote mainly for the eyes of her friends, lost interest in poetry. By 1842 she told Emerson that, while he could freely select from the verses she had written the previous summer, she had no new ones to offer him. Sturgis remained interested in the *Dial*, reading it "as if music fell upon my heart"; she saw the July 1843 *Dial* while sailing with Henry Channing and thought it well done. And the October 1843 number, she told Emerson, was even "a better mine of gems than the last."[13]

Sturgis did not contribute more to the *Dial* for a number of reasons. Fuller's resignation as editor and the marriage of her close friends made her feel lonely, and writing poetry only heightened this feeling by bringing back memories. As her poetic output declined, she met William Tappan and became more closely associated with New York, drifting away from the Boston-based *Dial*.

35
William Aspinwall Tappan

Nothing is known of William Aspinwall Tappan's early life. His connection to the *Dial* was directly through Henry David Thoreau and Ralph Waldo Emerson. Tappan first entered the *Dial*'s circle in February 1843 at New York, when he met Emerson, who was on a lecture tour. Emerson had probably heard of Tappan through Giles Waldo, a mutual acquaintance in Washington. The two spent "a very happy pair of hours," attending Henry Channing's lectures, and Emerson called his companion a "nonpareil" who gave him "great hope." He suggested the works of Michel Montaigne and Thomas Carlyle to Tappan, who later read them with great pleasure.

The young man impressed Emerson, for he mentioned Tappan to Charles Stearns Wheeler as a friend whom he greatly cherished, and he insisted that Henry James meet Tappan, for he was "on every account worth talking with." To Margaret Fuller Emerson called his new friend a person of great promise, and he told Thoreau that Tappan spoke "seldom but easily & strongly, & moves like a deer." Indeed, Emerson thought Tappan's only negative points were his lack of reading, which Emerson quickly moved to correct, and his complaint that "Tappan writes me never a word." Tappan's visit to Emerson in October 1843 made up for the lack of correspondence and cemented a friendship that lasted throughout their lives.[1]

It was through Emerson that Tappan met his future wife, Caroline Sturgis. Soon after he had met Tappan, Emerson mentioned him to Sturgis and sent some of his letters along. Emerson was motivated as much by his wish to introduce two of his good friends to each other as he was by a desire to give Sturgis someone else beside himself on whom to shower her affections — and problems. Sturgis saw "a most loving receptive child" depicted in the letters, and she expressed a desire to meet their writer. Emerson kept her interest up by asking Fuller to give her the letters she had by Tappan. Sturgis was definitely smitten — as much by the mystery as by the man: "I would rather see him than Webster because he is the greatest unknown to me now & objects in the distance always loom up." Although the two were not married until 1847, their interest in each other dated and increased from this time.[2]

Tappan's other close friend on the *Dial* was Thoreau. When informed by Emerson that Thoreau was going to live near him on Staten Island, Tappan replied that this could be an exciting opportunity. The two became friends at once: Thoreau liked Tappan's "looks and the sound of his silence," and Tappan told Emerson that Thoreau "*had* a friend" in him at New York. Thoreau no doubt reminded Tappan of an earlier promise to help with the *Dial*, and it was through Thoreau that Tappan made his only contribution, a poem called "The Sail." Tappan contributed nothing else because he was not a writer; all of his future activities were in the business world.[3]

36

John Francis Tuckerman

John Francis Tuckerman became a contributor to the *Dial* because he was a friend of many of its contributors, rather than because of any Transcendental leanings of his own. Tuckerman was born in Boston on 13 June 1817, the first child of a wealthy Boston merchant and his English wife. In 1833 he entered Harvard with the class that included Henry Thoreau and Charles Stearns Wheeler. There his interest in music led him to join the Pierian Sodality, where he met John Sullivan Dwight and Christopher Pearse Cranch. Along with his sister, he joined James Russell Lowell, William Wetmore Story, and Maria White in what they termed "The Club," an informal group of mutual acquaintances.[1]

Tuckerman was no doubt prompted to contribute his article on the "Music of the Winter" to the April 1841 *Dial* by his association with these people. His graduation from the Harvard Medical School in 1841 and his accepting a position as a naval surgeon probably made any further contributions from his pen unlikely.

37

Jones Very

Jones Very was unusual, even among the *Dial*'s contributors. Judged insane when the quantity and quality of his writing were greatest, when they declined he was thought quite competent. Very was born on 28 August 1813 at Salem, Massachusetts, the first of the six children of a sea captain and his common-law wife. At age ten Very accompanied his father on voyages to Russia and New Orleans, but his nautical career ended when his father died in 1823. He went to work in an auction house, later helped to teach school, and was admitted to Harvard in 1833 as a sophomore because he was well-tutored.

Very was an excellent student. Even though he belonged to the class that was briefly expelled for Dunkin's Rebellion in 1834, most thought him innocent of any wrongdoing. Upon his return Very settled into an active undergraduate life, joining the Institute of 1770, a debating club.[1] In 1835 he received a scholarship, and by the time he was graduated with second honors in August 1836 he had won the Bowdoin Prize twice, the first student to do so.

Also by that time he had found a solution to the mental anguish that he had been suffering for several years over the question of evil. Very had determined that, since evil could only come into existence through conscious thoughts, temptation was in part a function of will, and he concluded that if all thoughts were driven from the mind temptation would be eliminated. Very then set about trying to suspend his own will without giving any indication to other people of doing so. He partially succeeded but some people still wondered about him. Elliot Cabot—whom Very, as freshman tutor in Greek, was helping in 1837—thought him of "high and noble character and full of religious enthusiasm" but also "somewhat morbid and unbalanced."[2]

In December 1837 Very delivered one of his Bowdoin Prize essays several times as a lecture on "Why There Cannot be Another Epic Poem." He gave it at Salem and there made the first of the friendships that led to his connection with the *Dial*. Elizabeth Peabody, attracted by the title of the lecture, went to hear Very

Collection of Joel Myerson.

and was captivated by him. She wrote Ralph Waldo Emerson and inquired whether, as curator of the Concord Lyceum, he could invite Very to lecture there. Emerson thanked her for the suggestion and promptly began making arrangements for Very to come.[3]

Very was pleased at the opportunity, for he was familiar with Emerson's writings. In 1836 he had purchased *Nature* after hearing some of Emerson's lectures. He liked the book, especially the chapter on "Idealism," and he took it to Concord with him to have the author inscribe it. Very delivered his lecture on 4 April 1838 and, as was the custom, dined with the Emersons. This initial meeting was successful, and Very and two classmates returned the following week, when he surprised Emerson by his "devout sentiment." Very also accompanied Emerson to the meeting of the Transcendental Club on 20 May 1838, where he was a well-qualified participant in the discussion of "Is Mysticism an Element of Christianity?" Emerson must have also interested him in Thomas Carlyle; the following month Very signed the subscription list for Carlyle's *Critical and Miscellaneous Essays* that Charles Stearns Wheeler was circulating.[4]

Soon after his return to Harvard as freshman tutor in Greek, Very had completed, in his own mind, an "identification with Christ," and inevitably his unorthodox religious views became public knowledge. In early September Very startled his class with the apocalyptic cry, "Flee to the mountains, for the end of all things is at hand!"[5] He was quickly dismissed, and Wheeler took his place. The Salem Unitarians, in an attempt to disassociate Very from themselves, blamed his condition on his friendships with Emerson and the Transcendentalists and spirited him into the McLean asylum in Charlestown.[6]

Before he left Salem, however, Very did two important things. The first was to send his essay on Shakespeare to Emerson. Very's identification with Christ was by now complete, and he called the essay not his own words but "the teachings of the Holy Spirit." He also stopped by to "baptize" Peabody, who "trembled to the centre" when Very announced "I come to baptize you with the Holy Ghost & with fire." She was relieved when he left after completing his mission without harming her. And, in reporting the meeting to Emerson, confessed her fears that Very was indeed insane. Emerson received her letter while he was reading Very's paper and was distressed to hear that he was thought to be insane, for Very's essay certainly was not.[7]

Very was released from the McLean asylum on 17 October 1838, exactly one month after his being committed, and he immediately left for Concord to see Emerson. He was preceded there by a letter from Peabody, announcing that Very, who was bringing a paper on *Hamlet*, thought Emerson highly sympathetic to his own case since in his mind they were both being persecuted for their beliefs. Accordingly, Very was going to "deliver his revelation" to Emerson, and she told him to hear Very out and not to worry, for he was quite "harmless."

When Very arrived at the end of October, he stayed for nearly a week, and Emerson, though he felt Very's mind was not "in a natural & probably not in a permanent state," found him "a treasure of a companion."[8] He took Very's eccentric behavior in stride. Very declared one day to be "a day of hate," and he shrank from anyone in whom he discerned "the bad element." Emerson, remembering that "Sincerity is more excellent than flattery," brushed aside Very's actions by declaring that he "charmed us all by telling us he hated us all." After Very left Emerson reported to Peabody that he had found him "serene, intelligent, and true." He pronounced him "profoundly sane" and even wished "the whole world were as mad as he." Emerson also kept Very's two essays with him to read again.[9]

After he returned to Salem, Very sent Emerson two of his sonnets that had been printed in the *Salem Observer*. Emerson had not known that Very wrote poetry, and, when he returned Very's essays in November, he praised the latter's verses for their "so deep & true" sentiment and their simplicity of expression. He also suggested that Very collect his poetry and prose into a publishable volume, and he volunteered to act as editor. Very replied with gratitude but said that he could not publish his works until the Spirit had so ordered it.[10]

Very circulated among the Transcendentalists while he waited for the Spirit to suggest his next step. In December 1838 he wrote a letter to Bronson Alcott, giving his favorable views on Alcott's *Conversations with Children on the Gospels*, and soon followed this with a personal visit. Alcott thought Very "insane with God; diswitted in the contemplation of the holiness of Divinity," an example of "mysticism in its highest form," and, after accompanying him to a Transcendental Club meeting, he decided that Very would be "deemed insane by nearly every man." Fortunately, Alcott was not one of these men, and he continued to praise Very. In January 1839 Emerson lent him Very's essays, and Alcott stayed up late reading them and copying generous extracts into his journal. Alcott also saw Very's sonnets and felt them to be "remarkable literary productions."[11]

By the end of January, though, Alcott was distressed to find that Very's "look, tones, words, are all sepulchral," for having allowed the Spirit to control his actions. Very was now beginning to think of his temporal life as a past one. His present life, that of the Spirit, was becoming the only reality to him, and he spoke to Alcott of having once lived in the world, among men and things, but of "being now in the Spirit." He had discovered Nature to be "a charnal house, and the voices of men, echoes of the dead who haunt its dark chambers." Alcott was understandably disturbed and took Very with him to meet John Sullivan Dwight in an unsuccessful attempt to cheer him up. Although Alcott now found Very "less in the Spirit," he also found him "more spectral than ever" and worried for his health.[12]

Very obviously needed something to relieve the pressures of the evil that he felt himself to be struggling against. Emerson tried to do just this by renewing Very's interest in a literary career, and in January he sent some of Very's sonnets and his Shakespeare essays to Margaret Fuller. Her comments were not encouraging, for though she believed the *Hamlet* criticism contained excellent things and had a noble tone, because Very probed at rather than grasped his subject, the essay was, nevertheless, on the whole a somewhat *"inferior"* production.[13]

One bright spot was the *Western Messenger*. Very had sent James Clarke some of his sonnets for the magazine, and Clarke, who had met him earlier in

Boston,[14] remarked that "the charge of Insanity is almost always brought against any man who endeavours to introduce to the common mind any very original ideas." He defended Very's sanity and said that when they had met he had not noticed even a "partial derangement" in him. Yet soon Very had secluded himself in his rooms in Salem, and Emerson felt that he was either "dying or becoming hopelessly mad."[15]

However, in the summer of 1839, Very left his chambers and reentered the world. He stopped in Boston to see his former classmate Sam Ward, whom he urged to forget his business life, and he invited Ward to join him in the "banquet" of life. Ward politely declined and after this was convinced of Very's insanity. Emerson, on the other hand, found most of his fears dispelled when Very allowed him to become his editor and sent his manuscripts to him in early June. Very had previously given Peabody a "monstrous folio sheet" containing "four double columns of sonnets," which he said the Spirit had enabled him to write. He also had his brother write a letter to Emerson, instructing the latter to freely select those sonnets that he considered publishable. Peabody took this letter and the sonnets, and sent them to Emerson, with Very soon following them to Concord in person. Along the way he saw Alcott, who found him "much better both in body and soul," and who felt that his interest in man and nature was reviving.

Emerson had selected a third of the 200 poems for publication and expected few troublesome editorial matters to be raised. Therefore he was surprised when Very forbade any correction of his verses because he felt that they were not his but "the utterances of the Holy Ghost." Very's strictures applied even to spelling, and Emerson was quite vexed. As usual, however, he solved the problem diplomatically; by telling Very that the "Spirit should be a better speller" and by getting him to agree that they could not "permit the Holy Ghost to be careless (& in one instance) to talk bad grammar," Emerson gained "sovereign" editorial power and promised to "make out quite a little gem of a volume."[16] When Very's *Essays and Poems* appeared in September 1839, Lowell felt that some of the sonnets were "better poetry" than had yet been published in America, and Fuller even thought of reviewing the volume for Heraud's *Monthly Magazine*.[17] Two years later Emerson called attention to the "unquestionable stamp of grandeur" that the poems possessed when he reviewed them in the *Dial*.[18]

Soon after his book was published, Very was beset with even greater personal problems. The Spirit was in touch with him less often, and he suddenly found himself forced to abandon his position as its instrument. Others had objected earlier to his stance as false, but with the Spirit's silence Very's position quickly became untenable.[19] Alcott decided that Very now said "nothing worth repeating." Visits to Emerson in March 1840 and to the Transcendental Club meeting that May failed to help his despondency. He attended Fuller's Conversations but found no help and even animosity there. By September 1841 his literary activity had almost ended, and he reconciled himself to the quiet life of a preacher until his death nearly forty years later.[20]

Because most of Very's best poems were written during the years that the Spirit "dictated" to him and were collected by Emerson in *Essays and Poems*, few of his verses appeared in the *Dial*. Also, immediately after the Spirit's departure in 1840, Very wrote few poems. When one of his three poems in the *Dial*, "The Evening Choir," appeared "altered considerably" by Emerson from what Very had written, he was upset. But, since he no longer believed that the Spirit wrote his poems, Very protested only mildly, no doubt taking Emerson's editorial work to be a statement upon a deficiency in his own poetic talents.[21]

Very was "much pleased and satisfied" with "the occasional glances" he got of the *Dial*. He followed Alcott's trip to England in the October 1842 number, which he thought "a superior one," and he suggested that the *Dial* publish something on Heraud's lectures. However, Emerson, Very, and the *Dial* soon drifted apart, and Emerson, who had placed Very on the free list after his contribution to the ninth number, failed to send him any more copies after April 1843.[22]

By that date Emerson had decidedly given up on Very; subsequent references to him in Emerson's journal are always in the past tense, as if speaking of a dead man.[23] Emerson recognized that Very was no longer the "saint" he had earlier appeared to be, and, looking back, he saw him as "morbid" even then. In 1839 Emerson had drawn this picture of Very: "Here is Simeon the Stylite . . . in the shape of Jones Very, religion for religion's sake, religion divorced, detached from man, from the world, from science & art; grim, unmarried, insulated, accusing; yet true in itself, & speaking *things* in every word. The lie is in the detachment." Now, but a few years later, Emerson found him to be "lamentably sane."[24]

38
Samuel Gray Ward

Samuel Gray Ward was the wealthiest of the *Dial*'s contributors. When he was born in Boston on 3 October 1817, his father was well on his way to the half-million-dollar fortune he would leave at his death in 1858. Ward's early education was at the Boston Latin School, where he was first scholar, and the Round Hill school in Northampton, Massachusetts, where he met Ellery Channing. The boy's interest in learning was encouraged by his father, the treasurer of the Boston Athenæum. His father was also the treasurer of Harvard, and in 1832 Ward entered college there.

At Harvard Ward's classmates included Jones Very, and another undergraduate, Channing, became his friend. Upon his graduation Ward toured Europe.

When he returned to Boston in the summer of 1838, he entered his father's mercantile business and left to work at a branch in New Orleans. One reason

Samuel Gray Ward.

From Emerson's *Journals.*

why he chose New Orleans was Anna Barker, a beautiful young socialite there whom he had met at Cambridge, Massachusetts, and again in Europe. When spring came and Ward journeyed back to Boston, he found himself very much in love, and in May 1839 he returned to New Orleans to propose. Ward, who fancied himself a "student" and a "literary man," discovered that Miss Barker felt that there was "very little probability" of marriage unless his plans of "a scholar's life gave place to some lucrative profession."

Unwilling to trade art for commerce, Ward returned home, arriving at Boston in a state of health that worried his family. Although he insisted that "Anna used no influence," he also realized that he must "satisfy not only her feelings but her tastes," and when she came north in June, he proposed to her again with the full understanding that he was to provide material as well as spiritual comfort.[1] To this end Anna's father promised Ward a position in his banking firm. The engagement was formally announced, and Ward's father prepared a house on fashionable Louisburg Square in Boston for the young couple to live in after their October marriage.

Another woman in Ward's life was Margaret Fuller, whom he had first met in 1835. Although she did not immediately like him,[2] Ward took to her at once. And, when she moved to Boston in 1835, Ward wrote from London to tell his sister that *"by all means"* she should try to take lessons from Fuller, "a most delightful acquaintance and with a universality of knowledge." They corresponded, and he gratefully followed her guidance in his literary and artistic pursuits.[3] However, Fuller wished an emotional as well as an intellectual involvement, and Ward's engagement to Anna Barker both stunned and angered her.[4] Having known Anna for many years, Fuller was especially hurt because she thought Ward had chosen beauty over intelligence.[5] Even worse to her was his choosing the "dead wood" of a banker's desk as his profession.[6]

It was through Fuller that Ward met Ralph Waldo Emerson. After hearing him lecture in Boston Ward asked her for an introduction, and the two met for the first time in the summer of 1838. In October of the following year Ward introduced Emerson to Anna.[7] By 1840 the two were well on the way to a large correspondence, and Emerson found Ward "beautiful" to him among the "many ordinary & mediocre youths" of his acquaintance.[8]

Fuller also introduced Ward to Caroline Sturgis and Ellen Hooper, and their mutual friendship with Ellery Channing assured frequent meetings and letters.[9] Another uniting force was the *Dial*. Fuller would often copy Ward's poems for Sturgis to see, and from her supply of them she chose four to include in the *Dial's* first number. The *New-Yorker* thought well enough of his sonnet on Washington Allston to reprint it, and James Clarke especially asked about "The Shield."[10]

Ward's approaching marriage eclipsed any further literary activity, and he was absent from the October 1840 number. On the third of that month he married Anna: Emerson wrote a letter of congratulations[11] and Elizabeth Peabody, a friend of Anna's, thought Ward *"blest"* by having married her.[12] The capricious Channing, whose poetry Ward had shown to Emerson, bitterly lamented the marriage, complaining that now Ward should have "no place or need for him" in his affections.[13] Fuller remained silent.

Although Ward contributed a paper on Italian literature to the next *Dial*, his marriage and entrance into the business world soon took up all his time.[14] A friend's observation that Ward was "very well sewed up" in business was only too true.[15] Emerson still praised Ward as "a beautiful & noble youth of a most subtle & magnetic nature, made for an artist," but he noted: "For the present, he buys & sells."[16]

Ward bought and sold well enough to accumulate the beginnings of a good-sized fortune. The money not only brought the Wards material happiness but was also spent on friends, in such acts as Ward's backing of Channing's poems for publication. As Ward moved closer to relative financial independence, he again picked up his pen, and by September 1842 he had sent some pieces on art to Emerson for the *Dial*. But when Emerson told Sarah Clarke and Ellen Hooper who the author of the essays was, Ward withdrew most of them, leaving only one, "The Gallery," for the October number.[17] Ward apparently wanted most of the unfinished pieces back to revise, now that he knew that others were aware of his authorship. At any rate, Emerson was sure that he would publish the essays, for he put an "editorial muzzle" on himself, and he warned the others to preserve Ward's anonymity. To the letter of "warning" Emerson playfully added that, if they kept Ward's secret, "as many as six or seven subscribers to the Dial shall be kept in profound ignorance of our secret, & who knows but that the next Number may record the death of subscribers whom curiosity has burst."[18]

Ward wrote Emerson again in April 1843 about the article, and in May the *Dial*'s editor thanked him for the "good news" that he would again write for the magazine. When Emerson received Ward's "papers on art, &c" at the beginning of June, they were still unfinished, and he suggested that if Ward did not want to complete them they could be printed as "sketches." Thus Emerson, who had told Thoreau that the "good sense" of the pieces was "eminent," printed them in the July 1843 *Dial* as "Notes on Art and Architecture." For many readers the unfinished form of the "notes" did not detract from their value. Sophia Ripley praised their "sense & practical American talent," which were in a rare union with "taste & knowledge." Their "strength and sense" made Fuller "proud" as she reread them with Sarah Clarke.[19]

Ward's plan to "write on poetry" for the January 1844 *Dial* resulted in a review of a new translation of Dante.[20] To the *Dial*'s last number he contributed two poems, one of which, "The Consolers," may be a comment on his relations with Emerson.[21] In June 1844 the Wards left for Lenox, Massachusetts, since their personal worth of $35,000 now allowed them to live and work in the country for a while. Had the *Dial* continued longer, it is quite possible that Ward would have contributed more.

39

Charles Stearns Wheeler

Charles Stearns Wheeler, who contributed two letters of foreign intelligence to the *Dial*, was the most promising of the young contributors to the magazine. Even Henry Thoreau did not show the early promise that Wheeler had for writing and publishing. Wheeler's death in 1843 cut short this promise and left the pieces in the *Dial* his most lasting memorial.

Wheeler was born on 19 December 1816 at Lincoln, Massachusetts, near Concord. At fourteen he was attending school in Lincoln winters and spending summers at Phineas Allen's Concord Academy. In 1833 Wheeler and Thoreau were the only two students from their class whom Allen recommended for Harvard, and in August the two enrolled as roommates.

Wheeler's four years at Harvard were well spent. At seventeen he was older than most of the undergraduates and approached college with somewhat more seriousness. He made many important friends: over half of the Harvard-educated contributors to the *Dial* were in Cambridge at that time. Along with James Russell Lowell he became a charter member of Alpha Delta Phi, a secret fraternity. Wheeler financed his last two years by helping Jared Sparks on his *Library of American Biography*. Other jobs of teaching, editing, copying, and index-making earned him $600, a large sum in the 1830s.

A "quiet, teachable, and studious boy, a very diligent and patient student, and a great reader," Wheeler did well academically.[1] He coedited the undergraduate magazine *Harvardiana*, was elected to Phi Beta Kappa, and won the Bowdoin Prize in his senior year with an essay on "What Reasons Are There for Not Expecting Another Great Epic Poem?" He was graduated in 1837 with second honors.

That summer Wheeler taught a boys' school before returning in the fall as a resident graduate. He liked the intellectual atmosphere at Harvard and soon became engaged in a number of important projects.[2] As a copier and proofreader for the Cambridge printing firm of Metcalf, Torry, and Ballou, Wheeler helped LeBarron Russell and Ralph Waldo Emerson edit the American editon of Thomas Carlyle's *Sartor Resartus* in 1836. He also helped Emerson edit Carlyle's *French Revolution* and *Critical and Miscellaneous Essays* during the following two years. On his own, Wheeler edited the *Critical and Miscellaneous Essays* of Thomas Macaulay and, after writing for his permission, introduced Alfred Tennyson to America when he edited his *Poems* in 1842. In the same year he prepared an annotated edition of Herodotus that was adopted for classroom use at Harvard. An appointment as Greek tutor in 1838 to replace Jones Very

Charles Stearns Wheeler.

University of Georgia Press.

was enhanced by an instructorship in history the following year. Wheeler started giving teas in his room, and Emerson was glad to attend, for after his Divinity School Address the latter had received few invitations to come to Harvard. Soon Wheeler was becoming known as a member of the Transcendental circle.[3]

Wheeler made many acquaintances during this period and seems to have left a favorable impression on all of them. He often lent books to Margaret Fuller, and Theodore Parker respected him. Even though he had replaced Very, the two remained friends; Very often read his sonnets to him, and Wheeler helped Very sell his *Essays and Poems*. Emerson greatly appreciated him, both personally and for his help with the editions of Carlyle. But Wheeler's best friend was his old roommate, Thoreau, who liked Wheeler's "patient industry and energy—his reverent love of letters—and his proverbial accuracy." Wheeler had built a shanty at Flint's Pond—a mile east of Walden Pond—for "the purpose of economy," and Ellery Channing believed that Thoreau's visits there probably had a great deal to do with shaping his Walden sojourn.[4] Thoreau arranged for Wheeler to lecture before the Concord Lyceum, and when Thoreau briefly returned to Cambridge in late 1841 he again roomed with Wheeler.[5]

By 1842 Wheeler had saved enough money to realize his greatest ambition: a trip to Europe. After arranging his affairs, which included leaving Lowell in charge of Tennyson's interests, Wheeler went to Concord to say farewell to Emerson before he sailed on 8 August.[6] He arrived in Heidelberg, Germany, on 22 September and roomed with John Weiss while they studied at the university. In March they left for Göttingen and joined J. F. Heath and James Elliot Cabot in attending the lectures there.

European life agreed with Wheeler, though he did have some minor complaints. He soon discovered that the Germans assumed that a visiting American must by definition be rich, and he wrote home to warn others to wear old clothes in order to keep the beggars away and to get everything at a cheaper price. Wheeler also had trouble in obtaining copies of the *Dial*, and he told Emerson to give copies for him to "any youngster coming out to Germany," since it was too expensive to mail the entire number. The problem was partially solved by having Robert Bartlett occasionally "steal sheets" for Wheeler and send them on. Emerson helped out by mailing copies to Wheeler at his own expense.[7]

One reason why Emerson tried so hard to get the *Dial* to Wheeler was that he had become a valued contributor to the magazine. He had arranged with Wheeler in March to send letters of "foreign intelligence" for the *Dial*, and Wheeler had mailed Emerson his first batch of news in his letter of 20-23 October 1842.[8] Wheeler also was approached for contributions to the *Pioneer* when Lowell, as editor, had written him on 14 October.[9] Lowell's letter arrived after he had sent his first letter to Emerson for the *Dial*, and Wheeler replied that he would be "most happy to contribute." Although mentioning his promise to do the same thing for the *Dial*, Wheeler repeated many of the things he had told Emerson about, plus "a few facts which I have learned since," and instructed Lowell to make his peace with Emerson about using them.[10] Three days later Wheeler wrote another letter to Emerson to make his "conscience clear" by explaining the arrangement with Lowell, reassuring Emerson that Lowell would "knock into pi" Wheeler's intelligence if Emerson said the word to him.[11]

Emerson was happy with the "capital report" he received.[12] He told Wheeler of his contentment, adding that Henry Hedge had translated the introductory lecture of Friedrich Schelling that he had sent in October, and that all would appear in the January *Dial*. The situation with the *Pioneer* was also under control. Lowell, who had received another letter from Wheeler reminding him that the *Dial* had first choice, went to see Emerson about the matter, and, when Emerson told him not to use Wheeler's "intelligence," Lowell "behaved very magnanimously" and was content that the *Dial* "should publish all" and the *Pioneer* none. Accordingly, Emerson took Wheeler's letters of 20-23 October and 11 November 1842 and, upon Bartlett's suggestion, used parts of Wheeler's letters to him in putting together the "intelligence" that was printed in the January 1843 *Dial*.[13]

In January Wheeler sent a long letter to Emerson concerning recent events in Germany and enclosed an account of religious censorship in Prussia "on which text Parker or some other champion of freedom will perhaps be able to preach a sermon." Wheeler also expressed surprise at the "great importance" that Emerson had placed on his "intelligence." At the same time Wheeler sent some more "intelligence" to the *Pioneer* and repeated his warning to Lowell to check with Emerson first about using it.

Thoreau, who was editing the *Dial* in Emerson's absence, received Wheeler's letter at the end of February and prepared it for the press. He was, therefore, surprised when the March 1843 issue of the *Pioneer* also carried "intelligence" by Wheeler. Emerson also was surprised, for most of Wheeler's letter there was the same one that Lowell had promised not to print when he had seen Emerson in December. As Lowell was in New York recovering from an eye operation when the March issue of the *Pioneer* went to the printer, the piece had been inserted by his coeditor Robert Carter without Lowell's knowledge. Emerson knew that Lowell would not have broken his promise and certainly would not have written the *Pioneer*'s cutting introduction to the piece as "having appeared in a quarterly magazine of limited circulation," and he did not blame Lowell for the error.[14]

At the end of April Emerson wrote Wheeler a letter of thanks for his contributions, unaware that soon after leaving Göttingen for Leipzig Wheeler had become ill. Three weeks after his arrival Wheeler had been confined to bed with a violent "gastric fever," and Heath was called in to attend him. Although he gave encouragement to Wheeler's family, Heath confided his worst fears to Cabot: "I think it impossible that he can live. . . .The physicians. . . have given me to understand that they have no hope scarcely of a recovery . . . This morning there are symptoms of their worst fears being realized—that is, of the disease passing into a consumptive fever." Wheeler's condition worsened, and he died on 13 June 1843.

Emerson, when he heard the news, mourned the loss of "so much ingenuousness, perserverance, & generosity of mind." Thoreau was deeply moved by Wheeler's death, which "left a gap in the community not easy to be filled," and he felt both a sense of loss and of inspiration: "The literary enterprises he was planning for himself and friends remind one of an older and more studious time—so much more then remains for us to do who survive."[15]

40

William Dexter Wilson

William Dexter Wilson, like many of the contributors of the *Dial* who had ties to the Unitarian church, went through a period of religious doubt during the late 1830s and early 1840s. However, he was unique among that group in that he resolved his difficulties by converting to the Episcopal faith.

Wilson was born at Stoddard, New Hampshire, on 28 February 1816 and was educated at the Walpole (New Hampshire) Academy. After his graduation in 1831 he stayed on there for four years as a mathematics teacher. Following his graduation from Harvard Divinity School in 1838, he studied languages and became an unsettled preacher. By April 1842 he had become an Episcopalian, and later in that year he began his long settlement in Sherburne, New York, as minister to the church there. He was apparently unmarried.

Wilson's contributions to the *Dial* were made through Ralph Waldo Emerson. The two had probably first met at a Transcendental Club meeting, and in February 1838 Wilson thanked Emerson for the "profit & pleasure" he had received from attending his lectures in Boston. The next month Wilson was one of three divinity school students who invited Emerson to deliver an address to that year's graduating class. Emerson accepted with pleasure, and on 15 July 1838 he gave his famous Divinity School Address. In the days following the occasion Wilson reported back to Emerson that, while some of the class had disagreed with his views, they all thanked him for speaking to them, and he arranged with Emerson for the printing of the address.[1]

Wilson's generally favorable review in July 1840 of Théodore Jouffroy's *Introduction to Ethics*, which Henry Channing had translated for George Ripley's *Specimens of Foreign Standard Literature* series, was the result of the study of German he had undertaken since leaving Cambridge. His thirty-five-page article on "The Unitarian Movement in New England" in April 1841 was also a product of these years, and into it he poured his own growing religious doubts. In effect spelling out the reasons why he would eventually leave the faith, Wilson called Unitarianism barren and lifeless and warned that its future hopes depended on the reform elements within it remaining active. Most of the article traced the philosophical and theological roots of Unitarianism, and it was this part that impressed most readers. Few agreed with Henry Bellows that it was "very crude," and in England William Forster thought it a "striking and most powerful article." James Murdock, in writing a book on contemporary philosophy, quoted extensively from Wilson's piece in his chapter on Unitarianism, and he referred his readers to it as "an elaborate and highly interesting article."[2]

Although Wilson later published many philosophical works, during the early 1840s he was involved in writing a study of the Episcopal church. Both the subject and the time spent upon it, and his distance from Boston, probably stopped him from any further work for the *Dial*.[3]

Notes

The following abbreviations are used throughout the Notes:

ABA   Amos Bronson Alcott

AL   *American Literature*

AlcAuInd   A. Bronson Alcott, "Autobiographical Index," Houghton Library, Harvard University.

AlcDiJaJn39   A. Bronson Alcott, "Diary January-June 1839," Houghton Library, Harvard University.

AlcDiJyDec39   A. Bronson Alcott, "Diary July-December 1839," Houghton Library, Harvard University.

AlcJ38   A. Bronson Alcott, "Journal for 1838," Houghton Library, Harvard University.

AlcL   A. Bronson Alcott, *The Letters of A. Bronson Alcott,* ed. Richard L. Herrnstadt (Ames, Iowa: Iowa State University Press, 1969).

AlcSc40   Joel Myerson, "Bronson Alcott's 'Scripture for 1840,' " *ESQ: A Journal of the American Renaissance* 20 (IV Quarter 1974): 236-59.

BAL   Jacob Blanck, comp., *Bibliography of American Literature,* 6 vols. to date (New Haven, Conn.: Yale University Press, 1955-).

Bo   Boston, Massachusetts

CCS   Scripps College Library

CKN   Charles King Newcomb

CPC   Christopher Pearse Cranch

CS   Caroline Sturgis

CSW   Charles Stearns Wheeler

CSmH   Henry E. Huntington Library, San Marino, California

ClAuDiCor   James Freeman Clarke, *Autobiography, Diary and Correspondence* ed. Edward Everett Hale (Boston: Houghton, Mifflin, 1891).

ClLetMF   James Freeman Clarke, *The Letters of James Freeman*

	Clarke to Margaret Fuller, ed. John Wesley Thomas (Hamburg: Cram, de Gruyter, 1957).
ClLetSister	Sarah Clarke, "Letters of a Sister," proof sheets, Houghton Library, Harvard University.
CoHiBi	George Willis Cooke, *An Historical and Biographical Introduction to Accompany* The Dial, 2 vols. (Cleveland: The Rowfant Club, 1902).
CtY	Yale University Library, New Haven, Connecticut
CuEarlyLetDw	George William Curtis, *Early Letters of George Wm. Curtis to John S. Dwight: Brook Farm and Concord*, ed. George Willis Cooke (New York: Harper's, 1898).
DLC	Library of Congress, Washington, D.C.
EH	Elizabeth Hoar
EPP	Elizabeth Palmer Peabody
ESQ	*Emerson Society Quarterly*
EmCorTC	Ralph Waldo Emerson, *The Correspondence of Emerson and Carlyle*, ed. Joseph Slater (New York: Columbia University Press, 1964).
EmJ	Ralph Waldo Emerson, *The Journals of Ralph Waldo Emerson*, ed. Edward Waldo Emerson and Waldo Emerson Forbes, 10 vols. (Boston: Houghton Mifflin, 1909-14).
EmJMN	Ralph Waldo Emerson, *The Journals and Miscellaneous Notebooks of Ralph Waldo Emerson,* ed. William H. Gilman et al, 14 vols. to date (Cambridge, Mass.: Harvard University Press, 1960 -).
EmL	Ralph Waldo Emerson, *The Letters of Ralph Waldo Emerson*, ed. Ralph L. Rusk, 6 vols. (New York: Columbia University Press, 1939).
EmRecLiFr	Ralph Waldo Emerson, *Records of a Lifelong Friendship, 1807-1882: Ralph Waldo Emerson and William Henry Furness,* ed. H[orace]. H[oward]. F[urness]. (Boston: Houghton Mifflin, 1910).
EmW	Ralph Waldo Emerson, *The Complete Works of Ralph Waldo Emerson,* ed. Edward Waldo Emerson, The Centenary Edition, 12 vols. (Boston: Houghton Mifflin, 1903-4).
FHH	Frederic Henry Hedge
FrWHC	Octavius Brooks Frothingham, *Memoir of William Henry Channing* (Boston: Houghton, Mifflin, 1886).
FuJ42	Joel Myerson, "Margaret Fuller's 1842 Journal: At Concord with the Emersons," *Harvard Library Bulletin* 21 (July 1973):320-40.
FuNbD	Margaret Fuller, "Notebook for the *Dial*," Houghton Library, Harvard University.

FuW	Margaret Fuller, "Works," copies of her manuscripts, Houghton Library, Harvard University.
GR	George Ripley
HDT	Henry David Thoreau
HawAmNb	Nathaniel Hawthorne, *The American Notebooks,* ed. Claude M. Simpson (Columbus, Ohio: Ohio State University Press, 1972).
HigMF	Thomas Wentworth Higginson, *Margaret Fuller Ossoli* (Boston: Houghton, Mifflin, 1884).
HoMif	Houghton Mifflin Publishers
ICM	Meadville Theological School Library, Chicago, Illinois
ICN	The Newberry Library, Chicago, Illinois
ICU	University of Chicago Library, Chicago, Illinois
InNd	University of Notre Dame Library, Notre Dame, Indiana
JFC	James Freeman Clarke
JRL	James Russell Lowell
JSD	John Sullivan Dwight
LMC	Lydia Maria Child
LU	Louisiana State University Library, Baton Rouge, Louisiana
LdE	Lidian Emerson
Lo	London, England
MB	Boston Public Library, Boston, Massachusetts
MBG	Isabelle Stuart Gardner Museum, Boston, Massachusetts
MBilHi	Billerica Historical Society, Billerica, Massachusetts
MCR-S	The Arthur and Elizabeth Schlesinger Library on the History of Women in America, Radcliffe College, Cambridge, Massachusetts
MH	Harvard University Libraries (mainly the Houghton Library), Cambridge, Massachusetts
MHarF	Fruitlands Museums, Harvard, Massachusetts
MHi	Massachusetts Historical Society Library, Boston, Massachusetts
MSaE	Essex Institute Library, Salem, Massachusetts
MWelC	Wellesley College Library, Wellesley, Massachusetts
MeBa	Bangor Public Library (collection of the Bangor Historical Society), Bangor, Maine
MemMF	Ralph Waldo Emerson, William Henry Channing, and James Freeman Clarke, *Memoirs of Margaret Fuller Ossoli*, 2 vols. (Boston: Phillips, Sampson, 1852).
NBu	Buffalo and Erie County Public Library, Buffalo, New York.
NEQ	*New England Quarterly*
NIC	Cornell University Library, Ithaca, New York
NN-B	New York Public Library (Henry W. and Albert A. Berg

	Collection), New York City, New York
NN-M	New York Public Library (Manuscripts Division), New York City, New York
NNPM	The Pierpont Morgan Library, New York City, New York
NNU	New York University Library, New York City, New York
NPV	Vassar College Library, Poughkeepsie, New York
NRU	University of Rochester Library, Rochester, New York
NY	New York City, New York
NjP	Princeton University Library, Princeton, New Jersey
PkJ	Theodore Parker, "Journal" (vols. 1 and 2), Andover-Harvard Theological School Library, Cambridge, Massachusetts
RNR	Redwood Library and Athenæum, Newport, Rhode Island
RPB	Brown University Library, Providence, Rhode Island
RWE	Ralph Waldo Emerson
RuLiEm	Ralph L. Rusk, *The Life of Ralph Waldo Emerson* (New York: Scribner's, 1949).
SC	Sarah Clarke
SGW	Samuel Gray Ward
SR	Sophia Ripley
SaHaABA	F. B. Sanborn and William T. Harris, *A. Bronson Alcott: His Life and Philosophy,* 2 vols. (Boston: Roberts, 1893).
SaRec	F. B. Sanborn, *Recollections of Seventy Years,* 2 vols. (Boston: Richard G. Badger, 1909).
ScLiLetCPC	Leonora Cranch Scott, *The Life and Letters of Christopher Pearse Cranch* (Boston: Houghton Mifflin, 1917).
TC	Thomas Carlyle
TP	Theodore Parker
ThCor	Henry David Thoreau, *The Correspondence of Henry David Thoreau,* ed. Walter Harding and Carl Bode (New York: New York University Press, 1958).
ThJ	Henry David Thoreau, *Journal,* ed. Bradford Torrey and Francis H. Allen, vols. 7-20 of *The Writings of Henry David Thoreau,* The Walden Edition, 20 vols. (Boston: Houghton Mifflin, 1906).
TxU	University of Texas Library, Austin, Texas
ViU-B	University of Virginia Library (Clifton Waller Barrett Library), Charlottesville, Virginia
WHC	William Henry Channing
WmE	William Emerson

Introduction

1. Frank Luther Mott, *A History of American Magazines 1741-1850* (Cambridge, Mass.: Harvard University Press, 1957 [1939]), p. 368.

2. JRL to G. W. Cooke, 30 Nov. 1885, MHarF; see also "The Transcendental Club and the Dial," Boston *Commonwealth*, 24 Apr. 1863, p. 1; TP, *Experience as a Minister* (Bo: Rufus Leighton, 1859), p. 58; "Music a Means of Culture," *Atlantic Monthly* 26 (Sept. 1870):323; "Editor's Easy Chair," *Harper's New Monthly Magazine* 43 (Nov. 1871):930; "The Destinies of Ecclesiastical Religion," *Christian Examiner* 82 (Jan. 1867):13; "Memoir of Ralph Waldo Emerson," *Proceedings of the Massachusetts Historical Society*, 2d ser., 2 (June 1885):114; JFC, *Epochs and Events in Religious History* (Bo: Osgood, 1883), pp. 295-96; RWE to W. B. Greene, ca. 5[?] July[?], in *EmL*, 6:244; and "Historic Notes of Life and Letters in New England," in *EmW* 10:343-44 (written in 1867).

3. RWE to Chapman, 30 Mar. 1845, in *EmL*, 3:288; see also Duyckinck to RWE, 13 Aug. 1845, RWE to Duyckinck, 25 Aug. and 5 Sept. 1845, and Duyckinck to RWE, 20 Sept. 1845, in ibid., pp. 297n, 297, 301; MH (Landor) Duyckinck to RWE, 2 Oct. 1845, in *EML*, 3:308n; John Chapman, "Preface," in *Characteristics of Men of Genius* (Bo: Otis, Broaders; Lo: John Chapman, 1847), 1:ii; 29, 31 Dec. 1846, Sterling Library, Univ. of London.

4. *American Whig Review* 1 (Apr. 1845):370; *Broadway Journal* 2 (12 July 1845):2; "Tale-Writing—Nathaniel Hawthorne," *Godey's Lady's Book* 35 (Nov. 1845):256; Nathaniel Hawthorne, *The Centenary Edition of the Works of Nathaniel Hawthorne*, ed. William Charvat et al. (Columbus, Ohio: Ohio State University Press, 1964), 3:52; Howard Vincent, *The Trying-Out of "Moby-Dick"* (Bo: HoMif, 1949), p. 259n; Herman Melville, *The Writings of Herman Melville*, ed. Harrison Hayford et al. (Evanston, Ill.: Northwestern University Press, 1971), 7:280; *Independent* 25 (18 Dec. 1873):1569.

5. Raymond L. Kilgour, *Messrs. Roberts Brothers Publishers* (Ann Arbor, Mich.: University of Michigan Press, 1952), pp. 132, 198; "Prospectus" dated 1 June 1882, reprinted in "A Reprint of 'The Dial,'" *Journal of Speculative Philosophy* 16 (July 1882):329-30; Kilgour, *Roberts Brothers*, p. 198. The Rowfant Club's edition is truly a collector's item—the *Dial* was reprinted in numbers, each of which was boxed, as were the two volumes of Cooke's study. And, strangely, the 1961 photo-offset reprint by Russell & Russell of New York used the Rowfant Club's edition, rather than the original, to copy from.

Chapter 1: The Transcendental Club and the *Dial*

1. "The Celebration at Cambridge," *Boston Courier*, 10 Sept. 1836, in Kenneth Walter Cameron, *Companion to Thoreau's Correspondence* (Hartford, Conn.: Transcendental Books, 1964), pp. 163-66; CoHiBi, 1:48 (Willard's); RWE to FHH, 20 July 1836, in *EmL*, 2:29; 14 June 1836, in Joel Myerson, "Frederic Henry Hedge and the Failure of Transcendentalism," *Harvard Library Bulletin* 23 (Oct. 1975):400-401.

2. *SaRec*, 2:445 (Concord); *ClLetMF*, p. 7.

3. FHH to Cabot, n.d., in James Elliot Cabot, *A Memoir of Ralph Waldo Emerson* (Bo: HoMif, 1887), 1:244-45. Because Hedge had invited only ministers, Bronson Alcott, though in Cambridge for the celebration, was not permitted to attend. Emerson had tried unsuccessfully to convince Hedge to change his mind, urging him to overlook "the professional limits" and to admit Alcott, "a God-made priest" (20 July 1836, in *EmL*, 2:29).

4. The Boston public was very suspicious of Alcott's educational reforms, since his desire to discuss all subjects, including religion and sex, was not shared by his contemporaries. He also treated children as intelligent human beings, feeling it was his job to draw out their natural genius rather than to instill a rote education, and, accordingly, he rarely used the then-popular method of corporal punishment. As Alcott described it, "Our life is to be devoted to the amelioration of our

fellow beings, in attempts to establish the reign of truth and reason — and arrange society — our systems of education — in accordance with the laws of our nature, as we find it in its incipient state." Others saw this philosophy in a different light. Harriet Martineau, after visiting Alcott's school, was left with the impression that he was doing mischief to his pupils "by relaxing their bodies, [and] pampering their imaginations. . . .His system can be beneficial to none, and must be ruinous to many" (14 June [1828], in ABA, "Journal for 1828," p. 271, MH: Harriet Martineau, *Society in America* [NY: Saunders and Otley, 1837], 2:278).

5. When Charles Lane once asked Brownson to list the "profoundest men in America," Brownson unhesitatingly named himself as one. Emerson characterized him thus: "Brownson never will stop & listen, neither in conversation but what is more, not in solitude" (late Oct. 1842, in *EmJMN*, 8:305).

6. Once, when a lady complained to Francis about Emerson's "insanity," he indignantly replied, "Madam, I wish I were half as sane." He thought that the Transcendentalists in general "will be laughed at, perhaps, for things that will appear visionary and crude," but eventually "the great cause of spiritual truth will gain far more by them than by the others" (Mrs. Sarah Ripley to Mary Moody Emerson, 4 Sept. 1833, in [Elizabeth Hoar], *Mrs. Samuel Ripley* [Philadelphia: J. B. Lippincott, 1855], p. 51; journal entry, 1836, in John Weiss, *Discourse Occasioned by the Death of Convers Francis* [Cambridge, Mass.: Privately printed, 1863], p. 29).

7. 11 Sept. 1836, in Joel Myerson, "Bronson's Alcott's 'Journal for 1836,' " in *Studies in the American Renaissance 1978*, ed. Joel Myerson (Bo: Twayne, 1978), p. 72; 20 Sept. 1836, *EmJMN*, 5:195; ABA, "The Transcendental Club and the Dial," Boston *Commonwealth*, 24 Apr. 1863, p. 1 ("silent"); 20 Sept. 1836, in *EmJMN*, 5:194-95; FHH to Cabot, n.d., in James Elliot Cabot, *A Memoir of Ralph Waldo Emerson*, 1:245 (journal); RWE to MF, 20 Sept. 1836, in *EmL*, 2:37; 19 Sept. 1836 in Myerson, "Alcott's 'Journal for 1836,' " p. 77.

8. 3 Oct. 1836, in Myerson, "Alcott's 'Journal for 1836,' " p. 80; 3 Oct. 1836, in Joel Myerson, "Convers Francis and Emerson," *AL* 50 (Mar. 1978):23; *EmJMN*, 5:218; 3 Oct. 1836, in Myerson, "Alcott's 'Journal for 1836,' " p. 80. A list of those who attended each meeting, as well as a complete enumeration of all known Transcendental Club gatherings, will be found in Joel Myerson, "A Calendar of Transcendental Club Meetings," *AL* 44 (May 1972):197-207.

9. ABA to RWE, 9 May 1837, in *AlcL*, p. 32 (re-assemble); Week 21, May 1837, in ABA, "Journal for 1837," pp. 381-82, MH; 24 May 1837, in *AlcL*, p. 33.

10. 30 May 1837, in *EmJMN*, 5:338. "Symposeum" (Alcott's spelling), "Transcendental Club," and "Hedge's Club" were used interchangeably in describing this group. I have chosen to use the most common designation, "Transcendental Club," throughout this book.

11. 29 May 1837, in Myerson, "Francis and Emerson," 24; Henry F. Brownson, *Orestes A. Brownson's Early Life: From 1803 to 1844* (Detroit, Mich.: H. F. Brownson, 1898), p. 308; RWE to MF, 30 May 1837 in *EmL*, 2:78.

12. Quoted in Odell Shepard, *Pedlar's Progress: The Life of Bronson Alcott* (Bo: Little, Brown, 1937), pp. 194-95; William Charvat, *Emerson's American Lecture Engagements* (NY: New York Public Library, 1961), p. 16 (unless otherwise noted, all references to dates, places, and titles of Emerson's lectures are from this source); W. V., "Opening of the Greene-St. School," *Providence Daily Journal*, 17 June 1837, p. 2; 27 June 1837, in Annie Russell Marble, "Margaret Fuller as Teacher," *Critic* 43 (Oct. 1903):340.

13. Quoted in Madeleine B. Stern, *The Life of Margaret Fuller* (NY: Dutton, 1942), p. 153. Holmes later denied saying this (see Moncure Daniel Conway, *Autobiography, Memories, and Experiences* [Bo: HoMif, 1904], 1:384).

14. Perry Miller, ed., *The Transcendentalists: An Anthology* (Cambridge, Mass.: Harvard University Press, 1950), p. 189; "Emerson," in ibid., p. 432-33.

15. "Oration on Genius" and "Observations on the Growth of the Mind," in ibid., pp. 49-59.

16. "Likeness to God," in ibid., p. 23; "Remarks on the Four Gospels," in ibid., pp. 124-29; "Dudleian Lecture," in ibid., p. 158; "The New School in Literature and Religion," in ibid., pp. 193-96; "Emerson's Nature," in ibid., pp. 173-76; "To Andrews Norton" and "The Latest Form of Infidelity Examined," in ibid., pp. 160-63, 213-20; "Francis Bowen," in ibid., pp. 183-86; "A Discourse on the Transient and Permanent in Christianity," in ibid., pp. 271, 272.

17. RWE to MF, 17 Aug. 1837, in *EmL*, 2:95; 13 Sept. 1837, in *EmJMN*, 5:373. Lidian Emerson

felt herself to be "honoured with the opportunity of administering to the earthly comfort of the whole transcendental coterie," and believed that her "all-day party," which seated eighteen at the dining table, went off "very satisfactorily" (LdE to EPP, 22 Aug. 1837, MH: LdE to Lucy Brown, 2 Sept. 1837, MH).

18. At age fifteen she read literary and philosophical works in three foreign languages during a day that lasted from five in the morning until eleven at night. The only break in this routine was the few hours reserved for walking, singing, and playing the piano. Fuller remembered her childhood as an unhappy one: "I was sent to bed several hours too late, with nerves unnaturally stimulated. The consequence was a premature development of the brain, that made me a 'youthful prodigy' by day, and by night the victim of spectral illusions, nightmare, and somnambulism" (*HigMF*, pp. 23-24; *MemMF*, 1:15).

19. *MemMF*, 1:236. Fuller used to tell her friends, "I now know all the people worth knowing in America, and I find no intellect comparable to my own." So well known was her opinion of herself that years later Oscar Wilde could say that when she wrote an essay on Emerson, the printer had to send out for extra cases of capital "I"'s. Sometimes even she realized the dangers of her egotism: "God forbid that any one should conceive more highly of me than I myself" (*MemMF*, 1:234; "Mr. Pater's Last Volume," *Speaker* 1 [22 Mar. 1890]:319-20; quoted in Mason Wade, *Margaret Fuller: Whetstone of Genius* [NY: Viking, 1940], p. 94).

20. MF to Almira Barlow, 6 Oct. 1834, in *FuW*, 1:17; MF to FHH, 1 Feb. 1835, MH; *MemMF*, 1:202; 12 Aug. 1836, in *EmJMN*, 5:188; 13 Aug. 1836, in ibid., 5:190 (egotism); 4 May 1837, in ibid., 5:319; Emerson endorsed Fuller's letter of 30 May 1837 with: "What shocking familiarity" (Harry R. Warfel, "Margaret Fuller and Ralph Waldo Emerson," PMLA 50 [June 1935]:582).

21. 6 Sept. 1837, in *EmJMN*, 5:375; Charles Godfrey Leland, *Memoirs* (NY: Appleton, 1893), p. 77; 6 Oct. 1836, in *EmJMN*, 5:218 (Barlow); Week 4, Jan. 1838, in *AlcJ38*, p. 81.

22. Of course, the Transcendentalists did little to help their own cause and quite innocently provided their detractors with ammunition. Alcott's "Orphic Sayings" acted as a lightning rod in drawing down ridicule upon the *Dial*, and an attempt to be objective about Brook Farm can easily be shattered when one is asked at dinner, "Is the butter within the sphere of your influence?" As late as 1844, when Samuel Longfellow thought of sending a friend's son to Brook Farm for schooling, he inquired of Dwight: "Would a boy of fourteen necessarily imbibe any *very wild* notions, such as are so conveniently classed under the *opprobrious epithet* Transcendental?" (Lindsay Swift, *Brook Farm* [NY: Macmillan, 1900], p. 57; 19 Feb. 1844, MB).

23. Weeks 18-21, May 1838, in *AlcJ38*, pp. 251-54; TP to George E. Ellis, 27 May 1838, MHi.

24. RWE to ABA, 28 June 1838, in *EmL*, 2:138-41. Emerson complained of its generalities, its "prophetic pretension," and the archaic language it employed, much as later reviewers would do to Alcott's "Orphic Sayings."

25. The best discussions of this controversy are in Miller, *The Transcendentalists*; William R. Hutchison, *The Transcendentalist Ministers* (New Haven, Conn.: Yale University Press, 1957), pp. 64ff; and Charles Crowe, *George Ripley* (Athens, Ga.: University of Georgia Press, 1967), pp. 97-123.

26. Week 48, Nov. 1838, in *AlcJ38*, pp. 411-12.

27. Parker also wrote this in his journal: "When examined to the Bottom is [Alcott] anything more than a very spiritual & highly religious Dogmatist" (ca. 15 Nov. 1838, in *PkJ*, 1:74-75).

28. Week 48, Nov. 1838, in *AlcJ38*, pp. 412-13.

29. Week 49, Dec. 1838, in ibid., pp. 427-28.

30. Alcott, whose very nature demanded that he be a major participant in any conversation, somewhat stifled a more general involvement in the discussion by his overbearing presence. He recognized that more often than not there was "monologue rather than dialogue," but he gave this reason: "Indeed, it has come to this, that I am ⟨to⟩ ⟨expected to⟩ ↑ relied on for ↓ most of the talking" (8 May 1839), in *AlcDiJaJn39*, p. 747). Angle brackets (⟨ ⟩) indicate cancellations in the manuscript, arrows (↑ ↓) insertions.

31. 9 May 1839, in *PkJ*, 1:144; 8 May 1839, in *AlcDiJaJn39*, pp. 745-48; 10 May 1839, in *EmJMN*, 7:194.

32. Editors' statement, in *EmJ*, 5:202; Francis to TP, 24 May 1839, in Clarence L. F. Gohdes, *The*

Periodicals of American Transcendentalism (Durham, N.C.: Duke University Press, 1931), p. 223; 22 May 1839, in *AlcDiJaJn39*, pp. 803-6; Francis to TP, 24 May 1839, in Gohdes, *Periodicals*, p. 223.

33. JSD to ABA, 12 Sept. 1839, copy by ABA, in *AlcDiJyDec39*, p. 239; 16 Sept. 1839, in *PkJ*, 1:232; 16 Sept. 1839, in *AlcDiJyDec39*, p. 242.

34. 18 Sept. 1839, in *AlcDiJyDec39*, p. 249; 18 Sept. 1839, in *PkJ*, 1:232; Feb. 1840, in *AlcSc40*, p. 242.

35. 12 Mar. 1839, in *AlcDiJaJn39*, p. 464; Hawthorne to Longfellow, 12 Jan. 1839 in Samuel Longfellow, *Life of Henry Wadsworth Longfellow* (Bo: Ticknor, 1886), 1:312; Edward Everett Hale, *James Russell Lowell and His Friends* (Bo: HoMif, 1899), p. 265; W. W. Story to his father, 25 Jan. 1840, in Henry James, *William Wetmore Story and His Friends* (Bo: HoMif, 1903), 1:52 ("milk"); CPC to Julia Myers, 4 Feb. 1840, *ScLiLetCPC*, p. 47; Gohdes, *Periodicals*, p. 13.

36. As Emerson viewed it, if as many as 20,000 copies of Addison and Steele's *Spectator* were sold in a day, and if four persons read each copy, then "each of those moral lessons" was read by "more than 50,000 persons." And since then, Emerson reckoned, "the number has indefinitely multiplied" (Oct. 1824, in *EmJMN*, 2:279).

37. 27 Jan. 1837, in *EmJMN*, 5:284 ("aristocracy"); 1846, in ibid., 6:18; 19 Nov. 1832, in *EmL*, 1:358; *RuLiE*, p. 166 (Emerson was so ill that his brother Charles wrote Ezra Ripley that he seemed "as white & thin as a ghost" [10 Dec. 1832, MH]); RWE to Edward Emerson, 22 Dec. 1833, in *EmL*, 1:402; Charles Emerson to WmE, 9 Sept. 1833, in ibid., 1:402n.

38. 27 Feb. 1835, in *ClLetSister;* WHC's statement, quoted in *FrWHC*, p. 109; RWE to TC, 30 Apr. 1835, in *EmCorTC*, p. 125 (title); Mar. 1835, in ABA, "Journal for 1835," p. 104 (editors); MF to FHH, 6 Mar. 1835, MH; RWE to TC, 12 Mar. 1835, in *EmCorTC*, p. 119; 12[?] Apr., in *EmL*, 1:443; 30 Apr. 1835, in *EmCorTC*, p. 125; 13 May 1835, in *EmCor TC*, pp. 129-30; RWE to FHH, 25 June 1835, in *EmL*, 1:446 (Buove); EPP to JSD, NRU, where it is dated "1837" (however, internal evidence clearly places the date of the letter as 1836).

39. S. G. Goodrich, *Recollections of a Lifetime* (Auburn and NY: Miller, Orton, and Mulligan, 1856), 2:382-83n (1842); letter, 1836, in *MemMF*, 1:168.

40. Review of the *Lowell Offering* 4 (Sept. 1844):286; "Prospectus" for the *Pioneer*, in *The Pioneer: A Literary Magazine*, ed. Sculley Bradley (NY: Scholars' Facsimiles & Reprints, 1947); "Literary Periodicals," *Boston Weekly Magazine* 3 (21 Nov. 1840):78 ("depraved tastes"); M. F. W., "Popular Literature of the Day," *Evergreen* 1 (Jan. 1844):17 (art); *Literary Messenger* 1 (15 Oct. 1841):62; W. W. Story to J. F. Heath, 28 Mar. 1843, ViU-B ("namby pamby"); HDT to RWE, 14 Sept. 1843, in *ThCor*, p. 139; quoted in *Providence Daily Journal*, 29 Oct. 1842, p. 2; Channing to Mrs. E. L. Follen, 21 Dec. 1841, in William Henry Channing, *Memoir of William Ellery Channing* (Bo: Crosby and Nichols, 1848), 3:372; 13 Apr. 1839 in *AlcDiJaJn39*, p. 639; 21 Apr. 1846, in ABA, "Diary for 1846," p. [74], MH; E[vert]. A. D[uyckinck]., "Literary Prospects of 1845," *American Whig Review* 1 (Feb. 1845):146.

41. [D. Newell], "The Influence of Light Literature Upon the Family Circle," *Christian Family Magazine* 2 (Jan. 1843):110; *Mother's Assistant*, in "The Character of Periodicals," *Boston Weekly Magazine* 3 (13 Mar. 1841):205; Newell, "Light Literature," 112. See also Caroline John Garnsey, "Ladies' Magazines to 1850: The Beginnings of an Industry," *Bulletin of the New York Public Library* 58 (Feb. 1954):81-88; and Bertha Monica Stearns, "Philadelphia Magazines for Ladies: 1830-1860," *Pennsylvania Magazine of History and Biography* 69 (July 1945):207-19.

42. "American Monthly Literature," *Christian Examiner* 36 (Jan. 1844):142 (like the *North American Review*, this religious magazine also considered literature as falling within its realm of knowledge); "Magazine Literature" *Arcturus* 2 (Nov. 1841):342, 344; review of the *North American Review, Knickerbocker* 15 (Jan. 1840):81.

43. 27 Mar. 1839, in *AlcDiJaJn39*, p. 542. Concerning German philosophy, the *Christian Examiner* had this to say: "We greatly mistake the American mind if these attenuated speculations ever take deep root among us. That mind is too clear-sighted, keen, and practical to be enamored of a cloud. . . .The splendid but inane diction of [Transcendentalism] will find few admirers among us. While therefore the American scholar will estimate the deep research of the Germans above all price,

for their theories he will have little respect" (G. W. B[urnap]., "German Theology," *Christian Examiner* 32 [July 1842]:324).

44. John White Chadwick, *Theodore Parker* (Bo: HoMif, 1901), p. 277; TP to George E. Ellis, 7 Aug. 1838, MHi; Hale, *Lowell*, pp. 59-60; *Daily Picayune*, 4 July 1840, p. 2; 13 June 1838, in *EmJMN*, 7:18; 27 Mar. 1839, in *AlcDiJaJn39*, p. 542.

45. *CoHiBi*, 1:58; 26 Sept. 1839, in *AlcDiJyDec39*, p. 261; 1 Nov. 1839, in ibid., ρ. 374 (Emerson); 18 Nov. 1839, in ibid., p. 409 (friends); 1 Nov. 1839, in ibid., p. 375; 24 Oct., 1 Nov. 1839, in ibid., pp. 333, 375 (*Dial*). The major reason why Alcott liked Heraud's magazine was, in Alcott's own words: "Many of the articles seem. . .like passages from my own thought." Emerson, however, was glad when Heraud's magazine was passed over as a model, especially after he received this description of its editor from Carlyle: "Heraud is a loquacious scribacious little man, of middle age, of parboiled greasy aspect. . .He picked up a notion or two from Coleridge many years ago; and has ever since been rattling them in his head, like peas in an empty bladder" (30 Oct. 1839, in *AlcDiJyDec39*, p. 444. See also especially John A. Heraud, "Education," *Monthly Magazine*, 3d ser., 3 [Apr. 1840]:341-53; and 1 Apr. 1840, in *EmCorTC*, p. 264).

46. During the last half of 1840 the *Monthly Magazine* favorably reviewed Ripley's *Specimens of Foreign Standard Literature* series, the Norton-Ripley papers, Emerson's Divinity School Address, and the *Dial* ([John A. Heraud], "Census of Foreign Literature," *Monthly Magazine*, 3d ser., 4 [July, Aug., Oct., Dec. 1840]:1-14, 112-28, 331-38, 628-37).

47. JFC to MF, 1833, in *ClLetMF*, p. 52 ("principles"); JFC to MF, 20 Feb. 1835, in ibid., p. 88 ("free"); "Western Poetry, No. I.," *Messenger* 1 (June 1835): 60; "Introductory," ibid., p. 1; "Our New Volume," *Messenger* 3 (June 1837): 854 ("Christianity"); Saul Hounchell, "The Principal Literary Magazines of the Ohio Valley to 1840," Ph.D. diss., George Peabody College, 1934, passim. Clarke, Cranch, Henry Channing, Emerson, Fuller, Ripley, Dwight, Hedge, Elizabeth Peabody, Brooks, Caroline Sturgis, Very, Alcott, and Parker were all published by the *Messenger*; Alcott even unsuccessfully submitted his manuscript "Psyche" to it (Gohdes, *Periodicals*, pp. 28-31; "Plans and Prospects," *Messenger* 8 [June 1840]:91).

Chapter 2: The Publication of the *Dial*

1. 19 Sept. 1839, in *PkJ*, 1:233; 26 Sept. 1839, in *EmL*, 2:225.

2. 28 Sept. 1839, in *AlcDiJyDec39*, p. 264; RWE to MF, 16 Oct. 1839, in *EmL*, 2:229.

3. RWE to MF, 16 Oct. 1839, *EmL*, 2:229 (unpublished writings); 25 Sept. 1839, in MF, "Notebook for 1840," MH; 16 Oct. 1839, in *EmL*, 2:229.

4. Orestes Brownson to Victor Cousin, 15 Nov. 1836, in Daniel Ramon Barnes, "An Edition of the Early Letters of Orestes Brownson," Ph.D. diss., University of Kentucky, 1970, p. 136; "Brownson's Writings," *Dial* 1 (July 1840):31. Clarence L. F. Gohdes reports that the following *Dial* contributors also wrote for Brownson's journal: Alcott, Henry Channing, Dwight, Fuller, Parker, Elizabeth Peabody, and Ripley (*The Periodicals of American Transcendentalism* [Durham, N.C.: Duke University Press, 1931], p. 48).

5. Brownson began his magazine with this announcement to his readers: "I undertake this Review, then, for myself; not because I am certain that the public wants it, but because I want it" ("Introductory Remarks" *Boston Quarterly Review* 1 [Jan. 1838]:4).

6. 27 Mar. 1839, in *AlcDiJaJn39*, pp. 541-42.

7. 28 Sept. 1839, in ibid., p. 264 ("literature"); 19 Oct. 1839, in ibid., p. 320.

8. 20 Oct. 1839, in ibid., p. 321; 21 Oct. 1839, *EmJMN*, 7:273; 21 Oct. 1839, in *AlcDiJyDec39*, p. 322; *EmL*, 2:231.

9. Mason Wade, *Margaret Fuller: Whetstone of Genius* (NY: Viking, 1940), p. 70; *MemMF*, 1:336 (noon); Helene G. Baer, *The Heart is Like Heaven: The Life of Lydia Maria Child* (Philadelphia: University of Pennsylvania Press, 1964), p. 119 ($200).

10. 5 Dec. 1839, in *AlcDiJyDec39*, p. 456; W. E. Channing to EPP, [summer 1840], in her *Reminiscences of Rev. Wm. Ellery Channing* (Bo: Roberts, 1880), p. 411. David P. Edgell in his biography of Channing correctly assumes that Channing's objections were those of "any carefully conscientious man who has developed the habit of weighing every word and thought. He found the glowing intuitions of the Transcendentalists insufficiently considered" (*William Ellery Channing: An Intellectual Portrait* [Bo: Beacon, 1955], p. 121).

11. Peabody, *Reminiscences*, p. 370.

12. Emerson was evidently unhappy with these early poetic attempts; he wished them to be published without his signature, not wanting to "own any of them." Nor was he interested enough to find out if they were scheduled to be published, for the day before the first *Dial* came out he wrote Carlyle that he did not know if his "few verses" had been inserted (RWE to MF, 30 May 1840, in *EmL*, 2:299; 30 June 1840, in *EmCorTC*, p. 273).

13. He believed that "we all feel much alike in regard to this Journal; we all wish it to be, but do not wish to be in any way personally responsible for it" (12 Dec. 1839, in *EmL*, 2:242-43).

14. 22 Dec. 1839, in ibid., p. 245.

15. RWE to MF, 14 Nov. 1839, in ibid., p. 234; 17 Feb. 1838, in *EmJMN*, 5:453. Many people thought they saw both a physical and a literary resemblance between the two. Parker, who never did like Thoreau, thought his *A Week on the Concord and Merrimack Rivers* "full of beautiful things," but he suspected some of them "from their family likeness" to be Emerson's. He also believed that the "good deal of affectation in the book" was due to Thoreau's trying to be "R. W. Emerson, & not being contented with his own mother's son." Carlyle felt that Thoreau had "formed himself a good deal upon one Emerson" but did not "want abundant fire and stamina of his own." While rusticating in Concord in 1838, Lowell wrote a friend that Thoreau imitated Emerson's "tone & manner" so successfully that he would not know them apart with his eyes shut. Ednah Dow Cheney also commented upon the way that Thoreau seemed to copy Emerson's mannerisms: "He is all overlaid by an imitation of Emerson; talks like him, puts out his arm like him, brushes his hair in the same way, and is even getting up a caricature nose like Emerson's." Emerson himself realized their intellectual similarities: "I am very familiar with all his thoughts, — they are my own quite originally drest." On the other hand, Joel Porte has argued that they were essentially in opposition, Emerson being basically "metaphysical" and Thoreau more "passional" (TP to RWE, 15 June 1849, in *EmL*, 4:151n; TC to RWE, 18 May 1847, in *EmCorTC*, p. 422; JRL to G. B. Loring, 12 July 1838, in Joel Myerson, "Eight Lowell Letters from Concord in 1838," *Illinois Quarterly* 38 [Winter 1975]:28; journal entry, 15 Jan. 1848, in *SaRec*, 2:469; Sept. 1841, in *EmJMN*, 8:96; Joel Porte, *Emerson and Thoreau: Transcendentalists in Conflict* [Middletown, Conn.: Wesleyan University Press, 1966], p. 192).

16. According to Rusk, Charles acted as a sobering influence upon young Waldo's ideas as well as a sounding board for his thoughts. The latter valued his criticisms and always tried to consult Charles for his opinions. After a number of years of being with Thoreau, Emerson recorded in his journal: "I have sometimes fancied my friend's wisdom rather corrective than initiative, an excellent element in conversation to counteract the common exaggerations & preserve the sanity, but chiefly valuable so & not for its adventure & exploration or for its satisfying peace" (*RuLiE*, p. 231; ca. 19 Apr. 1842, in *EmJMN*, 8:237).

17. Emerson told his brother William that Thoreau would become a "great poet" and told Aunt Mary that Thoreau wrote "genuine poetry." To Fuller he praised Thoreau's "good poetry & better prose," and he told Carlyle that Thoreau had produced "the truest verses" he had seen (26 Sept. 1839, 22 Dec. 8[?] Feb. 1839, in *EmL*, 2:225, 244, 182; 8 Aug. 1839, in *EmCorTC*, P. 246).

18. MB; 1 Jan. 1840, MH; SC to JFC, 30 Jan. 1840, in *ClLetSister*.

19. 16 Jan. 1840, MH; JFC to SC, 8 Feb. 1840, MH; 25 Feb. 1840, in *FrWHC*, pp. 167-68.

20. RWE to MF, 17[?] Jan. 1840, in *EmL*, 2:249; 20 Jan. 1840, in ibid., p. 248n.

21. ca. Feb. 1840, in *PkJ*, 1:298; MF to RWE, 20 Jan. 1840, in *EmL*, 2:248n.

22. James Clarke had read these poems in early 1836 and called them better than any other of her verses that he had seen, mainly because they had "more singleness of purpose" and "more unity" than the others (JFC to MF, 28 Mar. 1836, in *ClLetMF*, p. 118).

23. When Thoreau gave "Sympathy" to him in August, Emerson had called it the "purest strain & the loftiest" that had yet "pealed from this unpoetic American forest." He told Ward of the poem in October, before mentioning it to Fuller, and in November he copied it for Ward, instructing him to forward it to Fuller after he had read it (1 Aug. 1839, in *EmJMN*, 7:230-31; 3 Oct. 1839, in RWE, *Letters from Ralph Waldo Emerson to a Friend 1838-1853*, ed. Charles Eliot Norton [Bo: HoMif, 1899], p. 12; 14 Nov. 1839, in *EmL*, 2:234; 26 Nov. 1839, in *Letters to a Friend*, p. 17).

24. Thoreau had finished the piece in February, and Emerson thought it to be a "fine critique" of Flaccus. In 1848, when H. G. O. Blake reread the article after meeting Thoreau, he was impressed by the depth of its thought and wrote a letter of praise to its author, who replied that Blake's sympathetic response gave him pleasure (10 Feb. 1840 in *ThJ*, 1:117; RWE to MF, 3 Mar. 1840, in *EmL*, 2:259; mid-Mar., 27 Mar. 1848, in *ThCor*, pp. 213-14).

25. 3 Mar. 1840, in *EmL*, 2:258; RWE to Henry Barnard, 2 Mar. 1840, NNU. W. H. S. Jordan had started in 1836 as a magazine agent and proprietor of "W. H. S. Jordan's Literary Rooms." That year he succeeded to the publishing business of Samuel Colman and in 1839 joined forces with J. H. and W. A. Weeks, who had begun publishing books the previous year (Robert W. Flint, "The Boston Book Trade, 1835-1845: A Directory," library school thesis, Simmons College).

26. As he told Cranch: "Within a year my contemporaries have risen very much in my respect, for, within that period, I have learned to know the genius of several persons who now fill me with pleasure and hope" (4 Mar. 1840, in *ScLiLetCPC*, p. 59).

27. RWE to Henry Barnard, 2 Mar. 1840, NNU; 18 Mar. 1840, in *EmCorTC*, p. 261.

28. MF to FHH, 10 Mar. 1840, in *HigMF*, p. 150; MF to WHC, 22 Mar. 1840, MB; RWE to MF, 30 Mar. 1840, in *EmL*, 2:271. She had written Hedge on 10 March that "I could make a number myself with the help Mr. E. will give" (*HigMF*, p. 150). However, on 4 March Emerson began a series of nine lectures on "The Present Age" at the Concord Lyceum; on 10 March he delivered the first of three lectures in New York; and on 20 March he began a series of six lectures on "Human Life" in Providence, Rhode Island.

29. She confidently said: "A perfectly free organ is to be offered for the expression of individual thought and character. There are no party measures to be carried, no particular standard to be set up. A fair calm tone, a recognition of universal principles will, I hope pervade the essays. . .I hope there will neither be a spirit of dogmatism nor of compromise. That this periodical will not aim at leading public opinion, but at stimulating each man to think for himself, to think more deeply and more nobly by letting them see how some minds are kept alive by a wise self-trust."

30. 22 Mar. 1840, MB.

31. 30 Mar. 1840, in *EmL*, 2:270-71. Others promising aid included Ellery Channing, Sarah Clarke, Cranch, Dwight, Parker, Ripley, Thomas Stone, Caroline Sturgis, Thoreau, and Ward.

32. Apr. 1840, in *AlcSc40*, pp. 244-45.

33. This last piece, which never appeared in the *Dial*, was possibly meant as a sequel to her two anonymous "Literary Notices—Chat in Boston Bookstores" that had appeared in the January and July *Boston Quarterly Reviews* of that year.

34. *FuNbD*; RWE to MF, 15 Apr. 1840, in *EmL*, 2:282.

35. ABA to Hannah Robie, 26 Apr. 1840, MH; 7 Apr. 1840, in *EmJMN*, 7:341-42; the information probably came directly from W. H. S. Jordan of Weeks, Jordan & Co., who was the *New-Yorker*'s agent at Boston until mid-April ("Agents," *New-Yorker* 9 [18 Apr. 1840]:79); [J. C. Pennell], "Boston Notions," in *Footprints: or, Fugitive Poems* (Philadelphia: John Pennington, 1843), pp. 90-92; Andrews Norton to J. G. Palfrey, 22 Apr. 1840, MH.

36. 17 Apr. 1840, in *FuNbD*; 19 Apr. 1840, MB.

37. Fuller had always considered herself rejected by society because, she believed, others were envious of her intellectual accomplishments. She was to a large extent correct; women disliked her because she had adopted an unconventional and, to them, unfeminine role, and men disliked her for competing with them on their own intellectual terms—and often coming away victorious. Only after her romance with Ossoli, who accepted her purely as a woman, did she successfully integrate the various facets of her personality.

38. RWE to MF, 8 Apr. 1840, in *EmL*, 2:275 (Alcott); RWE to MF, 15 Apr. 1840, in ibid., p. 281;

see RWE to MF, 31[?] July 1839, in ibid., p. 211, and 7 Nov. 1839, *FuW*, 1:581; RWE to MF, 9 Sept. 1839, in *EmL*, 2:223; RWE to MF, 8 Apr. 1840, in ibid., p. 275 (S. Clarke); 15 Apr. 1840, in ibid., p. 281.

39. RWE to MF, in ibid., pp. 280-81; RWE to MF, 21[?] Apr. 1840, in ibid., p. 287; 23 Apr. 1840, in ibid., p. 290 ("re-written"); RWE to MF, 27[?] Apr. 1840, in ibid., p. 293.

40. RWE to WmE, 20 Apr. 1840, in ibid, p. 284; 24 Apr. 1840, in *PkJ*, 1:349; 21 Apr. 1840, in *EmCorTC*, p. 269; 21[?] Apr. 1840, in *EmL*, 2:286-87.

41. *EmL*, 2:285-86; 25 Apr. 1840, in ibid., p. 290n; see late Sept. 1839, in *EmJMN*, 7:243; 27[?] Apr. 1840, in *EmL*, 2:292-93; see late Apr. 1840, in *EmJMN*, 7:344-45; 8 May 1840, in *EmL*, 2:294.

42. F. DeWolfe Miller, "Christopher Pearse Cranch," Ph.D. diss., University of Virginia, 1942, p. 59, and Stanley M. Vogel, *German Literary Influences on the American Transcendentalists* (New Haven, Conn.: Yale University Press, 1955), p. 96 (Goethe); Mar. 1840, in *AlcAuInd*; RWE to MF, 8 Apr. 1840, in *EmL*, 2:276; RWE to MF, 15 Apr. 1840, in ibid., p. 280; 24 Apr. 1840, in ibid., pp. 291-92; RWE to MF, 8 May 1840, in ibid., p. 294; May 1840, in *AlcSc40*, p. 245 (visit); MF to RWE, 31 May 1840, in *EmL*, 2:297n.

43. Ripley was probably the author of the "Prospectus," according to Higginson and to Richard Henry Dana, Jr., who wrote his father that a friend called it "a clumsy piece of English & a palpable imitation of Emerson." One person who definitely had no hand in it was Henry Channing; parts of his unused, highly "Transcendental" prospectus show why: "This work aims to awaken a new interest in the Soul, or mind, or faculties, or being of man, or whatever we choose to call that higher part of our nature, which distinguishes us from the animal. . . . it would give free play to obscurity of conception . . . It waits for a new Prophet; . . . It does not know but what this Prophet is now alive, & may come forth in its pages" (*HigMF*, p. 151; 16 June 1840, in Lloyd Wilfred Griffin, "Selected Letters of Richard Henry Dana, Jr. (1815-82)," M.A. thesis, University of Maine, 1947, p. 60; n.d., MH).

44. As no single-copy price was announced, it is possible that Weeks, Jordan & Co. had decided against selling the *Dial* either by the number or through a combination of single and subscription sales, as Ripley had suggested to Little and Brown earlier.

45. The only copies of the extremely rare "Prospectus" that I have been able to find are at MH; two copies are laid into volume one of *AP8.D5410(A), and one copy is pasted in ABA, "Scripture for 1840," p. 79, MH. No copy has subscribers' names written on it. The "Prospectus" was later printed on the *Dial*'s wrappers.

46. May 1840, in *AlcSc40*, p. 245; 6 May 1840, in *EmJMN*, 7:346; see RWE to MF, 8 May 1840, in *EmL*, 2:293, and RWE to Bartol, 8 May 1840, ViU-B; May 1840 in *AlcSc40*, p. 245; 28 May 1840, in *EmJMN*, 7:360 ("Methodist"); George Ripley and George P. Bradford, "Philosophic Thought in Boston," in *The Memorial History of Boston*, ed. Justin Winsor (Bo: Osgood, 1882), 4:323n. Father Taylor is known primarily today as being Melville's probable model for Father Mapple in *Moby-Dick*.

47. RWE to MF, 8 May 1840, in *EmL*, 2:293-94; 1 June 1840, in *EmJMN*, 7:364; RWE to MF, 30 May 1840, in *EmL*, 2:299; on 7 April 1840 Clarke had promised two poems for the *Dial*, but on 20 June he said that he had been unable to revise them well enough for publication (JFC to SC, MH; *ClLetMF*, p. 140); 20 June 1840, in ibid, p. 140; JFC to MF, 24 May 1840, in ibid., p. 138; MF to RWE, 31 May 1840, in *EmL*, 2:298n; 7 June 1840, in ibid., p. 304. The lack of subscribers gives an air of credibility to a statement ascribed to a daughter of Father Taylor: "The transcendentalists soar into the illimitable, dive into the infinite, and never pay cash!" (quoted in Frank Luther Mott, *A History of American Magazines 1741-1850* [Cambridge, Mass.: Harvard University Press, 1957 (1939)], p. 708).

48. 21 June 1840, in *EmL*, 2:305-6; 30 June 1840, in *EmCorTC*, pp. 272-73.

49. The first printed notice of publication I have found states that the *Dial* was "Published this day" on 1 July 1840, the same day that Emerson received a copy from Alcott. Since no printing records have been found from the *Dial*'s various publishers, in the absence of references in contemporary letters and journals to the dates on which the *Dial* first became available, I will use contemporary booksellers' and publishers' advertisements to determine these dates. Also, when no other information is available, I will assume that the *Dial* was officially placed on sale — or published — on the day

that printing and binding were completed (*Boston Daily Advertiser*; RWE to MF, 2 July 1840, in *EmL*, 2:310).

50. GR to JSD, 7 July 1840, MB; MF to [Almira Barlow], [July 1840], in *FuW*, 1:23; SC to JFC, 7 July 1840, in *ClLetSister*; MF to RWE, 5 July 1840, in *HigMF*, p. 155; HDT to Rufus Griswold, 9 Oct. 1841, in *ThCor*, p. 54: one error in "Sympathy" resulted from Emerson's miscopying "posts" for "ports" (RWE to MF, 21 July 1840, in *EmL*, 2:317); RWE to MF, 2 July 1840, in ibid., p. 311; Thoreau, on the other hand, maintained that he had never received proof (RWE to MF, 21 July 1840, in ibid., p. 317); MF to RWE, 5 July 1840, in *HigMF*, p. 155.

51. JRL to G. B. Loring, 28 June 1840, MH; 14 July 1840, Philip Graham, "Some Lowell Letters," *Texas Studies in Literature and Language* 3 (Winter 1962):576; Hale to JRL, 4 July 1840, MH.

52. Hedge said of it: "There has been nothing done in English rhyme like this since Milton." A reviewer of the 1843 edition of Griswold's *Readings in American Poetry* complained of the omission of "The Problem," which he then quoted from "an old number of the *Dial*." Longfellow also liked the poem, and in 1846, while assembling an anthology of verse, he asked Emerson's permission to include it (quoted in Joseph Henry Allen, *Our Liberal Movement in Theology* [Bo: Roberts, 1882], p. 216; *Pathfinder* 1 [29 Apr. 1843]:149; 25 Nov. 1846, in *EmL*, 2:365n).

53. Clarke was struck by such phrases as "the vast solitudes of prayer," "It has the step of Fate," and "the sphere in the ecliptic." Also, "the confidence & valor of the tone" were surely Emerson's (JFC to SC, 8 July 1840, MH).

54. 12 Sept. 1840, in *EmJMN*, 7:395; SR to JSD, 1 Aug. 1840, MB.

55. Samuel Treat, Jr., to CSW, 13 July 1840, in Kenneth Walter Cameron, "Emerson, Transcendentalism, and Literary Notes in the Stearns Wheeler Papers," *American Transcendental Quarterly*, no. 20 (Fall 1973), supplement 76; WmE to RWE, 28 Aug. 1840, in *EmL*, 2:312n; TC to RWE, 26 Sept. 1840, in *EmCorTC*, p. 280: after reading this letter, Emerson manfully told Fuller that Carlyle "faintly praises The Dial Number 1" (20 Oct. 1840, in *EmL*, 2:349); F. Appleton to I. A. Jewett, 6 July 1840, in *Mrs. Longfellow: Selected Letters and Journals of Fanny Appleton Longfellow*, ed. Edward Wagenknecht (Lo: Peter Owen, 1959), p. 69; Charles R. Crowe, "Transcendentalism and 'The Newness' in Rhode Island," *Rhode Island History* 14 (Apr. 1955):39 (intellectual); R. Newcomb to CKN, 6 July 1840, RPB.

56. SR to JSD, 1 Aug. 1840, MB.

57. 10 Aug. 1840, in *PkJ*, 1:431. One such humorous entry compared the *Dial*'s younger writers to "awk[ward] and lurching" dancing school pupils, while complaining of the "uncouth & barbarous" words that they used, some of which were "virginal in respect to English language still" (ca. 29 June 1840, in ibid., pp. 410-11).

58. 23 Sept. 1840, in ibid., p. 467.

59. Copies by ABA, Sept. 1840, in *AlcSc40*, pp. 248-51; 31 Oct. 1840, copy by ABA, "Scripture for 1840," p. 181, MH. In addition to the people mentioned above, Alcott sent copies to James Pierrepont Greaves and Henry G. Wright (July 1840, in *AlcSc40*, p. 247).

60. Full bibliographical references to and a discussion of all the reviews and notices of and reprints from the *Dial* will be found in Joel Myerson, "The Contemporary Reception of the Boston *Dial*," *Resources for American Literary Study* 3 (Autumn 1973):203-20.

61. n.d., pasted in ABA, "Scripture for 1840," p. 108.

62. James Elliot Cabot tentatively identified the reviewer, "W.J.P.," as a William J. Potter. But it was actually William Pabodie of Providence, who had expressed similar views on Fuller's work to Rhoda Newcomb after the *Dial* first came out, and who is identified as the author by Sarah Helen Whitman. Ripley thought Pabodie's "series of living pictures" of the contributors to be "not without discrimination," but Emerson commented negatively upon this review: "The piece seems to be written by a woman. It begins with round sentences but ends in Oh's & Ah's." The *Boston Courier* (28 July 1840) reprinted a negative section dealing with Emerson's philosophy in order to inform its readers in "plain and unsophisticated language" what Transcendentalism "really is" (J. E. Cabot, "Ledger," p. 270, MH; R. Newcomb to CKN, 6 July 1840, RPB; S. H. Whitman to Orestes Brownson, 19 Nov. 1840, InNd; GR to JSD, 6 Aug. 1840, MB; 31 July 1840, in *EmJMN*, 7:388).

63. Alcott's cause was not helped any by the *Dial*'s omission of the bracketed word in the following

sentence: "The poles of things are not integrated: creation [not] globed and orbed" (ABA's correction, "Scripture for 1840," p. 109).

64. MF to RWE, 5 July 1840, in *HigMF*, p. 155; RWE to MF, 2 July 1840, in *EmL*, 2:311; July 1840, in *AlcAuInd*; reprinted in "Transcendentalism," *Boston Daily Bee*, 11 Apr. 1843, p. 2. A full discussion of the furor Alcott aroused is in Joel Myerson, "'In the Transcendental Emporium': Bronson Alcott's 'Orphic Sayings' in the *Dial*," *English Language Notes* 10 (Sept. 1972):31-38.

65. 27 Aug. 1840, in Thomas Holley Chivers, *The Correspondence of Thomas Holley Chivers*, ed. Emma Lester Chase and Lois Ferry Parks (Providence, R.I., Brown University Press, 1957), p. 10; CPC to JSD, 16 Aug 1840, in Miller, "Cranch," p. 124; 16 Sept. 1840, in *EmL*, 2:312n; 30 Aug. 1840, in *EmCorTC*, p. 277; Ward to Longfellow, 15 Oct. 1840, in Maud Howe Elliott, *Uncle Sam Ward and His Circle* (NY: Macmillan, 1938), p. 274.

Chapter 3: The *Dial* Under Margaret Fuller

1. Emerson also requested that Thoreau be sent copies as a contributor and not as a subscriber, that Alcott get free copies for his English friends, and that free copies go to Thomas Stone and Cranch as inducements for them to contribute in the future (2 July 1840, in *EmL*, 2:310-11).

2. Specifically, Fuller replied that Thoreau would receive free copies, but Cranch, like Clarke, was already a subscriber and therefore would not need to have extra copies sent him. Stone's name was not on the free list because Fuller was being very strict, and not even her own good friends Ellen Hooper, Caroline Sturgis, and Charles Newcomb received complimentary copies.

3. 5 July 1840, in *HigMF*, pp. 154-55; 8 July 1840, in *EmL*, 2:313.

4. MF to [Almira Barlow], [July 1840], in *FuW*, 1:23; MF to RWE, 19 July 1840, in *HigMF*, p. 158; MF to John Neal, 28 July 1840, ViU-B; RWE to MF, 27 July 1840, in *EmL*, 2:319; RWE to MF, 21 July 1840, in ibid., p. 316.

5. RWE to MF, 27 July 1840, in *EmL*, 2:319 (review); RWE to MF, 21 June 1840, in ibid., p. 306; 21 July 1840, in ibid., pp. 315-16.

6. In late April 1840 Emerson had sent a "little tract" by Edward Palmer, *A Letter to those who Think*, to the *Dial* for review. Ripley, who was doing most of the reviews for October, praised Palmer as a "sincere thinker" but disagreed with many of his ideas. Apparently, Ripley had overextended himself in this number, for one of his other reviews was merely a reprint of the *Boston Daily Advertiser*'s account of Dr. Walker's talk at the Harvard Divinity School, even though Ripley had attended it himself (RWE to MF, 21[?] Apr. 1840, in *EmL*, 2:287; *Dial*, 1:251; GR to JSD, 6 Aug. 1840, MB).

7. *FuNbD*; RWE to MF, 21 July 1840 in *EmL*, 2:315. The essay was the genesis of Thoreau's "The Service," and the poem, "When winter fringes every bough," was later incorporated into his "A Winter Walk" in the October 1843 *Dial* (see *The Service*, ed. F. B. Sanborn [Bo: Charles E. Goodspeed, 1902]; and Walter Harding, *The Days of Henry Thoreau* [NY: Knopf, 1966], p. 114).

8. 21 July 1840, in *EmL*, 2:315.

9. Of this poem Parker later said: "[A] pine-tree which should talk as Mr. Emerson's tree talks would deserve to be plucked up and cast into the sea." Others thought better of the poem: Lowell told Emerson that "Woodnotes" was "beautiful" to him, and Fuller reported that the poem had been heard with "delight" by her friends. In all probability, this "Woodnotes" was composed of "old rhymes" that Emerson had "tacked" together to send Fuller in late April. He said that she could print "only one of them or two at two times"; the second "Woodnotes" was published in October 1841 (quoted in Thomas Wentworth Higginson, "Emerson," *Nation* 34 [4 May 1882]: 376; 18 Nov. 1841 in James Russell Lowell, *New Letters of James Russell Lowell*, ed. M. A. DeWolfe Howe [NY: Harper's, 1932], p. 6; MF to RWE, 7 Nov. 1840, in *EmL*, 2:354n; 23[?] April 1840 in ibid., p. 288).

10. RWE to TC, 21 Apr. 1840, in *EmCorTC*, p. 269; 7 June 1840, in *EmL*, 2:303; MF to RWE, 5 July 1840, in *HigMF*, p. 156 (set in type); RWE to WmE, 30 June 1840, in *EmL*, 2:308; 30 June 1840, in *EmCorTC*, p. 271; MF to RWE, 5 July 1840, in *HigMF*, p. 156; RWE to MF, 8 July 1840, in *EmL*, 2:313; 19 July 1840, in *HigMF*, pp. 157-58; RWE to MF, 21 July 1840, in *EmL*, 2:315-16. That

Fuller was in complete control can be seen in these sentences she wrote to Emerson: "I think when you look again you will think you have not said what you meant to say. The 'eloquence' and 'wealth,' thus grouped, have rather *l'air bourgeois*" (19 July 1840, in *HigMF*, p. 157).

11. 31 July 1840, in *EmJMN*, 7:388. Emerson did not necessarily mean that the *Dial* should concern itself with particular topics or events; what he wanted were general essays on "the subjects of 'Labor,' 'Farm,' 'Reform,' 'Domestic Life,' etc.," and not on specific controversies such as the one that had evolved over his Divinity School Address (RWE to MF, 4 Aug. 1840, in *EmL*, 2:322).

12. GR to JSD, 6 Aug. 1840, MB; ABA to S. J. May, 10 Aug. 1840, in *AlcL*, p. 53; SR to JSD, 1 Aug. 1840, MB. Such misleading initials were "Z." for Caroline Sturgis and "J." for Ward.

13. Aug. 1840, in *AlcAuInd*; 10 Aug. 1840, in *PkJ*, 1:431.

14. 1-2 Sept. 1840, in *PkJ*, 1:442; EPP to JSD, 20 Sept. 1840, MB ("Atheism"); RWE to EPP, 8 Sept. 1840, in *EmL*, 2:329; CPC to JSD, 12 Sept. 1840, in F. DeWolfe Miller, "Christopher Pearse Cranch," Ph.D. diss., University of Virginia, 1942, pp. 126-27.

15. By the end of July Alcott was preparing about fifty of his "Sayings" for Fuller, and in August he transcribed them for submission. Apparently she rejected his offer of help when he saw her in the middle of the month (RWE to MF, 21 July 1840, in *EmL*, 2:316; Aug. 1840, in *AlcSc40*, p. 248; RWE to MF, 16 Aug. 1840, in *EmL*, 2:324).

16. 1-2 Sept. 1840, in *PkJ*, 1:446.

17. EPP to JSD, 20 Sept. 1840, MB.

18. George Bradford, who had sent in an article on "Friendship," found it omitted from the number because of the many other contributions. As early as July he had offered to write a piece on abolition, and though he was translating Fenelon, possibly to give to the *Dial*, he was never published by the *Dial* (RWE to MF, 27 July 1840, in *EmL*, 2:318; RWE to CS, 25 Sept. 1840, MH).

19. Emerson's optimism concerning how little was expected of him was amazing. Not learning from his experience on the October number, he told Fuller: "Then in the following number [January] a sonnet will suffice." In reality, he contributed two poems, a review, and two articles to the October *Dial* (8 July 1840, in *EmL*, 2:313).

20. RWE to SGW, [26 Aug. 1840], MH; RWE to MF, 13 Sept. 1840, *EmL*, 2:332; *Boston Daily Advertiser*.

21. 11 Oct. 1840, in Henry Wadworth Longfellow, *The Letters of Henry Wadsworth Longfellow*, ed. Andrew Hilen (Cambridge, Mass.: Harvard Univeristy Press, 1966-), 2:254; George Keats to JFC, 25 Nov. 1840, in Madeleine B. Stern, "Four Letters from George Keats," *PMLA* 56 (Mar. 1941): 211; Oct. 1840, in *EmJMN*, 7:517.

22. And when Fanny Appleton met him, Carlyle called the *Dial* "a ghost of a book" and doubted whether "it would ever attain a body . . . without which it could do little in this world" (TC to RWE, 9 Dec. 1840, in *EmCorTC*, p. 287; journal entry, 3 June 1841, in Fanny Appleton Longfellow, *Mrs. Longfellow: Selected Letters and Journals of Fanny Appleton Longfellow (1817-1861)*, ed. Edward Wagenknecht [Lo: Peter Owen, 1959], p. 76).

23. 17 Oct. 1840, MH. Much the same effect was wrought on Ripley, who, after reading Emerson's article on "Modern Literature," told him of the "true joy" he had in finding someone else confirming his own "faith in the objects for which I am just now living" ([Oct. 1840], MH).

24. WmE to RWE, 15 Nov. 1840, MH; Hildreth to CSW, 27 Oct. 1840, in Kenneth Walter Cameron, "Emerson, Transcendentalism, and Literary Notes in the Stearns Wheeler Papers," *American Transcendental Quarterly*, no. 20 (Fall 1975): supplement 72.

25. Emerson was upset with the *Advertiser*'s review. He was already angry because the *Dial* was trying to compete with other journals on their own terms when it should be unique in tone and format, and he wrote: "Go, dear soul, and be scales & a sword, an accusation and a terror, a Day of doom & a Future to the . . . fat & easy & conceited world, the cultivated & intellectual world [that] takes the prophets by the hand and affects to be of their part" (27 Oct. 1840, in *EmJMN*, 7:407).

26. 7 Nov. 1840, in *EmL*, 2:354n; MF to Albert G. Greene, 2 Oct. 1840, RPB; RWE to Daniel Parker, 10 Nov. 1840, MBilHi; Parker to RWE, 30 Nov. 1840, MH; RWE to Daniel Parker, 2 Dec. 1840, MBilHi.

27. MF to RWE, 6 Dec. 1840, in *EmL*, 2:363n ("volunteers").

28. Even though Fuller denied it, one possible reason for their exclusion was that she thought that Emerson should prefix a "fitting word" to the poems, while he believed that they should be printed "without any other commentary" than that they were from the "New Poet" of the last number (MF to RWE, 6 Dec. 1840, in *EmL*, 2:363n; MF to RWE, 7 Nov. 1840, in ibid., p. 354n; RWE to MF, 4 Nov. 1840, in ibid., p. 355).

29. 15 Nov. 1840, MH; 1[?] Dec. 1840, in *EmL*, 2:363; Dec. 1840, MH; 6 Dec. 1840, in *EmL*, 2:362n; 8 Dec. 1840, in ibid., p. 366; 10 Dec. 1840, TxU.

30. RWE to MF, 8 July 1840, in *EmL*, 2:313; RWE to MF, 24 Oct. 1840, in ibid., p. 353; 4 Nov. 1840, in ibid., p. 355; MF to RWE, 7 Nov. 1840, in ibid., p. 354n; RWE to WmE, 9 Nov. 1840, in ibid., pp. 357-58; late Nov. 1840, in ibid, p. 366n; RWE to MF, 1[?] Dec., 21 Dec. 1840, in ibid., pp. 362-63, 372 (revising); RWE to MF, 8 Dec. 1840 in ibid., pp. 365-66. Emerson was revising his 1836 lecture on "Art" for use in *Essays, First Series* at the time, and he probably gave Fuller "the balance of the manuscript of the lecture, possibly with additions but with little further editing" for the *Dial*. This would account for the need for subsequent revision (see RWE, *The Early Lectures of Ralph Waldo Emerson*, ed. Stephen E. Whicher et al. [Cambridge, Mass.: Harvard University Press, 1959-1972], 2:41). Convers Francis considered "Thoughts on Art" admirable. Writing to Parker, he praised the article's "aesthetical thinking" and said that it contained in a few pages "more profound and striking truth" than he had seen in whole volumes. And in New York, Henry Bellows called it "beautiful & impressive" ([Jan. 1841], in *SaHaABA*, 2:368; H. Bellows to W. Bellows, 22 June 1841, MHi).

31. See 25 May 1840, in *EmJMN*, 7:354-57; RWE to MF, 24 Nov. 1840, in *EmL*, 2:361; RWE to CS, 21 Dec. 1840, MH.

32. 7 Nov. 1840, in *EmL*, 2:354n; Nov. 1840, in *AlcSc40*, p. 254; MF to RWE, 6 Dec. 1840, in *EmL*, 2:362n; 1 Dec. 1840, in *ThCor*, pp. 41-42; 21 July 1840, in *EmL*, 2:315; 27 July 1840, in ibid., p. 318, 320 (title). Emerson may have been less than straightforward in his dealings with Thoreau over this poem. After Fuller returned her criticisms, Emerson showed them to Thoreau, who "boggled" over the word "relumes." He insisted, Emerson said, on "his own honest 'doth have,'" which Emerson restored, telling Fuller that "our tough Yankee must have his tough verse." What happened, it seems, was that Emerson, without Thoreau's knowledge, had substituted "relumes" for "doth have," and when Thoreau found out he told him that it was Fuller's suggestion. That Emerson said "relumes" always sounded "sacred" to him — and that the poem appears with "doth have" in Thoreau's journal — seems to confirm this view (RWE to MF, 4 Aug. 1840, *EmL*, 2:322; 24 July 1839, in *ThJ*, 1:87; and Carl Bode's examination of the manuscript in his edition of HDT, *Collected Poems of Henry Thoreau*, enl. ed. [Baltimore, Md.: Johns Hopkins University Press, 1964], p. 297).

33. In 1836 Fuller had praised Hawthorne's "The Gentle Boy" for its "grace and delicacy of feeling," which she thought so refined that she assumed the author to be a woman (quoted in Moncure Daniel Conway, *Emerson at Home and Abroad* [Bo: Osgood, 1882], p. 260).

34. MF to [WHC?], 19 Oct. 1840, in *MemMF*, 2:47-49; MF to [WCH], 8 Nov. 1840, MB. Emerson found "beauty & wit" in this essay, thinking it written with more than Fuller's usual "spirit & elegance," and to her he called it "rich and sad" and of "permanent value" (RWE to CS, 13 Jan. [1841], MH; 19 Jan. 1841, *EmL*, 2:378).

35. MF to RWE, 6 Dec. 1840, in *EmL*, 2:363n.

36. *Boston Daily Advertiser* and *Boston Morning Post*; 13 Jan. [1841], MH; 12 Jan. 1841, in *EmL*, 2:376; JSD to his sister, 12 Jan. 1841, in George Willis Cooke, *John Sullivan Dwight* (Bo: Small, Maynard, 1898), p. 39; 27 Jan. 1841, MH; Harding, *Thoreau*, p. 103; George Keats to JFC, 17 Jan. 1841, in Stern, "Keats," p. 213; F. Appleton to I. A. Jewett, 25 Jan. 1841, in Longfellow, *Mrs. Longfellow*, p. 75; 18 Jan. 1841, in James Marsh, *Coleridge's American Disciples: The Selected Correspondence of James Marsh*, ed. John J. Duffy (Amherst, Mass.: Univeristy of Massachusetts Press, 1973), p. 251; W. Bellow to H. Bellows, 9 Jan. 1841, MHi; H. Bellows to W. Bellows, 22 June 1841, MHi.

37. [2] Feb. 1841, MB; Mason Wade, *Margaret Fuller: Whetstone of Genius* (NY: Viking, 1940), p. 76 ($600).

38. MF to RWE, 6 Dec. 1840, *EmL*, 2:363n; RWE to CS, 13 Jan. 1841, MH. Emerson had suggested that the poem, which had apparently been given to him with the title "The Guardian the Lover & the

Maid," be called "The Maiden: the Adopted Father: the Adopted Mother: the Lover." Fuller met his suggestion halfway by using his title as the poem's subtitle in the *Dial* (RWE to MF, 7 Nov. 1840, 9 Feb. 1841, in *EmL*, 2:355, 381).

39. RWE to CS, 13 Jan. 1841, MH.

40. When Fuller first heard the name "Leila" she knew, "from the very look and sound, it was mine." Although the reviewers did not like this piece, the Brook Farmers did, and two years later Emerson told her that "some choice spirits" at West Roxbury were reading it when he arrived (quoted in *MemMF*, 1:219; 11 July 1843, *EmL*, 3:183).

41. Fuller chose the dialogue form because she felt it would "excuse incompleteness and imperfections," and because it gave her "an opportunity to be sketchy or elaborate" as she pleased (MF, "Notebook for 1840," MH).

42. RWE to MF, 12 Jan. 1841, in *EmL*, 2:376 (*Essays*); 9 Feb. 1841, in ibid., p. 381; RWE to TC, 28 Feb. 1841, in *EmCorTC*, p. 291; RWE to MF, 2 Mar. 1841, in *EmL* 2:384 (corrections); RWE to WmE, 22 Mar. 1841, in ibid., p. 387; MF to WHC, [2] Feb. 1841, MB. Jones Very took "pleasure" from the published lecture, and Carlyle, after Alcott had left his home during his 1842 trip to England, told Emerson that the best thing Alcott did while he stayed was to circulate copies of the English edition of Emerson's lecture. Also in England, Thomas Ballantyne read the lecture and wrote Emerson that it was far superior to his *Essays* in "practical utility" (Very to RWE, 21 Nov. 1841, MWelC; 17 Nov. 1842, in *EmCorTC*, p. 334; 3 Dec. 1842, MH).

43. *Boston Daily Advertiser*, 14 Sept. 1841, p. 3.

44. Although the *Boston Morning Post* of 12 April 1841 stated that the *Dial* was "published April 1st," it is more likely that Jordan's advertisement in the Boston *Atlas* announcing that the *Dial* was for sale on 5 April is correct.

45. RWE to MF, 22 Apr. 1841, in *EmL*, 2:395; RWE to Mary Moody Emerson, 4 May 1841, in ibid., p. 398; 30 Apr. 1841, in *EmCorTC*, p. 293; James Marsh to H. Raymond, 1 Mar. 1841, in Ronald Vale Wells, *Three Christian Transcendentalists: James Marsh, Caleb Sprague Henry, and Frederic Henry Hedge* (NY: Columbia University Press, 1943), p. 167; William Forster to B. Fox, n.d., in T. Wemyss Reid, *Life of. . . . William Edward Forster* (Lo: Chapman and Hall, 1888), 1:147.

46. In an attempt to show the "Origin of Transcendentalism," the *Salem Observer* (17 Apr. 1841) printed extracts from the "Chaldean Oracles," coincidentally the same text used in the "Ethnical Scriptures" for the April 1844 *Dial* (in Alfred Felix Rosa, "A Study of Transcendentalism in Salem with Special Reference to Nathaniel Hawthorne," Ph.D. diss., University of Massachusetts, 1971, pp. 94-95).

47. 14 June 1841, in *AlcAuInd*; E. B., "American Correspondence," *Monthly Magazine*, 3d ser., 5 (May 1841): 477; RWE to WmE, 1 June 1841, in *EmL*, 2:402; RWE to LdE, 14 June 1841, in ibid., p. 404.

48. RWE to LdE, 14 June 1841 in *EmL*, 2:405-6; RWE to LdE, 22 June 1841, in ibid., p. 407; Sturgis had argued against publishing "Woodnotes," while Fuller had made no comment, a silence which disturbed Fuller, and she soon wrote Emerson to say that he did have her support after all (21 June 1841, in ibid., pp. 408-9n).

49. RWE to MF, 15 June 1841, in ibid., p. 405. Later Very wrote Emerson that he was thankful for "the high eulogism" that he considered the review to be (21 Nov. 1841, MWelC).

50. TP to MF, 1841, in John Weiss, *Life and Correspondence of Theodore Parker* (NY: Appleton, 1864), 1:303.

51. On 25 May 1841 she wrote her brother Richard: "He [Thoreau] has a great deal of practical sense, and as he has bodily strength to boot, he may look to be a successful and happy man" (MH).

52. On 22 April 1841 Emerson had asked Fuller: "Will you not print . . . Henry Thoreau?" Emerson reportedly told Sanborn that in 1837 Mrs. Lucy Brown, his wife's sister, had brought the verses to him after Thoreau had tossed them, "tied round a bunch of violets," into her window. When Thoreau died, Alcott chose this poem to read at his funeral (*EmL*, 2:395; F. B. Sanborn, *Life of Henry David Thoreau* [Bo: HoMif, 1917], p. 129; *CoHiBi*, 1:118).

53. Emerson was not alone in liking the Goethe article: John Morley later called it "fresh, cordial, and frank," and Hedge, who thought it "one of the best criticisms extant of Goethe," as well as one of

the best things Fuller ever wrote, later chose it as one of the few secondary sources to include in his *Prose Writers of Germany* (RWE to WmE, 3 July 1841, in *EmL*, 2:413; Morley, *Critical Miscellanies* [Lo: Macmillan, 1886], 1:310; *MemMF*, 1:96; Hedge, *Prose Writers of Germany*, third edition [NY: C. S. Francis, 1855], pp. 266, 269).

54. *Boston Daily Advertiser* and *Boston Atlas*.

55. MF to RWE, 8 Sept. 1841, in *EmL*, 2:446n. The surplus contributions from the July number were apparently not as good as Fuller implied in her note "To Contributors" in that issue.

56. Another English comment on Transcendentalism at this time was not published. Elizabeth Peabody, in a questionable decision, sent a copy of Emerson's *Essays*, with a letter praising them, to William Wordsworth. After reading them he disgustedly compared Emerson with Carlyle as examples of the "weakness of our age," and he asked an American friend, Henry Reed of Philadelphia, "Where is the thing that now passes for philosophy at Boston to stop?" Reed replied that Peabody, whom he had never heard of, must have "strangely misapprehended" Wordsworth's "ways of thinking and feeling and writing" to send Emerson's writings to him. Reed had himself read little in Emerson or Carlyle, but from what he had read he had decided that "the dialect they employ is an intolerable corruption of our mighty language," and he believed that "there is a desperate unsoundness in their philosophical and theological views." As to Wordsworth's question, Reed answered that the natural conclusion of the philosophy at Boston would be "infidelity and pantheism" (16 Aug. 1841, 29 Nov. 1841, in William Wordsworth, *Wordsworth & Reed: The Poet's Correspondence with His American Editor, 1836-1850*, ed. Leslie Nathan Broughton [Ithaca, N.Y.: Cornell University Press, 1933], pp. 57, 60).

57. RWE, *Essays* (Lo: John Fraser, 1841), pp. ix-x: the "Preface" is dated 11 Aug. 1841; reprinted in *Boston Recorder*, 6 Aug. 1841, p. 127.

58. When Joseph Evans Snodgrasse, after reading this story, asked Poe if he had a "quarrel" with the *Dial,* he was answered in the negative: "My slaps at it were only in 'a general way.' The tale in question is a mere Extravaganza levelled at no one in particular, but hitting right & left at things in general" (19 Sept. 1841, in Edgar Allan Poe, *The Letters of Edgar Allan Poe*, ed. John Ward Ostrom [Cambridge, Mass.: Harvard University Press, 1948], 1:183).

59. RWE to MF, 22 Apr. 1841, in *EmL*, 2:395; 6 July 1841, in ibid., pp. 414-15; 19 Aug. 1841, in ibid., p. 442. An example of Miss Woodbridge's talent, and of why Emerson rejected her work, can be seen in this selection from her "The Temperance Tree," sung at the anniversary of the New York State Temperance Society:

> "That noble tree—we need not tell
> Its dear, its honor'd name—
> Glad millions know and love it well,
> It needs no trump of fame."

("Poetry," *Boston Recorder*, 2 Apr. 1841, p. 56)

60. Emerson wanted "[t]hose verses which in a manner cost the poet his life, which make the poet a new creature, react with equal virtue on other men & we must listen and be changed whether we will or will not" (7 July 1841, MBilHi).

61. 19 Aug. 1841, in *EmL*, 2:442 (Rusk tentatively identifies the author as Oliver Jordan Fernald, a Harvard freshman): ibid. Emerson had met Orne in June, when he had invited him to Concord (RWE to LdE, 22 June 1841, in ibid., pp. 407-8); Emerson incorrectly told his Aunt Mary that White would be in the October number: I have been unable to identify White (21 Sept. 1841, in ibid., p. 452).

62. Brownson published some "Orphic Sayings" in the October *Boston Quarterly Review*, causing his friend Alexander H. Everett, the president of Jefferson College in Louisiana, to ask: "What is the meaning of this? Is the Dial defunct? Does that mysterious Horologue no longer 'report the progress of the hours of the day?'" (18 Oct. 1841, InNd).

63. After Alcott was introduced to More's work by Convers Francis in November 1840, he showed the poem to Emerson, who recommended it to Fuller for the *Dial*. Alcott then sent it to her, but she already had too many original contributions to consider it. Emerson was probably instrumental in

getting the selection printed: he had asked Fuller, "Will you not print Henry More?" and after its publication, he told his brother William that it well deserved "a Sunday afternoon" (ABA to A. Q. Thaxter, 3 Nov. 1840, copy by ABA, in *AlcSc40*, p. 252; 4 Nov. 1840, in *EmL*, 2:354-55; Nov. 1840, in *AlcSc40*, p. 254; 22 Apr. 1841, in *EmL*, 2:395; 7 Oct. 1841, in ibid., pp. 454-55).

64. *Boston Morning Post*, 14 Sept. 1841, p. 2; Sept. 1841, in *EmJMN*, 8:92; RWE to WmE, 1 June 1841, in *EmL*, 2:402; 10 Jan. 1840, in *ThJ*, 1:110-13; RWE to MF, 19 Aug. 1841, in *EmL*, 2:442; RWE to LdE, 20[?] July 1841, in ibid., p. 432: RWE to MF, 27 July 1841, in ibid., p. 435; RWE to MF, 19 Aug. 1841, in ibid., p. 442; RWE to MF, 8 Sept. 1841, in ibid., p. 445 (rejected); RWE to MF, 13 Sept. 1841, in ibid., p. 447; RWE to MF, Nov[?] 1839[?], in ibid., p. 242; RWE to MF, 27 July 1841, in ibid., p. 435; HDT to Mrs. Lucy Brown, 8 Sept. 1841, in *ThCor*, p. 46; RWE to MF, 19 Aug. 1841, in *EmL*, 2:442.

65. On 25 September Emerson wrote to Rufus Griswold, a compiler of anthologies, to call Thoreau to his attention: "Unless I am greatly mistaken, Mr. Thoreau already deserves and will more and more deserve your attention as a writer of American Poetry" (Rufus W. Griswold, *Passages from the Correspondence and Other Papers of Rufus W. Griswold*, [ed. W. M. Griswold] [Cambridge, Mass.: W. M. Griswold, 1898], p. 99).

66. RWE to MF, 19 Aug. 1841, in *EmL*, 2:442; RWE to MF, 27 July 1841, in ibid., p. 435; 19 Aug. 1841, in ibid., p. 442; 27 July 1841, in ibid., p. 435 (prose); RWE to MF, 8 Sept. 1841, in ibid., p. 445; MF to RWE, 8 Sept. 1841, in ibid., p. 446n; RWE to MF, 8 Sept. 1841, in ibid., p. 445; see 4 Sept. 1841, in *EmJMN*, 8:49 (E. Hoar); RWE to MF, 13 Sept. 1841, in ibid., p. 447; MF to RWE, 16 Sept. 1841, in ibid., p. 449n. The *Arcturus* later singled out the Landor article as evidence that Emerson was one of "the best critics in the country." Carlyle sent it to an "Editorial Friend" to be "put into the Newspapers here," since Landor was "not often so well praised among us, and deserves a little good praise" ("Criticism in America," *Arcturus* 3 [May 1842]: 406; TC to RWE, 19 Nov. 1841, in *EmCorTC*, p. 313).

67. 27 July 1841, in *EmL*, 2:435; MF to RWE, 8 Sept. 1841, in ibid., p. 446n. Perhaps, also, in her extensive quoting, Fuller indirectly expressed her agreement with Caroline Sturgis on the poem: "It is like a vast cloud, full of gorgeous lights & gloomy shadows . . . I do not believe you will know what half of it means" (CS to RWE, 4 Sept. 1841, MH).

68. 17[?] Sept. 1841, in *EmL*, 2:450; 12 Sept. 1841, in *ScLiLetCPC*, p. 60; 1 Oct. 1841, in ibid., p. 61-63. Other printer's errors in the October *Dial* included two misprints in Thoreau's poem (see HDT to Rufus Griswold, 9 Oct. 1841, in *ThCor*, p. 54).

69. The *Dial* was announced as published "yesterday" by the 1 October 1841 *Boston Courier*, on 1 October by the *Boston Atlas*, and on 2 and 3 October by bookstore advertisements in the *Boston Morning Post*; however, Emerson's letter to Cranch of 1 October makes it clear that the *Dial* was to be published that day (*ScLiLetCPC*, p. 62).

70. *Boston Daily Advertiser*, 14 Sept. 1841, p. 3; this policy appeared in July and October on the recto of the back wrapper.

71. TC to RWE, 19 Nov. 1841, in *EmCorTC*, p. 312; 8 Oct. 1841, in George Templeton Strong, *The Diary of George Templeton Strong*, ed. Allan Nevins and Milton Halsey Thomas (NY: Macmillan, 1952), 1:169.

72. MF to CKN, 2 Oct. 1841, MH; MF to Richard Fuller, 17 Nov. 1841, MH (teaching).

73. As Emerson put it, one difference between them was that "I like to hear of my faults and you do not like to hear of yours." Also, the following journal entry could possibly refer to Fuller's attitude at this time: "The best persons hold themselves aloof, they feel the disproportion between their faculties & the work offered them, & they prefer to go into the country & gaze at the skies & the waters & perish of ennui" (Oct., late Oct. 1841, in *EmJMN*, 8:108, 120).

74. RWE to CPC, 1 Oct. 1841, in *ScLiLetCPC*, p. 63.

75. 6 Oct. 1841, in *EmL*, 2:457-58n. Such arrangements, especially with subscription lists, were common at this time. The very successful *Christian Examiner* changed publishers in 1837 and sold its stock, title, and subscription list for $2,350. When Brownson stopped his *Boston Quarterly Review* in October 1842 to join the *Democratic Review*, the new publisher purchased Brownson's subscription list for $200. However, only 100 people transferred to the *Democratic Review*, and when Brownson left in 1843 to start his own journal again, his subscription list and the title "Boston Quarterly

Review" were offered to him for the same $200. Brownson apparently refused to pay and, assuming that his own name would be enough, published the first number of *Brownson's Quarterly Review* in Januay 1844 (contract between Charles Bowen and James Munroe & Co., 1 Feb. 1844, MHi; John L. O'Sullivan to Brownson, 9 Oct. 1843, in Edward John Power, "Orestes A. Brownson," *Records of the American Catholic Historical Society of Philadelphia* 62 [June 1951]:85).

76. MF to Richard Fuller, 5 Nov. 1841, MH; RWE to MF, 9 Nov. 1841, in *EmL*, 2:461-62; 9 Nov. 1841 in *EmL*, 2:461-61n; RWE to MF, ca. 14[?] Nov. 1841, in ibid., p. 464. Although Fuller promised to give Emerson "a precise account of the new agreement," I have been unable to locate such a document.

77. RWE to MF, 9 Nov. 1841, in ibid., p. 462; Emerson was unhappy with the title of the article, thinking it too "presbyterian" (RWE to MF, 20 Dec. 1841, in ibid., p 471); RWE to MF, ca. 14[?] Nov. 1841, in ibid., p. 464; ABA to MF, 6 Dec. 1841, in *Dial* 2 (Apr. 1842):409; 18 Oct. 1841, in *ThCor*, pp. 56-57.

78. The only bright spot for Thoreau in his work on the *Dial* at this time was his receipt of a letter from Isaiah T. Williams of Buffalo, who had read some of Thoreau's poetry in the *Dial* and was struck by its "childhood" or "playful" quality (27 Nov. 1841, in *ThCor*, p. 60).

79. MF to [WCH?], 19 Oct. 1840, in *MemMF*, 2:47-49.

80. Ellery Channing praised her article; Emerson found Bettina "more witty" than either George Sand or Madame de Staël, and "as profound & greatly more readable"; but Carlyle said that he was "sorry" to find in the review "a decided weariness!" (Ellery Channing to MF, 8 Jan. 1842, MH; early Aug. 1842, in *EmJMN*, 8:194; TC to RWE, 17 Nov. 1842, in *EmCorTC*, p. 335).

81. MF to her mother, 25 Dec. 1841, MH; 21 Nov. 1841, MWelC.

82. Journal entry, 21 Jan. 1842, typescript, MBilHi. The first notice announcing the *Dial* for sale that I have been able to find is in the *Boston Atlas* on 3 January. Apparently Peabody distributed the *Dial* more slowly and to fewer stores than Jordan had; I have found no mention of the *Dial* in any advertisements for Peabody's own bookstore.

83. 18 Dec. 1841, InNd; TC to T. Ballantyne, 31 Dec. 1841, in TC, *New Letters of Thomas Carlyle*, ed. Alexander Carlyle (Lo: John Lane, 1904), 1:245-46 ("ghostly"); TC to John Sterling, 18 Dec. 1841, in ibid., pp. 243-44.

84. MF to [EH], [8?] Mar. 1842, in *MemMF*, 1:310; for Emerson, with young Waldo's death, "all that is glad & festal & almost all that is social even," had departed "from this world" (RWE to EPP, 28 Jan. 1842, *EmL*, 3:8); RWE to FHH, 23 Mar. 1842, in ibid., p. 36; RWE to WmE, 26 Mar. 1842, in ibid., p. 39 (subscribers); RWE to FHH, 23 Mar., *EmL*, 3:36 ($750).

85. ca. 17 Mar. 1842, in *HigMF*, pp. 168-69 (the date is from Rusk, *EmL*, 3:33n).

86. Quoted in George Willis Cooke, "'The Dial': An Historical and Biographical Introduction, with a List of the Contributors," *Journal of Speculative Philosophy* 19 (July 1885):231; 18 Mar. 1842, in *EmL*, 3:33-34.

87. RWE to TC, 31 Mar. 1842, in *EmCorTC*, pp. 320-21 (misgivings); *EmL*, 3:35-36.

88. RWE to WmE, 26 Mar. 1842, in *EmL*, 3:39; RWE to FHH, 23 Mar. 1842, in ibid., p. 37 ("portfolio"); 20 Mar. 1842, in *EmJMN*, 8:203.

89. RWE to MF, 18[?] Mar. 1842, in *EmL*, 3:33 (New York); RWE to CPC, 3 May 1843, typescript, MHi (Delf); RWE to MF, 18[?] Mar. 1842, in *EmL*, 3:33.

90. RWE to FHH, 23 Mar. 1842, in *EmL*, 3:37-38.

91. RWE to WmE, 19 Feb. 1842, in ibid., pp. 13-14.

92. *Boston Morning Post*, 28 Mar. 1842. The fact that the *Dial* was published ahead of schedule allowed an errata slip to be inserted for Alcott's paper, rather than let it go totally uncorrected, as had happened to Fuller, Dwight, and Thoreau earlier. Another good sign was that the authors of "several works" had sent their books to the *Dial* for review (*Dial* 2 [April 1842]:544; see also William Everts to RWE, 12 Mar. 1842, MH).

93. Peabody also asked subscribers to send their money and their names directly to her rather than to the *Dial's* agents, thus saving on commissions. And people were encouraged to subscribe, who were currently in the habit of buying single numbers, so that she could determine with greater accuracy the number of copies to be printed.

94. Some magazines simply inserted at the end of each number the names of those subscribers who had not paid. The *Western Messenger* constantly reminded its subscribers to pay up and inserted a slip in its final issue stating that "delinquent subscribers" were a major reason why it was ceasing publication (8 [Apr. 1841]).

95. J.E. Snodgrass, "Transcendentalism. A Miniature Essay," *Magnolia* 4 (Apr. 1842):214-15.

96. Emerson may have been quite innocently at fault for this. Greeley had decided to report on his New York lecture series at length and probably felt that this not only was the best sampling of the Transcendentalists' writings for that month, but also enough.

97. Journal entry, 28 May 1842, in Caroline Fox, *Memories of Old Friends*, ed. Horace N. Pym (Lo: Smith, Elder, 1882), 1:295.

Chapter 4: The *Dial* Under Emerson

1. MF to Mary Rotch, 7 Apr. 1842, MH; 9 Apr. 1842, in *EmL*, 3:45-46n; 6 Apr. 1842, in ibid., p. 44; 7 Apr. 1842, MH.

2. RWE to MF, 10 Apr. 1842, in *EmL*, 3:46.

3. Emerson once described himself to his fiancée as "a poet, of low class without doubt yet a poet." Personally, he told friends, he had "no sweeter experiences" than those which came from "reading poetry." And as late as 1877 he prized his own poetry above his prose (RWE to Lydia Jackson, 1 Feb. 1835, in ibid., 1:435; RWE to SGW, 27 Oct. 1839, MH; quoted in *FrWHC*, p. 402).

4. See F. B. Sanborn, "Biographical Introduction," in William Ellery Channing, *Poems of Sixty-Five Years* (Philadelphia and Concord: James H. Bentley, 1902), pp. xxiii-xxiv; 9 Apr. 1842, in *EmL*, 3:45n; RWE to MF, 10 Apr. 1842, in ibid., p. 47.

5. Junius Alcott had shown the prayer to his brother, who brought it to Emerson's attention. Emerson thought it well done and especially liked these "three good things": "*first*, that it was a prayer, written in this prayerless age; second, that he thanks God for the continuance of their love[;] . . . and *third*, he thanks him for the knowledge he has attained of him by his Sons." A third prayer that Emerson quoted in the article was probably selected by Thoreau (5 Apr. 1842, in *EmJMN*, 8:221; Sophia Thoreau to Ricketson, 18 May 1863, in Anna and Walton Ricketson, eds., *Daniel Ricketson and His Friends* [Bo: HoMif, 1902], p. 157).

6. After seeing the poems in the *Dial*, Henry Channing praised their "delicate, clear-cut, medallion-like nakedness," so sharply defined, to Channing's senses, as to be "unique." He had also liked "The Times" piece when he had heard Emerson deliver it as a lecture, but only after reading it did he feel that he had realized the "good sense and humanity and large wisdom" that it contained (WHC to MF, 7 July 1842, in *FrWHC*, pp. 183-84).

7. 22 Apr. 1842, in *EmJMN*, 8:238-40. See also RWE to CS, 7 July 1841, MH; July 1841, in *EmJMN*, 8:14, 28; and Roger Chester Mueller, "The Orient in American Transcendental Periodicals (1835-1886)," Ph.D. diss., Univeristy of Minnesota, 1968, p. 26.

8. Since Emerson often thought that "almost all half bred scholars belong to little cliques, read particular journals & text books, extol one or two poets & philosophers, talk in their own vocabulary, & ignore the whole world beside," the "readiest remedy" was to use contemporary literature sparingly and to "plunge deep . . . into some distant school." Although Fuller liked the "Ethnical Scriptures" series enough to request that Emerson send "extra sheets" of them to her, Parker railed against the "absurdities in the Indian Vedas." Calling them "improbable," he later told Convers Francis that Emerson had "come upon them *late*, and both exaggerates their merits, and misleads himself by their *bizarréries*" (RWE to Edward A. Washburn, 17 Apr. 1839, TxU; RWE to MF, 31 Dec. 1842, in *EmL*, 3:108; 22 Feb. 1858, in John Weiss, *Life and Correspondence of Theodore Parker* [NY: Appleton, 1864], 1:364).

9. See ca. 23 Mar. 1842 on George H. Colton, *Tecumseh*, and 5 Apr. 1842, on Borrow, in *EmJMN*, 8:206, 223; RWE to WmE, 2 Apr. 1842, in *EmL*, 3:41-42; see RWE to MF, 2[?] Apr. 1842, and MF to RWE, 9 Apr. 1842, in ibid., pp. 42-43, 45n.

10. RWE to TP, 11 May 1842, in *EmL*, 3:55; RWE to FHH, 23 Mar. 1842, and RWE to TP, 11 May 1842, in ibid., pp. 37, 55.

11. RWE to MF, 9 May 1842, in ibid., p. 54. Hawthorne praised the "true, minute, and literal" observations that Thoreau had made, and he felt that this was his best piece of writing to date. He later referred to this article when recommending Thoreau as "a genuine and exquisite observer of nature" to Epes Sargent for his *New Monthly Magazine*. Alcott thought the article "worthy of Isaac Walton himself," and he considered it a "classic" description of the woods around Concord (1 Sept. 1842, in *HawAmNb*, p. 355; 21 Oct. 1842, in Edward C. Sampson, "Three Unpublished Letters by Hawthorne to Epes Sargent," *AL* 34 [Mar. 1962]:103; ABA to his wife, 2 Aug. 1842, in *AlcL*, p. 88).

12. TP to RWE, 7 Apr. 1842, MH; RWE to MF, 10 Mar. 1842, in *EmL*, 3:30 (article); RWE to WmE, 26 Mar. 1842, in ibid., p. 38; RWE to MF, 9 May 1842, in ibid., p. 54 (upset); RWE to WmE, 29 May 1842, in ibid., p. 56.

13. *Boston Morning Post*, 4 Jan. 1842, p. 2, and "The Bible Convention," 31 Mar. 1842, p. 1 (Scriptures). Emerson wrote that "Madmen, madwomen, men with beards, Dunkers, Muggletonians, Come-outers, Groaners, Agrarians, Seventh-day-Baptists, Quakers, Abolitionists, Calvinists, Unitarians, and Philosophers, — all came successively to the top, and seized their moment, if not their *hour*, wherein to chide, or pray, or preach, or protest." As Emerson's description indicates, the conventions were a hodge-podge of various delegates furthering all manner of causes; the *Boston Daily Advertiser* called the speeches "exceedingly incongruous, irrational, absurd, and even nonsensical," and the *New York Evening Post* reported the meetings under the title "Philosophy Run Mad" (3:101; quoted in *SaHaABA*, 1:326; 11 Jan. 1842, p. 2). One reason why Whiting failed to write more for the *Dial* was his poor financial condition. The *Dial* could not pay its contributors, and Whiting spent most of his time working or writing to support his family (see Whiting to the editors, 14 Mar. 1841, *Plain Speaker* 1 [Apr. 1841]:11).

14. Brisbane must have sent his article in soon after the date he had promised Emerson in late May. Brisbane did not, as he later claimed, write "occasionally for the *Dial*"; this was his sole "contribution" (postscript to Greeley to RWE, 26 May 1842, MH; quoted in Redelia Brisbane, *Albert Brisbane: A Mental Biography* [Bo: Arena, 1893], p. 208).

15. RWE to CKN, 7 May 1842, in *EmL*, 3:51; RWE to MF, 3 June 1842, in ibid., p. 58; MF to RWE, 9 Apr. 1842, in ibid., p. 45n; 9 June 1842 in ibid., p. 62.

16. RWE to Mary Moody Emerson, 22 June 1842, in ibid., p. 65; RWE to WmE, 26 June 1842, in ibid., p. 68; RWE to TP, 30 June 1842, in ibid., pp. 68-69; 2 July 1842, MH; *Boston Daily Advertiser*.

17. MF to RWE, 23 June 1842, in *EmL*, 3:72n; MF to CKN, 1 July 1842, MH; WHC to MF, 7 July 1842, in *FrWHC*, p. 183; ABA to his wife, in *AlcL*, p. 88; 19 July 1842, in RWE, *A Letter of Emerson*, ed. Willard Reed (Bo: Beacon, 1934), p. 24; Emerson, in reply, said that he was glad if "only" three articles had offended Parker (8 July 1842, MH; 17 July 1842, in *EmL*, 3:71); 29 Aug. 1842, in *EmCorTC*, pp. 328-29.

18. Greeley later apologized for reprinting the lecture without first asking Emerson's permission but said that he had done so in the hope that it would be "rather beneficial both to [the *Dial*] and the sale of your Lectures when they appear in a volume" (20 July 1842, MH).

19. 1 July 1842, in *EmCorTC*, p. 323: Carlyle's reply concerning the contents of the *Dial* was: "*Perge, Perge*, nevertheless" (19 July 1842, in ibid., p. 327); RWE to TP, 17 July 1842, in *EmL*, 3:70.

20. RWE to John Sterling, 15 Aug. 1842, NN-B; RWE to WmE, 22 Aug., 8 Sept. 1842, in *EmL*, 3:82, 85.

21. Jones Very liked them all "pretty well," Fuller told Emerson that they had "read well" to her, and Hawthorne thought that, though they might appear to some as being "very careless and imperfect," Thoreau's poems were really as "true as bird-notes" (Very to RWE, 23 Nov. 1842, MWelC; 16 Oct. 1842, in *EmL*, 3:90n; Hawthorne to Epes Sargent, 21 Oct. 1842, in Sampson, "Hawthorne Letters," p. 103).

22. Emerson gave one of these poems, "Dirge," its title before sending it to the printer (21 Aug. 1842, in *FuJ42*, p. 325).

23. RWE to EH, 7 May 1842, in *EmL*, 3:49.

24. RWE to WmE, 5 Oct. 1842, in ibid., p. 88 ("ethics"); 24 Aug. 1842, in *FuJ42*, p. 326. Fuller definitely liked the poem, and she felt that Emerson had "put more of himself into Saadi . . . than in any thing he has written before" (19-20 Sept. 1842, in *FuJ42*, p. 338).

25. RWE to WmE, 22 Aug. 1842, in *EmL*, 3:82; RWE to SC, 30 Sept. 1842, MH; RWE to TP, 8 Sept. 1842, in *EmL*, 3:86-87.

26. RWE to MF, 9 June 1842, in *EmL*, 3:62; 19 July 1842, in ibid. p. 75; 17-24 Aug. 1842, in *FuJ42*, pp. 322-27; RWE to TP, 8 Sept. 1842, in *EmL*, 3:87. Emerson felt Fuller had made "a fine selection & translation," and he recommended the article highly to his brother William (RWE to SGW, 30 Sept. 1842, MH; 8 Sept. 1842, in *EmL*, 3:85).

27. "Editor's Table," *Union* 20 (Aug. 1842):201: reprinted from a review of Francis Bowen, *Critical Essays*, in *Christian Examiner* 32 (July 1842), 398; Kenneth Walter Cameron, "Emerson, Thoreau and the Town Athenaeum," in his *The Transcendentalists and Minerva* (Hartford, Conn.: Transcendental Books, 1958), 3:892.

28. Late June 1842, in *EmJMN*, 8:181.

29. Carlyle knew an unusual man was coming when Emerson advised him of Alcott's visit in this manner: "If you have heard his name before, forget what you have heard. Especially if you have ever read anything to which this name was attached, be sure to forget that." When Alcott arrived and saw "the restless melancholy, the memory feeding on hope" that Carlyle presented, he wrote his wife that "The man is sick; he needs rest." Carlyle was amused by this "venerable Don Quixote," "bent on saving the world by a return to acorns and the golden age," and he felt that Alcott's "present *sally* into modern existence . . . evidently gives him pain." He did go out of his way to be hospitable to Alcott, even to the extent of cooking his vegetarian guest "unimaginable messes according to our best understanding" of his dietary habits — but all for naught. Once, while Carlyle was eating his potatoes for breakfast, the fresh strawberries he had ordered to please Alcott arrived, and his visitor blithely plopped them down in the same plate with his own potatoes, "where the two juices ran together and fraternized." Carlyle was so "shocked" that he left his meal and "stormed up and down the room instead." At their last meeting, the "Potato Quixote" and he came to a "sheer rupture"; when Carlyle asked "When shall I see you again?" Alcott's answer was "Never, I guess!" (31 Mar. 1842, in *EmCorTC*, p. 320; 2 July 1842, in *AlcL*, p. 78; TC to RWE, 19 July 1842, in *EmCorTC*, p. 326; TC to John Sterling, 23 July 1842, in TC, *Letters of Thomas Carlyle to John Stuart Mill, John Sterling and Robert Browning*, ed. Alexander Carlyle [Lo: T. Fisher Unwin, 1923], p. 256; TC's recollection told to Henry James, Sr., quoted in Annie Fields, journal entry, 28 July 1864, in M. A. DeWolfe Howe, *Memories of a Hostess* . . . [Bo: Atlantic Monthly Press, 1922], p. 75; TC to Sterling, 29 Aug. 1842, in Carlyle, *Letters to Mill &c*, p. 257).

30. ABA to RWE, 2 July 1842, in *AlcL*, pp. 81-82; 10 Aug. 1842, in ABA, *The Journals of Bronson Alcott*, ed. Odell Shepard (Bo: Little, Brown, 1938), p. 169; 21 July 1842, in ibid., p. 166 ("too broad"); 27 Aug. 1842, *FuJ42*, p. 328.

31. ABA to his wife, 2 July 1842, in *AlcL*, p. 79 ("distribution"); 12 June 1842, in ibid., p. 71; ABA to RWE, 2 July 1842, in ibid., pp. 81-82.

32. 2 July 1842, in ibid., p. 81. Alcott was quite confident that Emerson would accept these manuscripts, for the advertisement of the *Dial* in the August *Healthian* mentioned Lane, Heraud, Henry G. Wright, and Francis Barnham, all of England, as "contributors" to the American magazine (1:72).

33. RWE to SGW, 30 Sept. 1842, MH. One, "a paper of Hermes Trismegistus," probably served as the basis for the "Ethnical Scriptures" selections in January 1844, as Emerson had indeed promised in his "Editor's Table" in October (ABA to his wife, 2 Aug. 1842, in *AlcL*, p. 88).

34. RWE to FHH, 1 Sept. 1842, in *EmL*, 3:84-85.

35. See TP to RWE, 8 July, 3 Sept. 1842, MH. Emerson reviewed Brownson's *A Letter to Rev. Wm. E. Channing*, which he had received from Elizabeth Peabody in June. At that time he merely complained of its "idolatrous" message, but by October the ideas proposed by Brownson — who was rapidly becoming a convert to Roman Catholicism — had become so abhorrent to Emerson that he devoted two pages in the *Dial* to refuting them (RWE to EPP, 9 June 1842, in *EmL*, 3:63-64).

36. RWE to SGW, 30 Sept. 1842, MH. Thoreau apparently was careless, for Fuller's review of Tennyson appeared with such typographical errors as "infamy" for "infancy" and "abstraction" for

"obstruction." She was "*a little* vexed," since she had hoped that Tennyson would see the review. In apologizing for him, Emerson said that Thoreau had corrected errors elsewhere in the magazine, and he either did not see the mistakes in her review or "concluded that it was good Dialese" (MF to RWE, 16 Oct. 1842, in *EmL*, 3:90n; 11 Oct. 1842, in ibid., p. 91).

37. *Boston Daily Advertiser*, 3 Oct. 1842.

38. Charles Dickens, *American Notes for General Circulation* (Lo: Chapman and Hall, 1842), 1:134.

39. Quoted in CSW to J. F. Heath, 14 Nov. 1842, MH; Jones Very to RWE, 23 Nov. 1842, MWelC; quoted in CSW to J. F. Heath, 14 Nov. 1842, MH.

40. RWE to TP, 7[?] Nov. 1842, in *EmL*, 3:95 (invited); RWE to FHH, 1 Sept. 1842, in ibid., p. 85; Cameron, "Emerson, Thoreau and Town Athenaeum," 3:894; RWE to FHH, 1 Sept. 1842, in *EmL*, 3:85.

41. 16 Oct. 1842, in ibid., p. 90n; Emerson had been trying to get Sturgis's poem for the *Dial* for over a year (see RWE to MF, 22 Apr. 1841, in ibid., 2:395); see TP to RWE, 8 July 1842, 3 Sept. 1842, MH, RWE to TP, 8 Sept. 1842, in *EmL*, 3:87, and TP to RWE, [late 1842], MH, where the date "[1843]" is supplied: however, internal evidence clearly dates the year as 1842; RWE to MF, 12 Dec. 1842, in *EmL*, 3:103 (Channing); and Ellen Louisa Tucker Emerson, *One First Love: The Letters of Ellen Louisa Tucker to Ralph Waldo Emerson*, ed. Edith W. Gregg (Cambridge, Mass.: Harvard University Press, 1962), pp. 130-31.

42. Nearly two years later Cornelius Mathews wrote Emerson to complain that his review of *The Career of Puffer Hopkins* in the January 1843 *Dial* had done him a "great injustice" by calling his book of "the school of Dickens," for it was, to Mathews, of "no man's school," but true to the author's own "point of observation and design" (11 Nov. 1844, MH).

43. MF to FHH, 17 Dec. 1842, MH ("cold"); 16 Nov. 1842, in *EmL*, 3:97; RWE to MF, 12 Dec. 1842, in ibid., p. 102; RWE to WmE, 25 Nov. 1842, in ibid., p. 100; 16 Dec. 1842, MH ("clearly"); RWE to CSW, 13 Dec. 1842, MH.

44. See 30 May 1836, in *EmJMN*, 5:165; see 31 May, 7 June, 1 Sept. 1841, in *ThJ*, 1:261, 264, 279; HDT to Isaiah T. Williams, 14 Mar. 1842, in *ThCor*, p. 68, and *Dial* 3:335; and RWE to CSW, 13 Dec. 1842, MH. Thoreau considered his translation to be so successful that he even thought of doing more, and Hedge rejoiced when he read it in the *Dial*. Greeley felt that Thoreau's work created a "deserved sensation," and when in 1849 a new translation of Aeschylus was published at least two reviewers thought to compare it with Thoreau's: Cornelius C. Felton, in the *North American Review* (October 1842), believed Thoreau's attempt to have been "executed with ability," and the *Boston Semi-Weekly Advertiser* (29 Sept. 1842) praised his "bold translation" (HDT to RWE, 15 Feb. 1843, in *ThCor*, p. 88; RWE to LdE, 20 Jan. 1843, in *EmL*, 3:129; Greeley to Griswold, 25 Aug. 1845, in Rufus W. Griswold, *Passages from the Correspondence and Other Papers of Rufus W. Griswold*, [ed. W. M. Griswold] [Cambridge, Mass.: W. M. Griswold, 1898], p. 207).

45. RWE to WmE, 13, 15 Jan. 1816, in *EmL*, 1:15-16; RWE to Gould, 21 Dec. 1842, in ibid., 3:106.

46. TP to RWE, [late 1842], MH. Parker was so concerned about this error, which misattributed a quotation, that he also wrote a letter of correction to the *Boston Daily Advertiser*, which printed it on 7 October 1842.

47. RWE to LdE, 6 Jan. 1843, in *EmL*, 3:111-12.

48. *Boston Daily Advertiser*; FHH to MF, 5, 12 Jan. 1843, MH. Emerson was now listed as editor on the recto of the back wrapper. Another new feature on the *Dial*'s cover was the printing of its title, for, as he had wanted to do earlier, Emerson dropped the subtitle, "A Magazine of Literature, Philosophy, and Religion," in order to print "The Dial" in large bold letters.

49. 12 Jan. 1843, in *EmL*, 3:121; TP to RWE, 20 Jan. 1843, MH; 12 Feb. 1843, in *EmL*, 3:146-47; 23 Feb. 1843, in ibid., p. 148; Hawthorne later thought "Canova" was one of the few good pieces in its number (9 Apr. 1843, in *HawAmNb*, p. 373; 1843, in *EmJMN*, 8:529).

50. RWE to HDT, 12 Feb. 1843, in *ThCor*, p. 85; 15 Feb. 1843, in ibid., pp. 87-88 (the Etzler review later appeared in the November 1843 *Democratic Review*); [1 Mar. 1843], in *ThCor*, p. 89, where it is incorrectly dated "16 Feb. 1843" (see Kenneth Walter Cameron, *Companion to Thoreau's Correspondence* [Hartford, Conn.: Transcendental Books, 1964], p. 225).

51. EPP to HDT, 26 Feb. 1843, ViU-B; 5 Mar. 1843, in *EmL*, 3:154; RWE to W. H. Furness, 11 Mar. 1843, in *EmRecLiFr*, p. 19.

52. RWE to MF, 20[?] Mar. 1843, in *EmL*, 3:159-60; 21 Mar. 1843, MH.

53. 1843, in *EmJMN*, 8:529; RWE to MF, 20[?] Mar. 1843, in *EmL*, 3:160-61 (Channing); Thoreau may have used Emerson's own journals, and the extracts in them, in making his selections: see Mueller, "Orient in American Transcendental Periodicals," pp. 58-59, and HDT, *Early Essays and Miscellanies*, ed. Joseph J. Moldenhauer (Princeton, N.J.: Princeton University Press, 1975), pp. 382-83. These poems were probably Thoreau's revision of the verses that had pleased Emerson by their "honest truth" when Thoreau had read them to him in November 1842 (*EmJMN*, 8:257); RWE to MF, 12 Feb. 1843, in *EmL*, 3:147.

54. Mar. 1843, in *EmJMN*, 8:370, 375.

55. RWE to EPP, 25[?] Mar.[?] 1843, in *EmL*, 3:162. Carlyle was unable to comment on the January *Dial* because it had been mailed incorrectly, and when it arrived with "a guinea of postage" he had refused to pay. Carlyle went on to say, in his manner of complimenting the *Dial*, that while there was "not indeed anything, except the Emersonian papers," which he "properly speaking *liked*," there was "much that [he] did not dislike" (11 Mar. 1843, in *EmCorTC*, p. 337).

56. HDT to RWE, [1 Mar. 1843], in *ThCor*, p. 89; RWE to MF, 20[?] Mar. 1843, in *EmL*, 3:160; Apr. 1843, in *EmJMN*, 8:388.

57. *Boston Daily Advertiser*; William Story to J. F. Heath, 28 Mar. 1843, ViU-B.

58. H. James to RWE, 11 May 1843, in Ralph Barton Perry, *The Thought and Character of William James* (Bo: Little, Brown, 1935), 1:47; 8 Apr. 1843, in *HawAmNb*, p. 371.

59. RWE to TC, 29 Apr. 1843, in *EmCorTC*, p. 343 ("friends"); RWE to MF, 20 Apr. 1843, in *EmL*, 3:165-66 ("volunteer"); RWE to TC, 29 Apr. 1843, in *EmCorTC*, p. 343 ("careless"). One example of Munroe's business sense was his decision to raise the prices of back numbers from the thirty-seven and a half cents per copy and five dollars per three-volume set that Peabody had charged to forty-two cents each for numbers one through eight, sixty-two and a half cents each for numbers nine through twelve, and six dollars for the set of three volumes (verso of back wrapper).

60. RWE to SGW, 3 May 1843, MH; 19 May 1843, in *EmJMN*, 8:400; *United States Magazine, and Democratic Review* 12 (May 1843):519-20.

61. RWE to SGW, 3 May 1843, MH (Channing); 29 Apr. 1843, in *EmL*, 3:170.

62. RWE to MF, 20 Apr. 1843, in *EmL*, 3:165; RWE to MF, 11 May 1843, in ibid., p. 174. Thoreau called Fuller's piece "a noble piece, rich extempore writing"; Sophia Ripley found it "rich in all good things"; and a friend told Parker that he considered it "the best piece that has seen the light in the Dial." Ellery Channing recommended it "without qualification," and Emerson felt it to be "quite an important fact in the history of Woman." The radical woman's rights advocate Mary Gove earnestly thanked Emerson for printing Fuller's call to arms. Only Sophia Hawthorne disliked "the speech which Queen Margaret Fuller has made," and it seemed to her that if Fuller were "married truly, she would no longer be puzzled about the rights of woman," since marriage, to Sophia, was "woman's true destiny and place" (HDT to the Emersons, 8 July 1843, in *ThCor*, pp. 124-25; SR to RWE, 5 July 1843, MH; TP to RWE, 2 Aug. 1843, MH; RWE to MF, 11 July 1843, in *EmL*, 3:183; 15 Aug. 1843, MH; n.d., Julian Hawthorne, *Nathaniel Hawthorne and His Wife* [Bo: HoMif, 1884], 1:257).

63. 21 May 1843, in *ThCor*, p. 102; 23 May 1843, in ibid., p. 107 (ill); 8 June 1843, in ibid., p. 112; 15 June 1843, in ibid., p. 118.

64. Alcott also believed it was "wicked to eat animal food," but when he lectured the boys of Concord on this subject, wearing as he was "a very comfortable pair of calfskin boots," they could not reconcile the words with the deed and so "thought Mr. Alcott rather stupid" (George F. Hoar, *Autobiography of Seventy Years* [NY: Scribner's, 1903], 1:73).

65. Frederick L. H. Willis, *Alcott Memoirs* (Bo: Richard G. Badger, 1915), p. 83.

66. After Alcott and his English friends had arrived in Concord, Emerson noted in his journal that, though fine men, they were "too desultory, ignorant, imperfect, and whimsical to be trusted for any progress. Excellent springs, worthless regulators." As for Alcott's chances to be "the founder of a family or institution," Emerson would just as soon collect "money for a madman." And when Alcott asked him how he could make Fruitlands succeed with his own wife and family to maintain, Emerson answered that "he was not the person to do it, or he would not ask the question." Emerson was right,

for the community failed at the end of the year (26 Oct., 14 Nov. 1842, in *EmJMN*, 8:300, 310).

67. When Fuller read this letter, it made her "laugh till [she] cried," so "whimsically" did it contrast with the "strong instincts and imperative necessities" of Chicago, where she was then staying (MF to RWE, 4 Aug. 1843, in *EmL*, 3:194n).

68. RWE to MF, 7 June 1843, in ibid., p. 179; RWE to EH, June[?] 1843]?], in ibid., p. 181 ("panegyric"); ca. 10 June 1843, in *EmJMN*, 8:422. Thoreau thought that Emerson had "spoken a good word" for Carlyle, and the review was, according to Sophia Ripley, "regally" done. Mrs. Hawthorne praised it as "noble," and only the reformers, Henry Channing and Greeley, while "much pleased," had a criticism to make, that Emerson had overlooked the book's "practical aim and merits." Carlyle himself thanked Emerson for the review, which he considered the "most dangerous thing" he had read on himself in some years because of the "decided likeness" of him "recognizable in it." He also said that everyone who spoke of it called it the "beautifullest piece of criticism" they had read, and he even purchased an extra copy of that number to send to his mother (HDT to the Emersons, 8 July 1843, in *ThCor*, p. 125; SR to RWE, 5 July 1843, MH; n.d., Hawthorne, *Hawthorne and His Wife*, 1:256; HDT to RWE, 7 Aug. 1843, in *ThCor*, p. 133; 31 Oct. 1843, in *EmCorTC*, pp. 349-50).

69. Fuller found the poem "Gifts" to be "charming" and was also pleased by "To Rhea." Carl Strauch feels that the last poem represents "Emerson's Platonic advice to Margaret, by way of parable, that she raise her unreturned love [of him] up to the celestial and thereby improve the universe" (MF to RWE, 4 Aug. 1843, in *EmL*, 3:194n; "Hatred's Swift Repulsions: Emerson, Margaret Fuller, and Others," *Studies in Romanticism* 7 [Winter 1968]:96).

70. Emerson felt that Hunt's "Abou Ben Adhem" promised "its own immortality beyond all the contemporary poems." The poem might have been brought to his mind by Elizabeth Peabody, who had quoted from these "beautiful lines" in an article in the April 1842 *Boston Quarterly Review* (late May 1842, in *EmJMN*, 8:174; "Mr. Parker and the Unitarians," *Boston Quarterly Review* 5:208-9).

71. 6 May 1843, in Perry, *William James*, 1:45; 29 Apr. 1843, in *EmCorTC*, pp. 343-44; 14 May 1843, MH; 1 June 1843, MH ("sonnets"); 10 May 1843, in *EmJ*, 6:393; Mary Gove to RWE, 15 Aug. 1843, MH; [1843], in Thomas Wentworth Higginson, "The Personality of Emerson," *Outlook* 74 (23 May 1903): 221.

72. RWE to HDT, 10 and 15 June 1843, in *ThCor*, p. 118. Although the first advertisements for the *Dial* which I have been able to find announced it as just received at Ticknor's on 3 July, personal letters clearly indicate an earlier publication date.

73. 11 July 1843, in *EmL*, 3:183; CS to RWE, 5 July 1843, MH; SR to RWE, 5 July 1843, MH; HDT to the Emersons, 8 July 1843, in *ThCor*, p. 124; MF to RWE, 4 Aug. 1843, in *EmL*, 3:194n; TP to RWE, 2 Aug. 1843, MH.

74. 1 Nov. 1842, MH; [24 July 1843], in Leo Stoller, "Christopher A. Greene: Rhode Island Transcendentalist," *Rhode Island History* 22 (Oct. 1963):108; RWE to EH, 7 May 1842, in *EmL*, 3:49 (E. Hooper); RWE to SGW, 30 Sept. 1843, MH (Channing); Tappan's poem was probably in the "pacquet" referred to by Emerson on 21 May 1843 in writing to Thoreau (*ThCor*, p. 102); RWE to LdE, 19 July 1843, in *EmL*, 3:187.

75. RWE to MF, 7 Aug. 1843, in *EmL*, 3:197; 1 Sept. 1843, in ibid., p. 204-5; CKN to RWE, 8 Sept. 1843, MH; MF to RWE, 4 Aug., and RWE to MF, 7 Aug. 1840, in *EmL*, 2:194n, 198; RWE to CKN, 1 Sept. 1843, in ibid., 3:204.

76. HDT to RWE, 23 May 1843, in *ThCor*, p. 107; HDT to the Emersons, 8 July 1843, in ibid., p. 125; Sept. 1843, in *EmJMN*, 9:9-10, and repeated by Emerson in his obituary of Thoreau (*EmW*, 10:479); RWE to HDT, 8 Sept. 1843, in *ThCor*, pp. 137-38 (F. B. Sanborn prints part of the verses that Emerson removed in his *The Life of Henry David Thoreau* [Bo: HoMif, 1917], pp. 261-64); HDT to RWE, 14 Sept. 1843, in *ThCor*, p. 139. Thoreau's bad luck with printers followed him again, and after the number appeared he told Emerson that "[t]here are some sad mistakes in the printing" (17 Oct. 1843, in ibid., p. 145).

77. HDT to RWE, 14 Sept. 1843, in *ThCor*, p. 139. Probably Emerson was more responsible for this installment in the "Ethical Scriptures" than Thoreau was; at best, Thoreau assembled the pieces from Emerson's journals and from the markings in Emerson's own copy of the book being used.

78. Although Fuller considered the "Ode to Beauty" to be a fine poem, Thoreau found a "good deal

of fault" with it, especially its poor rhyme and "stereotyped lines" (MF to HDT, 25 Sept. 1843, in William White, "Three Unpublished Thoreau Letters," *NEQ* 33 [Sept. 1960]:373; HDT to RWE, 17 Oct. 1843, in *ThCor*, pp. 145-46).

79. Thoreau declared that, as he read the "lecture" on "The Comic," it was "as good as to be in our. . . Lyceum once more" (HDT to RWE, 17 Oct. 1843, in *ThCor*, p. 146).

80. Emerson gave a lengthy extract from the *Deutsche Snellpost* and "probably" provided the translation from Theodor Mundt's *Geschichte der Literatur der Gegenwart*. Both Fuller and Wheeler had sent Emerson copies of this last book with their recommendation that it be used in the *Dial* (*EmJMN*, 8:350, n5; MF to RWE, 4 Aug. 1843, in *EmL*, 3:194-95n; RWE to CSW, 30 Apr. 1843, ViU-B).

81. RWE to CS, 29 Sept. 1843, MH.

82. *Boston Daily Advertiser* and *Boston Post;* John Sterling to RWE, 20 Feb. 1844, in his *A Correspondence Between John Sterling and Ralph Waldo Emerson*, ed. Edward Waldo Emerson (Bo: HoMif, 1897), p. 83, CS to RWE, 10 Oct. 1843, MH; MF to RWE, 12 Nov. 1843, in *HigMF*, p. 166 (Parker).

83. TP to RWE, 2 Aug. 1843, MH; 31 Oct. 1843, in *EmCorTC*, p. 349, RWE to SGW, 28 Nov. 1843, MH, where the date "[1844]" is supplied: however, internal evidence clearly places the year as 1843; "Call of the Present — No. 2. — Science of Unity," *Present* 1 (15 Nov. 1843):76; RWE to SGW, 23 Oct. 1843, MH; 25 Oct. 1843, in *ThCor*, p. 149.

84. RWE to MF, 17 Dec. 1843, in *EmL*, 3:229.

85. One reason for the *Dial's* poor finances was the almost total lack of help from English sales. Peabody had often failed entirely to get the *Dial* off to England. Under Munroe, who sent fifty copies "duly to London," no account of their sales was received, even though Charles Mudie had the *Dial* prominently displayed in the window of his well-known bookstore. The change from John Green as the *Dial's* English publisher to the reliable John Chapman, who had "succeeded to the business" of Green, came with the *Dial's* last number — too late to make any difference (RWE to SGW, 23 Oct. 1843, MH; Guinevere L. Griest, *Mudie's Circulating Library and the Victorian Novel* [Bloomington, Ind.: Indiana University Press, 1970], p. 19; Henry G. Wright to RWE, 30 July 1844, MH).

86. RWE to SGW, 23 Oct. 1843, MH; 6 Oct. 1843, RWE, "Account Book 1840-44," MH; 2 Dec., 25 Nov. 1843, 5 June 1844, in ibid.; RWE to WmE, 17 Dec. 1843, in *EmL*, 3:229 (essays); RWE to WmE, 3 Dec. 1843, in ibid., p. 227.

87. Moses George Thomas to RWE, 25 Nov. 1843, MH; 4 Dec. 1843, CSmH; Thomas to RWE, 16 Dec. 1843, MH; 30 Dec. 1843, MH. Clarke later reviewed Thomas, *A Rejected Article, in Reply to Parker's Review of "Hennell on the Origin of Christianity." Offered First to the Dial; then to the Christian Examer* (Bo: Benjamin H. Greene, 1844), and praised Thomas for noticing what Clarke called the distinction between Parker's "Negative Transcendentalism," which could not exist with Christianity, and Emerson's "Positive Transcendentalism," which could. He also felt that Thomas well maintained his position that Parker's thoughts were "sheer infidelity" (*Christian World* 2[3 Feb. 1844]:3).

88. See mid-Nov. 1839, in *EmJMN*, 7:297; one poem, "The Times," was a fragment that he had left off working on that summer (John D. Gordan, comp., "Ralph Waldo Emerson, 1803-1882: Catalogue of an Exhibition from the Berg Collection," *Bulletin of the New York Public Library* 57 [Sept. 1953]: 441); RWE to SGW, 28 Nov. 1843, MH.

89. MF to RWE, 12 Nov. 1843, in *EmL*, 3:220n; RWE to MF, 18 Oct., 5 Nov. 1843, in ibid., pp. 215, 222; RWE to TC, 31 Dec. 1843, in *EmCorTC*, p. 355. Although Emerson later told Fuller that her paper was "an infinite refreshment to me to see it in the dry stone 'Dial,'" he was somewhat more pointed to Sterling. To him, Emerson apologized for the article being "inadequate" and asked his indulgence if Fuller's pen should "ramble a little." Emerson mentioned that she had been ill while writing the article, but he concluded: "Corinna never can write" (6 Jan. 1844, copy by RWE, in *EmJMN*, 11:459; 31 Jan. 1844, in Sterling, *Sterling-Emerson Correspondence*, p. 79).

90. RWE to MF, 17 Dec. 1843, in *EmL*, 3:230; see Walter Harding, *The Days of Henry Thoreau* (NY: Knopf, 1966), pp. 155-56; 20 July 1843, in *ThCor*, pp. 126-27; HDT to RWE, 7 Aug. 1843, in ibid., p. 133; RWE to HDT, 25 Oct. 1843, in ibid., p. 149. Because Thoreau described himself in October as having "weathered so many epics of late," he also possibly sent in his translation of

Aeschylus's *Seven Against Thebes* to Emerson at that time. Sanborn thinks that Thoreau may have also submitted at this time the poetic sequel to "The Service" that Sanborn prints on pp. 363-64, but a subsequent examination of the manuscript gives Sanborn's arguments much less force (HDT to RWE, 17 Oct. 1843, in ibid., p. 145; Harding, *Thoreau*, p. 119; Sanborn, *Thoreau* [1917]. See also Laurence A. Cummings, "Thoreau Poems in Bixby-Washington University Manuscripts," *ESQ*, no. 26 [I Quarter 1962]: 26).

91. *Boston Daily Advertiser*. By 31 December 1843 Emerson had not even seen Fuller's article, and the *Dial* was published too late to go on the steamer to England that left on 1 January (RWE to TC, in *EmCorTC*, p. 355; RWE to Sterling, 31 Jan. 1844, in Sterling, *Sterling-Emerson Correspondence*, p. 78).

92. RWE to LMC, 8 Jan. 1844, NNPM; 10 Feb. 1844, MH; 26 Feb. 1844, in *EmL*, 3:243 (Fuller); see Apr. 1843, in *EmJMN*, 8:527 ("Ethnical Scriptures"); 26 Feb. 1844, in *EmL*, 3:243.

93. RWE to WmE, 1 Apr. 1844, in ibid., p. 245; RWE to EPP, [Mar.? 1844?], in Lilian Whiting, *Boston Days* (Bo: Little, Brown, 1911), p. 21; Mar. 1844, *EmJMN*, 9:82 ("nervous"); *EmL*, 3:245.

94. *Boston Daily Advertiser*.

95. George William Curtis to JSD, 8 Apr. 1844, in *CuEarlyLetDw*, p. 167; Cornelius Mathews to RWE, 11 Nov. 1844, MH; RWE to W. H. Furness, 4 Apr. 1844, in *EmRecLiFr*, pp. 33-34; W. A. Jones, "Criticism in America," *Democratic Reivew* 15:247.

Chapter 5: Charles Timothy Brooks

Note: Biographical information is from Charles W. Wendte, "Memoir," in Charles T. Brooks, *Poems, Original and Translated*, ed. W. P. Andrews (Bo: Roberts, 1885), pp. 3-114.

1. Wendte, "Memoir," p. 41.

2. Brooks to JSD, 11 May 1837, MH. Wendte erroneously states that Brooks was ordained on 14 June 1837.

3. Apparently Brooks tried, without success, to get George Ripley to publish the translation of *William Tell* in his *Specimens of Foreign Standard Literature* (see Brooks to JSD, 26 Feb. 1838, NBu); CKN, *The Journals of Charles King Newcomb*, ed. Judith Kennedy Johnson (Providence, R.I.: Brown University Press, 1946), pp. 15-16.

4. 28 Mar. 1840, in *EmL*, 2:265.

5. 30 Mar. 1840, in *EmL*, 2:269. For an assessment of Brooks's writings, see Henry A. Pochmann, *German Culture in America* (Madison, Wis.: University of Wisconsin Press, 1957), p. 452.

Chapter 6: James Elliot Cabot

Note: Biographical information is from James Elliot Cabot, "Reminiscences," typescript, MCR-S, which was used in three useful published sketches of Cabot: Edward Waldo Emerson, *The Early Years of the Saturday Club 1855-1870* (Bo: HoMif, 1918), pp. 260-68; Thomas Wentworth Higginson, "James Elliot Cabot," *Proceedings of the American Academy of Arts and Sciences* 39 (1903-1904): 649-55; and Thomas Wentworth Higginson, "Memoir of James Elliot Cabot," *Proceedings of the Massachusetts Historical Society*, 2d ser. 20 (1906-1907): 526-33.

1. Cabot, "Reminiscences," pp. 16-17.

2. Henry A. Pochmann, *German Culture in America* (Madison, Wis.: University of Wisconsin Press, 1957), p. 638n (Longfellow); Cabot, "Reminiscences," p. 17 ("contempt"); John Olin Eidson, *Charles Stearns Wheeler: Friend of Emerson* (Athens, Ga.: University of Georgia Press, 1951), p. 67; Cabot, "Reminiscences," p. 31. Cabot may not have found his role in life while abroad, but he certainly did not waste his chance for an education. Pochmann calls Cabot more thoroughly schooled in Kant, Schelling, and Hegel than even Hedge. Higginson remembered that when he went to Cabot's

room at Harvard complaining of "not understanding Kant's 'Critique of Pure Reason,' in English, [Cabot] answered tranquilly that he could not; that having read it twice in German he had thought he comprehended it, but that Meiklejohn's translation was beyond making out" (Pochmann, *German Culture*, p. 253; Thomas Wentworth Higginson, *Cheerful Yesterdays* [Bo: HoMif, 1898], p. 105).

3. JRL to W. W. Story, Jan. 1844, in Robert Browning, *Browning to His American Friends: Letters Between the Brownings, the Storys and James Russell Lowell*, ed. Gertrude Reese Hudson (Lo: Bowes and Bowes, 1965), p. 220; L. Vernon Briggs, *History and Genealogy of the Cabot Family* (Bo: Charles E. Goodspeed, 1927), 2:643. Very had not yet been removed from Harvard when Cabot was an undergraduate, and, although they lost touch after Very's dismissal, Cabot remembered Very favorably, especially a meeting of theirs under strained circumstances. At that time it was against the rules for students to have guns for hunting, so a common ruse was to carry guns slung in two parts under the coat until reaching a safe distance from Cambridge. One afternoon Cabot and a friend were doing just this when they met Very, who "looked at us sorrowfully, no doubt penetrating our disguise, but was too high-minded to call us to question" (Cabot, "Reminiscences," p. 18). Later, Cabot, who was Louis Agassiz's assistant in 1847, corresponded with Thoreau about the samples he was sending to the Harvard naturalist (see *ThCor*, pp. 177ff).

4. *EmJMN*, 8:385, where the editors state that this is "probably" Cabot. Cabot's name was earlier printed in full for this entry in *EmJ*, 6:384. Although there is a remote possibility that this visitor was indeed Cabot, it is unlikely that he would have omitted such a meeting from his "Reminiscences," sent his article for the *Dial* anonymously to Emerson, and not pursued a correspondence with a man he both admired and respected.

5. *EmL*, 3:243. Higginson was also impressed and years later recalled this article as "the simplest and most effective statement" on Kant he had ever encountered (Higginson, "Cabot," p. 652).

6. N.d., MCR-S: although endorsed by Emerson "J. E. Cabot / 1845," this letter was obviously written to Emerson before Emerson's letter to Ward the previous December; Dec. 1844, in Emerson, *Saturday Club*, p. 262; 24 Mar. 1845, in *EmL*, 3:280, where Rusk states that this was apparently Emerson's first letter to Cabot (279n); 30 May 1845, in ibid., p. 288.

Chapter 7: William Ellery Channing

Note: Biographical information is from Frederick T. McGill, Jr., *Channing of Concord: A Life of William Ellery Channing II* (New Brunswick, N.J.: Rutgers University Press, 1967), and Robert N. Hudspeth, *Ellery Channing* (NY: Twayne, 1973), which prints letters not in McGill. F. B. Sanborn, who allowed Channing to live at his house during the last years of the poet's life, utilized many of Channing's reminiscences in his own writings.

1. At one meeting Fuller recorded in her journal the queer impression that he made upon her: "Ellery Channing was there; I concluded from what M. had said that he came to see *me*; however after looking at me for a while between his fingers he fairly turned his back upon me and began talking in a whisper to Wm. When I got up to go away he jumped up and walked home with me" ("December 1836 Journal," MH).

2. McGill, *Channing*, p. 21 ("rhapsody"); F. B. Sanborn, "Biographical Introduction," in William Ellery Channing, *Poems of Sixty-Five Years* (Philadelphia and Concord: James H. Bentley, 1902), p. xv ("The Spider"); ibid., pp. xxiii-xxiv (fifty); 3 Oct. 1839, in *EmL*, 2:227-28; RWE to SGW, 27 Oct. 1839, MH; 30 Jan. 1840, in *EmL*, 2:253; RWE to MF, 8 Apr. 1840, in ibid., p. 276; RWE to MF, 23[?]Apr. 1840, in ibid., p. 288.

3. 16 June 1840, MH; 21 June 1840, in *EmL*, 2:306; 5 July 1840, in *HigMF*, p. 156; RWE to SGW, 14 July 1840, MH; RWE to MF, 27 July 1840, in *EmL*, 2:320.

4. 12 Sept. 1840, in *EmL*, 2:331; 13 Sept. 1840, MH; RWE to MF, 13 Sept. 1840, in *EmL*, 2:332.

5. Late May 1840, in *EmJMN*, 7:359. The same feelings were expressed in the *Dial* article.

6. *Dial* 1:220-32. In Providence Sarah Helen Whitman read the article and wrote Orestes Brownson that if he did not have the "patience to read it all pray do not forget to read the last piece of poetry." Although she thought the poems "beautiful and noble thoughts," she felt that for the

most part they were "very crudely & affectedly expressed" (19 Nov. 1840, InNd). Channing's "Our Birth Days" always stayed with Emerson, and, years later, when emerging from the Mammoth Cave into the night, he quoted from it in his comment on the scene: "We had lost one of the 'days of our bright lives'" (RWE to LdE, 16 June 1850, in *EmL*, 4:213).

7. His cousin William Henry Channing had also always been upset at his behavior, believing him "disposed to insanity" (James Perkins to his wife, 4-10 June 1838, in McGill, *Channing*, p. 26).

8. F. B. Sanborn, *The Personality of Emerson* (Bo: Charles E. Goodspeed, 1903), p. 109.

9. 5 Sept. 1841, MH; MF to Channing, 3 Oct. 1841, in McGill, *Channing*, pp. 60-61; Channing to MF, 20 Mar. 1842, MH. Channing's desire for the family's approval was merely for form since he married Ellen before Margaret's reply reached them. She had apparently consulted Emerson, but his only response was to wish the couple "great happiness." Caroline Sturgis, who still clung to the romantic aura that had surrounded her and Channing at Curzon's Mill, was severly disappointed by his marriage. Although she felt "affectionately" toward Ellen, she thought her not "noble enough to be his wife" (13 Sept. 1841, in *EmL*, 2:447; CS to MF, 9 Sept. 1841, MH).

10. Mrs. Fuller to MF, 15 May 1842, in McGill, *Channing*, p. 67; 15 Mar. 1842, MH; 20 Mar. 1842, MH. Among those who had copies of his verses were Fuller, Ward, Sophia Ripley, Caroline Sturgis, and Henry Channing.

11. Hawthorne's letter to Fuller was a model of diplomacy: " . . . [M]y conclusion is, that the comfort of both parties would be put in great jeopardy. In saying this, I would not be understood to mean anything against the social qualities of Mr. and Mrs. Channing — my objection being wholly independent of such considerations. Had it been proposed to Adam and Eve to receive two angels into their Paradise, as *boarders*, I doubt whether they would have been altogether pleased to consent. . . . the whole four would have been involved in an unnatural relation — which the whole system of boarding out essentially and inevitably is" (25 Aug. 1842, CSmH).

12. 7 Apr. 1843, in *HawAmNb*, p. 369; RWE to CSW, 30 Apr. 1843, ViU-B.

13. Channing's "Manuscript Poetry," in *RuLiEm*, p. 233. At other times Channing could call Alcott an "execrable compound of sawdust & stagnation" (letter to HDT, 5 Mar. 1845, in *ThCor*, p. 162).

14. Mar. 1843, in *EmJMN*, 8:352; G. W. Curtis to S. H. Whitman, late summer 1845, in Caroline Ticknor, *Poe's Helen* (NY: Scribner's, 1916), p. 28.

15. Mar. 1843, in *EmJMN*, 8:352; journal entry, n.d., in *FuW*, 1:597; Oct. 1842, in *EmJMN*, 8:289 ("indirections"); 28 Aug., in *FuJ42*, p. 329.

16. MF to HDT, 25 Sept. 1843, in William White, "Three Unpublished Thoreau Letters," *NEQ* 33 (Sept. 1960):373; Channing to MF, 21 May 1843, MH. Channing himself later admitted about Thoreau, "I have never been able to understand what he meant by his life," his only conclusion being, "Something peculiar I judge." And he wrote in his copy of Alcott's *Concord Days* (Bo: Roberts, 1882) that Thoreau had "few passions & these were directed against not for others" (notebook entry, n.d., in Herbert Cahoon, "Some Manuscripts of Concord Authors in the Pierpont Morgan Library," *Manuscripts* 18 [Fall 1966]:48-49; MHarF).

17. F. B. Sanborn, *Henry D. Thoreau* (Bo: HoMif, 1882), pp. 177-78; 8 Nov. 1851, in *ThJ*, 3:99; 15 Nov. 1851, in ibid., p. 118. This same impression of Channing's writing stayed with Thoreau, and he mentioned it to Sanborn soon after their first meeting (F. B. Sanborn, *The Personality of Thoreau* [Bo: Charles E. Goodspeed, 1901], p. 63).

18. 5 Aug. 1842, in *HawAmNb*, p. 316 ("gnome"). "Nevertheless," Hawthorne later wrote, "the lad himself seems to feel as if he were a genius; and, ridiculously enough, looks upon his own verses as too sacred to be sold for money. Prose he will sell to the highest bidder; but measured feet and jingling lines are not to be exchanged for gold — which, indeed, is not very likely to be offered for them. I like him well enough, however; but after all, these originals in a small way, after one has seen a few of them, become more dull and common-place than even those who keep the ordinary pathway of life. They have a rule and a routine, which they follow with as little variety as other people do *their* rule and routine" (2 Sept. 1842, in *HawAmNb*, p. 357).

19. 7 Apr. 1843, in ibid., p. 369; 2 Sept. 1842, in ibid., p. 357.

20. Hubert Hoeltje's suggestion in his book that Channing "in a degree filled the vacancy left long ago by the death of Charles [Emerson]" is much too strong. Charles provided valuable criticisms of Emerson's works and a deep and truthful friendship, neither of which the younger Channing could

supply. His arrival in Concord just as Thoreau, Emerson's regular walking companion, was leaving for Staten Island, greatly accelerated their acquaintance (*Sheltering Tree: A Story of the Friendship of Ralph Waldo Emerson and Amos Bronson Alcott* [Durham, N.C.: Duke Univ. Press, 1943], p. 61).

21. 18[?] Mar. 1842, in *EmL*, 3:33; early Sept. 1841, in *EmJ*, 6:46; late Sept. 1842, in *EmJMN*, 8:276; Mar. 1843, in ibid., p. 352.

22. RWE to CS, 5 Aug. 1842, MH. Years later Emerson was still saying that Channing had "more poetic genius than any one" he knew, while at the same time admitting that he had "some defects" that had "prevented him from writing a single good poem" (RWE to William Allingham, 14 July 1851, in Kenneth Walter Cameron, "A Garland of Emerson Letters," *ESQ*, no. 10 [I Quarter 1958], p. 38).

23. Mar. 1843, in *EmJMN*, 8:352; early Sept. 1841, in *EmJ*, 6:46 ("artist"); journal entry, 15 Nov. 1856, in Thomas Wentworth Higginson, "Walks with Ellery Channing," *Atlantic Monthly* 90 (July 1902):32. Channing's lack of interest in perfectly completing a task may be seen in this statement to Thoreau: "*I* am universal; I have nothing to do with the particular and definite" (8 Nov. 1851, in *ThJ*, 3:99).

24. Mar. 1843, in *EmJMN*, 8:351; on 8 April Emerson repeated this opinion to Hawthorne, and in August Thoreau entered this comment into his journal (*HawAmNb*, p. 371; 25 Aug., in Thomas William Blanding, "The Text of Thoreau's Fragmentary Journals of the 1840's," B. A. thesis, Marlboro College, 1970, p. 22).

25. Mar. 1843, in *EmJMN*, 8:351; Sept. 1842, in ibid., 7:468.

26. Or in Emerson's words, he was "too much a lover of agreeable sensations ever to carry his verses to a high finish" (RWE to SGW, 28 Nov. [1843], MH, where the date "1844" is supplied: however, internal evidence clearly dates the year as 1843).

27. 20 Sept. 1846, in Higginson, "Walks with Channing," p. 28.

28. Channing to RWE, 9 Feb. 1845, CSmH ("child"); n.d., in David P. Edgell, "A Note on a Transcendental Friendship," *NEQ* 24 (Dec. 1951): 530; Channing to Higginson, 1849, in F. B. Sanborn, "A Concord Note-Book: Ellery Channing and his Table-Talk, Second Paper," *Critic* 47 (Aug. 1905): 122. Channing was much like a spoiled child and always demanded the full and complete attention of his friends. Fuller quickly realized that he would for this reason be less than happy in his relations with Emerson: "Ellery was in such a mood as I have not seen him before, from his disappointment at finding Mr E. engrossed with those Englishmen [Lane and Wright]. He'll have enough of that sort to bear, if he lives near our intellectual friend." She concluded that Emerson "does not understand Ellery, though he likes him much, & keeps him before him as an object of smiling contemplation" (journal entry, 30 Oct. 1842, in *FuW*, 1:435; 24 Aug. [1842], in *FuJ42*, p. 326).

29. T. W. Higginson, "Two 'Dial' Poets," *Literature*, 5 Jan. 1899, p. 179.

30. Channing called his verses "proper love poems" because "they were really genuine fruits of a fine, light, gentle, happy intercourse with his friends" (Dec. 1842, in *EmJMN*, 8:318).

31. 21-23 Aug. [1842], in *FuJ42*, p. 325 ("music"); MF to RWE, 16 Oct. 1842, in *EmL*, 3:90n.

32. RWE to WmE, 3 July 1841, in *EmL*, 2:413. See also RWE to MF, 12 Dec. 1842, 20[?] Mar. 1843, in ibid., 3:103, 160-61. The poem to Emerson was "Sonnet to — —" and those to Elizabeth and Caroline were most likely "To***" and "To— —" (*Dial*, 2:121, 3:507-9). The poem "Anna" was clearly written to Anna Ward; Mrs. Ward's daughter preserved a copy of it and labelled it as such (ibid., p. 326; MH).

33. RWE to SGW, 19 Dec. 1841, MH ("good"); RWE to MF, 12 Dec. 1842, in *EmL*, 3:103 ("beauties"); 30 Apr. 1843, ViU-B (Wheeler); 17 Nov. 1843, in *EmCorTC*, p. 352; HDT to RWE, 17 Oct. 1843, in *ThCor*, p. 145; 31 Dec. 1843, *HigMF*, p. 183.

34. 11 July 1843, in *EmL*, 3:184; RWE to HDT, 10 June 1843, in *ThCor*, p. 118 ("vivacity"); SR to RWE, 5 July [1843], MH; HDT to the Emersons, 8 July 1843, in *ThCor*, p. 124 (installments); HDT to RWE, 17 Oct. 1843, in ibid., p. 145; CS to RWE, 5 July 1843, MH.

35. 6 Apr. 1843, MH; 19 June 1843, MH.

36. *SaRec*, 2:335; RWE to MF, 12 Feb. 1843, in *EmL*, 3:146; *BAL*, 2:129.

37. The copies were sent by a distinguished messenger, Henry James, Sr., to whom Emerson had also given letters of introduction to Carlyle and Sterling (RWE to James, 11 Oct. 1843, in Ralph Barton

Perry, *The Thought and Character of William James* [Bo: Little, Brown, 1935], 1:53).

38. 30 June 1843, *EmL*, 3:181; 20 Feb. 1844, in John Sterling, *A Correspondence Between John Sterling and Ralph Waldo Emerson*, ed. Edward Waldo Emerson (Bo: HoMif, 1897), p. 83; "P.'s Correspondence," *United States Magazine, and Democratic Review* 16 (Apr. 1845):344.

39. Fuller was also glad about Channing's success, for, as she put it, her own "constellation seems full now he is added, his life casts light on all the others" ("November 1841 Journal," MH).

40. EH to Richard Fuller, 8 July 1843, MH.

41. "Our Amateur Poets. No. III.—William Ellery Channing," *Graham's Magazine* 23:113-17; "Mr. Channing's Poems," *Democratic Review* 13:309-14.

42. Emerson wrote in late 1846 that "no more than 250 copies" had been sold (RWE to John Chapman, 29, 31 Dec., Sterling Library, University of London).

43. Three of Channing's poems were in the 1844 *Gift*, which was published in October 1843. Emerson's other attempt at this time to place Channing's poems in the *Gift* failed (*BAL*, 2:129; see 11 Mar., 19 Mar. 1843, in *EmRecLiFr*, pp. 18-20; RWE to MF, 20[?] Mar. 1843, in *EmL*, 3:160; and RWE to SGW, 23 Oct. 1843, MH).

44. Apparently, only Thoreau and Channing received cash for their contributions to the *Dial*. Emerson has these notations in his "Account Book 1840-44": "To W.E.C. for a poem 10.00" and "Cash to W.E.C. for Dial papers 10.00" (25 Nov. 1843, 5 June 1844, MH).

45. RWE to LdE, 24 July 1843, in *EmL*, 3:188.

46. Emerson asked Ward: "Is it quite hopeless to think of giving Ellery the charge of the Dial" (beginning in July 1844). Emerson had been cheered up by "sundry signs of its making an impression" and thought that the magazine might continue into a fifth volume. On the whole, Emerson's idea must be regarded more as a hopeful passing wish than as a considered offer (23 Oct. 1843, MH).

47. 10 Feb. 1844, "Account Book 1840-44," MH.

48. Letter, [1855], in Sanborn, *Thoreau* (1882), p. 179. As Higginson later concluded, Channing "would not bring out the best side of people" (letter to Sanborn, 10 Aug. 1895, MHarF).

Chapter 8: William Henry Channing

Note: Biographical information is from *FrWHC*.

1. *ClAuDiCor*, p. 35.

2. *MemMF*, 2:8 ("friend"); Madeleine B. Stern, *The Life of Margaret Fuller* (NY: Dutton, 1942), p. 58 (Fuller and Hedge).

3. Earl Morse Wilbur, *An Historical Sketch of the Independent Congregational Church, Meadville, Pennsylvania* (Meadville, Pa.: n.p., 1902), p. 29; Thomas Wentworth Higginson, "William Henry Channing," in *Heralds of a Liberal Faith*, ed. Samuel A. Eliot (Bo: American Unitarian Association, 1910), 3:61.

4. *ClAuDiCor*, pp. 35-36; RWE to WmE, 29 Dec. 1837, in *EmL*, 2:104 (Carlyle); [July? 1838?], in *FrWHC*, p. 142; quoted in Octavius Brooks Frothingham, *Theodore Parker* (NY: Putnam's, 1880), p. 105; TP to G. E. Ellis, 7 Aug. 1838, MHi.

5. Once again Clarke was instrumental in persuading Channing to move to the West. Soon after Channing had settled in New York, George Ripley reported to Clarke that Channing had "little occupation" and that he might be talked into moving to Ohio. Knowing that if Channing did move, he would go either to Boston or the West, Clarke told him that he had heard that Boston was "a perfect Inquisition" and suggested Cincinnati instead. Clarke continued to write in this vein until Channing accepted (15 Mar., 29 Mar. 1837, MH).

6. 27 Feb. 1839, in Oliver Wendell Holmes, *Ralph Waldo Emerson* (Bo: HoMif, 1884), p. 131. Channing himself wrote H. J. Huidekoper that he was happy in his new position (24 Apr. 1839, ICM). Earlier he had submitted some German translations for John Sullivan Dwight's *Select Minor*

Poems of Goethe and Schiller. Channing was not only happy with his translations ("the hardest fight with words I ever had") but also with the "great pleasure" in being "united with one whom I love in a good work" (see WHC to JSD, 28 May 1837, Dorris Harris Catalogue no. 18, item 36; WHC to JSD, 22 Sept. 1838, CtY).

7. 25 Feb. 1840, in *FrWHC*, p. 168. Because of such letters, Fuller doubted that Channing would ever fully carry out his plans. She summed up her impressions of him in this manner: "Perfect honesty, worth, & all goodness stamped upon his face. — & earnest, — but not great" (journal entries, Oct. 1842, n.d., in *FuW*, 1:427, 557).

8. Frederick T. McGill, Jr., *Channing of Concord: A Life of William Ellery Channing II* (New Brunswick, N.J.: Rutgers University Press, 1967), p. 56n (antislavery); [10 June 1841], NPV; *HigMF*, p. 206 (Greeley). As Sophia Ripley saw it, Channing was "exchanging words for deeds" (SR to JSD, 6 May 1841, MB).

9. Nov. 1842, in *EmJMN*, 8:250; 8 June 1843, in *ThCor*, p. 111; HDT to Helen Thoreau, 21 July 1843, in ibid., p. 128; Isaac Hecker to Orestes Brownson, 6 Sept. 1843, InNd; 16 Oct. 1843, in *ThCor*, p. 143 (confession); HDT to Helen Thoreau, 18 Oct. 1843, in ibid., p. 147. Thoreau may have commented disparagingly upon the *Present* because of such associationist rhetoric employed there as "couply consociated" for the more normal "married" (see Lindsay Swift, *Brook Farm* [NY: Macmillan, 1900], p. 118).

10. LMC to E. G. Loring, 12 June 1843, NN-M; LMC to E. G. Loring, 26 Sept. 1843, NN-M.

11. F. B. Sanborn, *Henry D. Thoreau* (Bo: HoMif, 1882), p. 174 ("Friend"); MB; 25 Feb. 1840, in *FrWHC*, pp. 167-68. Channing was probably stirred into writing by his recent reading of De Wette's *Theodore; or, the Skeptic's Conversion.* That the article was in Channing's mind at this early date makes it seem unlikely that Isaac Hecker, rather than Channing himself, served as the model for Ernest, as George William Curtis later told Hecker (Henry A. Pochmann, *German Culture in America* [Madison, Wis.: University of Wisconsin Press, 1957], p. 242; see Curtis to Elliott, 28 Feb. 1890, in Walter Elliott, *The Life of Father Hecker* [NY: Columbus Press, 1891], p. 55).

12. 22 Mar. 1840, MB; JFC to SC, 8 July 1840, MH.

13. RWE to TP, 30 June 1842, in *EmL*, 3:69; TP to RWE, 16 May 1842, MH, where Parker optimistically tells Emerson that Channing could "furnish a valuable paper immediately"; RWE to MF, 29 May 1842, in *EmL*, 3:58; 8 Sept. 1842, in ibid., p. 87. As early as July, Parker had felt that Channing would fail to produce the review, and because of his own enthusiasm about Hennell's book he had volunteered to write the review himself (TP to RWE, 8 July 1842, MH).

14. 7 July 1842, in *FrWHC*, p. 183; "Call of the Present — No. 2. — Science of Unity," *Present* 1 (15 Nov. 1843):76; "The Democratic Review and O. A. Brownson," ibid. (15 Oct. 1843):72.

15. Lindsay Swift, *Brook Farm* (New York: Macmillan, 1900), p. 227; WHC's notations, in his copy of the *Spirit of the Age*, ICN; quoted in Caroline Dall, *Transcendentalism in New England* (Bo: Roberts, 1897), p. 27.

Chapter 9: Lydia Maria Child

Note: Biographical information is from Helene G. Baer, *The Heart is Like Heaven: The Life of Lydia Maria Child* (Philadelphia: University of Pennsylvania Press, 1964).

1. [1859], John White Chadwick, *Theodore Parker* (Bo: HoMif, 1901), p. 353; quoted in Lilian Whiting, *Boston Days* (Bo: Little, Brown, 1911), p. 56.

2. 10 Jan. 1827, in *MemMF*, 1:55; quoted in Baer, *Child*, p. 113.

3. David's ill fortune was so well known that, when a friend of Mrs. Child's found out that he was carrying stone for the railroad and losing ten cents a cart on the transaction, she said, "Oh — well — now — Mrs. Child, *if* your husband has got hold of any *innocent occupation*, by which he *only* loses ten cents on a load, *for heaven's sake, encourage him in it!*" (Susan I. Lesley, *Recollections of My Mother: Mrs. Anne Jean Lyman . . .* [Bo: HoMif, 1899 (1875)], p. 355).

4. LMC to John Pierpont, 9 Mar. [1842], LU ("power"); LMC to E. G. Loring, 28 Sept. 1841, in

Martin Duberman, *James Russell Lowell* (Bo: HoMif, 1966), p. 84 ("cause"); Ethel K. Ware, "Lydia Maria Child and Anti-Slavery," *Boston Public Library Quarterly* 3 (Oct. 1951):273.

5. She also attended Alcott's Conversations, where she first met George Ripley and Caroline Sturgis (see Week 9, Feb., in *AlcJ38*, p. 147); Frederick L. H. Willis, *Alcott Memoirs* (Bo: Richard G. Badger, 1915), p. 23; LMC to Lewis J. Cist, 27 Feb. 1838, CCS; LMC to E. G. and Louisa Loring, 19 July 1840, MCR-S ("good"); LMC to F. G. Shaw, [Sept.?] 1840 in LMC, *Letters of Lydia Maria Child. . .*[ed. Harriet Winslow Sewall] (Bo: HoMif, 1883), p. 37 ("missionary"); 20 Oct., NIC; 23 Apr. 1844, ViU-B.

6. Copies of the *Dial* bearing the names of the *National Anti-Slavery Standard* and "L. M. Child" are at CtY and NjP; LMC to E. G. Loring, 12 June 1843, NN-M; LMC to G. B. Loring, 25 Aug. 1840, in Horace Elisha Scudder, *James Russell Lowell* (Bo: HoMif, 1901), 1:80. Mrs. Child had given Emerson his copy of *Philothea* as an expression of her gratitude for the "pleasure & benefit" his writings had given her. Mrs. Alcott, a friend of Mrs. Child, also liked the novel and helped her daughters to dramatize it and to act it out (LdE to Lucy Brown, [29? Oct.? 1838?], MH; Sandford Salyer, *Marmee: The Mother of Little Women* [Norman, Okla.: University of Oklahoma Press, 1949], pp. 75-76).

7. 12 Apr. 1842, in Henry James, *William Wetmore Story and His Friends* (Bo: HoMif, 1903), 1:49; review of H. W. Longfellow, *Poems on Slavery*, *Pioneer* 1 (Feb. 1843):92.

8. LMC to JSD, 23 Apr. 1844, ViU-B. A few months before she had written Augusta King that she had grown "less and less inclined" to seek aid from "any of these wandering prophets," because she had not gained "a morsel of spiritual food" from any of them. All her "real progress" had been made "in the quietude of my own spirit," and more and more she sought "to be *alone*" (19 Sept. 1843, NIC).

9. 7 Oct., *EmCorTC*, pp. 137-38. Earlier that year Mrs. Child had asked Carlyle to give a series of lectures in the United States, since she thought the Americans were intellectually undernourished people who "go about with mouths wide open, like the young ravens seeking food" (7 Apr., in Rodger L. Tarr, "Emerson's Transcendentalism in L. M. Child's Letter to Carlyle," *ESQ*, no. 58 [I Quarter 1970], p. 114).

10. LMC to LdE, 22 May n.y., in *RuLiEm*, p. 215; JRL to G. B. Loring, 25 Aug. 1840, in Scudder, *Lowell*, 1:80; 14 Sept. 1832, in *EmJMN*, in 4:40.

11. LMC to Augusta King, 30 Oct. 1844, NIC. She said much the same thing about the Transcendentalists in general: "they *strive* to build anew; but their structures seem to me to be like castles of piled up clouds . . . overarched by the rainbow of promise. In other words, their pulling down is distinct, while their building up is vague, though beautiful" (LMC to C. Francis, 8 Jan. 1841, NIC).

12. Milton Meltzer, *Tongue of Flame: The Life of Lydia Maria Child* (NY: Crowell, 1965), p. 87.

13. *EmL*, 3:151. After Emerson had visited her, Mrs. Child told a friend that he had been "very cordial and hearty," and had given her tickets for the course of lectures he was delivering (LMC to E. G. Loring, 21 Feb. 1843, NN-M).

14. She had turned down her brother's request in 1840 to submit an article on "Gospels of Beauty," both because she felt the editors of the *Dial* had not "the least wish for such an article" and because she herself had "no particular sympathy" with the Transcendentalists as a whole. In 1844 Emerson returned one of her manuscripts, which she had submitted when Fuller was editing the *Dial*, and said that "we have usually had so much new matter to choose from, that I believe I have never used any of this traditional stock" (LMC to C. Francis, 20 Oct., NIC; 8 Jan., NNPM).

15. Emerson told her that it was "a family book" at his house and altogether "a most salutary infusion of love" into American literature; T. W. Higginson said that it was "eagerly read by us young Transcendentalists"; and Fuller not only favorably reviewed the book in the *Dial*, but also wrote a personal letter of praise in case Mrs. Child had not seen the review in "that generally eschewed periodical" (8 Jan. 1844, NNPM; Higginson, *Cheerful Yesterdays* [Bo: HoMif, 1898], p. 102; 18 Mar. 1844, MHarF).

Chapter 10: Eliza Thayer Clapp

Note: Biographical information is from *CoHiBi*, 2:101-12. Many of Miss Clapp's writings were collected posthumously in her *Essays, Letters, and Poems* (Bo: Privately printed [Riverside Press], 1888).

1. Ebenezer Clapp, comp., *Record of the Clapp Family in America* (Bo: David Clapp & Son, 1876), p. 264.

2. Letter, 24 Oct. 1887, in Clapp, *Essays &c*, pp. 122-23; E. T. Clapp to Cooke, n.d., in *CoHiBi*. 2:109 (Parker); letter, 2 Apr. 1888, in Clapp, *Essays &c*, p. x (Hedge); 24 Oct. 1887, in ibid., p. 124 ("helpful"); letter, 20 Sept. 1887, in ibid., p. 118; E. T. Clapp to Cooke, n.d., *CoHiBi*, 2:101.

3. RWE to MF, 20 Oct. 1840, in *EmL*, 2:350 (unimpressed); 5 Oct. 1840, DLC.

4. RWE to MF, 1[?] Dec.[?] 1840, in *EmL*, 2:364.

5. 8 Feb. [1841], DLC; RWE to MF, 22 Apr. 1841, in *EmL*, 2:395.

6. Hedge and Frederic Dan Huntington printed it as Emerson's in their *Hymns for the Church*; Samuel Longfellow and Samuel Johnson did the same in their *Hymns of the Spirit*; and James Martineau also credited it to Emerson in his *Hymns of Praise and Prayer* (*CoHiBi*, 2:106-7).

7. 23 Feb. 1842, DLC; RWE to FHH, 23 Mar. 1842, in *EmL*, 3:37 (retitled); RWE to EPP, 2 July 1842, MH (free *Dial*).

Chapter 11: James Freeman Clarke

Note: Biographical information is from Arthur S. Bolster, Jr., *James Freeman Clarke* (Bo: Beacon, 1954), and *ClAuDiCor*. Bolster was forced to leave out notes and a bibliography of Clarke's writings from his book: they are available in his "The Life of James Freeman Clarke," Ph.D., diss., Harvard University, 1953.

1. Mary Peabody to Sophia Peabody, 27 Feb. 1833, in Josephine Elizabeth Roberts, "A New England Family: Elizabeth Palmer Peabody. . .Mary Tyler Peabody. . .Sophia Amelia Peabody. . .," Ph. D. diss., Western Reserve University, 1937, p. 75. In commenting upon her to Fuller in 1835, Clarke said that Peabody knew "too little of the world," and that her manners seemed to him "not the best" (*Cl LetMF*, p. 135).

2. Diary entry, 12 Sept. 1831, in *ClLetMF*, p. 7; *MemMF*, 1:114; 8 Sept. 1834, in *ClLetMF*, p. 79.

3. Caroline Dall to T. W. Higginson, 19 June 1884, MB. This understanding did not stop Fuller from entering into Clarke's romantic life. After he had quarreled with a Miss Elizabeth Randall, he wrote her a note of apology that Fuller intercepted and destroyed without his knowledge. Thinking the girl had spurned his attempt at a reconciliation when he received no answer to his note, Clarke forever put her out of his mind, just as Fuller, who disliked the girl, had wanted him to do (Bolster, *Clarke*, p. 61).

4. [1832], in *ClLetMF*, p. 35.

5. 1832, JFC's "Autobiography," in Stanley M. Vogel, *German Literary Influences on the American Transcendentalists* (New Haven, Conn.: Yale University Press, 1955), p. 127; 5 Dec. 1832, JFC's "Journal of Understanding," in ibid., p. 159.

6. He wrote Fuller: "I thought that here I could be myself, not being perverted by the demands (praise and blame) of conventional opinions. I find that I can be myself in nothing—that I must make myself over, body and soul, to the requisitions of Kentucky taste" (12 Aug. 1833, in *ClLetMF*, p. 57).

7. 25 Nov. 1834, in Oliver Wendell Holmes, *Ralph Waldo Emerson* (Bo: HoMif, 1884), p. 79. Emerson may have mentioned Clarke's piece to Carlyle: one of the few copies of *Sartor Resartus* that

Carlyle sent to Emerson for his American friends went to Clarke (SC to JFC, 27 Feb. 1835, in *ClLet-Sister*).

8. JFC to MF, 1833, in *ClLetMF*, p. 52; 20 Feb. 1835, in ibid., p. 88; JFC to MF, 12 Apr. 1835, in ibid., p. 91; JFC to Allen, [17 Feb. 1835], in Joseph Henry Allen, *Sequel to "Our Liberal Movement"* (Bo: Roberts, 1897), p. 99; JFC, journal entry, 11 Dec. 1832, in John Wesley Thomas, *James Freeman Clarke* (Bo: John W. Luce, 1949), p. 29; 29 Mar. 1838, in *ClLetMF*, p. 130.

9. See JFC to MF, 20 Nov. 1837, in *ClLetMF*, p. 128; JFC to RWE, 30 Apr. 1838, MH.

10. JFC to MF, 29 Mar. 1838, in *ClLetMF*, p. 131; JFC, lecture at his church, 8 Jan. 1865, quoted in George Willis Cooke, *Ralph Waldo Emerson* (Bo: Osgood, 1882), p. 48; 24 Sept. 1838, MSaE.

11. 29 Dec. 1838, in *ClAuDiCor*, p. 124.

12. 30 Jan. 1840, in *ClLetSister*; 8 Feb. 1840, MH; JFC to SC, 7 Apr. 1840, MH; JFC to SC, 27 Apr. 1840, MH ("review"); 24 May 1840, in *ClLetMF*, p. 138; 20 June 1840, in ibid., p. 140. Fuller did not list Clarke as a probable contributor to the first number, though she did list "Crossing the Alleghenies" and "Picture poems," both by "J.F.C.," for the second number (*FuNbD*).

13. 8 July 1840, MH; JFC to Frederic Huidekoper, 28 Sept. 1840, ICM.

14. RWE to MF, 22 Apr. 1841, in *EmL*, 2:395; SC to JFC, 7 July 1840, in *ClLetSister*; Thomas, *Clarke*, pp. 48-50.

15. Among the original members were the three Peabody sisters, although Elizabeth soon left to join Theodore Parker's congregation.

16. Originally Emerson planned to print just John Keats's notes, but Clarke later sent in the accompanying introduction on George, whom Clarke thought "one of the best men in the world" (RWE to CSW, 13 Dec. 1842, MH; RWE to LdE, 26 Feb. 1843, in *EmL*, 3:151).

17. "Memoir of Ralph Waldo Emerson," *Proceedings of the Massachusetts Historical Society*, 2d ser., 2 (June 1885):113-14. And to G. W. Cooke he wrote that the period of the *Dial* was marked by "youth" and "pleasure" (4 Dec. 1881, MHarF).

Chapter 12: Sarah Clarke

Note: Biographical information is from Arthur S. Bolster, Jr., *James Freeman Clarke* (Bo: Beacon, 1954), and Joel Myerson, "'A True & High Minded Person': Transcendentalist Sarah Clarke," *Southwest Review* 59 (Spring 1974): 163-72.

1. 6 Sept. 1837, in *EmJMN*, 5:375; *MemMF*, 1:207; Sophia Peabody to ABA, 9 June 1837, in *SaHaABA*, 1:223; SC to JFC, 7 July 1840, in *ClLetSister*.

2. JFC to MF, [1838], in *ClLetMF*, p. 135; Louise Hall Tharp, *The Peabody Sisters of Salem* (Bo: Little, Brown, 1950), p. 150; SC to JFC, 28 Apr. 1836, in *ClLetSister* (Hedge); SC to JFC, 5 Feb. 1835, in ibid.

3. SC to JFC, 27 Apr. 1835, in *ClLetSister;* SC to JFC, 23 July 1838, in ibid; RWE to MF, 24 May 1843, in *EmL*, 3:176; 12 Sept. 1840, in *EmJMN*, 7:395; 30 Mar. 1840, in *EmL*, 2:271.

4. RWE to MF, 8 May 1840, in *EmL*, 2:293; MF to RWE, 5 July 1840, in *HigMF*, p. 155.

5. 8 July 1840, MH. She specifically rejected Fuller's comment that in Allston's picture of the dead man raised by the touch of the prophet's bones there was "a want of artist's judgment in the very choice of the subject." Emerson, however, agreed with Fuller (*Dial*, 1:76; RWE to MF, 8 Apr. 1840, in *EmL*, 2:275).

6. 20 July 1840, in *ClLetSister*; 13 July 1840, MH.

7. RWE to CS, 5 Oct. 1840, MH. Emerson took her comment seriously, and he also entered it into his journal (12 Sept. 1840, in *EmJMN*, 7:395).

8. SC to JFC, [ca. Oct. 1838], in *ClLetSister.*

Chapter 13: Christopher Pearse Cranch

Note: Biographical information is from F. DeWolfe Miller, "Christopher Pearse Cranch: New England Transcendentalist," Ph.D. diss., University of Virginia, 1942; parts of this appeared with new information in Miller's *Christopher Pearse Cranch and His Caricatures of New England Transcendentalism* (Cambridge, Mass.: Harvard University Press, 1951). *ScLiLetCPC* is still of value since Miller did not have access to some of the primary material used in it.

1. Quoted in Octavius Brooks Frothingham, *Theodore Parker* (NY: Putnam's, 1880), p. 44.

2. JSD and others to CPC, 27 July 1837, typescript, MHi; JSD to CPC, 12 Aug. 1837, typescript, MHi.

3. Other opinions of Cranch's verse of this period were not so kind. Miller describes it as being marked by "jejune religiosity," and Dwight thought his poetry was "always beautiful, but feeble" (Miller, *Cranch*, p. 10; JSD to CPC, 12 Aug. 1837, typescript, MHi).

4. 14 Oct. 1837, in *ScLiLetCPC*, p. 38.

5. Arthur S. Bolster, Jr., *James Freeman Clarke* (Bo: Beacon, 1954), p. 112; JFC to A[nna]. H[uidekoper]., 3 Feb. 1839, in *ClAuDiCor*, p. 126; Hazen C. Carpenter, "Emerson and Christopher Pearse Cranch," *NEQ* 37 (Mar. 1964):22.

6. This scrapbook contains Cranch's extant drawings from among the 20 or 30 illustrations of "some of Mr. Emerson's queer sayings" that he and Clarke did between them. It was collected and titled by Clarke in 1844 and is reproduced in full in Miller, *Cranch*. Sarah Clarke believed that the drawings met with "the most distinguished success," and on 11 March 1839 her brother told Emerson of the "sketches not of the gravest character" that Cranch had drawn, but which he thought that Emerson would like inasmuch as "the gravest things have also a comic side." It is also clear from this letter that Emerson had not yet personally met Cranch (JFC, "Notebook 1839-40," MH; SC to JFC, 10 Feb. 1839, in *ClLetSister; EmL*, 2:190).

7. 12 Oct. 1839, in *PkJ*, 1:250; CPC, 30 Dec. 1839, "Manuscript Autobiography," in Miller, "Cranch," p. 97; CPC to Margaret Cranch Brooks, 1 Aug. 1839, in Miller, "Cranch," p. 98. After one of their meetings, Parker wrote a poem on the "Beauty of C.P.C." Cranch later drew a delightful caricature of Parker entering a German bookstore and making a headlong dash for the shelves, to the frightened surprise of the proprietor and oblivious to two dogs barking at him (*PkJ*, 1:169-70; Miller, *Cranch*, figure 18).

8. CPC to Julia Myers, 4 Feb. 1840, in *ScLiLetCPC*, p. 47; 22 Dec. 1836, in Miller, "Cranch," p. 53; ca. 15 July 1838, "Manuscript Autobiography," in ibid., p. 81; "Emerson's Oration," *Western Messenger* 4 (Oct. 1837):184-89; 5 Apr. 1833, in *EmJMN*, 4:156.

9. "Enosis," which was influenced by Cranch's reading of *Nature*, Thomas Carlyle's *Sartor Resartus*, and Furness's *Remarks on the Four Gospels*, was originally called "Communion" and appeared in the *Dial* as "Stanzas." Its later title of "Gnosis" resulted from editors' misreadings of the German-style typography of its title in Cranch's *Poems* (see Miller, *Cranch*, p. 9; CPC to Margaret Cranch Brooks, 7 Mar. 1840, in ibid., p. 105; Sidney E. Lind, "Christopher Pearse Cranch's 'Gnosis': An Error in Title," *Modern Language Notes* 62 [Nov. 1947]:486-88).

10. *ScLiLetCPC*, p. 58.

11. *EmL*, 2:258. Emerson remembered these poems, for in December 1841 he wrote: "Transcendentalism is likened to. . .the Aurora Borealis." Cranch seems not to have known Fuller until later. He sent her a presentation copy of his *Poems* in 1844, and it was at his house that she stayed when she first visited New York (*EmJMN*, 8:156).

12. 4 Mar. 1840, in *ScLiLetCPC*, pp. 59-60.

13. 14 Apr. 1840, in "Manuscript Autobiography," in Miller, "Cranch," p. 97; 20 Apr. 1840, in ibid., p. 110; 23 May 1840, in Carpenter, "Emerson and Cranch," p. 23n; 19 June 1840, in Miller, "Cranch," p. 75; *PkJ*, 1:273, 340.

14. JFC to SC, 8 July 1840, MH; CPC to JSD, 16 Aug. 1840, in Miller, "Cranch," pp. 123-24; CPC to JSD, 12 Sept. 1840, in ibid., pp. 126-27. Elizabeth Peabody gives a full account of the Boston meeting in a letter to Dwight and does not mention Cranch's presence (20 Sept. 1840, MB).

15. 11 July 1840, in *ScLiLetCPC*, pp. 50-51; 2 Aug. 1840, in John Quincy Adams, *Memoirs of John Quincy Adams*, ed. Charles Francis Adams (Philadelphia: J. B. Lippincott, 1874-77), 10:345; LMC to Augusta King, 21 Oct. 1840, NIC.

16. When Fuller left her ship in Liverpool at the start of her European journey in 1846, she was surprised to find that the director of the local Mechanics' Institute had incorporated "Musings of a Recluse" into the lecture he was giving (Margaret Fuller, *At Home and Abroad*, ed. Arthur B. Fuller [Bo: Crosby, Nichols, 1856], p. 122).

17. 17 Nov. 1840, in Joel Myerson, "Transcendentalism and Unitarianism in 1840: A New Letter by C. P. Cranch," *CLA Journal* 16 (Mar. 1973):366-67; CPC to JSD, 20 Nov. 1840, in *ScLiLetCPC*, p. 58.

18. Keats wrote Clarke on 17 January 1841: "I did somewhere meet with that passage that so tenderly brings into linked feelings the timid hares, the sylvan woods, the fireside and the human heart, but in my worldly progress it drew from me, and excited in me but one pleasing reflection, and I passed it by" (Madeleine B. Stern, "Four Letters from George Keats," *PMLA* 56 [Mar. 1941]:213).

19. CPC to JSD, 22 July 1841, in Miller, "Cranch," pp. 131-32; CPC to JSD, 17 Nov. 1840, in Myerson, "A New Cranch Letter," p. 368.

20. Miller, "Cranch," p. 134 (Parker); CPC to Catherine Myers, 4 Oct. 1841, in *ScLiLetCPC*, p. 75 (W. H. Channing); 12 Sept. 1841, in ibid., p. 60; 17[?] Sept. 1841, in *EmL*, 2:450; 1 Oct. 1841, in *ScLiLetCPC*, pp. 61-63. That "Inworld" was really half of a poem did not occur to the *Boston Morning Post* (15 Oct. 1841) either, for they cited it in a review of the *Dial* as an example of that magazine's fine poetry.

21. "Inworld" and "Outworld" were reprinted in the January 1842 *Dial* as Emerson had promised. "Silence and Speech," which was probably based on Thomas Carlyle's antithesis, "Speech is silvern, Silence is golden," was in the April 1841 issue (see William Silas Vance, "Carlyle and the American Transcendentalists," Ph. D. diss. University of Chicago, 1941, p. 170).

22. *Dial* 1(Oct. 1840):195. This drawing is quite rightly a favorite of scholars: Scott and Miller both reproduce it.

23. Julia Ward Howe, *Reminiscences 1819-1899* (Bo: HoMif, 1899), p. 145 (that Cranch had done this drawing is clear from his letter to G. W. Cooke, 18 Nov. 1885, MHarF); *SaHaABA*, 2:359n ("glee"); Miller, *Cranch*, p. 62. Cranch was also possibly the writer of this "Epigram on the Dial":

> A. Our Dial shows the March of light
>   O'er cities, woods & meadows —
> B. Not so — and yet you name it right,
>   It marks the flight of shadows

(JFC, "Notebook 1839-40," MH).

24. 21 Apr. 1843, MB (Cranch suggested "To the Aurora Borealis," "The Ocean," and "Endymion" for publication); 3 May 1843, typescript, MHi, for Furness's connection with Carey and Hart, see *EmRecLiFr*, pp. 18-19; *BAL*, 2:320; 7 June 1844, in *ScLiLetCPC*, p. 64.

25. And forty years later, when Cranch could clearly recall his contributions to the first two numbers of the *Dial*, he "quite forgot" whether he had anything in the last two (CPC to G. W. Cooke, 2 June 1884, MHarF).

26. *Godey's Lady's Book*, 33:18-19. Reviewers of Cranch's *Poems* often took pains to separate him from what they considered the stigma of being too closely associated with the *Dial*. The *Southern Quarterly Review* told its readers that Cranch did not "appear to have been deeply bitten by the mania" of Transcendentalism; in fact, his "labors in the cause of American transcendentalism, have never amounted to more than a laudable effort to allegorize a truism, and convert a precious common-place into something like a revelation" (6 [July 1844]:260).

27. Henry James, *William Wetmore Story and His Friends* (Bo: HoMif, 1903), 1:110.

Chapter 14: George William Curtis

Note: Biographical information is from Gordon Milne, *George William Curtis & the Genteel Tradition* (Bloomington, Ind.: Indiana University Press, 1956), and Edward Cary, *George William Curtis* (Bo: HoMif, 1894). *CuEarlyLetDw* also provides much material on the *Dial* period.

1. George William Curtis, "An Autobiographical Sketch," *Cosmopolitan* 17 (Oct. 1894):703 (poems); quoted in Milne, *Curtis*, p. 20; Ora Gannett Sedgwick, "A Girl of Sixteen at Brook Farm," *Atlantic Monthly* 85 (Mar. 1900):400.

2. George William Curtis, "Editor's Easy Chair," *Harper's New Monthly Magazine* 38 (Jan. 1869):270; see Cary, *Curtis*, p. 17.

3. See Curtis to JSD, 11 Nov. 1843, 12 Jan. 1845, in *CuEarlyLetDw*, pp. 112, 200; Curtis, "Editor's Easy Chair," *Harper's New Monthly Magazine* 84 (Apr. 1892):800 (Cranch); Curtis to JSD, 18 Jan. 1844, in *CuEarlyLetDw*, p. 144; Curtis, "Editor's Easy Chair" (1869), p. 270.

4. Curtis to Anna Shaw, 1 May 1856, in Milne, *Curtis*, p. 250n; Curtis to Daniel Ricketson, 23 Apr. 1856, in ibid., pp. 228-29.

5. Curtis to G. W. Cooke, 9 June 1882, MHarF; Curtis to JSD, 18 Jan. 1844, in *CuEarlyLetDw*, p. 144; Curtis to S. H. Whitman, 28 June 1845, in George William Curtis, "Some Early Letters of George William Curtis," ed. Caroline Ticknor, *Atlantic Monthly* 114 (Sept. 1914):368; 5 July [1843], MH.

6. Curtis to JSD, 3 Mar. 1844 in *CuEarlyLetDw*, pp. 153-54 ("social"); Curtis, "Editor's Easy Chair" (1869), p. 270; Curtis to JSD, 8 Apr. 1844, in *CuEarlyLetDw*, p. 165.

Chapter 15: Charles Anderson Dana

Note: Biographical information is from James Harrison Wilson, *The Life of Charles A. Dana* (NY: Harper's, 1907).

1. Dana to Dr. Flint, 16 Jan. 1840, in Wilson, *Dana*, p. 19. Although Ripley had married Sophia Dana, she was no relation to Charles Dana's branch of the family (Mary Caroline Crawford, *Famous Families of Massachusetts* [Bo: Little, Brown, 1930], 1:26n).

2. Wilson states that he could not discover any word from Dana indicating "complete confidence" in Brook Farm's success (*Dana*, p. 34).

3. Dana to Dr. Flint, 21 Nov. 1840, in Wilson, *Dana*, p. 27; Charles S. Rosebault, *When Dana was "The Sun"* (NY: Robert M. McBride, 1931), p. 20 (individuality); George Willis Cooke, *John Sullivan Dwight* (Bo: Small, Maynard, 1898), p. 53 (secretary); John Thomas Codman, *Brook Farm: Historic and Personal Memories* (Bo: Arena, 1894), p. 10; Lindsay Swift, *Brook Farm* (NY: Macmillan, 1900), p. 146 ("Professor").

4. Dana was involved in the running series of associationism lectures being sponsored by Greeley, John Sullivan Dwight, Ripley, and Henry Channing throughout the later years of Brook Farm. Among the topics were "Mans Destiny on the Planet," "Practical Organization," and "Spiritual Foundation of Association" (WHC to Greeley, 21 Dec. 1846, RNR).

5. Dana was apparently aware of other literary activities of the Transcendentalists, for he purchased a copy of Jones Very's *Essays and Poems* upon its publication in 1839 (The Current Company, catalogue one, item 48).

6. GR to Brownson, 18 Dec. 1842, InNd.

7. 13 Aug. [1843], MH; 31 Oct. 1843, MH. Emerson wrote this about Bartlett's death: "It is a great grief to me, who was learning every year to value him more, though there has been something curious, as well as valuable, in his unfolding" (RWE to CSW, 30 Apr. 1843, ViU-B).

8. Dana to G. W. Cooke, 17 May 1882, MHarF; 5 July [1843], MH.

9. Dana reluctantly put aside a translation of Aeschylus's *Agamemnon* he was preparing for the *Dial* since "a multitude of duties" pressed upon him. However, he was "not a little consoled" about it

when he compared his own "lame & halting version" with Aeschylus's "solemn & stately measures" (Dana to RWE, 10 Feb. 1844, MH).

10. In 1844 Dana gave "A Lecture on Association, In Its Connection with Religion," before the New England Fourier Society in Boston. Dwight, who had become his friend at Brook Farm, gave a similar lecture on education, and both lectures were printed as *Association, in Its Connection with Education and Religion* . . . (Bo: Benjamin H. Greene, 1844) one month later. Just a short time before this, Dana had assumed his office on the business committee of the "Friends of Fourier," along with Ripley, Henry Channing, Albert Brisbane, and Greeley (*Boston Post* [12 Apr., 9 Apr. 1844]).

Chapter 16: John Sullivan Dwight

Note: Biographical information is from George Willis Cooke, *John Sullivan Dwight* (Bo: Small, Maynard, 1898), and Walter L. Fertig, "John Sullivan Dwight: Transcendentalist and Literary Amateur of Music," Ph.D. diss., University of Maryland, 1952.

1. Dwight did not preach while at Meadville, even though there was no regular minister there during his stay and the members of the congregation took turns in delivering the sermon (Earl Morse Wilbur, *An Historical Sketch of the Independent Congregational Church, Meadville, Pennsylvania* [Meadville: n.p., 1902], p. 28).

2. After their graduation, Parker and Dwight kept in touch, and their correspondence included this interesting character sketch of Dwight by Parker: "You have a deep love of the beautiful, strong likings and keen dislikings, a quick discernment, a deep love of freedom. . . . But . . . You do not always see the beautiful clearly. . . .so you love vagueness, mistaking the indefinite for the Infinite. . . You are deficient in will. This is the most important statement I have to make. . . .you are not a patient thinker. This proceeds from want of will. . . . I admire your imagination . . . but it makes you dream when you should do" (14 Mar. 1837, in Cooke, *Dwight*, pp. 11-13). Cranch and Dwight would often visit T. W. Higginson's house to play their flutes with his sister. In 1837 Dwight led others in extending to Cranch an invitation to join the Pierian Sodality for "the promotion of musical taste" at Harvard (Thomas Wentworth Higginson, *Cheerful Yesterdays* [Bo: HoMif, 1898], p. 18; 27 July, typescript, MHi).

3. JSD to JFC, 10 Mar. 1837, MB, and JSD to CPC, 12 Aug. 1837, typescript, MHi; RWE to MF, 24 May 1838, in *EmL*, 2:135; 2 Dec. 1838, in *EmCorTC*, p. 209. Dwight's letter of 2 Oct. 1838 to Carlyle is printed in *A Select Assembly of Notable Books and Manuscripts from the Allison-Shelley Collection of Anglica Americana Germanica* (University Park, Pa.: Pennsylvania State University Library, 1972), pp. 36-37. Carlyle's reply of 18 Oct 1838 is at CtY.

4. Although the book was not officially mentioned as published until April 1839, the evidence above and the presence of a presentation copy dated December 1838 point to a late 1838 or early 1839 publication date (see *BAL*, 1:127).

5. 14 Mar. 1839, in Cooke, *Dwight*, p. 27; 19 Mar. 1839, in *EmCorTC*, pp. 219-20; 17 Apr. 1839, in ibid., p. 226.

6. Longfellow to Sam Ward [of New York], 5 Jan. 1839, in Maud Howe Elliott, *Uncle Sam Ward and His Circle* (NY: Macmillan, 1938), p. 243, FHH to JSD, 21 Mar. 1837, MHarF.

7. GR to [JSD], 6 Apr. 1838, in Stanley M. Vogel, *German Literary Influences on the American Transcendentalists* (New Haven, Conn.: Yale University Press, 1955), p. 113; TP to JSD, 10 Jan. 1839, in Fertig, "Dwight," p. 61.

8. See RWE to JSD, 3 June 1837, in *EmL*, 2:79, and Stanley T. Williams, "Unpublished Letters of Emerson," *Journal of English and Germanic Philology* 26 (Oct. 1927):476. When Bronson Alcott saw him at this time, Dwight was holding weekly meetings with "the people who seemed deeply interested in seeking the truth" (Aug. [1839], in *AlcDiJyDec39*, p. 176).

9. Edward Waldo Emerson, *The Early Years of the Saturday Club 1855-1870* (Bo: HoMif, 1918), p. 48; RWE to MF, 17[?] Jan. 1840, in *EmL*, 2:250.

10. Ripley's *The Claims of the Age on the Work of the Evangelist* (Bo: Weeks, Jordan, 1840),

preached at Dwight's ordination, makes it clear that George Willis Cooke and others, following Cooke, were incorrect in assigning Dwight's ordination to 1839.

11. On 19 June 1840 Cranch thanked Dwight for his account of his "delightful environment" and added, "I hear so much of Northampton" (*ScLiLetCPC*, p. 56).

12. NPV. In fact, Dwight even forgot to prepare his ordination day sermon and had to prepare it hurriedly the day before the ceremony (Emerson, *Saturday Club*, p. 48).

13. Although one minister reported that Dwight's parishioners would "lament his preaching often as an affliction which they had not deserved," he did have some defenders. Mrs. Anne Lyman wrote: "Nobody could allege anything against Mr. Dwight, with truth, except that he was a Transcendentalist. And that they knew when they ordained him" (Mr. Peabody to Henry Ware, 24 Dec. 1840, MHi; Mrs. Lyman to Mrs. Greene, 4 Jan. 1842, in Susan I. Lesley, *Recollections of My Mother: Mrs. Anne Jean Lyman . . .* [Bo: HoMif, 1899 (1875)], p. 375).

14. GR to JSD, 7 July 1840, MB; JFC to SC, 8 July 1840, MH; *CuEarlyLetDw*, p. 44; GR to JSD, 7 July 1840, MB: perhaps Ripley was influenced in his judgment by some of the blatant typographical errors that had crept into the article (see *CoHiBi*, 2:187); JFC to SC, 8 July 1840, MH; RWE to Daniel Parker, 2 Dec. 1840, MBilHi; GR to JSD, 7 July 1840, MB; ca. 9 Apr. 1840, in *PkJ*, 1:338 (Parker included the subsequent title of the poem, "Rest," after which he later wrote in pencil, "Afterwards printed. . .by the Dial"); Cooke, *Dwight*, p. 42; SR to JSD, 1 Aug. 1840, MB.

15. 7 July 1840, MB; *CuEarlyLetDw*, p. 44; Henry Bellows to JSD, 5 Oct. 1841, MB; 9 Apr. 1841, MB.

16. 12 Jan. 1841, in Cooke, *Dwight*, p. 39; JSD to Caroline Dall, 26 June 1855, MHi; 7 Oct. 1842, ViU-B.

17. 1845, in Cooke, *Dwight*, p. 74. Lowell had written to Duyckinck on 28 June 1845 to recommend Dwight as "well worthy" of Duyckinck's "prompt attention." The publisher's desire to "disseminate the pure principles" of Dwight's sermons in order to make Dwight's name known sounds much like Duyckinck's own view of his role with the Wiley and Putnam's series (James Russell Lowell, "Letters of James Russell Lowell, 1843-54," *Bulletin of the New York Public Library* 4 [Oct. 1900]:341).

18. John Sullivan Dwight, "Music a Means of Culture," *Atlantic Monthly* 26 (Sept. 1870):323.

Chapter 17: Edward Bliss Emerson, Charles Chauncy Emerson, and Ellen Louisa Tucker Emerson

Note: Biographical information is from *RuLiEm*, Henry F. Pommer, *Emerson's First Marriage* (Carbondale, Ill.: Southern Illinois University Press, 1967), and Ellen Louisa Tucker Emerson, *One First Love: The Letters of Ellen Louisa Tucker to Ralph Waldo Emerson*, ed. Edith W. Gregg (Cambridge, Mass.: Harvard University Press, 1962).

1. RWE to MF, 23 Apr. 1840, in *EmL*, 2:290; RWE to MF, 24 Apr. 1840, in ibid., p. 292; MF to RWE, 25 Apr. 1840, in ibid., p. 290n. The stanza is:

> Farewell, thou fairest one,
> Unplighted yet to me,
> Uncertain of thine own
> I gave my heart to thee.
> That untold early love
> I leave untold to-day.
> My lips in whisper move
> Farewell to . . . . . !
> Far away, far away.

Since the poem was described in the *Dial* as "Lines written while sailing out of Boston Harbor for the West Indies," Emerson believed that some readers would assume one of his brothers to be the author. Indeed,

James Clarke, for one, correctly guessed that Edward wrote it (*EmW*, 9:260; JFC to SC, 8 July 1840, MH).

2. Quoted in James Elliot Cabot, *A Memoir of Ralph Waldo Emerson* (Bo: HoMif, 1887), 1:138; 9 Nov. 1835, MH; 10 July 1828, in *EmJMN*, 3:137.

3. Soon after their engagement, Charles wrote Elizabeth that it seemed to him that "a rose light showed on the very pages" of his law books. Although the two were very much in love, Charles, who was aware of his family's history of consumption, was sometimes gloomy: "I miss you as I miss the great Future for which I hope, the virtue I have not yet domesticated, the happiness I have not yet deserved." Charles confessed these fears only to Elizabeth, and when Waldo read their letters after Charles's death, he was "harrowed" by so "much contrition, so much questioning, so little hope, [and] so much sorrow" (ca. Aug. 1833, ca. Apr. 1834, copies by RWE, 19 Mar. 1837, in *EmJMN*, 5:389, 157, 288).

4. The possibility that Charles and Elizabeth would settle in Concord after their marriage was a major factor in deciding Waldo Emerson to move there. He even built an addition to his house in anticipation of their living with him. The intellectual arrangement would also have been nice, for Charles had earlier declared that if he were "a metaphysician of any sort it should be of the transcendental school," which was "grand & true" (Charles Emerson to Mary Moody Emerson, 7 Mar. 1833, MH).

5. 25 Mar. 1855, in F. B. Sanborn, "Manuscript Diary of Franklin B. Sanborn," ed. Kenneth Walter Cameron, in his *Transcendental Climate* (Hartford, Conn.: Transcendental Books, 1963), 1:221; Oliver Wendell Holmes, "Poetry; a Metrical Essay," in his *Poems* (Bo: Otis, Broaders; and NY: George Dearborn, 1836), p. 37; Fuller, "Lines . . . On the Death of C. C. E.," *Boston Daily Centinel & Gazette*, 17 May 1836, p. 1; 20 Oct. 1835, ABA, "Journal for 1835," p. 442, MH; described by a Mr. Waterston in his letter to EPP, quoted in EPP to Mary Peabody, 15 May 1836, in *EmL*, 2:19n; 17 Sept. 1836, in *EmCorTC*, p. 148; 16 May 1836, in *EmJMN*, 5:151.

6. RWE to WmE, 8 Aug. 1836, in *EmL*, 2:31; RWE to R. C. Winthrop, 15 Aug. 1836, in ibid., p. 34; see 11 Mar. 1837, in *EmJMN*, 6:256, and RWE to WmE, 20 Mar. 1837, in *EmL*, 2:59; RWE to MF, 15 Apr., 23 Apr. 1840, in ibid., p. 282, 290; *FuNbD* (first number); JFC to SC, 8 July 1840, MH; RWE to MF, 4 Nov. 1840, in *EmL*, 2:355; Emerson had thought of doing this earlier when he had assumed the *Dial*'s editorship (RWE to WmE, 22 Aug. 1842, in ibid., 3:83); 4 Aug. 1843, in ibid., p. 194n; HDT to the Emersons, 8 July 1843, in *ThCor*, p. 124.

7. Soon after their engagement, Emerson wrote in his journal: "She has the purity & confiding religion of an angel. . . . Will God forgive me my sins & aid me to deserve this gift of his mercy" (17 Jan. 1829, in *EmJMN*, 3:149).

8. Hedge recalled Ellen as "a beautiful fragile figure" with "a complexion that indicated feeble health & forboded early death." Charles Emerson felt that even before his brother married Ellen he knew that she was dying; he thought that she was "too lovely to live long," but Waldo said that if she dies "tomorrow" it would have been his blessing to have loved her (FHH to Cabot, 14 Sept. 1882, MH; Charles Emerson to WmE, 22 Jan. 1829, in *EmL*, 1:259n).

9. *FuNbD*; Ellen's "I've done with grief now / I shan't tell why." — an obvious reference to Emerson's coming into her life — became in the *Dial*,". . .a clear voice spoke, — / And my tears are dry.", — making the instrument of her relief God's voice (Emerson, *One First Love*, p. 153).

10. RWE to MF, 21 July 1840, in *EmL*, 2:316; MF to RWE, 7 Nov. 1840, in ibid., p. 354n.

Chapter 18: William Batchelder Greene

Note: Biographical information is from Louis Brownell Clarke, comp., *The Greenes of Rhode Island* (NY: Knickerbocker Press, 1903), pp. 694-95; Charles Carleton Coffin, "Memoir of Nathaniel Greene," *New-England Historical and Genealogical Register* 32 (Oct. 1878):373-78; and *CoHiBi*, 2:117-28. See also Rudolf Rocker, *Pioneers of American Freedom* (Los Angeles, Calif.: Rocker Publication Committee, 1949), pp. 97-112, for an account of Greene's later years.

1. Elizabeth Palmer Peabody, *Reminiscences of Rev. Wm. Ellery Channing* (Bo: Roberts, 1880), p. 438 (doctors); Greene was described as being at one time a "personal disciple" of Brownson (I. T. Hecker, "Dr. Brownson in Boston," *Catholic World* 45 [July 1887]:468).

2. Peabody, *Reminiscences*, p. 435. Louise Hall Tharp asserts that Greene was both "the young man [Peabody] had hoped to meet twenty-five years earlier" and "the son she knew now she would never have." Robert L. Straker, who carefully combed Tharp's book for errors, calls insinuations of a romance pure "poppycock" and states that the extant letters between Greene and Peabody show that "their interests were entirely theological" (*The Peabody Sisters of Salem* [Bo: Little, Brown, 1950], p. 219, where she misdates their first meeting by nearly a decade; Robert L. Straker, "A Gloss Upon Glosses," pp. 33, 34, typescript, NN-M).

Tharp's first statement is a romantic obfuscation of actual events, yet Straker's explanation is also incomplete. Peabody complained to Brownson that Greene thought "transcendentalism produced a *certain coldness* with respect to individual relations;—that people approached one another for purely intellectual purposes & without sufficiently considering the happiness of individuals; as if every one was all sufficient to himself, & nobody had any duties to others." As a result of his constantly commenting with "perfect nonchalance" on her "various intellectual, religious,—& even *moral* deficiencies," Peabody thought that Greene felt that she had "no feelings to be wounded, and no *respectability!*" (n.d., InNd).

There is more truth in Tharp's second statement. When Greene returned from Florida, Peabody nursed him at home, where she "adopted *the feelings* as well as the manners of his mother." Thus his comments also disturbed her because he paid no attention to "*that deference* due to sixteen years advance of him in point of time." In fact, said Peabody, "in those years when the bent & cast of *my* character[,] moral, intellectual, religious were formed. . .*he* was two three & four years old!" It should also be added that Peabody was fond of "adopting" people and causes, and that Greene was merely one of the many, including Jones Very and Nathaniel Hawthorne, whom she at one time sponsored (EPP to Brownson, n.d., InNd).

Greene very early in their friendship regretted allowing Peabody to become "so well acquainted" with him, as he told Brownson; she took his general comments for personal attacks on herself, and she expected too much, intellectually, from him. Like Hawthorne, Greene soon became uneasy around Peabody and at last commented, "She is a strange character—entirely too hard for me" (24 Aug. [1842], InNd).

3. Thomas Wentworth Higginson, *Cheerful Yesterdays* (Bo: HoMif, 1898), p. 106; quoted in *SaHaABA*, 2:401.

4. Peabody, *Reminiscences*, p. 435; 9 Nov. 1841, in *EmL*, 2:462n.

5. Afterward, Mrs. Cheney asked Louisa Alcott whether her father's action was intentional. Louisa replied, "Oh, he knew well enough what he was about" (*SaHaABA*, 2:401-2).

6. A sheet of paper with Emerson's notation "More First Principles," containing thoughts on conscience and poetry by Greene, is still laid in the back of Emerson's "Notebook T" (see *EmJMN*, 6:399n).

7. Green sent Emerson a volume of German tales translated by his father in 1843, and his *Transcendentalism* (1849) was dedicated to Emerson (LdE's postscript, HDT to RWE, 20 Feb., in *ThCor*, p. 91; [West Brookfield, Mass.: Oliver S. Cooke]).

8. Greene married Anna Shaw, whose brother Francis Shaw had married a cousin of Ellen and Caroline Sturgis. The Shaws's daughter later married George William Curtis (Granville Hicks, "A Conversation in Boston," *Sewanee Review* 39 [Apr.-June 1931]:137; John Ward Dean, "Descendants of the Rev. Daniel Rogers·of Littleton, Mass.," *New-England Historical and Genealogical Register* 39 [July 1885]:226).

9. One of Greene's other publications was a revision and expansion of his *Dial* article as *The Doctrine of Life. With Some of Its Theological Applications* (Bo: B.H. Greene, 1843). In his preface to this book, Greene stated that the "germs of this essay may be found" in his *Dial* article and, although since writing that article his views had undergone "a slight change," he was still willing to be held answerable for what he then wrote (p. [iii]).

Chapter 19: Frederic Henry Hedge

Note: Biographical information is from O. W. Long, *Frederic Henry Hedge* (Portland, Me.: Southworth-Anthoensen Press, 1940); Joel Myerson, "Frederic Henry Hedge and the Failure of Transcendentalism," *Harvard Library Bulletin* 23 (Oct. 1975): 396-410; and Martha Ilona Tuomi, "Dr. Frederic Henry Hedge: His Life and Works to the End of His Bangor Pastorate," M.A. thesis, University of Maine, 1935.

1. WHC's statement, in *FrWHC*, p. 109; Mar. 1835, in ABA, "Journal for 1835," p. 104, MH.

2. One reason why Hedge made Emerson his friend was that he respected his views. Hedge thought Emerson's American Scholar address "as sweet a song as had been sung . . . in many a year" (quoted in Arthur S. Bolster, Jr., *James Freeman Clarke* [Bo: Beacon, 1954], p. 108).

3. FHH to J. G. Palfrey, 16 June 1833, MH; 12 July 1834, MeBa.

4. Myerson, "Hedge," pp. 400-401; RWE to FHH, 20 July 1836, in *EmL*, 2:29.

5. Week 22, June 1837, in ABA, "Journal for 1837," p. 409, MH; Week 18, May 1837, in ibid., p. 319.

6. ABA to RWE, 9 May 1837 in *AlcL*, p. 32. Emerson made this wish come true when he invited Alcott to stay with him at Concord while Hedge was there (RWE to MF, 17 Aug. 1837, in *EmL*, 2:94).

7. Week 22, June 1837, in ABA, "Journal for 1837," p. 409; FHH to Caroline Dall, 1 Feb. 1877, in Dall, *Transcendentalism in New England* (Bo: Roberts, 1897), p. 17. Hedge's reply to Parker (9 Aug. 1838) listing what books to get is still preserved, carefully laid into Parker's journal (*PkJ*, vol. 1, between pp. 23 and 24).

8. 19 Sept. 1839, in *PkJ*, 1:233.

9. 1 Feb. 1865, in Joel Myerson, "Caroline Dall's Reminiscences of Margaret Fuller," *Harvard Library Bulletin* 22 (Oct. 1974): 427; MF to FHH, 6 Mar. 1835, MH; 1 Jan. 1840, MH.

10. 16 Jan. 1840, MH.

11. *FuNbD*; 10 Mar. 1840, in *HigMF*, p. 150; FHH to MF, 24 Mar. 1840, described in James Elliot Cabot, "Notebook," MH; 30 Mar. 1840, *EmL*, 2:270-71.

12. 25 Nov. 1840, in Madeleine B. Stern, "Four Letters from George Keats," *PMLA* 56 (Mar. 1942): 211.

13. RWE to MF, 12 Jan. 1841, in *EmL*, 2:376. The poem's transcendental qualities may be inferred from the fact that it was often reprinted as "The Idealist." Emerson printed "Questionings" over Hedge's name in his edition of *Parnassus* (George Willis Cooke, ed., *The Poets of Transcendentalism* [Bo: HoMif, 1903], p. 314; [Bo: Osgood, 1875], pp. 91-92).

14. 23 Mar. 1842, in *EmL*, 3:37; 11 May 1842, in ibid., p. 55; 27 Aug. 1841, in *EmJMN*, 8:31; 1 Sept. 1842, in *EmL*, 3:84.

15. 20-23 Oct. 1842, MH; RWE to FHH, 21 Nov. 1842, *EmL*, 3:97-98; RWE to CSW, 13 Dec. 1842, MH; FHH to MF, 5, 12 Jan. 1843, MH.

16. FHH to C. Francis, 26 Jan. 1842, MHi.

17. Henry Wadsworth Longfellow, after once hearing Hedge preach, wrote in his journal: "His organ of self-esteem is so large that it seems sometimes as if it would lift him off his legs" (13 Apr. 1846, in Long, *Hedge*, p. 21).

18. FHH to C. Francis, 26 Jan. 1842, MHi.

19. Elizabeth Palmer Peabody, *Reminiscences of Rev. Wm. Ellery Channing* (Bo: Roberts, 1880), p. 371; 2 Sept. 1840, in *PkJ*, 1:442.

Chapter 20: Elizabeth Hoar

Note: Dr. Elizabeth Maxfield-Miller of the Concord Academy is currently writing a biography of Elizabeth Hoar; some of her findings have appeared in "Emerson and Elizabeth of Concord," *Harvard Library Bulletin* 19 (July 1971):290-306.

1. Oct. 1841, in *EmJMN*, 8:105.

2. 25 Mar. 1855, in F. B. Sanborn, "Manuscript Diary of Franklin B. Sanborn," ed. Kenneth Walter Cameron, in his *Transcendental Climate* (Hartford, Conn.: Transcendental Books, 1963), 1:221; James Elliot Cabot, *A Memoir of Ralph Waldo Emerson* (Bo: HoMif, 1887), 1:381.

3. 13 Sept. 1837, in *EmJMN*, 5:373; Randall Stewart's comment, in his edition of Nathaniel Hawthorne, *The American Notebooks by Nathaniel Hawthore* (New Haven, Conn.: Yale University Press, 1932), p. 313n; MF to CKN, 1 July 1842, MH; Curtis to CPC, 14 May 1844, typescript, MHi; 5 Aug. 1842, in *HawAmNb*, p. 316; Lane to RWE, 14 Dec. 1843, MH.

4. However, Sturgis was not humbled by Hoar, adding that she could not have "pulled half as well as I did" (CS to RWE, 17 Oct. [1840?], MH).

5. 9 Feb. 1839, in *AlcDiJaJn39*, pp. 268-69; RWE to CS, 13 Oct. 1840, MH.

6. Late Mar. 1843, in *EmJMN*, 8:352; EH to Richard Fuller, 8 July 1843, MH.

7. Elizabeth Maxfield-Miller, "Elizabeth Hoar of Concord and Thoreau," *Thoreau Society Bulletin*, no. 106 (Winter 1969):1. When Hoar was in the same class as Thoreau and Charles Stearns Wheeler, Sarah Ripley told Mary Moody Emerson that "she keeps up with them well" (4 Sept. 1833, in [Elizabeth Hoar], *Mrs. Samuel Ripley* [Philadelphia: J. B. Lippincott, 1877], p. 51).

8. EH to HDT, 2 May 1843, in *ThCor*, p. 98; Mar. 1843, in *EmJMN*, 8:375.

9. 4 Sept. 1842, in *FuJ42*, p. 334; MF to CKN, 1 July 1842, MH ("refinement"); 21 July 1850, in *EmJ*, 8:119; Oct. 1841, in *EmJMN*, 8:105.

10. George F. Hoar, *Autobiography of Seventy Years* (NY: Scribner's, 1903), 1:60; quoted in *RuLiEm*, p. 91 (1821); ibid., p. 221; RWE to TC, 15 May 1839, in *EmCorTC*, p. 233 ("nun"); *SaRec*, 2:370; 6 June 1836, in *EmJMN*, 5:170; W. E. Channing to T. W. Higginson, in F. B. Sanborn, "A Concord Note-Book: Ellery Channing and His Table-Talk, Second Paper," *Critic* 27 (Aug. 1905):122.

11. RWE to MF, 20[?] Mar. 1843, in *EmL*, 3:160; Oct. 1841, in *EmJMN*, 8:105. Much later Emerson praised the "pure force" of Hoar's poem "George Nidiver," which he included, unsigned, in his 1870 *Society and Solitude* (RWE to EH, 17 Jan. 1870, in Carroll A. Wilson, *Thirteen Author Collections of the Nineteenth Century . . .* , ed. Jean C. S. Wilson and David A. Randall [NY: Scribner's, 1950], 1:33; *EmW*, 7:277-80, 435n).

Chapter 21: Ellen Sturgis Hooper

Note: Biographical information is from *CoHiBi*, 2:54-61, supplemented by genealogies and biographical dictionaries.

1. Roger Faxton Sturgis, ed., *Edward Sturgis of Yarmouth, Massachusetts 1613-1695 and his Descendants* (Bo: Stanhope Press, 1914), pp. 42-43; Stanley J. Kunitz and Howard Haycraft, eds., *American Authors 1600-1900* (NY: H. W. Wilson, 1938), p. 380 (education); Charles Henry Pope and Thomas Hooper, comps., *Hooper Genealogy* (Bo: Charles H. Pope, 1908), p. 155. The Hoopers's third and last child grew up to marry Henry Adams (see Marion Hooper Adams, *The Letters of Mrs. Henry Adams 1865-1883*, ed. Ward Thoron [Bo: Little, Brown, 1936], p. xiii).

2. Louise Hall Tharp, *The Peabody Sisters of Salem* (Bo: Little, Brown, 1950), p. 88; MF to [WHC?], 8 Nov. [1840], MB; quoted in *CuEarlyLetDw*, p. 38; Clarke later named one of his daughters after Ellen Hooper (Arthur S. Bolster, Jr., *James Freeman Clarke* [Bo: Beacon, 1954], p. 194); quoted in *CuEarlyLetDw*, p. 38; JRL to Nathan Hale, Jr., 25 July 1840, in Philip Graham, "Some Lowell Letters," *Texas Studies in Literature and Language* 3 (Winter 1962):577; RWE to SC, 30 Sept. 1842, MH.

3. Many of Mrs. Hooper's poems were collected in 1872 by Edward William Sturgis, who had them privately printed for distribution to friends. A great many variants exist between this printing and that of the *Dial*. It is impossible to say with absolute certainty which version is closer to her original manuscript, but the fact that later reprints of her poems preferred the 1872 texts, which often have entire stanzas not present in the *Dial*, may indicate that for the *Dial* printings Emerson or Fuller ex-

ercised editorial license. On the other hand, Mrs. Hooper may have revised the poems after they were published in the *Dial*, and the 1872 text may have come from the manuscripts of these later revisions.

4. RWE to CS, [184?], MH; RWE to MF, 21 June 1840, in *EmL*, 2:306; MF to CS, 10 Feb. 1840, MH.

5. 17 Oct. 1843, in *ThCor*, p. 145; Henry David Thoreau, *Walden*, ed. J. Lyndon Shanley, in *The Writings of Henry D. Thoreau*, ed. Walter Harding et al. (Princeton, N.J.: Princeton University Press, 1971), pp. 254-55; CPC to Griswold, 21 Apr. 1843, MB.

6. JFC to SC, 8 July 1840, MH; *CoHiBi*, 2:55, 194. Wendell Phillips liked "I slept . . . " enough to copy it for friends; one such copy has been offered for sale as a poem by him (*The Flying Quill* [Autographs at Goodspeed's], 1 June 1972, item 142).

7. RWE to EH, 7 May 1842, in *EmL*, 3:49. She once told Emerson that "she sympathized with the Transcendental movement, but she sympathized even more with the objectors" (1845, in *EmJMN*, 9:111).

Chapter 22: Benjamin Peter Hunt

Note: Biographical information is from "The Late Benjamin P. Hunt, of Philadelphia," *Twenty-Fifth Annual Report of the Trustees of the [Boston] Public Library* (Boston: n.p., 1877), pp. 119-23; *CoHiBi*, 2:176-80; and Samuel Cutler, "Necrology of the New-England Historic, Genealogical Society," *New-England Historical and Genealogical Register* 32 (Oct. 1878):430-34.

1. Hunt later confessed to one of his former pupils that he had not been "at all fitted to be a schoolmaster," for, even though he had read a great deal, he felt that he lacked "the minor or petty earnestness of character . . . necessary for such work." One of his former pupils disagreed: "[H]e certainly made all of us who were above idiocy think and live in thought above the ordinary range of school-boy life" (Charles Godfrey Leland, *Memoirs* [NY: Appleton, 1893], p. 69).

2. RWE to W. H. Furness, 24 Oct. 1837, in *EmRecLiFr*, p. 2; Emerson carefully copied Hunt's address into his journal (*EmJMN*, 3:202); 1 Sept. 1833, in ibid., 4:78-79.

3. RWE to W. H. Furness, 24 Oct. 1837, in *EmRecLiFr*, pp. 2-3; further enticements at Concord were Bronson Aclott, whom Hunt took to at once, and Fuller (ibid., p. 3; RWE to MF, 31 Jan. 1843, in *EmL*, 3:137).

4. RWE to LdE, 1 Feb. 1843, in *EmL*, 3:139. References to James Franklin, *The Present State of Hayti. . .*, and Charles MacKenzie, *Notes on Haiti. . .*, were made by Emerson in his journal, but neither book was reviewed in the *Dial* (see *EmJMN*, 8:521-22).

5. 10 June 1843, in *ThCor*, p. 118; 8 Aug. 1843, in *EmL*, 3:198-99. As was the case with Wheeler's letters, Hunt's narrative was kept in a diarylike manner and style. Therefore, to make it more readable Emerson did a good deal of editorial work on it. He changed little of its substance, though, and most of his efforts were directed toward condensing the bulky manuscript and tying the chronological arrangement together with a narrative line. Hunt told Emerson that he was "well pleased" that he had taken the trouble of "re-writing" it (20 Sept. 1843, MH; Hunt's manuscript is at MH).

6. 8 Aug. 1843, in *EmL*, 3:199; SR to RWE, 5 July [1843], MH; HDT to the Emersons, 8 July 1843, in *ThCor*, p. 125; MF to RWE, 4 Aug. 1843, in *EmL*, 3:194n.

7. 8 Aug. 1843, in *EmL*, 3:199-200. Hunt refused this offer, fearing that, had it been consummated, "it would have turned out a loss to somebody" (Hunt to RWE, 20 Sept. 1843, MH).

8. Hunt to RWE, 20 Sept. 1843, MH.

Chapter 23: Charles Lane

Note: Biographical information is from Roger William Cummins, "The Second Eden: Charles Lane and American Transcendentalism," Ph.D. diss., University of Minnesota, 1967.

1. RWE to EH, 4 Nov. 1839, in *EmL*, 2:231; July 1840, in *AlcSc40*, p. 247, 12 June 1842, in *AlcL*,

p. 70; 26 Dec. 1842, in ibid., p. 95.

2. Although many later accounts of the experiment present a ludicrous picture of Alcott and Lane, they definitely took themselves seriously. Lane wrote to an English journal that Fruitlands would be "an attempt at something which will entitle transcendentalism to some respect for its practicability," adding: "I seriously hope we are forming the basis for a really progressive movement" ("Practical Transcendentalism," *New Age* 1 [1 July 1843]:59).

3. 27 Nov. 1842, InNd; 4 Apr. 1843, MHi; C. Francis to FHH, 24 Jan. 1843, MeBa; journal entry, 9 May 1843, in John Joseph McDonald, "Hawthorne at the Old Manse," Ph.D. diss., Princeton University, 1971, p. 65n.

4. *MemMF*, 1:321 (asceticism); MF to FHH, 17 Dec. 1842, MH. Lane in turn glowingly called Fuller a "rare woman" (Lane to William Oldham, 28-30 Jan. 1843, in William Harry Harland, "Bronson Alcott's English Friends," typescript, MHarF).

5. Quoted in CSW to J. F. Heath, 3 Feb. 1843, MH; LMC to Augusta King, 19 Sept. 1843, NIC; LMC to E. G. Loring, 26 Sept. 1843, NN-M. Mrs. Child also felt that Lane would go so far as to cast off his linen clothing for a "primitive fig-leaf" if his "scruples" demanded it. "Even *this*," David Child thought, "might be cast aside before his visit was concluded, should it happen to occur to him that it was used for purposes of hiding, and that hiding, being all a sham, would have no place in the diviner unconscious state" (LMC to E. G. Loring, 26 Sept. 1843, NN-M).

6. 1 Nov. 1839, in *AlcDiJyDec39*, p. 374 (liked); RWE to MF, 16 Nov. 1842, in *EmL*, 3:96; RWE to CSW, 13 Dec. 1842, MH ("superior"); Sept. 1842, in *EmJMN*, 8: 261; Dec. 1842, in ibid., 7:477 ("manner"); RWE to CSW, 13 Dec. 1842, MH; 23 Mar. 1843, in *EmJMN*, 8:367; 25 May 1843, in ibid., p. 404 ("influence"); RWE to CS, 29 Sept. 1843, MH.

7. Lane to ABA, 31 Oct. 1840, copy by ABA, in his "Scripture for 1840," p. 181, MH; 1 (1 Aug. 1842):166-68; RWE to SGW, 30 Sept. [1842], MH.

8. RWE to WmE, 8 Sept. 1842, in *EmL*, 3:85 (printer); RWE to TC, 15 Oct. 1842, in *EmCorTC*, p. 331. Emerson told Carlyle that he might see "a certain shadow or mask" of himself in the Cromwell article, for Emerson guessed that its author was familiar with Carlyle's lectures and had "profited thereby" (15 Oct. 1842, in ibid., p. 331).

9. 2 July 1842, in *AlcL*, p. 82. Lane's article on Greaves brought back old memories to Carlyle: "I knew old Greaves myself; and can testify, if you will believe me, that few greater blockheads (if 'blockhead' may mean 'exasperated imbecil' and the ninth-part of a thinker) broke the world's bread in his day" (TC to RWE, 11 Mar. 1843, in *EmCorTC*, p. 338).

10. ca. 1 Dec. 1842, in *AlcAuInd*; 13 Dec. 1842, MH; RWE to LdE, 6 Jan. 1843, in *EmL*, 3:111-12.

11. 12 Feb. 1843, in *ThCor*, p. 85; HDT to RWE, in ibid., pp. 87-88; HDT to RWE, [1 Mar. 1843], in ibid., p. 89.

12. Thoreau mentioned Lane's wish for offprints to Emerson on 20 Feb. (ibid., p. 90) and Emerson arranged for the article on Alcott to be printed as a separate pamphlet, *The Law and Method in Spirit-Culture; an Interpretation of A. Bronson Alcott's Idea and Practice at the Masonic Temple, Boston* (Bo: James Munroe, 1843), which appeared three days before the *Dial* itself. The pamphlet was printed from the same plates used in the *Dial* with minor differences, such as the renumbering of pages. Emerson was not so gracious with the "Catalogue of Books," merely instructing the printer to send any pages he may have left over to Lane (*Boston Daily Advertiser* [5 Apr. 1843]; RWE to EPP, 14 Apr. [1843], in William White, "Two Unpublished Emerson Letters," *AL* 31 [Nov. 1959]:335).

13. HDT to RWE, [1 Mar. 1843], in *ThCor*, p. 89. Alcott enthusiastically recommended the review to his friends (see ABA to Hannah Robie, 2 Apr. 1843, MH).

14. RWE to MF, 20[?] Mar. 1843, in *EmL*, 3:159-60.

15. 20 Feb. 1843, in *ThCor*, p. 90. One such phrase omitted from the *Dial* version was: "To Emerson, in his own circle, is but slowly accorded a worthy response" (*SaHaABA*, 1:350).

16. RWE to LdE, 26 Feb. 1843, in *EmL*, 3:150-51; HDT to RWE, 20 Feb. 1843, in *ThCor*, p. 90; n.d., pasted in ABA, "Correspondence 1836-50," p. 102, MH; 9 Apr. 1843, in *HawAmNb*, p. 374; 6 Apr. 1843, MH.

17. RWE to WmE, 26 Oct. 1842, in *EmL*, 3:93 ("collection"); RWE to FHH, 21 Nov. 1842, in ibid., p. 98; RWE to CSW, 13 Dec. 1842, MH; 15 Feb. 1843, in *ThCor*, p. 87; HDT to RWE, 20 Feb. 1843, in ibid., p. 90; FHH to MF, 5, 12 Jan. 1843, MH.

18. RWE to MF, 11 May 1843, in *EmL*, 3:173; RWE to HDT, 10 June 1843, in *ThCor*, p. 118; MF to RWE, 4 Aug. 1843, in *EmL*, 3:194n; 17 Oct. 1843, in *ThCor*, p. 145.

19. A notice of "Thoughts on Spiritual Subjects, translated from François Fenelon," written by Lane in February, had been "crowded out by the unexpected length" of the other articles in the July number. The translation was by George Bradford, but I have found no evidence of its having been published (HDT to RWE, 20 Feb. 1843, in *ThCor*, p. 90; *Dial*, 4:133).

20. The original letter began: "In former numbers we have intimated the designs and efforts of Messrs Alcott and Lane . . . " Such verbose comments as one saying that the farm's original owner had "suddenly and unsought proffered his possessions" to allow Lane and Alcott to liberate "this tract from human ownership" were omitted by Emerson. He also shortened, for example, "Nearly the whole [farm] is irrigated by rivulets whose sources are in the hill slopes," to "watered by small streams" in the *Dial* (Lane and ABA to RWE, 12 June 1843, MH).

21. RWE to MF, 7 Aug. 1843, in *EmL*, 3:196; RWE to HDT, 8 Sept. 1843, in *ThCor*, p. 138; RWE to SGW, 30 Sept. [1842], MH. Emerson no doubt had the *Dial* article in mind when he later said that Lane had "rendered a valuable service to the Shakers by his residence among them." Lane very much liked this topic: in April 1844 he promised "A month with the Shakers" to the English *New Age*, and by August it had grown to a "Six Months' Residence" among them, though he delivered neither (RWE to William Bennett, 30 June 1845, in Dawson's of Pall Mall, catalogue 215, item 256; "On Sexual Communion," *New Age* 1 [1 Apr. 1844]:201; "Being Good and Doing Good," *New Age* 1 [1 Aug. 1844]:263).

22. Lane to RWE, 14 Dec. 1843, MH; RWE to MF, 26 Feb. 1844, in *EmL*, 3:243; 15 Mar. 1844, MH.

Chapter 24: James Russell Lowell

Note: Biographical information is from Martin Duberman, *James Russell Lowell* (Bo: HoMif, 1966), and Horace Elisha Scudder, *James Russell Lowell*, 2 vols. (Bo: HoMif, 1901).

1. Ethel Golann, "A Lowell Autobiography," *NEQ* 7 (June 1934):359.

2. Edward Everett Hale, *James Russell Lowell and His Friends* (Bo: HoMif, 1899), p. 30; JRL to T. S. Perry, 2 Mar. 1875, in James Russell Lowell, *Letters of James Russell Lowell*, ed. Charles Eliot Norton, 2 vols. (NY: Harper's, 1894), 2:136.

3. 25 June 1838, in Faculty Records, 11:346, MH; Scudder, *Lowell*, 1:30; JRL to G. B. Loring, [1 July 1838], in Joel Myerson, "Eight Lowell Letters from Concord in 1838," *Illinois Quarterly* 38 (Winter 1975):23; JRL to G. B. Loring, 25 July 1838, in ibid., p. 32.

4. Frost was capable of such oddities as this sentence from a Thanksgiving sermon: "We have been free from the pestilence that walketh in darkness, and the destruction that wasteth at noonday; it is true we have had some chicken-pox and some measles." He was also a somewhat unusual teacher. Lowell told a friend that one day Locke's book "made the remark that it was impossible for the mind ever to be without an idea of some sort. [Frost] immediately attacked it & said 'Why, I myself frequently have no idea in my mind!' 'Yes Sir, very likely' remarked I with a very lamblike aspect. Alas! [Frost] was happy in his dulness[:] he didn't perceive the wit" (quoted in Hale, *Lowell*, p. 45; JRL to Nathan Hale, Jr., 23 July 1838, in Joel Myerson, "Lowell on Emerson: A New Letter from Concord in 1838," *NEQ* 44 [Dec. 1971]:651-52).

5. JRL to G. B. Loring, 12 July 1838, in Myerson, "Lowell Letters," p. 28. Lowell's later uncomplimentary comments on Thoreau cost him many friends. After reading Lowell's review of Thoreau's *Letters to Various Persons* in 1865, Bronson Alcott, who had just published his small and limited edition of *Emerson*, wrote to a friend: "Lowell shall have none [of *Emerson*], were the edition a million; think of that paper of his on Thoreau . . . and call him E's friend afterwards!" (*North American Review* 101 [Oct. 1865]:597-608; ABA to Mary Stearns, 22 Oct. 1865, in *AlcL*, p. 377).

6. Lowell always made a distinction between the public, or "Transcendental," Emerson and the

private man: "[I]f his head be sometimes in thin and difficult air, his heart never is" (JRL to Leslie Stephen, 3 May 1873, in Scudder, *Lowell*, 2:167).

7. 8 July 1838, in Philip Graham, "Some Lowell Letters," *Texas Studies in Literature and Language* 3 (Winter 1962):559; 23 July 1838, in Myerson, "Lowell on Emerson," p. 651; JRL to G. B. Loring, 9 Aug. 1838, in Myerson, "Lowell Letters," p. 35.

8. 1 Sept. 1838, MH; RWE to JRL, 3 Sept. 1838, in *EmL*, 2:159; Lowell afterward commented upon the occasion in these lines:

> Behold the baby arrows of that wit
> Wherewith I dared assail the woundless Truth!
> Love hath refilled the quiver, and with it
> The man shall win atonement for the youth!

(JRL to W. Field, 13 Dec. 1885, in Lowell, *Letters*, 2:302).

9. James Russell Lowell, "Some Letters of Walter Savage Landor," *Century Magazine* 35 (Feb. 1888):511; Kenneth Walter Cameron, "Early Records of the Concord Lyceum," in his *Transcendental Climate* (Hartford, Conn.: Transcendental Books, 1963), 3:692; JRL to G. B. Loring, 2 Dec. 1838, MH.

10. James Russell Lowell, *Uncollected Poems of James Russell Lowell*, ed. Thelma M. Smith (Philadelphia: University of Pennsylvania Press, 1950), p. 249; JRL to G. B. Loring, 28 June 1840, MH.

11. 1[?] Dec.[?] 1840, in *EmL*, 2:363; 6 Dec. 1840, in ibid., p. 363n; 10 Dec. 1840, in ibid., p. 367; RWE to MF, 15 Dec. 1840, in ibid.

12. Wheeler's review was actually embarrassing: "We have had little heart to look for faults and blunders, since one or two experiments in that line resulted in the discovery of fresh beauties." Lowell told a friend that this puff had "amounted only to a compliment to the family" (*Christian Examiner* 30 [Mar. 1841]:131-34; JRL to J. F. Heath, 12 Mar. 1841, NN-B).

13. JRL to G. B. Loring, 18 Feb. 1841, MH.

14. *Dial* 2:133-34; RWE to EH, 18 July 1841, in *EmL*, 2:429. In *Papers on Literature and Art* Fuller described Lowell as "absolutely wanting in the true spirit and tone of poesy. . . . his verse is stereotyped; his thought sounds no depth, and posterity will not remember him." This and the *Dial* notice were probably in Lowell's mind when he drew Fuller as Miranda, with an "I-turn-the-crank-of-the-Universe air," in his 1848 *A Fable for Critics*. That same year Lowell drew this other, less famous picture of Fuller:

> Her eye, — it seems a chemic test,
> And drops upon you like an acid;
>
> . . . .
>
> There, you are classified; she's gone
> Far, far away into herself;
> Each with its Latin label on,
> Your poor components, one by one,
> Are laid upon their proper shelf
> In her compact and ordered mind,
>
> . . . .
>
> One problem still defies thy art; —
> Thou never canst compute . . .
> The distance and diameter
> Of any simple human heart.

([NY: Wiley & Putnam, 1846], 2:132; [NY: G. P. Putnam], p. 53; "Studies for Two Heads," in James Russell Lowell, *Poems, Second Series* [Cambridge, Mass.: George Nichols; NY: B. B. Mussey], pp. 136-37).

15. In the *Dial* the poem is erroneously dated "April, 1819"; in the extant manuscript the sonnet is dated "April, 1841" (enclosed with JRL to RWE, 19 Nov. 1841, MH).

16. 19 Nov. 1841, MH; RWE to JRL, 25 Nov. 1841, in *EmL*, 2:467; 27 Nov. 1841, in James Russell Lowell, *New Letters of James Russell Lowell*, ed. M. A. DeWolfe Howe (NY: Harper's, 1932), pp. 7-8; 4 Dec. 1841, in *EmL*, 2:470. Emerson accepted Lowell's revisions in the manuscript of "Only as thou herein . . . ," but one substantive change was made in the *Dial*'s text. Later, when the situations were reversed and Lowell was associated with the *Atlantic Monthly*, it was he who suggested that Emerson change "hypocritical" to "hypocritic" in his "Days" (*Uncollected Poems*, p. 28n; RWE to F. H. Underwood, 24 Sept. 1857, in Bliss Perry, *Park-Street Papers* [Bo: HoMif, 1908], p. 245).

17. JRL to JSD, 7 Oct. 1842, ViU-B ("carte blanche"); "Prospectus" for the *Pioneer*, reprinted in Sculley Bradley, ed., *The Pioneer: A Literary Magazine* (NY: Scholars' Facsimilies & Reprints, 1947), n.p.; "Introduction," in ibid., p. xxvi (collapse); RWE to CSW, 13 Dec. 1842, and JRL to RWE, 16 Dec. 1842, MH; *Pioneer* 1 (Mar. 1843):143: a more detailed discussion of this episode is in the chapter on Wheeler.

18. JRL to G. W. Cooke, 30 Nov. 1885, MHarF.

Chapter 25: John Milton Mackie

Note: Biographical information is from James Grant Wilson and John Fiske, eds., *Appleton's Cyclopaedia of American Biography* (NY: Appleton, 1888-89), 4:135-36, and *CoHiBi*, 2:98.

1. Henry A. Pochmann, *German Culture in America* (Madison, Wis.: University of Wisconsin Press, 1957), p. 768n; RWE to MF, 22 Apr. 1841, in *EmL*, 2:395; RWE to John Chapman, 30 Oct. 1846, in ibid., 3:359: Chapman, however, thought it good enough to be one of the three articles from the *Dial* that he reprinted in his *Characteristics of Men of Genius* (Bo: Otis, Broaders; Lo: John Chapman, 1847).

Chapter 26: Charles King Newcomb

Note: Biographical information is from Charles King Newcomb, *The Journals of Charles King Newcomb*, ed. Judith Kennedy Johnson (Providence, R.I.: Brown University Press, 1946).

1. Sarah Newcomb to CKN, 11 Jan. 1838, in Newcomb, *Journals*, p. 14.

2. MF to CKN, 29 May 1839, MH; Rhoda Newcomb to CKN, 6 July 1840, RPB.

3. MF to RWE, 5 July 1840, in *EmL*, 2:310n.

4. Georgiana Bruce Kirby, *Years of Experience* (NY: Putnam's, 1887), p. 105 ("eccentric"); G. W. Curtis to G. W. Cooke, 9 June 1882, MHarF; Lindsay Swift, *Brook Farm* (NY: Macmillan, 1900), pp. 200, 201; Kirby, *Years of Experience*, p. 106 (Ellsler).

5. MF to CKN, 1 July 1842, MH; RWE to CS, [21? Feb.? 1842], MH; [Georgiana Bruce Kirby], "Reminiscences of Brook Farm," *Old and New* 3 (Apr. 1871):436; 6 June 1841, in Newcomb, *Journals*, p. 18; 12 June 1842, in ibid., p. 19; her comments written upon a letter to her by CKN, 2 Nov. 1841, in F. B. Sanborn, "The Friendships of Hawthorne," in *The Hawthorne Centenary at the Wayside* [ed. Thomas Wentworth Higginson] (Bo: HoMif, 1905), p. 178.

6. Curtis to G. W. Cooke, 9 June 1882, MHarF; "Hall of Fantasy," *Pioneer* 1 (Feb. 1843): 51 (this and other references to Hawthorne's contemporaries were omitted from later printings); HDT to B. B. Wiley, 26 Apr. 1857, in *ThCor*, p. 477.

7. 27 July 1840, in *EmL*, 2:319; Newcomb, *Journals*, p. 15; RWE to FHH, 23 Mar. 1842, in *EmL*,

3:37 ("genius"); RWE to CS, [21? Feb.? 1842], MH. Emerson also recorded in his journal that Newcomb made him "happy by his conversation" (21 Feb. 1842, in *EmJMN*, 8:201).

8. Newcomb, *Journals*, p. 8 (copy-book); ibid., p. 15 (the passage that is probably the germ of "Dolon" is given in ibid., pp. 22-23n); 2 Oct. 1841, MH.

9. 8 Mar. 1842, in *EmL*, 3:29n; RWE to MF, 10 Mar. 1842, in ibid., p. 30; 18 Mar. 1842, in ibid., p. 35; 9 Apr. 1842, in ibid., pp. 45-46; ibid., p. 51; 9 May [1842], MH; 22[?] May 1842, in *EmL*, 3:55.

10. MH; 8 June 1842, in *EmL*, 3:61; 16 June 1842, in *EmJMN*, 8:179; 20 June 1842, in *EmL*, 3:66-67; 21 June 1842, MH.

11. F. B. Sanborn, "Thoreau, Newcomb, Brook Farm," *Springfield Daily Republican*, 2 Dec. 1896, p. 5. Newcomb's sister later wrote this perfect parody of "Dolon":

> "As 'Dolon' loved to go & sit on a large rock within a wood which bordered on an old potatoe-moss-hilled field, separated from the house by a large hay field' . . . [he] may again be seated on the same rock beneath the sky, the clouds, the branches & leaves, pondering, not upon the nature of the root which was one day to materially contribute to the satisfying of some hungry body, (for Dolon was too spiritual to eat,) but upon the expansion of his soul into a transparent eye ball, as the genial rays of the sun were vivifying & expanding & maturing the useful plant on which his physical eye now dwelt, while as he thought of . . . reason & the ideal world, of the future passings of his disembodied etherealized spirit from planet to planet, from star to star . . . Dolon . . . was mortified to find himself guilty of a sensation resembling what in the days of his infancy he had heard spoken of as hunger. And yet could it be? for his spirit was so pure, so truthful, so aspiring, so searching, so ardent, he enjoyed such precious communion with stars & waves & trees & blue skies & petrified forests. . . . with lizards scorpions, cock-roaches & cabbage-leaves." (Sarah Newcomb Gallagher to CKN, [8] Mar. 1843, RPB).

12. 30 July 1842, MH; WHC to MF, 7 July 1842, in *FrWHC*, p. 184; quoted in CSW to J. F. Heath, 14 Nov. 1842, MH; RWE to MF, 19 July 1842, in *EmL*, 3:74; 9 June 1842, in ibid., p. 63 ("sentences"); 17 July 1842, in ibid., p. 71; RWE to EPP, 2 July 1842, MH.

13. See RWE to CKN, 22[?] May, 20 June 1842, in *EmL*, 3:55-56, 66-67; *EmJMN*, 8:179n, where the connection is suggested by the editors; CKN to RWE, 21 June 1842, MH.

14. MF to CKN, 1 July 1842, MH; CS to RWE, 29 July 1842, MH; *EmL*, 3:82; [19 Aug. 1842], MH. Newcomb's mother also felt that he was dissipating, for she asked if he had "given up the 2d Dolon for the next Dial?" (6 Sept. 1842, RPB).

15. 16 Jan. 1843, in Josephine Elizabeth Roberts, "A New England Family: Elizabeth Palmer Peabody . . . Mary Tyler Peabody . . . Sophia Amelia Peabody . . . ," Ph.D. diss., Western Reserve University, 1937, p. 216; 1 Feb. 1843, MH; 8 Apr. 1843, in *HawAmNb*, p. 371.

16. [May 1843], MH; 9 May 1843, in *EmL*, 3:173; *EmJMN*, 8:428; 1 Sept., and CKN to RWE, 8 Sept. 1843, in *EmL*, 3:204-5, and MH; CKN to CS, 19 June [1844], MH. Still, the *Historical Catalogue of Brown University 1765-1904* listed Newcomb's occupations as "Engaged in literary pursuits" ([Providence, R.I.: Brown University, 1905], p. 174). Newcomb and Emerson remained in sporadic though constant touch throughout the rest of their lives. In 1849 Newcomb belatedly received from Emerson a copy of his *Historical Discourse* at Concord (1835). Emerson also used his remembrances of Newcomb in his work. He was the youth of "invalid habit, which had infected in some degree the tone of his mind" in *MemMF*. Emerson drew heavily upon him for his portrait of Benedict in the "Worship" chapter of *Conduct of Life*. To his friends, Emerson later confessed that "he doubted Newcomb's genius when he found that he did not care for an audience," and that, while he showed the "rich possibilities" of American writing, "his result is zero." Newcomb also appeared in "Historic Notes of Life and Letters in New England" as the "youth of the subtlest mind. . . puny in body and habit as a girl." And in 1872, when fire damaged Emerson's house, the now wealthy Newcomb wrote from Europe offering to lend or to give him the money necessary for repairs (copy in the Myerson collection; *MemMF*, 1:209; Apr. 1844, in *EmJ*, 6:506, and *EmW*, 6:234-36; Curtis to G. W. Cooke, 9 June 1882, MHarF; RWE to Caroline [Sturgis] Tappan, 13 Oct. 1857, in *EmL*, 5:87; *EmW*, 10:362-63, 582n; 23 Aug., MH).

Chapter 27: Theodore Parker

Note: Biographical information is from John Weiss, *Life and Correspondence of Theodore Parker*, 2 vols. (NY: Appleton, 1864); Octavius Brooks Frothingham, *Theodore Parker* (NY: Putnam's, 1880); and Henry Steele Commager, *Theodore Parker* (Bo: Little, Brown, 1936).

1. Parker became an omnivorous book collector, and at his death he left the Boston Public Library 12,000 volumes and 2,500 pamphlets; upon his wife's death, another 2,000 volumes were added. Parker's devotion to books is amply demonstrated in this letter to his fiancée shortly before their marriage: "I dreamed last night of being at a bookstore, and when the clerk showed me some book which I had long been seeking, and at a price most villainously cheap, 'Oh, no,' said I; 'I shall *never* buy more books; at any rate, never so cheap. *I am a-going to be married!*' and down went the corners of my mouth till they touched my stock" (Thomas Wentworth Higginson, "Report on the Parker Library," *Thirty-First Annual Report of the Trustees of the [Boston] Public Library* [Boston: n.p., 1883], p. 19; TP to Lydia Cabot, Feb. 1837, in Weiss, *Parker*, 1:97).

2. Quoted in Commager, *Parker*, p. 31; James Freeman Clarke, *A Look at the Life of Theodore Parker* (Bo: Walker, Wise, 1860), p. 7.

3. Nathaniel Hawthorne called her "a most comfortable woman to behold; she looks as if her ample person were stuffed full of tenderness – indeed, as if she were all one great, kind heart" (letter to Sophia Peabody, 13 Apr. 1841, in Nathaniel Hawthorne, *Love Letters of Nathaniel Hawthorne* [Chicago: Society of the Dofobs, 1907], 2:5).

4. In January[?] 1841 Dwight gave Parker this analysis of his character:

"Your life seems a succession of convulsive efforts, and the only wonder is to me that they don't exhaust you. . . . You feel that such sentiments as you cherish ought to triumph, but you find the world courting men who pursue inferior aims. Coupled with your high ideal is an impatient wish to see it immediately realized, – two things which don't go well together; for the one prompts you to love, the other, soured by necessary disappointment, prompts to hate . . . I think your love of learning is a passion, that it injures your mind by converting what is originally a pure thirst for truth into a greedy, avaricious, jealous striving, not merely to know, but to get all there is known." [George Willis Cooke, *John Sullivan Dwight* (Bo: Small, Maynard, 1898), pp. 14-15].

5. Journal entry, Dec. 1837, in Frothingham, *Parker*, p. 95.

6. Quoted in Henry David Gray, *Emerson: A Statement of New England Transcendentalism as Expressed in the Philosophy of Its Chief Exponent* (Stanford, Calif.: Stanford University, Press 1917), p. 63; winter 1836, in Frothingham, *Parker*, p. 63; 15 July 1838, in *PkJ*, 1:2.

7. Journal entry, n.d., in Weiss, *Parker*, 1:290; ca. 25 July 1839, in *PkJ*, 1:182. Years later, when Parker brushed aside the complaint that there was an absence of art in America, he likened it to "the stuff which Margaret Fuller used to twaddle forth on that theme" (TP to GR, 29 Oct. 1859, in Weiss, *Parker*, 2:377).

8. They first met at a party in 1837 when Fuller had "some pleasant talk with him," but, she complained, "before I could get to Spinoza, somebody seized on me and carried me off." Parker sometimes disliked her constant querying, but he also came to expect it of her, as this journal entry shows: "Saw Miss Fuller also; pleasantly disappointed in her, – no scoffing to-day" (MF to RWE, [1837], in *HigMF*, p. 86; 17 June 1839, in *SaRec*, 2:546).

9. Henry Channing said to those who were scared off by Parker's fierce exterior: "Do not be frightened by the stone dogs and griffins at the gate: within is a rare garden." Emerson analyzed Parker's public manner thus: "T.P. has beautiful fangs, & the whole amphitheatre delights to see him worry & tear his victim" (quoted in John White Chadwick, *Theodore Parker* [Bo: HoMif, 1901], p. 378, Sept. 1842, in *EmJMN*, 8:258).

10. 7 Aug. 1859, in Joel Myerson, "Caroline Dall's Reminiscences of Margaret Fuller," *Harvard Library Bulletin* 22 (Oct. 1974):416, 419-20; journal entry, [1840?], in *FuW*, 1:599.

11. 19 Sept. 1839, in *PkJ*, 1:233; ca. Feb. 1840, in ibid., p. 298.

12. Late May 1840 in *PkJ*, 1:381; ca. Feb. 1840, in ibid., p. 298.

13. When Parker had first preached the sermon, Sarah Clarke had told her brother that it was considered "utter heresy and abomination" (7 July 1840, in *ClLetSister*).

14. ca. 29 June 1840, in *PkJ*, 1:410-11.

15. ca. 25 July 1838, in ibid., p. 7-8; William Silas Vance, "Carlyle and the American Transcendentalists," Ph.D. diss., Unviersity of Chicago, 1941, p. 361; EPP to JSD, 20 Sept. 1840, MB. See also Arthur M. Schlesinger, Jr., *Orestes A. Brownson* (Bo: Little, Brown, 1939), p. 104; S. H. Whitman to Brownson, 19 Nov. 1840, InNd; ABA to S. J. May, 15 Nov. 1840, MH; WmE to RWE, 15 Nov. 1840, MH; journal entry, 21 Jan. 1842, typescript, MBilHi; RWE to Parker, 10 Nov. 1840, MBilHi; and Parker to RWE, 30 Nov. 1840, MH.

16. [ca. Jan. 1841], in *SaHaABA*, 2:367. William T. Harris, later editor of the *Journal of Speculative Philosophy*, credits this article with having started him on his study of German literature. In New York Henry Bellows registered a dissenting view, calling Parker's article "full of pedantry, presumption & party-sentiment" (Harris to [Hinsdale?], Mar. 1889, in B. A. Hinsdale, "Notes on the History of Foreign Influence Upon Education in the United States," *Annual Reports of the Department of the Interior for the Fiscal Year Ended June 30, 1898. Report of the Commissioner of Education* [Washington, D.C.: Government Printing Office, 1899], 1:613; H. Bellows to William Bellows, 22 June 1841, MHi).

17. H. S. Patterson to Brownson, 29 May 1841, InNd.

18. 1841, in Weiss, *Parker*, 1:303.

19. Fuller probably wrote this letter to Parker: "[D]o not hold it 'a baseness to write fair.' . . . A man so ready to avow his opinions in speech, ought not to conceal them so cunningly when he writes." At another time, Parker was told that the printer had refused to print from his handwriting: "[I]t must be copied, or he must be paid double" (both n.d., in Weiss, *Parker*, 2:46-47).

20. 7 Apr. 1842, MH.

21. N.d., in Commager, *Parker*, p. 87; 7 Apr. 1842, MH; Parker never finished the Strauss review for the *Dial* (see his letters to RWE, 7 Apr., 16 May, 8 July 1842, [1843], MH); RWE to TP, 11 May 1842, in *EmL*, 3:54-55; 16 May 1842, MH; 8 July 1842, MH; 17 July 1842, in *EmL*, 3:71.

22. One person who liked the article for exactly these reasons was Lydia Child, who called it "decidedly the best thing in the Dial" (LMC to E. G. Loring, 12 Oct. 1842, NN-M).

23. RWE to TP, 8 Sept. 1842, in *EmL*, 3:86-87.

24. 16 Oct. 1842, in ibid., p. 90n. Emerson told Ward that Fuller's "Romaic Ballads," Ellery Channing's verses, the pieces from England, and Ward's own contribution were all needed to balance "the grim parish politics" of Parker (30 Sept. [1842], MH).

25. Only a few ministers, including Pierpont and James Freeman Clarke, were brave enough to risk the wrath of parishioners and ministers alike by exchanging pulpits with him. Parker's solution was to rent his own hall, where he subsequently drew record crowds. This incident is reported, from Parker's journal, in Weiss, *Parker*, 1:188-93.

26. On one occasion Emerson was all set to print two of Parker's notices but found, upon arriving at the printer's, that there was simply no room for them. Emerson probably never seriously considered printing many of Parker's other reviews; the topics were too strictly theological for his tastes (RWE to TP, 30 June 1842, in *EmL*, 3:68-69).

27. TP to RWE, 8 July 1842, MH; TP to RWE, [1843], MH; RWE to TP, 17 July 1842, in *EmL*, 3:70-71, and see "Editor's Table," *Dial* 3:278; TP to RWE, 2 Aug. 1843, MH.

28. TP to RWE, 2 Aug. 1843, MH; 18 Aug. 1843, in *EmL*, 3:203.

29. TP to RWE, 8 July 1842, MH; 18 Dec. 1840, MB.

Chapter 28: Elizabeth Palmer Peabody

Note: Biographical information is from Josephine Elizabeth Roberts, "A New England Family: Elizabeth Palmer Peabody . . . Mary Tyler Peabody . . . Sophia Amelia Peabody . . . ," Ph.D. diss.,

Western Reserve University, 1937, and the romanticized accounts of her life in Gladys Brooks, *Three Wise Virgins* (New York: E. P. Dutton, 1957), and Louise Hall Tharp, *The Peabody Sisters of Salem* (Bo: Little, Brown, 1950).

1. The most famous picture of her in this vein was done by Henry James in *The Bostonians*. Although James vehemently denied that the Miss Birdseye of that novel was based upon Peabody, the resemblances were strong enough for a number of people to complain of the parody, thus giving James's characterization a ring of truth. James's character belonged to "the Short-Skirts League, as a matter of course; for she belonged to any and every league that had been founded for almost any purpose whatever. This did not prevent her being a confused, entangled, inconsequent, discursive old woman, whose charity began at home and ended nowhere, [and] whose credulity kept pace with it" ([Lo: Macmillan, 1886], p. 27. See also James to William James, 15 Feb. [1885], in Henry James, *The Letters of Henry James*, ed. Percy Lubbock [NY: Scribner's, 1920], 1:115-17, and F. O. Matthiessen, *The James Family* [NY: Knopf, 1947], pp. 325-27).

2. Henry Channing, on 16 May 1870, described Peabody in 1820 as being "fair and bright-cheeked, with brown hair neatly parted on her forehead, and rather slight and graceful in form and movement." Yet by the 1840s Elizabeth was well on her way to becoming the woman of "bulky form and pulpy face and watery eyes" that Moses Coit Tyler found in 1862 (quoted in *FrWHC*, p. 397; Tyler to his wife, 14 Dec. 1862, in *Moses Coit Tyler*, ed. Jessica Tyler Austen [Garden City, N.Y.: Doubleday, Page, 1911], p. 16).

3. EPP, "Emerson as Preacher," in *The Genius and Character of Emerson*, ed. F. B. Sanborn (Bo: Osgood, 1885), pp. 150-51.

4. EPP to Brownson, n.d., InNd; EPP, *Reminiscences of Rev. Wm. Ellery Channing* (Bo: Roberts, 1880), p. 10.

5. Quoted in Tharp, *Peabody Sisters*, pp. 50-51; Charles Emerson to Mary Moody Emerson, 11 Apr. [1833], MH.

6. Caroline Dall, "Studies toward the life of 'A business woman'," p. 65, MCR-S. This was probably the most famous boardinghouse in Boston: in addition to Mary and Elizabeth Peabody, James and Sarah Clarke, Jared Sparks, George Hilliard, and Horace Mann were all staying there at that time.

7. Mary Peabody to Sophia Peabody, 27 Feb. 1833, in Roberts, "A New England Family," pp. 75-76; Joel Myerson, "Sarah Clarke's Reminiscences of the Peabodys and Hawthorne," *Nathaniel Hawthorne Journal 1973*, ed. C. E. Frazer Clark, Jr. (Englewood, Col.: Microcard Editions, 1973), p. 131.

8. EPP, "Emerson as Preacher," pp. 151-52. Peabody had hoped that Emerson would start another school when he returned, and, if he did, she said that she would like a position in it (EPP to Mary Peabody, 8 Feb. 1834, in Josephine E. Roberts, "Elizabeth Peabody and the Temple School," *NEQ* 15 [Sept. 1942]:499).

9. EPP to Mary Peabody, n.d., in Roberts, "Elizabeth Peabody and the Temple School," p. 498; EPP, *Reminiscences*, p. 355; EPP to Mary Peabody, 11 Apr. 1835, in Roberts, "Elizabeth Peabody and the Temple School," pp. 505-6; quoted in Brooks, *Three Wise Virgins*, p. 110; 7 Aug. 1836, in Odell Shepard, *Pedlar's Progress: The Life of Bronson Alcott* [Bo: Little, Brown, 1937], pp. 187-89. When all was going well, Alcott named one of his girls Elizabeth Peabody Alcott, but after their close friendship had come to an end, Alcott changed the name to Elizabeth Sewall Alcott (see 22 May 1836, in Joel Myerson, "Bronson Alcott's 'Journal for 1836,'" *Studies in the American Renaissance 1978*, ed. Joel Myerson [Bo: Twayne, 1978], pp. 59, 99).

10. NRU, where the date "1837" is supplied: however, internal evidence clearly dates the letter as 1836; ABA to Sophia Peabody, 23 Aug. 1836, in *AlcL*, p. 29.

11. *RuLiEm*, p. 234. Yet when Emerson was collecting information about Fuller for his part in *MemMF*, Peabody sent him a letter beginning: "not counting myself among her intimate friends, as she decidedly wished I should not . . . " (n.d., copy by RWE, in *EmJMN*, 11:482).

12. To Lidian Emerson, Peabody once compared the three of them in this manner: "You know your husband's [difficulty] is *the love of thought*. Mine is the *love of truth* – & Very's own was *love of beauty. Angelic sins* are they not?" ([Dec. 1838], MSaE).

13. RWE to LdE, 23 Apr. 1836, in *EmL*, 2:12; Horace Mann to [EPP], 9 Dec. 1836, in [Mary Peabody Mann], *Life of Horace Mann* (Bo: Walker, Fuller, 1865), p. 51.

14. ca. 2 Aug. 1839, in *PkJ*, 1:187. Later, when Peabody was going about the country selling a chart that arranged the history of the world in chronological order, Parker asked Christopher Pearse Cranch for a picture: "Here is the subject: Elizabeth P. Peabody is looking at an expressman's slate and writing an order on it in the street. She has a bundle of Bem's Chronology under her arm, a parasol and her bonnet falling back etc., and the expressman is looking on with dire amaze" (n.d., typescript, MHi).

15. James Thornton to G. E. Ellis, 21 Sept. 1837, MHi.

16. Clarence L. F. Gohdes, *The Periodicals of American Transcendentalism* (Durham, N.C.: Duke University Press, 1931), p. 147.

17. 12 Oct. 1840, MSaE; 20 Oct. 1840, in *EmL*, 2:350.

18. At that time Peabody was printing Fuller's translation of *Günderode*, and Fuller had been correcting her many errors, including the advertisement for the book, which incorrectly identified Bettina's correspondent, a young poetess, as a *"nun"* (MF to RWE, Apr. 1842, copy, MB).

19. 3 Dec. 1836, in *EmJMN*, 5:262. Horace Mann charitably told Peabody that her fault lay in "the discrepancy between her power of seeing and feeling truth and of expressing it." Mrs. Mary Lowell Putnam was more direct. Writing to her brother, James Russell Lowell, about Peabody's forthcoming contribution to his *Pioneer*, she said: "I cannot think that her abilities qualify her to write a leading article for *any* periodical. Her name alone would be an injury to any work to which she should be a contributor . . . Surely it would be better even to delay this number a week or two than to disappoint the expectations which the introduction to your first number authorized the public to form of your work." Nevertheless, Lowell, who thought her piece very good, printed it, though his sister's views were shared by many people (15 J[?] 1834, in Roberts, "A New England Family," p. 144; 1 Feb. [1843], in Sculley Bradley, "Lowell, Emerson, and the *Pioneer*," *AL* 19 [Nov. 1947]:237; JRL to Robert Carter, 31 Jan. 1843, NN-B).

20. *CoHiBi*, 1:140; Very to RWE, 21 Nov. 1841, MWelC; quoted in Orestes A. Brownson, "Brook Farm," *United States Magazine, and Democratic Review* 11 (Nov. 1842):490. In Lockport, New York, a Mr. Johnson read Peabody's article in the New York *Tribune*, where it had been reprinted, and, inspired by it, he wrote Ripley to ask, "[C]an I and my children be admitted into your society, *and be better off than we are here?*" Similarly, an associationist in Ohio dated his "intense interest" in Ripley's community from his reading of Peabody's description of it (28 Oct. 1842, in John Thomas Codman, *Brook Farm: Historic and Personal Memories* [Bo: Arena, 1894], p. 281; Elijah P. Grant to GR, 7 Feb. 1844, ICU).

21. Harm Jan Huidekoper to Mrs. Anna Clarke, 16 Sept. 1841[?], in Nina Moore Tiffany and Francis Tiffany, *Harm Jan Huidekoper* (Cambridge, Mass.: Riverside Press, 1904), p. 288 (the dating of the letter is obviously in error; Anna Clarke, Huidekoper's daughter, was J. F. Clarke's wife); RWE to MF, 26 Feb. 1844, in *EmL*, 3:243; SR to JSD, 1 Aug. 1840, MB.

22. At one time she was apparently translating some French translations of "Bhuddist books" for the *Dial*, but nothing came of it (Lane to Isaac Hecker, 29 Dec. 1843, typescript of original at the Paulist Fathers' Archives in New York, MHarF).

23. James, *Bostonians*, p. 37.

Chapter 29: Benjamin Franklin Presbury

Note: Biographical information is from *CoHiBi*, 2:129-32, and Joseph Waite Presby, *William Presbrey of London, England, and Taunton, Mass., and His Descendants 1690-1918* (Rutland, Vt.: Tuttle, 1918), pp. 40-41.

1. *CoHiBi*, 2:129.

2. 9 Nov. 1841, in *EmL*, 2:462; 12 Nov. 1841, in William White, "Emerson as Editor: A Letter to Benjamin F. Presbury," *American Notes & Queries* 12 (Dec. 1973):59-60; 15 Nov. 1841, MH.

3. There are over a dozen substantive variants between Presbury's copy in his letter of 15 November 1841 and the version printed in the *Dial*.

4. Possibly one poem of his was simply lost. Emerson, on 10 April 1842, told Fuller that "Mr. Presbury's poem is not in the collection you gave me: I have therefore made no reply to his letter, I ought to have told you this earlier" (*EmL*, 3:46).

Chapter 30: George Ripley

Note: Biographical information is from Charles Crowe, *George Ripley* (Athens, Ga.: University of Georgia Press, 1967); Octavius Brooks Frothingham, *George Ripley* (Bo: HoMif, 1882); and Lisette Riggs, "George and Sophia Ripley," Ph.D. diss., University of Maryland, 1942.

1. However, in later years Ripley felt that he and Emerson had been on "quite a distant footing" while at college (letter of 14 May 1880, in Howard S. Mott Autographs, catalogue 192, item 60).

2. Crowe, *Ripley*, p. 21.

3. RWE to TC, 30 Apr. 1835, in *EmCorTC*, p. 126; Week 16, Apr. 1838, in *AlcJ38*, p. 233; Week 22, June 1837, in ABA, "Journal for 1837," p. 409, MH.

4. Fuller told Henry Channing: "His mind, though that of a captain, is not that of a conqueror." Alcott recorded in his journal: "He reasons more than feels; judges more than thinks. Genius, I doubt his [ability] of measuring. . . . He deals mainly in the treasures of other men's minds & having little original thought, save as prompted by others" (n.d., in Lindsay Swift, *Brook Farm* [NY: Macmillan, 1900], p. 131; Week 10, Mar. 1837, in ABA, "Journal for 1837," p. 170).

5. GR to TP, 28 Feb. 1856, in Crowe, *Ripley*, p. 79. When Ripley had to sell his library to pay for the debts of Brook Farm, he was somewhat gladdened when Parker bought most of it. Even so, Ripley said of the occasion, "I can now understand how a man would feel if he could attend his own funeral." A few months before his death Parker said to a friend: "If any one writes my life, I think it will be George Ripley: he, better than any one, understands my philosophy, and what I meant to do" (quoted in John Thomas Codman, *Brook Farm: Historic and Personal Memories* [Bo: Arena, 1894], p. 235; quoted in Octavius Brooks Frothingham, *Theodore Parker* [NY: Putnam's, 1880], p. v).

6. On 1 June 1835 Ripley had begun the correspondence with this somewhat jejune letter: " . . . the music of your soul-melody has sounded to this distant spot. . . . I have communed with your spirit in the utterance of its deep wisdom, and when I have felt the significance of your mystic sayings, my heart has leaped up with the response, 'This unknown Being is my Brother.'" Carlyle later described Ripley as one of the "Socinian Preachers [who] quit their pulpits . . . and retire into the fields to cultivate onion-beds, and live frugally on vegetables" (Joseph Slater, "George Ripley and Thomas Carlyle," *PMLA* 67 [June 1952]:341-42. The germ of Carlyle's statement, which appeared, without mentioning Ripley by name in his *Past and Present* [Boston: Charles C. Little and James Brown, 1843], p. 294, is in Emerson's letter of 30 October 1840 to Carlyle [*EmCorTC*, p. 284]. Ripley did realize that Carlyle was referring to him [letter, 20 May 1875, in Frothingham, *Ripley*, p. 290]).

7. 23 Feb. 1837, in James Marsh, *Coleridge's American Disciples: The Correspondence of James Marsh*, ed. John J. Duffy (Amherst, Mass.: Univeristy of Massachusetts Press, 1973), pp. 192-93. Of the eight titles published in this series during its four years of life, six were edited or translated by *Dial* contributors (Ripley, Henry Channing, Dwight, Fuller, James Clarke, and Charles Timothy Brooks).

8. Arthur S. Bolster, Jr., *James Freeman Clarke* (Bo: Beacon, 1954), p. 129; journal entry, 27 May 1840, in William C. Gannett, *Ezra Stiles Gannett* (Bo: Roberts, 1877), pp. 219-20; JFC to his wife, 25 Sept. 1840, in *ClAuDiCor*, p. 133.

9. 28 Sept. 1839, in *AlcDiJyDec39*, p. 264; *HigMF*, p. 151; JFC to SC, 8 July 1840, MH; *FuNbD*.

10. Fuller appreciated Ripley's ideas about what the critic's role should be since they were very similar to her own. Ripley thought: "It is the duty of every educated man to set his face against the innovations which disfigure the language; to exercise the functions of a committee of vigilance where no verbal tribunal forms a court of final appeal; and thus to aid in the creation of a body of common law which shall have the force of a statute" (quoted in Frothingham, *Ripley*, p. 217).

11. To Marsh Ripley was more subdued in his claims for the *Dial*: "[W]e have no aim but the spread

of a more generous culture and the illustration of cleaner and more healthy relations between man and man" (17 Oct. 1840, in Marsh, *Correspondence*, p. 239).

12. GR to JSD, 7 July 1840, MB ("unworthy"); GR to JSD, 6 Aug. 1840, MB.

13. GR, review of the *Massachusetts Quarterly Review*, *Harbinger* 7 (9 Sept. 1848):150. When Ripley's library was sold in 1846, he had only one volume — the first — of the *Dial* (Leonard Howe & Co., *Catalogue of a Select Private Library* . . . [Bo: Alfred Mudge, 1846], p. 2, in Kenneth Walter Cameron, *The Transcendentalists and Minerva* [Hartford, Conn.: Transcendental Books, 1958], 3:809).

14. Among his many objections to Brook Farm, Emerson felt that Ripley was unconsciously creating an aura of authority that threatened the individualism of each member. He also felt that Ripley enjoyed their struggling with an almost perverse pleasure, a fact that is borne out by Ripley's statement that he dreaded "the effect of being allowed not to struggle with poverty and other hardships." Ripley in turn criticized the youths who unconsciously worshiped Emerson too blindly and who, "like their master, express themselves confusedly" (early May 1843, in *EmJMN*, 8:393; GR to Dana, 18 Mar. 1842, in James Harrison Wilson, *The Life of Charles A. Dana* [NY: Harper's, 1907], p. 39; GR to Brownson, 18 Dec. 1842, InNd).

Chapter 31: Sophia Ripley

Note: Biographical information is from Charles Crowe, *George Ripley* (Athens, Ga.: University of Georgia Press, 1967): Henrietta Dana Raymond, "Sophia Willard Dana Ripley, Co-Founder of Brook Farm," M.A. thesis, Columbia University, 1949; and Lisette Riggs, "George and Sophia Ripley," Ph.D. diss., University of Maryland, 1942.

1. Ethel Golann, "A Lowell Autobiography," *NEQ* 7 (June 1934):359; Faith Chipperfield, *In Quest of Love: The Life and Death of Margaret Fuller* (NY: Coward-McCann, 1957), p. 88; Caryl Coleman, "A Forgotten Convert," *Catholic World* 122 (Nov. 1925):194.

2. Crowe, *Ripley*, p. 41.

3. Ora Gannett Sedgwick, "A Girl of Sixteen at Brook Farm," *Atlantic Monthly* 85 (Mar. 1900):395 ("self-control"); John Thomas Codman, *Brook Farm: Historic and Personal Memories* (Bo: Arena, 1894), p. 17; quoted in *CoHiBi*, 1:115. One of her Brook Farm students later described Mrs. Ripley as a woman of "majestic height and bearing," whom the younger scholars habitually addressed as Sophia without the slightest bit of disrespect (Mrs. Nora Blair, 22 Dec. 1892, in Joel Myerson, "Two Unpublished Reminiscences of Brook Farm," *NEQ* 48 [June 1975]:258).

4. EPP to JSD, [10 June 1841], NPV (Parker).

5. C. Francis to FHH, 12 Nov. 1838, MeBa. When Mrs. Ripley became ill in 1836, Francis wrote Hedge: "We have been so accustomed to the energy & greatness of her spirit in its present form, that we could not admit the thought of its passing into another form": as nice a way of wishing a recovery as has been penned (21 Mar. 1836, MeBa).

6. Granville Hicks, "A Conversation in Boston," *Sewanee Review* 39 (Apr.-June 1931):130; MF to WHC, 25-28 Oct. 1840, MB; June 1843, in *EmJMN*, 8:428; Crowe, *Ripley*, p. 76.

7. Mrs. Lyman to Catherine Robbins, 27 Feb. 1841, in Susan I. Lesley, *Recollections of My Mother: Mrs. Anne Jean Lyman* . . . (Bo: HoMif, 1899 [1875]), p. 374; 9 Jan. 1841, MHi; 22 June 1841, MHi; 3 July 1841, in *EmL*, 2:413.

8. SR to JSD, 1 Aug. 1840, MB; 5 July, MH.

Chapter 32: Jonathan Ashley Saxton

Note: Biographical information is from *CoHiBi*, 2:113-16, and George Sheldon, "History of 'Deerfield' — No. 138," *Greenfield [Massachusetts] Gazette and Courier*, 1885: collected under the binder's title, *History of Deerfield*, by G. Sheldon, p. 216, ICN F.844205.8.

1. MF to RWE, 12 Nov. 1843, in *HigMF*, p. 166; James Murdock, *Sketches of Modern Philosophy*

(Hartford, Conn.: John C. Wells), p. 181.

2. It is possible that Saxton was the "J.A.S." whose "Lady Mirbel's Dirge" was rejected by the *Dial* in July 1843 ("To Correspondents," *Dial* 4:136).

3. When he was eighty, Saxton wrote his son, whom he had sent to Brook Farm as an apprentice printer in 1845, that his own confidence in the idealistic "dream" of the Transcendentalists was "vivid still" (GR to Saxton, 31 Mar. 1875, in Arthur E. Bestor, Jr., *Brook Farm, 1841-1847: An Exhibition to Commemorate Its Founding*, mimeographed [NY: Columbia University Libraries, 1941], p. 6; [ca. 1875], in John Thomas Codman, *Brook Farm: Historic and Personal Memories* [Bo: Arena, 1894], p. 255).

Chapter 33: Thomas Treadwell Stone

Note: Biographical information is from James Grant Wilson and John Fiske, eds., *Appleton's Cyclopædia of American Biography*, (NY: Appleton, 1888-89), 5:703; J. Gardner Bartlett, *Simeon Stone Genealogy* (Bo: Stone Family Association, 1926); and *CoHiBi*, 2:87-93.

1. *CoHiBi*, 1:16; *General Catalogue of Bowdoin College . . . 1794-1912* (Brunswick, Me.: Bowdoin College, 1912), p. 65 (Andover); RWE to Mary Moody Emerson, 19 Aug. 1832, in *EmL*, 1:355.

2. "The Transcendental Club and the Dial; A Conversation by A. Bronson Alcott . . . ," Boston *Commonwealth*, 24 April 1863, p. 1.

3. 16 Jan. 1840, MH; Emerson's unlocated letter is described in *EmL*, 2:277; 22 Apr. 1840, MH, and RWE to MF, 27[?] Apr.[?] 1840, in ibid., p. 293; RWE to MF, 8 May 1840, in ibid.

4. RWE to MF, 8 May 1840, in ibid., p. 294; 31 May 1840, in ibid., p. 298n; 7 June 1840, in ibid., p. 304.

5. 21 July 1840, in ibid., p. 316; *FuNbD*. Assuming that the article was indeed ready for publication, Fuller's preference for her coeditor's articles (one of which was on her brother-in-law, Ellery Channing) and the conclusion of a two-part work appears understandable.

6. 12 Feb. 1841, in *ScLiLetCPC*, p. 69.

7. Mid-Sept. 1841, in *EmJMN*, 8:52; RWE to Mary Moody Emerson, 21 Sept. 1841, in *EmL*, 2:451.

8. 23 Mar. 1842, in *EmL*, 3:38.

Chapter 34: Caroline Sturgis

Note: Biographical information is from *CoHiBi*, 2:54-61; and Roger Faxton Sturgis, ed., *Edward Sturgis of Yarmouth, Massachusetts 1613-1695 and his Descendants* (Bo: Stanhope Press, 1914), pp. 42-43. Carl F. Strauch, "Hatred's Swift Repulsions: Emerson, Margaret Fuller, and Others," *Studies in Romanticism* 7 (Winter 1968):65-103, offers an interesting interpretation of Caroline Sturgis's relationship with Ralph Waldo Emerson.

1. Emerson called Sturgis's eyes "a compliment to the human race," and he declared that "a poet might well dedicate himself to the fine task of expressing their genius in verse." Lidian Emerson once wrote her husband that she was like "a supernatural being whose look was inspiration." When Henry James met her in the late 1850s, he found that even then she had "an admirable intelligence, of the incurably ironic or mocking order," and he called her a "socially impulsive presence (always for instance insatiably hospitable) . . . " Emerson felt that her "best poems were her pretty blasphemies, for she had much fault to find with the gods," and he said that she "blasphemed very prettily both in verse and prose" (late Dec. 1842, in *EmJMN*, 8:318; 30 Jan. 1843, MH; Henry James, *Notes of a Son and Brother* [NY: Scribner's, 1914], p. 213; n.d., in *EmJMN*, 8:174n).

2. In 1848 Sturgis wrote *Rainbows for Children* but let Mrs. Child edit and take public credit for it

(Helene G. Baer, *The Heart is Like Heaven: The Life of Lydia Maria Child* [Philadelphia: University of Pennsylvania Press, 1964], p. 177).

3. However, in later years Sarah Clarke thought Caroline "had not so much the poetic gift of expression" as her sister Ellen possessed (letter to T. W. Higginson, ca. 1889, MB).

4. She thought that "Thoreau imitates porcupines successfully" and told Fuller not to send a book to him for "he would only have given it to his squirrels to nibble" (n.d., MH).

5. Week 9, Feb. 1838, *AlcJ38*, p. 147; 17 Feb. 1839, *AlcDiJaJn39*, p. 313.

6. Newcomb complained that she lacked "all sort of reverence, uncongenial for me enough, such a closed thing, so that she comes too close, when I am open, & asks questions, & talks of character, & a type of a man, whilst I am lying in the indolent abandonment of self" (CKN, n.d., copy by RWE, in his "Notebook CKN," p. 95, MH).

7. But George Curzon recalled one time when Channing took her rowing and, after she had remained quiet the whole trip, he remarked, "Here have I wasted this evening in rowing a girl who won't talk to me – and not so very good looking either" (quoted in T. W. Higginson to F. B. Sanborn, 10 Aug. 1895, MHarF).

Sturgis wrote Emerson after Channing's marriage: "It seems as if the best people in being married only adopt children instead of taking equal friends." Nevertheless, their paths kept crossing. When Channing left Concord, Massachusetts, for New York in 1844, he shared a room with William Tappan, soon to be Sturgis's husband. The Channings named a daughter after her, and she and Tappan named their first child Ellen after Channing's wife (16 Oct. 1841, MH; Frederick T. McGill, Jr., *Channing of Concord: A Life of William Ellery Channing II* [New Brunswick, N.J.: Rutgers University Press, 1967], p. 108).

8. RWE to LdE, 19 Apr. 1836, in *EmL*, 2:10; RWE to MF, 4 May, 24 May 1838, in ibid., p. 129, 135; 28 June 1838, in ibid., p. 143; RWE to MF, 13 Sept. 1840, in ibid., p. 332; 11 Sept. 1840, MH; 9 Nov. 1840, MH.

9. Such an example is this passage: "I have not power to love the All – to throw myself upon the breast of the Universe. I want a home, I want to love One, but there is no One – And oh! it seems as if I should die because I have not a child to love" (CS to MF, 10 July 1841, MH).

10. See especially RWE to MF, 11 May 1843, in *EmL*, 3:175, and CS to RWE, 15 Aug. 1843, MH.

11. 10 Feb. 1840, MH; MF to RWE, 12 Apr. 1840, in *EmL*, 2:280; RWE to MF, 15 Apr. 1840, in ibid., p. 281; RWE to MF, 21 June 1840, in ibid., p. 306; RWE to MF, 21 July 1840, in ibid., p. 316; 21 July 1840, MH; 24 July 1840, MH. One reason why Emerson made corrections was that he felt that her verses, like Channing's, were "proper manuscript inspirations, honest, great, but crude," which had "never been filed" for "the eye that studies surface." The only extant evidence of his alterations seems to be in her poem "The Dream," in which Sturgis rejected more of Emerson's suggestions than she accepted (24 June 1840, in *EmJMN*, 7:372; RWE to MF, 27 July 1840, in *EmL*, 2:318-19).

12. 5 Oct. 1840, MH; 9 Oct. [1840], MH, where the date "184?" is supplied: however, internal evidence clearly dates the year as 1840; 13 Oct. 1840, MH; 10 Oct. 1843, MH.

13. CS to RWE, 9 Nov. 1840, MH; RWE to CKN, 7 May 1842, in *EmL*, 3:51; CS to RWE, 17 Oct. [1840?], MH, where the date "184?" is supplied: however, internal evidence makes it appear fairly certain that this was one of the series of letters Sturgis wrote to Emerson in October 1840 following her first publication in the *Dial*; CS to RWE, 5 July 1843, MH; 10 Oct. 1843, MH.

Chapter 35: William Aspinwall Tappan

1. RWE to HDT, Feb. 1843, in *ThCor*, p. 82; RWE to LdE, 11 Feb. 1843, in *EmL*, 3:144; RWE to LdE, 7 Feb. 1843, in ibid., p. 143 ("hope"); Mar. 1843, in *EmJMN*, 8:376; Tappan to RWE, 1 Mar. 1843, MH, and Giles Waldo to RWE, 14 May 1843, MH; 30 Apr. 1843, ViU-B; 11 Oct. 1843, in Ralph Barton Perry, *The Thought and Character of William James* (Bo: Little, Brown, 1935), 1:53; 10[?] Oct. 1843, in *EmL*, 3:211; 25 Oct. 1843, in *ThCor*, p. 149; RWE to HDT, 15 June 1843, in ibid., p. 118. (And commenting later on Tappan, a friend of T. W. Higginson described him as

"proverbially silent" [quoted in Higginson to F. B. Sanborn, 10 Aug. 1895, MHarF]).

2. CS to RWE, 23 Apr. 1843, MH; 11 May 1843, in *EmL*, 3:175; CS to RWE, 15 Aug. 1843, MH.

3. Giles Waldo to RWE, 14 May 1843, MH; HDT to RWE, 23 May 1843, in *ThCor*, p. 107; Giles Waldo to RWE, 18 Apr. 1843, MH; Giles Waldo to RWE, 14 May 1843, MH (promise); RWE to HDT, 21 May 1843, in *ThCor*, p. 102. Although Emerson told Fuller that Tappan "wrote the 'Sail' in the Dial," there is a chance that Tappan did not write the entire poem. Emerson, in his set of the *Dial* at MH, wrote Tappan's name by the poem's title, but he also marked "Giles Waldo" in the margin by the last stanza of the poem (10[?] Oct. 1843, in *EmL*, 3:211).

Chapter 36: John Francis Tuckerman

Note: Biographical information is from *CoHiBi*, 2:99-100, and Bayard Tuckerman, *Notes on the Tuckerman Family of Massachusetts and Some Allied Families* (Bo: Privately printed [Riverside Press], 1914), pp. 61-64.

1. See JSD and others to CPC, 27 July 1837, typescript, MHi; Edward Everett Hale, *James Russell Lowell and His Friends* (Bo: HoMif, 1899), pp. 70-72.

Chapter 37: Jones Very

Note: Biographical information is from William Irving Bartlett, *Jones Very: Emerson's "Brave Saint"* (Durham, N.C.: Duke University Press, 1942), and Edwin Gittleman, *Jones Very: The Effective Years 1833-1840* (NY: Columbia University Press, 1967).

1. Henry Thoreau was a later member of this club, and, although Kenneth Walter Cameron feels that the two never met, it is likely that they saw each other at the club's gatherings. After meeting Ellen Sewall, Thoreau remembered Very by choosing his *Essays and Poems* as a gift to send to her father ("Jones Very and Thoreau—The 'Greek' Myth," *ESQ*, no. 7 [II Quarter 1957], pp. 39-40; "Thoreau Discovers Emerson: A College Reading Record," *Bulletin of the New York Public Library* 57 [July 1953]:322; Walter Harding, *The Days of Henry Thoreau* [NY: Knopf, 1966], p. 98).

2. Gittleman, *Very*, p. 83 (question of evil); James Elliot Cabot, "Reminiscences," typescript, p. 17, MCR-S.

3. EPP to W. P. Andrews, 12 Nov. 1880, MWelC (much of this long letter was used by Andrews in his "Memoir," in Jones Very, *Poems by Jones Very* [Bo: HoMif, 1883], pp. 3-31; hereafter cited as "Andrews Letter"); RWE to Sophia Peabody, 20 Jan. 1838, in Rose Hawthorne Lathrop, *Memories of Hawthorne* (Bo: HoMif, 1897), p. 182. Elizabeth Peabody also introduced Very to Nathaniel Hawthorne.

4. 19 Apr. 1838, in *EmJMN*, 5:475; 26 Apr. 1838, in ibid., p. 480 ("sentiment"); CSW to RWE, 21 June 1838, MH.

5. Gittleman, *Very*, p. 187, p. 187 ("identification"); G. Bradford, Jr., "Jones Very," *Unitarian Review* 27 (Feb. 1887):111n. In Very's words, he now knew "by the Spirit of God" that he had been right in "cutting down the corrupt tree" that was his "former image" in order to prepare the way for "the One who came after" (Very to Henry Bellows, 24 Dec. 1838, in Harry L. Jones, "The Very Madness: A New Manuscript," *CLA Journal* 10 [Mar. 1967]:199).

6. Wheeler, for one, felt that attributing Very's insanity to "Emerson's notions" was incorrect: "Very bases all his insane notion of Christ's second coming in him upon the authority of the Bible. Emerson's faith allows no authority . . . to any man or book." Two years after Very's dismissal, Richard Henry Dana, Jr., commented that Very was "quite intimate with Emerson and the other Spiritualists . . . and his insanity has taken that shape accordingly." The unsympathetic Dana went on, "I am told that some of them are absurd enough to say that he is not insane—but that the world

does not understand him" (journal entry, 15 Sept. 1838, in John Olin Eidson, "Charles Stearns Wheeler: Emerson's 'Good Grecian,' " *NEQ* 27 [Dec. 1954]:478; Dana to William Cullen Bryant, 21 May 1840, in L. H. Butterfield, "Come with Me to the Feast: or, Transcendentalism in Action," *M[assachusetts]. H[istorical]. S[ociety]. Miscellany*, no. 6 [Dec. 1960], p. 5).

7. Sept. 1838, MWelC; "Andrews letter"; 24 Sept. 1838, MSaE; RWE to W. H. Furness, 20 Sept. 1838, in *EmRecLiFr*, p. 8.

8. 20 Oct. 1838, MSaE; RWE to MF, 9 Nov. 1838, in *EmL*, 2:173; in "Friendship," Emerson described Very as a man in a "religious frenzy" (*EmW*, 2:203, 415n).

9. 28, 29 Oct. 1838, in *EmJMN*, 7:122, 124; [ca. Oct. 1838], in Lilian Whiting, *Boston Days* (Bo: Little, Brown, 1911), p. 44 ("true"); RWE to EPP, 30 Oct. 1838, MBG.

10. 18 Nov. 1838, MWelC, 30 Nov. 1838, MWelC.

11. 8 Dec. 1838, MH; Week 50, Dec. 1838, in *AlcJ38*, p. 440: ibid., p. 446 ("insane"); 14 Jan. 1839, in *AlcDiJaJn39*, pp. 86-88; ibid., p. 103.

12. 29 Jan. 1839, in *AlcDiJaJn39*, pp. 207, 210; Very eventually became a friend of Dwight and occasionally sent him copies of his poems (Very to JSD, [25] Jan. 1840, MB); 27 Feb. 1839, in *AlcDiJa-Jn39*, p. 382. Hawthorne described Very's isolation by saying that he "stood alone, within a circle which no other of mortal race could enter, nor himself escape from" ("The Hall of Fantasy," *Pioneer* 1 [Feb. 1843]:53).

13. 18 Jan. 1839, in *EmL*, 2:179; MF to RWE, 4 Mar. 1839, copy, MB.

14. Clarke must have made a point of meeting Very after his sister Sarah called him "one of those self-sustained individuals" who were "remarkable for always speaking the truth and for believing in an Inward Voice" (5 Aug. 1838, in *ClLetSister*).

15. Clarke, "Religious Sonnets: By Jones Very," *Western Messenger* 6 (Mar. 1839):308-9; RWE to MF, 8 Mar. 1839, in *EmL*, 2:191.

16. Ward's account, [1839], in Butterfield, "Come with Me to the Feast," pp. 3-4; "Andrews letter"; Washington Very to RWE, 3 June 1839, MWelC; [June 1839], MSaE; 14 June 1839, in *AlcDiJaJn39*, p. 880; RWE to MF, 9 July 1839, in *EmL*, 2:209; EPP to [Sophia Peabody], 23 June 1839, in Lathrop, *Hawthorne*, p. 29 (correction; Lathrop does not identify Peabody's correspondent, but Whiting, in *Boston Days*, p. 29, says it is Sophia Peabody); "Andrews letter"; 16 May 1880, in ABA, "Journal for 1880," p. 160, MH ("speller"); "Andrews letter" ("grammar"); EPP to [Sophia Peabody], 23 June 1839, in Lathrop, *Hawthorne*, p. 29.

17. Written in his copy, MH; 18 Nov. 1839, in *AlcDiJyDec39*, p. 409.

18. *Dial* 2 (July 1841):130-31. Very was contributing to the *Dial* by this time, and Emerson helped him place his book on sale at Peabody's bookstore (Very to RWE, 21 Nov. 1841, MWelC).

19. Fuller observed that Very's state was "imperfect" because "he sometimes used his human will & understanding – & so falsifies his thought." Peabody felt that Very could not distinguish between "his own love of *obedience*" and the true voice of the Spirit (n.d., *FuW*, 1:607; EPP to LdE, [Dec. 1838], MSaE).

20. 6 Dec. 1839, in *AlcDiJyDec39*, p. 461; Fuller did not like him to attend because he tried to monopolize the talk (Gittleman, *Very*, p. 364); RWE to Rufus Griswold, 25 Sept. 1841, in Rufus W. Griswold, *Passages from the Correspondence and Other Papers of Rufus W. Griswold* [ed. W. M. Griswold] [Cambridge, Mass.: W. M. Griswold, 1898], p. 99. Charles Brooks could later say of the man whom Emerson had once described as being in a "religious frenzy" that he had a "peculiarly sweet smile, lighting up that face so singularly expressive of saintly simplicity and unselfish translucency of soul" (quoted in Andrews, "Memoir," p. 29).

21. Even though he felt that Emerson's corrections were "all improvements," Very said that he still preferred his own lines, for he felt "a little sad at the aspect of the piece" (23 Nov. 1842, MWelC).

22. Very to RWE, 21 Nov. 1841, MWelC; Very to RWE, 23 Nov. 1842, MWelC; RWE to EPP, 2 July 1842, MH. In 1855 Very owned numbers nine through twelve, which he said were the only ones Emerson had sent him (Very to Caroline Dall, 19 June 1855, MHi).

23. Bartlett, *Very*, p. 119. No doubt Emerson's companionship with Thoreau was a major reason why Emerson soon relegated Very to the past.

24. 17 Apr. 1843, in *EmJ*, 6:385; 16 June 1839, in *EmJMN*, 7:213; quoted in *SaRec*, 2:318.

Chapter 38: Samuel Gray Ward

Note: Biographical information is from Ward's own brief account of his life in *Ward Family Papers* ([Bo: Merrymount Press], 1900), and David Baldwin, "Puritan Aristocrat in the Age of Emerson: A Study of Samuel Gray Ward," Ph.D. diss., University of Pennsylvania, 1961.

1. Ward's statement, 2 Dec. 1843, in Baldwin, "Ward," p. 143-44; Faith Chipperfield, *In Quest of Love: The Life and Death of Margaret Fuller* (NY: Coward-McCann, 1957), p. 168 (health); Ward's statement, 2 Dec. 1843, in Baldwin, "Ward," p. 144.

2. On 27 July 1835, while on a boat trip near New York, Fuller had written in her journal: "About six, came out, & had a walk & a talk with Mr Ward: did not like him much" (copy by RWE, in *EmJMN*, 11:484).

3. SGW to Mary Ward, 8 Nov. 1836, in Baldwin, "Ward," p. 65; in 1873 Charles Eliot Norton noted in his journal that Ward had "listened much to her, and to good purpose" (*Letters of Charles Eliot Norton*, ed. Sara Norton and M. A. DeWolfe Howe [Bo: HoMif, 1913], 1:510).

4. In one of a series of letters to Ward Fuller stated: "You love me no more! . . . Why hide it from me?" In another she grieved that Ward had cut her from him in his "highest hour," and she moaned that the "world has separated us as intimates" (Sept. 1839, in *FuW*, 1:183; 15 Oct. 1839, MH).

5. James Clarke was pleased to hear Fuller talk favorably of Anna and was glad that she had "such a sweet creature to love." Rusk correctly assumes that in Anna, "a New Orleans beauty," Fuller saw "the unrealized half of what she herself wished to be" (12 May 1835, in *ClLetMF*, p. 94; *RuLiEm*, p. 253).

6. 21 Aug. 1842, MH.

7. On 7 October 1839 Emerson recorded in his journal that in Anna he had "enjoyed the frank & generous confidence of a being so lovely, so fortunate, & so remote from [his] own experiences" (*EmJMN*, 7:259).

8. 20 Apr. 1841, in ibid., p. 432; RWE, *Letters from Ralph Waldo Emerson to a Friend*, ed. Charles Eliot Norton [Bo: HoMif, 1899], prints only a small part of their total correspondence.

9. Ward actively promoted Channing to Fuller and quoted his words "whenever his own seemed inadequate, esteeming [Channing] of clearer insight, and, in some respects, of finer temper then himself" (MF to W. E. Channing, [3 Oct. 1841], MH).

10. MF to CS, 10 Feb. 1840, MH; JFC to SC, 8 July 1840, MH.

11. RWE to SGW and Anna Barker, Sept. 1840, in *EmL*, 2:338-39. In his journal Emerson wished his "beautiful, pure, & happy friends, – peace & beauty & power & the perpetuity & the sure unfolding of all the buds of joy that so thickly stud your branches" (5 Oct. 1840, in *EmJMN*, 7:404).

12. That night Peabody dreamed that it was John Sullivan Dwight, and not Ward, who married Anna, and she told Dwight that she "almost died of joy by way of sympathy" for him (EPP to JSD, 20 Sept. 1840, MB).

13. SGW to F. B. Sanborn, 9 June 1902, in *SaRec*, 2:576. To Fuller Channing said: "Why did he marry a fashionable woman, older than himself. And to marry a woman that had rejected him, what nonsense! There could have been no offering or rejecting, if the thing had been right." Yet T. W. Higginson later called Ward the "most patient & longsuffering of Ellery's early friends" (ca. 24 Aug. 1842, in *FuJ42*, p. 327; Higginson to Sanborn, 10 Aug. 1895, MHarF).

14. Emerson was "delighted" with this article but admitted that what his "beautiful friends" wrote he did not examine with "Aristotelian eyes but love it instead & thank God for the sunshine" (RWE to MF, 19 Jan. 1841, in *EmL*, 2:377).

15. F. M. Ward to Sam Ward, Jr., 24 Jan. 1842, in Maud Howe Elliott, *Uncle Sam Ward and His Circle* (NY: Macmillan, 1938), p. 222.

16. RWE to TC, 14 Nov. 1841, in *EmCorTC*, p. 310.

17. Emerson printed the piece without so much as an initial as a sign of authorship, calling it "one paper out of our folio" and mentioning that it had been detached "from its chapter" (*Dial* 3:269-72).

18. RWE to SC, 30 Sept. 1842, MH.

19. RWE to SGW, [ca. 29? Apr. 1843], in Edward Waldo Emerson, *The Early Years of the Saturday Club 1855-1870* (Bo: HoMif, 1918), p. 113: the date is by Rusk (*EmL*, 3:169); 3 May 1843, MH; RWE to MF, 7 June 1843, in *EmL*, 3:179; 10 June 1843, in *ThCor*, p. 118; SR to RWE, 5 July [1843], MH; MF to RWE, 4 Aug. 1843, in *EmL*, 3:194n.

20. RWE to SGW, 23 Oct. 1843, MH.

21. Baldwin suggests that Ward was "memorializing" his exchange with Emerson on spiritual matters in "The Consolers" ("Ward," pp. 172-73).

Chapter 39: Charles Stearns Wheeler

Note: Biographical information is from John Olin Eidson, *Charles Stearns Wheeler: Friend of Emerson* (Athens, Ga.: University of Georgia Press, 1951); also of value is the same author's "Charles Stearns Wheeler: Emerson's 'Good Grecian,' " *NEQ* 27 (Dec. 1954):472-83.

1. Wheeler's brother, quoted in Henry Williams, *Memorials of the Class of 1837 of Harvard University* (Bo: Geo. H. Ellis, 1887), p. 23.

2. Wheeler recorded in his class book that "To be one of so happy a crew was a lot too blessed for me." An example of Wheeler's industry was that he was licensed to preach on 14 June 1842 without having ever enrolled in the divinity school (ibid.).

3. These teas not only attracted Wheeler's Cambridge friends but also strangers passing through, and in this way George William Curtis and Charles King Newcomb met Wheeler. Not everyone was happy with Wheeler's friends. Henry Wadsworth Longfellow dryly noted that "the infected class" of the divinity school had gone, and "only one Transcendentalist, - and he a tutor!" remained in "all Cambridge." And an obituary of Wheeler complained that he was "sometimes too much absorbed with the whimsical novelties which the agitations of the age have brought to the surface of the foaming sea of philosophical and religious discussion" (Longfellow to Sam Ward [of New York], 1 Dec. 1840, in Henry Wadsworth Longfellow, *The Letters of Henry Wadsworth Longfellow*, ed. Andrew Hilen [Cambridge, Mass.: Harvard University Press, 1966-   ], 2:268; [Cornelius C. Felton], "Notices of Mr. Wheeler," *Christian Examiner* 35 [Nov. 1843]:238).

4. MF to RWE, 25 Apr. 1840, in *EmL*, 2:291n; TP to C. Francis, 12 June 1844, in John Weiss, *Life and Correspondence of Theodore Parker* [NY: Appleton, 1864], 1:241; Very to RWE, n.d., MWelC; HDT to Helen Thoreau, 21 July 1843, in *ThCor*, p. 129; W. E. Channing to Sanborn, 1883, in HDT, *Familiar Letters of Henry David Thoreau*, ed. F. B. Sanborn (Bo: HoMif, 1894), pp. 68-69n.

5. See HDT to CSW, 28 Nov. 1838, 3 Jan., 2 Mar. 1840, in Kenneth Walter Cameron, "Thoreau and Stearns Wheeler: Four Letters and a Reading Record," *ESQ*, no. 48 (III Quarter 1967), pp. 74-75.

6. RWE to CS, 5 Aug. 1842, MH. Emerson told Carlyle of the coming of his "good Grecian" Wheeler, but the two never met (1 July 1842, in *EmCorTC*, p. 323).

7. Quoted in Eidson, *Wheeler*, p. 64 (European life); 11 Nov. 1842, MH: one "youngster" who carried a *Dial* to Wheeler was Horace Mann (RWE to CSW, 30 Apr. 1843, ViU-B); CSW to RWE, 5, 24, 26 Jan. 1843, MH; RWE to LdE, 6 Jan. 1843, in *EmL*, 3:112.

8. RWE to FHH, 23 Mar. 1842, in *EmL*, 3:37-38.

9. Quoted in CSW to J. F. Heath, 14 Nov. 1842, MH. The best account of this incident is Sculley Bradley, "Lowell, Emerson, and the *Pioneer*," *AL* 19 (Nov. 1947):231-44.

10. Wheeler also suggested that Lowell print the item in "a different order, from that which I have used, [and] things would go vastly better." Ironically, Robert Carter did just that when he used the letter in the *Pioneer*'s unauthorized printing of it (8 Nov. 1842, MH).

11. 11 Nov. 1842, MH.

12. RWE to WmE, 25 Nov. 1842, in *EmL*, 3:100. Wheeler had told Emerson to make "any erasures, verbal insertions, transpositions of sentences, or other improvements . . . without the slightest feeling that the shadow of an apology is necessary." Since Wheeler wrote his newsletters over a period of

many days, the diarylike style he used was too choppy to be printed directly in the magazine. My own examination of these letters has borne out Eidson's findings:

> Emerson's insertions are rare, but his deletions are frequent. All passages relating the personal doings of Wheeler and his companions, most of which Wheeler did not intend for the *Dial*, are deleted. . . . Wheeler's exclamation points invariably disappeared, and his expressions of enthusiasm or astonishment either disappeared or assumed the dress of calm concise formality. . . . The readers of the *Dial* learned of Schlegel the writer but remained ignorant of Schlegel the man—as they did of the rowdiness of German university students and the filthiness of European beggars, on both of which topics Wheeler was voluble (5, 24, 26 Jan. 1843, MH; Eidson, *Wheeler*, p. 73).

13. 13 Dec. 1842, MH; 24 Nov. 1842, MH; RWE to CSW, 13 Dec. 1842, MH; Bartlett to RWE, 23 Dec. 1842, MH.

14. 5, 24, 26 Jan. 1843, MH; 20 Jan. 1842 [1843], MH; [1 Mar. 1843], in *ThCor*, p. 89; JRL to Carter, 17 Jan. 1843, NN-B (eye operation); "Letters from Germany," *Pioneer* 1:143-44. Lowell was still indirectly at fault. The day after he had anxiously inquired, "have you got any copy for the third number?" he sent Carter Wheeler's letter of 22 December 1842, suggesting that he could "get something" out of it "in spite of [Wheeler's] prohibition," by copying the "account of the beer drinking &c as far as I have marked in the letter." No doubt Carter took this to mean that he could indeed publish Wheeler's letter; or perhaps Lowell might not have made the situation concerning the *Dial*'s claims clear to Carter before he left for New York (letters of 19, [20], 24 Jan. 1843, NN-B).

15. 30 Apr. 1843, ViU-B; [Cornelius C.] F[elton]., "Charles Stearns Wheeler," *Boston Daily Advertiser*, 19 July 1843, p. 2; 4 June 1843, in Joel Myerson, "The Death of Charles Stearns Wheeler," *Concord Saunterer* 7 (Sept. 1972): 7 (Cabot); RWE to MF, 11 July 1843, in *EmL*, 3:183; HDT to Helen Thoreau, 21 July 1843, in *ThCor*, p. 129.

Chapter 40: William Dexter Wilson

Note: Biographical information is from James Grant Wilson and John Fiske, eds., *Appleton's Cyclopædia of American Biography* (NY: Appleton, 1888-89), 6:558, and *CoHiBi*, 2:51-53.

1. 26 Feb. 1838, MH; 21 Mar. 1838, in *EmL*, 2:147n; RWE to Wilson, Blake, and Simmons, 27 Mar. 1838, copy, in Kenneth Walter Cameron, *Ralph Waldo Emerson's Reading* (Raleigh, N.C.: Thistle Press, 1941), p. 130. See also Wilson to RWE, [16] July, 20 July 1838, MH.

2. Henry Bellows to William Bellows, 22 June 1841, MHi; Forster to Barclay Fox, n.d., in T. Wemyss Reid, *Life of . . . William Edward Forster* (London: Chapman and Hall, 1888), 1:147; James Murdock, *Sketches of Modern Philosophy* (Hartford, Conn.: John C. Wells, 1842), pp. 173-77.

3. In 1884 Wilson wrote to G. W. Cooke: "I knew but little about the origin of 'the Dial' &. . . .after it was started I lost all connection with it & all knowledge of it" (4 June, MHarF).

Appendix

This Appendix provides a list of the contents for each number of the *Dial*, followed by an alphabetical arrangement of the contributors and their contributions. A fully documented and complete report of the *Dial*'s contents is in Joel Myerson, "An Annotated List of Contributions to the Boston *Dial*," *Studies in Bibliography* 26 (1973):133-66.

Volume One   Number Two   **October 1840**

Volume One Number Three   **January 1841**

Volume One Number Four April 1841

Volume Two   Number One   **July 1841**

Volume Three Number Two   October 1842

Volume Four Number One   **July 1843**

Volume Four Number Two   **October 1843**

Volume Four   Number Three   **January 1844**

Page	*Title*	*Author*

Volume Four   Number Four   **April 1844**

Page	*Title*	*Author*

425-26	The Emigrants [translated]	C. T. Brooks
427-54	The Youth of the Poet and the Painter [Letters XIV-XXVIII]	W. E. Channing
455-57	The Twin Loves	S. G. Ward
458-69	Dialogue	M. Fuller
469	The Consolers	S. G. Ward
470-71	To Readers	W. E. Channing
471	The Death of Shelley	W. E. Channing
472	A Song of the Sea	W. E. Channing
473	To the Poets	W. E. Channing
473-83	Fourierism	E. P. Peabody
484-507	The Young American	R. W. Emerson
507-12	Herald of Freedom	H. D. Thoreau
513-14	Fragments of Pindar	H. D. Thoreau
515-21	The Tragic	R. W. Emerson
521-24	Saturday and Sunday Among the Creoles. A Letter from the West Indies.	B. P. Hunt
525-27	The Moorish Prince [translated]	C. T. Brooks
528	The Visit	R. W. Emerson
529-36	Ethnical Scriptures. Chaldæan Oracles. [selected]	R. W. Emerson
537-40	Millennial Church	C. Lane
540	[Review]	R. W. Emerson

Amos Bronson Alcott

Number	*Title*
I.1.85-98	Orphic Sayings
I.3.351-61	Orphic Sayings
II.4.409	*To the Editor of the Dial*
II.4.409-37	Days from a Diary
III.2.241	[Report of a Private Correspondent]

Charles Timothy Brooks

IV.4.425-26	The Emigrants [translated]
IV.4.525-27	The Moorish Prince [translated]

James Elliot Cabot

IV.4.409-15   Immanuel Kant

William Ellery Channing

I.2.187	["Why askest thou . . . "]
I.2.220-32	[Poems in "New Poetry"]
I.4.469	Hermitage
I.4.520-22	Theme for a World Drama. The Maiden — The Adopted Father — The Adopted Mother — The Lover
[?]I.1.52-53	Song
II.1.121	Sonnet to — — —
II.3.286	[Poetical Motto to "Yuca Filamentosa"]
III.1.40	Gifts
III.1.41	The Lover's Song
III.1.41	Sea Song
III.1.42	The Earth-Spirit
III.1.42-43	Prayer
III.1.43	After-Life
[?]III.1.81	To Shakespeare
III.2.256-58	Dirge
[?]III.2.264	The Poet
III.3.313	A Song of Spring
III.3.326	Anna
III.3.329	The River
III.3.329-30	Life
III.3.330	To — — —
III.3.340-42	Death
[?]III.4.506	Sonnets
III.4.507-8	To * * *
III.4.508-9	To — — —
III.4.509-11	The Friends
IV.1.48-58	The Youth of the Poet and the Painter [Letters I-IV]
[?]IV.1.62	Spring
[?]IV.1.63	The Song of Birds in Spring
IV.1.64	The Earth
IV.1.103	An Old Man
IV.1.106	The Journey
IV.1.115	The Glade
IV.2.174-86	The Youth of the Poet and the Painter [Letters V-IX]
IV.2.186-87	Autumn

IV.2.244	The Mother's Grief
IV.2.259	Allston's Funeral
IV.2.260-61	To the Muse
IV.2.261	William Tell's Song
IV.3.273-84	The Youth of the Poet and the Painter [Letters X-XIII]
IV.3.350	Autumn Woods
IV.3.364-73	The Fatal Passion, — A Dramatic Sketch
IV.4.427-54	The Youth of the Poet and the Painter [Letters XIV-XXVIII]
IV.4.470-71	To Readers
IV.4.471	The Death of Shelley
IV.4.472	A Song of the Sea
IV.4.473	To the Poets

William Henry Channing

I.1.48-58	Ernest the Seeker
I.2.233-42	Ernest the Seeker [continued]
II.1.45-47	Night and Day
II.1.48-52	Wheat Seed and Bolted Flour

Lydia Maria Child

III.4.490-92	What is Beauty?

Eliza Thayer Clapp

II.1.42-44	Two Hymns
II.1.55-57	Clouds
II.1.57-58	"The Future is Better than the Past"
II.1.58	August Shower
III.1.44-45	Autumn Leaves

James Freeman Clarke

I.2.159-60	First Crossing the Alleghanies
I.2.173-75	Nature and Art, or the Three Landscapes

I.3.292	Hymn and Prayer
I.3.312-13	To Nydia
I.4.443-45	Dream
I.4.468-69	Poems on Art. The Genuine Portrait. The Real and the Ideal.
II.3.385-93	Plan of Salvation
III.4.495-500	George Keats
III.4.500-504	Remarks on John Milton, by John Keats, Written in the Fly-Leaf of Paradise Lost. [edited]

Sarah Clarke

I.1.136	Dante

Christopher Pearse Cranch

I.1.11-12	To the Aurora Borealis
I.1.98	Stanzas
I.2.161-72	A Sign from the West
I.2.188-92	Musings of a Recluse
I.3.291	Endymion
I.3.298	The True in Dreams
I.3.379-81	Glimmerings
I.3.381	Correspondences
I.3.381-82	Color and Light
I.3.382-83	My Thoughts
I.3.383-84	The Riddle
I.3.384-85	The Ocean
II.1.47-48	The Blind Seer
II.2.271-72	Inworld
II.3.288-90	Inworld
II.3.290-91	Outworld
II.4.483-85	Silence and Speech
III.2.225-26	The Artist

George William Curtis

IV.1.87	A Song of Death

Charles Anderson Dana

II.4.528	Herzliebste
III.1.75	Eternity
IV.1.92	Manhood
IV.2.210	Via Sacra
IV.3.349	To R.B.

John Sullivan Dwight

I.1.17-22	The Religion of Beauty
I.1.22	["Sweet is the pleasure"]
I.1.124-34	The Concerts of the Past Winter
I.3.307-11	Ideals of Every-Day Life. No. I.
I.4.446-61	Ideals of Every-Day Life. No. II.

Charles Chauncy Emerson

I.1.13-16	Notes from the Journal of a Scholar
III.4.522-26	A Leaf from "A Voyage to Porto Rico"
IV.1.88-92	Notes from the Journal of a Scholar. No. II.

Edward Bliss Emerson

I.1.47	The Last Farewell

Ellen Louisa Tucker Emerson

I.1.72	Lines
I.3.314	The Violet

Ralph Waldo Emerson

I.1.1-4	The Editors to the Reader
I.1.84	To * * * *
I.1.122-23	The Problem
I.2.137-58	Thoughts on Modern Literature
I.2.158	Silence
I.2.220-32	New Poetry
I.2.242-45	Woodnotes
I.2.264-72	[Part of the Reviews]
I.3.339	The Snow-Storm
I.3.347	Suum Cuique
I.3.348-50	The Sphinx
I.3.367-78	Thoughts on Art
I.4.523-38	Man the Reformer
II.1.130-36	[Part of the Reviews]
II.2.205	Painting and Sculpture
II.2.205-6	Fate
II.2.207-14	Woodnotes. No. II.
II.2.262-71	Walter Savage Landor
II.3.373	The Park
II.3.373	Forbearance
II.3.373	Grace
II.3.374-79	The Senses and the Soul
II.3.382-84	Transcendentalism
III.1.1-18	Lectures on the Times [Introductory Lecture]
III.1.19	[Preliminary Note to "Natural History of Massachusetts"]
III.1.72-73	Tact
III.1.73	Holidays
III.1.73-74	The Amulet
III.1.77-81	Prayers
III.1.82-85	Veeshnoo Sarma [selected]
III.1.86-96	Fourierism and the Socialists
III.1.100-112	Chardon Street and Bible Conventions
III.1.123-26	Agriculture of Massachusetts
III.1.127-32	[Part of the Reviews]
III.1.132-36	[Intelligence]
III.2.181-97	Lectures on the Times. Lecture II. The Conservative.
III.2.227-47	English Reformers
III.2.247	[Introductory Note to "James Pierrepont Greaves"]
III.2.265-69	Saadi
III.2.269	[Introductory Note to "The Gallery"]
III.2.273-78	[Part of the Reviews]

III.2.278-80	[Editor's Table]
III.3.297-313	Lectures on the Times. Lecture III. The Transcendentalist.
III.3.327-28	To Eva at the South
III.3.387	[Literary Intelligence]
III.3.387	[Introductory Note to "Letter from Germany"]
III.3.404-16	[Part of the Reviews]
III.4.511-21	Europe and European Books
III.4.529-31	Friendship. From Chaucer's "Romaunt of the Rose" [selected]
III.4.532-40	[Part of the Reviews]
IV.1.59-62	Ethnical Scriptures. Extracts from the Desatir. [selected]
IV.1.62	Abou Ben Adhem. By Leigh Hunt. [selected]
IV.1.93-95	Gifts
IV.1.96-102	Past and Present
IV.1.104-6	To Rhea
IV.1.107	[Introductory Note to "Notes on Art and Architecture"]
IV.1.133	[Notice to Correspondents]
IV.1.134-35	[Reviews]
IV.1.136	To Correspondents
IV.2.205-10	Ethnical Scriptures. Chinese Four Books. [selected]
IV.2.226	The Three Dimensions
IV.2.247-56	The Comic
IV.2.257-59	Ode to Beauty
IV.2.262-70	A Letter
IV.2.270-72	[Reviews]
IV.3.357-63	Tantalus
IV.3.379	[Introductory Note to "Pindar"]
IV.3.401	Eros
IV.3.402-4	Ethnical Scriptures. Hermes Trismegistus. [selected]
IV.3.405-6	The Times. A Fragment.
IV.3.407-8	[Part of the Reviews]
IV.4.484-507	The Young American
IV.4.515-21	The Tragic
IV.4.528	The Visit
IV.4.529-36	Ethnical Scriptures. Chaldæan Oracles. [selected]
IV.4.540	[Review]

Margaret Fuller

I.1.5-11	A Short Essay on Critics
I.1.73-83	A Record of Impressions Produced by the Exhibition of Mr. Allston's Pictures in the Summer of 1839.
[?]I.1.84	"To Allston's Picture, 'The Bride'"
I.1.134	A Dialogue

I.1.135	Richter
I.1.135	*Some murmur at the "want of system" in Richter's writings*
I.1.135	The Morning Breeze
[?]I.1.136	A Sketch [I]
[?]I.1.136	A Sketch [II]
[?]I.1.136	["Did you ever admire . . . "]
[?]I.2.172	Angelica Sleeps [translated]
I.2.260-63	The Atheneum Exhibition of Painting and Sculpture
I.2.264-72	[Part of the Reviews]
I.3.293-98	Meta
I.3.299-305	The Magnolia of Lake Pontchartrain
I.3.340-47	Menzel's View of Goethe
I.3.401-8	[Part of the Reviews]
I.4.462-67	Leila
I.4.494-96	A Dialogue. Poet. Critic.
II.1.1-41	Goethe
[?]II.1.53-55	Need of a Diver
II.1.130-36	[Part of the Reviews]
II.1.136	To Contributors
II.2.137	[Introductory Notes to "Cupid's Conflict"]
II.2.148-203	Lives of the Great Composers, Haydn, Mozart, Handel, Bach, Beethoven
II.2.231-61	Festus
II.3.286-88	Yuca Filamentosa
II.3.313-57	Bettine Brentano and Her Friend Günderode
II.3.380-82	Epilogue to the Tragedy of Essex [translated]
II.3.393-408	[Part of the Reviews]
[?]II.4.437-83	Marie van Oosterwich [translated]
II.4.544	[Notice to Correspondents]
III.1.46-72	Entertainments of the Past Winter
III.1.127-32	[Part of the Reviews]
III.2.137-80	Romaic and Rhine Ballads
III.2.273-78	[Part of the Reviews]
III.3.404-16	[Part of the Reviews]
III.4.454-83	Canova
III.4.532-40	[Part of the Reviews]
IV.1.1-47	The Great Lawsuit. Man *versus* Men. Woman *versus* Women.
IV.3.307-49	The Modern Drama
IV.3.407-8	[Part of the Reviews]
IV.4.458-69	Dialogue

William Batchelder Greene

II.3.273-85	First Principles

Frederic Henry Hedge

I.2.175-82	The Art of Life, — The Scholar's Calling
I.3.290-91	Questionings
III.1.74-75	The Castle by the Sea [translated]
III.3.398-404	Schelling's Introductory Lecture in Berlin [translated]

Elizabeth Hoar

III.3.314-26	Discoveries in the Nubian Pyramids [translated]

Ellen Sturgis Hooper

I.1.123	["I slept, and dreamed that life was Beauty"]
I.2.187	"The Poor Rich Man"
I.2.193	The Wood-Fire
I.2.194	The Poet
I.2.216	Wayfarers
I.3.400	To the Ideal
[?]I.4.461	Listen to the Wind
I.4.519	The Out-Bid
I.4.544	Farewell
II.3.358-59	The Hour of Reckoning
IV.2.245	Sweep Ho!

Benjamin Peter Hunt

IV.1.116-33	Voyage to Jamaica
IV.2.227-44	Voyage to Jamaica [concluded]
IV.4.521-24	Saturday and Sunday Among the Creoles. A Letter from the West Indies.

Charles Lane

[?]III.2.242-43	[Reformation]
III.2.247-55	James Pierrepont Greaves

III.2.258-64	Cromwell
III.3.281-96	James Pierrepont Greaves [concluded]
III.3.404-416	[Part of the Reviews]
III.4.417-54	A. Bronson Alcott's Works
III.4.532-40	[Part of the Reviews]
III.4.545-48	Catalogue of Books
IV.1.65-86	Social Tendencies
IV.1.135-36	Fruitlands
IV.2.165-73	A Day with the Shakers
IV.2.188-204	Social Tendencies [concluded]
IV.3.351-57	Brook Farm
IV.3.373-78	Interior or Hidden Life
IV.4.415-25	Life in the Woods
IV.4.537-40	Millennial Church

James Russell Lowell

I.3.366	Sonnet. To a Voice Heard in Mt. Auburn, July, 1839
II.1.129	Sonnet. "To die is gain"
II.3.357	Sonnet ["When in a book . . . "]
II.3.357	Sonnet ["Only as thou herein . . . "]
II.3.358	Sonnet To Irene on Her Birthday

John Milton Mackie

I.4.470-93	Shelley

Charles King Newcomb

III.1.112-23	The Two Dolons. From the Ms. Symphony of Dolon. The First Dolon.

Theodore Parker

I.1.58-70	The Divine Presence in Nature and in the Soul
I.2.196-216	A Lesson for the Day; or the Christianity of Christ, of the Church, and of Society

I.2.218-19	Truth Against the World. A Parable of Paul.
I.2.264-72	[Part of the Reviews]
I.3.315-39	German Literature
I.4.497-519	Thoughts on Labor
II.1.59-76	The Pharisees
II.1.77	Protean Wishes
II.3.292-313	Primitive Christianity
II.4.485-528	Thoughts on Theology
II.4.529-44	[Reviews]
III.2.201-21	Hollis Street Council
III.2.273-78	[Part of the Reviews]
III.3.343-62	The Life and Character of Dr. Follen
IV.2.137-65	Hennell on the Origin of Christianity

Elizabeth Palmer Peabody

II.2.214-28	A Glimpse of Christ's Idea of Society
II.3.361-72	Plan of the West Roxbury Community
II.3.393-408	[Part of the Reviews]
IV.4.473-83	Fourierism

Benjamin Franklin Presbury

II.3.359	Sonnet To Mary on Her Birthday
II.3.360	Music To Martha.

George Ripley

I.1.22-46	Brownson's Writings
I.2.183-87	Letter to a Theological Student
I.2.246-56	[Reviews]
I.2.256-60	Professor Walker's Vindication of Philosophy
I.2.264-72	[Part of the Reviews]
I.3.401-8	[Part of the Reviews]

Sophia Ripley

I.3.362-66	Woman
II.1.78-81	Painting and Sculpture
II.1.122-29	Letter

Jonathan Ashley Saxton

II.1.83-121   Prophecy — Transcendentalism — Progress

Thomas Treadwell Stone

I.3.273-89   Man in the Ages
II.3.382-83   [Calvinist's Letter]

Caroline Sturgis

I.2.193   The Day Breaks
I.2.195   Life
I.2.195   Evening
[?]I.2.216   From Goethe
I.2.217   Pæan
I.2.217-18   Lyric
[?]I.2.219   Waves
[?]I.2.219   ["On the surface by the waves . . . "]
I.2.232   Art and Artist
I.2.245   Life and Death
I.2.263-64   "The Dream"
I.3.289   Afternoon
I.3.305   Love and Insight
I.3.305   Sunset
I.3.306   Give Us an Interpreter
I.3.306   ["Birds shooting swiftly . . . "]
[?]I.4.461   The Wind Again
I.4.469   The Angel and the Artist
II.1.82   Bettina!
II.1.129   Lines
II.2.203   Light and Shade
II.2.230-31   Windmill
III.1.126   Outward Bound
III.3.328   The Brook
IV.3.306   Lines

William Aspinwall Tappan

IV.2.246   The Sail

Henry David Thoreau

I.1.71-72	Sympathy
I.1.117-21	Aulus Persius Flaccus
I.3.314	Stanzas
II.1.81-82	Sic Vita
II.2.204-5	Friendship
III.1.19-40	Natural History of Massachusetts
III.1.79-80	[Metrical prayer]
III.2.180	The Black Knight
III.2.198-99	The Inward Morning
III.2.199	Free Love
III.2.200	The Poet's Delay
III.2.200	Rumors from an Æolian Harp
III.2.222	The Moon
III.2.222-24	To the Maiden in the East
III.2.224-25	The Summer Rain
III.3.331-40	The Laws of Menu [selected]
III.3.363-86	The Prometheus Bound [translation]
III.4.484-90	Anacreon
[?]III.4.493-94	Ethnical Scriptures. [Sayings of Confucius] [selected]
III.4.505	To a Stray Fowl
III.4.505-6	Orphics. I. Smoke. II. Haze.
III.4.527-29	Dark Ages
IV.2.211-26	A Winter Walk
IV.3.290-305	Homer. Ossian. Chaucer.
IV.3.379-90	Pindar
[?]IV.3.391-401	The Preaching of Buddha [selected]
IV.4.507-12	Herald of Freedom
IV.4.513-14	Fragments of Pindar

John Francis Tuckerman

I.4.539-44	Music of the Winter

Jones Very

III.1.97-100	Poems for the Dial ["The Evening Choir" and "The World"]

Samuel Gray Ward

I.1.83	"To W. Allston, On Seeing His 'Bride'"
I.1.84	Song
I.1.121	The Shield
I.1.123	Come Morir?
I.3.386-400	Letters from Italy on the Representatives of Italy
III.2.269-72	The Gallery
IV.1.107-15	Notes on Art and Architecture
IV.3.285-90	Translation of Dante
IV.4.455-57	The Twin Loves
IV.4.469	The Consolers

Charles Stearns Wheeler

III.3.388-97	[Letter from Germany]
III.4.541-44	[Letter from Heidelberg]

William Dexter Wilson

I.1.99-117	Channing's Translation of Jouffroy
I.4.409-43	The Unitarian Movement in New England

Unknown

II.2.228-30	Poems on Life
II.3.359	De Profundis Clamavi
III.1.76-77	Vespers
III.1.85	["I asked the angels to come to me . . . "]
III.2.265	Lines

Bibliography

Adams, John Quincy. *Memoirs of John Quincy Adams*. Edited by Charles Francis Adams. 12 vols. Philadelphia: J. B. Lippincott, 1874-77.

Adams, Marian Hooper. *The Letters of Mrs. Henry Adams 1864-1883*. Edited by Ward Thoron. Boston: Little, Brown, 1936.

"Aeneas, Jr." "A Visit to Hades." *Dartmouth* 3 (November 1841):108-19.

"Agents." *New-Yorker* 9 (18 April 1840):79.

Alcott, A. Bronson. *Concord Days*. Boston: Roberts, 1882.

— —. *The Journals of Bronson Alcott*. Edited by Odell Shepard. Boston: Little, Brown, 1938.

— —. *The Letters of A. Bronson Alcott.* Edited by Richard L. Herrnstadt. Ames: Iowa State University Press, 1969.

— —. "Reminiscences of the Transcendental Club." *Boston Book Bulletin* 1 (December 1877, March 1878):3-5, 30.

— —. "The Transcendental Club and the Dial; A Conversation by A. Bronson Alcott, Boston, Monday Evening, March 23, 1863." *The Commonwealth* [Boston], 24 April 1863, p. 1.

Alcott, Louisa M. "Transcendental Wild Oats." *Independent* 25 (18 December 1873):1569-71.

Allen, Joseph Henry. *Our Liberal Movement in Theology*. Boston: Roberts, 1882.

— —. *Sequel to "Our Liberal Movement."* Boston: Roberts, 1897.

"American Monthly Literature." *Christian Examiner* 36 (January 1844):141-42.

Andrews, William P. "Memoir." In Jones Very, *Poems of Jones Very*, pp. 3-31. Boston: Houghton, Mifflin, 1883.

Austen, Jessica Tyler, ed. *Moses Coit Tyler*. Garden City, N.Y.: Doubleday, Page, 1911.

B., E. "American Correspondence." *Monthly Magazine*, 3d ser., 5 (May 1841):477.

Baer, Helene G. *The Heart is Like Heaven: The Life of Lydia Maria Child*. Philadelphia: University of Pennsylvania Press, 1964.

— —. "Mrs. Child and Miss Fuller." *New England Quarterly* 26 (June 1953):249-55.

Baldwin, David. "Puritan Aristocrat in the Age of Emerson: A Study of Samuel Gray Ward." Ph.D. dissertation, University of Pennsylvania, 1961.

Barnes, Daniel Ramon. "An Edition of the Early Letters of Orestes Brownson." Ph.D. dissertation, University of Kentucky, 1970.

Bartlett, J. Gardner. *Simeon Stone Genealogy.* Boston: Stone Family Association, 1926.

Bartlett, William Irving. *Jones Very: Emerson's "Brave Saint."* Durham, N.C.: Duke University Press, 1942.

Bestor, Arthur E., Jr. *Brook Farm, 1841-1847: An Exhibition to Commemorate Its Founding.* [New York: Columbia University Libraries, 1941]. Mimeographed.

"The Bible Convention." *Boston Morning Post*, 4 January 1842, p. 2.

"The Bible Convention." *Boston Morning Post*, 31 March 1842, p. 1.

Blackburn, Charles E. "Some New Light on the *Western Messenger.*" *American Literature"* 26 (November 1954):320-36.

Blanck, Jacob. *Bibliography of American Literature.* 6 vols. to date. New Haven, Conn.: Yale University Press, 1955-.

Blanding, Thomas William. "The Text of Thoreau's Fragmentary Journals of the 1840's." B.A. thesis, Marlboro College, 1970.

Bolster, Arthur S., Jr. *James Freeman Clarke: Disciple to Advancing Truth.* Boston: Beacon, 1954.

— —. "The Life of James Freeman Clarke." Ph.D. dissertation, Harvard University, 1953.

Bowdoin College. *General Catalogue of Bowdoin College and the Medical School of Maine 1794-1912.* Brunswick, Me.: Bowdoin College, 1912.

Bradford, G., Jr. "Jones Very." *Unitarian Review* 27 (February 1887):111-18.

Bradley, Sculley. "Introduction." In *The Pioneer: A Literary Magazine*, pp. v-xxix. New York: Scholars' Facsimiles & Reprints, 1947.

— —. "Lowell, Emerson, and the *Pioneer.*" *American Literature* 19 (November 1947):231-34.

Briggs, L. Vernon. *History and Genealogy of the Cabot Family 1475-1927.* 2 vols. Boston: Charles E. Goodspeed, 1927.

Brisbane, Redelia. *Albert Brisbane: A Mental Biography.* Boston: Arena, 1893.

Brooks, Gladys. *Three Wise Virgins.* New York: E. P. Dutton, 1957.

Brown University. *Historical Catalogue of Brown University 1774-1904.* Providence, R.I.: Brown University, 1905.

Brownson, Henry F. *Orestes A. Brownson's Early Life: From 1803 to 1844.* Detroit, Mich.: H. F. Brownson, 1898.

Brownson, Orestes A. "Brook Farm." *United States Magazine, and Democratic Review* 11 (November 1842):481-96.

— —. "Introductory Remarks." *Boston Quarterly Review* 1 (January 1838):1-8.

B[urnap]., G. W. "German Theology." *Christian Examiner* 32 (July 1842):319-37.

Butterfield, L. H. "Come with Me to the Feast; or, Transcendentalism in Action." M[assachusetts]. H[istorical]. S[ociety]. *Miscellany*, no. 6 (December 1960), pp. 1-5.

Cabot, James Elliot. *A Memoir of Ralph Waldo Emerson.* 2 vols. Boston: Houghton, Mifflin, 1887.

Cahoon, Herbert, "Some Manuscripts of Concord Authors in the Pierpont Morgan Library," *Manuscripts* 18 (Fall 1966):44-50.

Cameron, Kenneth Walter. *Companion to Thoreau's Correspondence.* Hartford, Conn.: Transcendental Books, 1964.

— —. "Early Records of the Concord Lyceum." In *Transcendental Climate*, 3:641-731. Hartford, Conn.: Transcendental Books, 1963.

— —. "Emerson, Thoreau and the Town Athenaeum." In *The Transcendentalists and Minerva*, 3:890-95. Hartford, Conn.: Transcendental Books, 1958.

— —. "Emerson, Transcendentalism, and Literary Notes in the Stearns Wheeler Papers." *American Transcendental Quarterly*, no. 20 (Fall 1973), supplement, part 1, pp.69-98.

— —. "A Garland of Emerson Letters." *Emerson Society Quarterly*, no. 10 (I Quarter 1958), pp. 32-41.

— —. "Jones Very and Thoreau — The 'Greek' Myth." *Emerson Society Quarterly*, no. 7 (II Quarter 1957), pp. 39-40.

— —. Junius J. Alcott, Poet and Transcendentalist." *Emerson Society Quarterly*, no. 14 (I Quarter 1959), pp. 57-76.

— —. *Ralph Waldo Emerson's Reading*. Raleigh, N.C.: The Thistle Press, 1941.

— —. "Thoreau and Stearns Wheeler: Four Letters and a Reading Record." *Emerson Society Quarterly*, no. 48 (III Quarter 1967), pp. 73-81.

— —. "Thoreau Discovers Emerson: A College Reading Record." *Bulletin of the New York Public Library* 57 (July 1953):319-34.

— —. *The Transcendentalists and Minerva*. 3 vols. Hartford, Conn.: Transcendental Books, 1958.

Carlyle, Thomas. *Letters of Thomas Carlyle to John Stuart Mill, John Sterling and Robert Browning*. Edited by Alexander Carlyle. London: T. Fisher Unwin, 1923.

— —. *New Letters of Thomas Carlyle*. Edited by Alexander Carlyle. 2 vols. London: John Lane, 1904.

— —. *Past and Present*. Boston: Charles C. Little and James Brown, 1843.

— —. "Preface by the English Editor." In Ralph Waldo Emerson, *Essays*, pp. v-xiii. London: John Fraser, 1841.

Carpenter, Hazen C. "Emerson and Christopher Pearse Cranch." *New England Quarterly* 37 (March 1964):18-42.

Carson, Barbara Harwell. "Proclus' Sunflower and *The Dial*." *English Language Notes* 11 (March 1974):200-202.

Cary, Edward. *George William Curtis*. Boston: Houghton, Mifflin, 1894.

"The Celebration at Cambridge." *Boston Courier*, 10 September 1836.

Chadwick, John White. *Theodore Parker: Preacher and Reformer*. Boston: Houghton, Mifflin, 1901.

Channing, William Ellery. *Poems*. Boston: Charles C. Little and James Brown, 1843.

Channing, William Henry. "Call of the Present — No. 2. — Science of Unity." *Present* 1 (15 November 1843):73-80.

— —. "The Democratic Review and O. A. Brownson." *Present* 1 (15 October 1843):72.

— —. *Memoir of William Ellery Channing, with Extracts from his Correspondence and Manuscripts*. 3 vols. Boston: Wm. Crosby and H. P. Nichols, 1848.

Chapman, John. "Preface." *Characteristics of Men of Genius*. 2 vols. Boston: Otis, Broaders; London: Chapman Brothers, 1847.

"The Character of Periodicals." *Boston Weekly Magazine* 3 (13 March 1841):205.

Charvat, William. *Emerson's American Lecture Engagements: A Chronological List.* New York: New York Public Library, 1961.

Child, Lydia Maria. *Letters of Lydia Maria Child with a Biographical Introduction by John G. Whittier and an Appendix by Wendell Phillips*. [Edited by Harriet Winslow Sewall]. Boston: Houghton, Mifflin, 1883.

Chipperfield, Faith. *In Quest of Love: The Life and Death of Margaret Fuller*. New York:

Coward-McCann, 1957.

Chivers, Thomas Holley. *The Correspondence of Thomas Holley Chivers 1838-1858.* Edited by Emma Lester Chase and Lois Ferry Parks. Providence, R.I.: Brown University Press, 1957.

Christy, Arthur. *The Orient in American Transcendentalism.* New York: Columbia University Press, 1932.

Clapp, Ebenezer, comp. *Record of the Clapp Family in America.* Boston: David Clapp & Son, 1876.

Clapp, Eliza Thayer. *Essays, Letters and Poems.* Boston: Privately printed [Riverside Press], 1888.

Clarke, James Freeman. *Autobiography, Diary and Correspondence.* Edited by Edward Everett Hale. Boston: Houghton, Mifflin, 1891.

— —. *Epochs and Events in Religious History.* Boston: James R. Osgood, 1883.

— —. *The Letters of James Freeman Clarke to Margaret Fuller.* Edited by John Wesley Thomas. Hamburg: Cram, de Gruyter, 1957.

— —. *A Look at the Life of Theodore Parker.* Boston: Walker, Wise, 1860.

— —. "Memoir of Ralph Waldo Emerson, LL. D." *Proceedings of the Massachusetts Historical Society,* 2d ser., 2 (June 1885):107-17.

— —. "Religious Sonnets: By Jones Very." *Western Messenger* 6 (March 1839):308-14.

— —. [Review of *Select Minor Poems of Goethe and Schiller,* translated by John S. Dwight]. *Western Messenger* 6 (February 1839):259-65.

— —. [Review of Moses George Thomas, *A Rejected Article* . . .]. *Christian World* 2 (3 February 1844):3.

Clarke, Louise Brownell, comp. *The Greenes of Rhode Island.* New York: Knickerbocker Press, 1903.

Codman, John Thomas. *Brook Farm: Historic and Personal Memories.* Boston: Arena, 1894.

Coffin, Charles Carleton. "Memoir of Nathaniel Greene." *New England Historical and Genealogical Register* 32 (October 1878):373-78.

Coleman, Caryl. "A Forgotten Convert." *Catholic World* 122 (November 1925):192-203.

Commager, Henry Steele. *Theodore Parker.* Boston: Little, Brown, 1936.

Conway, Moncure Daniel. *Autobiography, Memories and Experiences of Moncure Daniel Conway.* 2 vols. Boston: Houghton, Mifflin, 1904.

— =. *Emerson at Home and Abroad.* Boston: James R. Osgood, 1882.

Cooke, George Willis. " 'The Dial': An Historical and Biographical Introduction, with a List of the Contributors." *Journal of Speculative Philosophy* 19 (July 1885):225-65.

— —. "'The Dial' and Corrigenda" *Journal of Speculative Philosophy* 19 (July 1885):322-23.

— —. *An Historical and Biographical Introduction to Accompany* The Dial. 2 vols. Cleveland, Ohio: The Rowfant Club, 1902.

— —. *John Sullivan Dwight: Brook-Farmer, Editor, and Critic of Music.* Boston: Small, Maynard, 1898.

— —. *Ralph Waldo Emerson: His Life, Writings, and Philosophy.* Boston: James R. Osgood, 1881.

— —. ed. *The Poets of Transcendentalism.* Boston: Houghton, Mifflin, 1903.

Cranch, Christopher Pearse. "Emerson's Oration." *Western Messenger* 4 October 1837): 1 84-89.

— —. *Poems.* Philadelphia: Carey and Hart, 1844.

Crawford, Mary Caroline. *Famous Families of Massachusetts.* 2 vols. Boston: Little, Brown, 1930.

"Criticism in America." *Arcturus* 3 (May 1842):401-6.

Crowe, Charles. *George Ripley: Transcendentalist and Utopian Socialist.* Athens, Ga.: University of Georgia Press, 1967.

— —. "Transcendentalism and 'The Newness' in Rhode Island." *Rhode Island History* 14 (April 1955):33-46.

Cummins, Roger William. "The Second Eden: Charles Lane and American Transcendentalism." PH.D. dissertation, University of Minnesota, 1967.

Cummings, Laurence A. "Thoreau Poems in Bixby-Washington University Manuscripts." *Emerson Society Quarterly*, no. 26 (I Quarter 1962), pp. 9-28.

Curtis, George William. "An Autobiographical Sketch." *Cosmopolitan* 17 (October 1894):703-5.

— —. *Early Letters of George William Curtis to John S. Dwight: Brook Farm and Concord.* Edited by George Willis Cooke. New York: Harpers, 1898.

— —. "Editor's Easy Chair." *Harper's New Monthly Magazine* 38 (January 1869):268-71.

— —."Editor's Easy Chair." *Harper's New Monthly Magazine* 43 (November 1871):929-33.

— —. "Editor's Easy Chair." *Harper's New Monthly Magazine* 84 (April 1892):797-801.

— —. "Some Early Letters of George William Curtis." Edited by Caroline Ticknor. *Atlantic Monthly* 114 (September 1914):363-76.

Cutler, Samuel. "Necrology of the New England Historic, Genealogical Society." *New England Historical and Genealogical Register* 32 (October 1878):430-34.

Dall, Caroline. *Transcendentalism in New England: A Lecture.* Boston: Roberts, 1897.

Dana, Charles A. *A Lecture on Association, in Its Connection with Religion.* Boston: Benjamin H. Greene, 1844.

Dean, John Ward. "Descendants of the Rev. Daniel Rogers of Littleton, Mass." *New England Historical and Genealogical Register* 39 (July 1885):225-30.

Dickens, Charles. *American Notes for General Circulation.* 2 vols. London: Chapman and Hall, 1842.

Duberman, Martin. *James Russell Lowell.* Boston: Houghton Mifflin, 1966.

D[uyckinck]., E[vert]. A. "Literary Prospects of 1845." *American Whig Review* 1 (February 1845):146-51.

Dwight, John S. *A Lecture on Association, in Its Connection with Education.* Boston: Benjamin H. Green, 1844.

— —. "Music a Means of Culture." *Atlantic Monthly* 26 (September 1870): 321-31.

— —. [Review of Schiller, *William Tell*, translated by Charles T. Brooks]. *Christian Examiner* 25 (January 1839):385.

Edgell, David P. "A Note on a Transcendental Friendship." *New England Quarterly* 24 (December 1951):528-32.

— —. *William Ellery Channing: An Intellectual Portrait.* Boston: Beacon, 1955.

"Editor's Table [on Holmes's "Terpsichore"]." *Knickerbocker* 23 (January 1844):98-99.

"Editor's Table [on "Transcendentalism"]." *Knickerbocker* 20 (August 1842):201.

Eidson, John Olin. "Charles Stearns Wheeler: Emerson's 'Good Grecean.'" *New England Quarterly* 27 (December 1954):472-83.

— —. *Charles Stearns Wheeler: Friend of Emerson.* Athens, Ga: University of Georgia Press, 1951.

Elliott, Maud Howe. *Uncle Sam Ward and His Circle.* New York: Macmillan, 1938.

Elliott, Walter. *The Life of Father Hecker.* New York: Columbus Press, 1891.

Emerson, Edward Waldo. *The Early Years of the Saturday Club 1855-1870.* Boston: Houghton Mifflin, 1918.

Emerson, Ellen Louisa Tucker. *One First Love: The Letters of Ellen Louisa Tucker to Ralph Waldo Emerson.* Edited by Edith W. Gregg. Cambridge, Mass.: Harvard University Press, 1962.

Emerson, Ralph Waldo. *The Complete Works of Ralph Waldo Emerson.* Edited by Edward Waldo Emerson. The Centenary Edition. 12 vols. Boston: Houghton, Mifflin, 1903-4.

— —. *The Correspondence of Emerson and Carlyle.* Edited by Joseph Slater. New York: Columbia University Press, 1964.

— —. *The Early Lectures of Ralph Waldo Emerson.* Edited by Stephen E. Whicher, Robert E. Spiller, and Wallace E. Williams. 3 vols. Cambridge, Mass.: Harvard University Press, 1959-72.

— —. *The Journals and Miscellaneous Notebooks of Ralph Waldo Emerson.* Edited by William H. Gilman et al. 14 vols. to date. Cambridge, Mass.: Harvard University Press, 1960-.

— —. *Journals of Ralph Waldo Emerson.* Edited by Edward Waldo Emerson and Waldo Emerson Forbes. 10 vols. Boston: Houghton Mifflin, 1909-14.

— —. *A Letter of Emerson . . .* Edited by Willard Reed. Boston: Beacon, 1934.

— —. *Letters from Ralph Waldo Emerson to a Friend 1838-1853.* Edited by Charles Eliot Norton. Boston: Houghton, Mifflin, 1899.

— —. *The Letters of Ralph Waldo Emerson.* Edited by Ralph L. Rusk. 6 vols. New York: Columbia University Press, 1939.

— —. "Mr. Channing's Poems." *United States Magazine, and Democratic Review* 13 (September 1843):309-14.

— —. *Records of a Lifelong Friendship, 1807-1882: Ralph Waldo Emerson and William Henry Furness.* Edited by H[orace]. H[oward]. F[urness]. Boston: Houghton Mifflin, 1910.

— —, ed. *Parnassus.* Boston: James R. Osgood, 1875.

— —, Channing, William Henry and Clarke, James Freeman. *Memoirs of Margaret Fuller Ossoli.* 2 vols. Boston: Phillips, Sampson, 1852.

F[elton, Cornelius C.]. "Charles Stearns Wheeler." *Boston Daily Advertiser,* 19 July 1843, p. 2.

— —. "Notices of Mr. Wheeler." *Christian Examiner* 35 (November 1843): 232-44.

— —. [Review of *The Prometheus and Agamemnon of Aeschylus,* translated by Henry William Herbert]. *North American Review* 69 (October 1849):407-21.

Fertig, Walter L. "John Sullivan Dwight: Transcendentalist and Literary Amateur of Music." Ph.D. dissertation, University of Maryland, 1952.

Flint, Robert W. "The Boston Book Trade, 1835-1845." Library school thesis, Simmons College, n.d.

Fox, Caroline. *Memories of Old Friends.* Edited by Horace N. Pym. 2 vols. London: Smith, Elder, 1882.

Frothingham, Octavius Brooks. *George Ripley.* Boston: Houghton, Mifflin, 1882.

— —. *Memoir of William Henry Channing*. Boston: Houghton, Mifflin, 1886.

— —. *Theodore Parker: A Biography*. New York: Putnams, 1880.

— —. *Transcendentalism in New England*. New York: Putnams, 1876.

Fuller, Margaret. *At Home and Abroad*. Edited by Arthur B. Fuller. Boston: Crosby, Nichols, 1856.

— —. "Lines . . . On the Death of C. C. E." *Boston Daily Centinel & Gazette*, 17 May 1836, p. 1.

— —. *Papers on Literature and Art*. 2 vols. New York: Wiley & Putnam, 1846.

G., J. E. "The Latterlights and Their Progeny. Or Doings in the City of the Savans." *Knickerbocker* 17 (June 1841):499-506.

Gannett, William C. *Ezra Stiles Gannett*. Boston: Roberts, 1877.

Garnsey, Caroline John. "Ladies' Magazines to 1850: The Beginnings of an Industry." *Bulletin of the New York Public Library* 58 (February 1954):74-88.

Gittleman, Edwin. *Jones Very: The Effective Years 1833-1840*. New York: Columbia University Press, 1967.

Glick, Wendell P. "Thoreau and the 'Herald of Freedom.'" *New England Quarterly* 22 (June 1949):193-204.

Godley, John Robert. *Letters from America*. 2 vols. London: John Murray, 1844.

Gohdes, Clarence L. F. *The Periodicals of American Transcendentalism*. Durham, N.C.: Duke University Press, 1931.

Golann, Ethel. "A Lowell Autobiography." *New England Quarterly* 7 (June 1934):356-64.

Goodrich, S. G. *Recollections of a Lifetime*. 2 vols. Auburn, N.Y.: Miller, Orton, and Milligan, 1856.

Gordan, John D. "Ralph Waldo Emerson, 1803-1882: Catalogue of an Exhibition from the Berg Collection." *Bulletin of the New York Public Library* 57 (August, September 1953):392-408, 433-60.

Graham, Philip. "Some Lowell Letters." *Texas Studies in Literature and Language* 3 (Winter 1962):557-82.

Gray, Henry David. *Emerson: A Statement of New England Transcendentalism as Expressed in the Philosophy of Its Chief Exponent*. Stanford, Calif.: Stanford University, 1917.

[Greene, William Batchelder]. *The Doctrine of Life. With Some of Its Theological Applications*. Boston: B. H. Greene, 1843.

— —. *Transcendentalism*. [West Brookfield, Mass.: Oliver S. Cooke, 1849].

Griest, Guinevere L. *Mudie's Circulating Library and the Victorian Novel*. Bloomington, Ind.: Indiana University Press, 1970.

Griffin, Lloyd Wilfred. "Selected Letters of Richard Henry Dana, Jr. (1815-1882)." M.A. thesis, University of Maine, 1941.

Griswold, Rufus W. *Passages from the Correspondence and Other Papers of Rufus W. Griswold*. [Edited by W. M. Griswold]. Cambridge, Mass.: W. M. Griswold, 1898.

— —, ed. *The Prose Writers of America*. New ed., rev. and enlg. Philadelphia: Porter and Coates, 1870.

Hale, Edward Everett. *James Russell Lowell and His Friends*. Boston: Houghton, Mifflin, 1899.

Harding, Walter. *The Days of Henry Thoreau*. New York: Alfred A. Knopf, 1966.

Harvard University. *Catalogue of the Officers and Members of the Hasty-Pudding Club in Harvard College*. Cambridge, Mass.: Metcalf, 1850.

— —. *Quinquennial Catalogue of the Officers and Graduates 1636-1920*. Cambridge, Mass.: Harvard University, 1920.

Hawthorne, Julian. *Nathaniel Hawthorne and His Wife*. 2 vols. Boston: Houghton, Mifflin, 1884.

Hawthorne, Nathaniel. *The American Notebooks by Nathaniel Hawthorne based upon the original manuscripts at the Pierpont Morgan Library*. Edited by Randall Stewart. New Haven, Conn.: Yale University Press, 1932.

— —. *The American Notebooks*. Edited by Claude M. Simpson. Vol. 8 of *The Centenary Edition of the Works of Nathaniel Hawthorne*, edited by William Charvat et al., 13 vols. to date. Columbus, Ohio: Ohio State University Press, 1972.

— —. *The Blithedale Romance*. Vol. 3 of *The Centenary Edition*. Columbus, Ohio: Ohio State Univerity Press, 1964.

— —. "The Celestial Railroad." *United States Magazine, and Democratic Review* 12 (May 1843):515-23.

— —. "The Hall of Fantasy." *Pioneer* 1 (February 1843):49-55.

— —. *Love Letters of Nathaniel Hawthorne*. 2 vols. Chicago: Society of the Dofobs, 1907.

— —. "P.'s Correspondence." *United States Magazine, and Democratic Review* 16 (April 1845):337-45.

Hecker, I. T. "Dr. Brownson in Boston." *Catholic World* 45 (July 1887):466-72.

Hedge, Frederic Henry. *Conservatism and Reform*. Boston: Charles C. Little and James Brown, 1843.

— —. "The Destinies of Ecclesiastical Religion." *Christian Examiner* 82 (January 1867):1-15.

— —. *Prose Writers of Germany*. 3d ed. New York: C. S. Francis, 1855.

Hennessy, Helen. "The *Dial*: Its Poetry and Poetic Criticism." *New England Quarterly* 31 (March 1958):66-87.

[Heraud, John A.]. "Census of Foreign Literature. Continental Philosophy in America" [No. 1. — Cousin's Ecclecticism; No. 2. — Victor Cousin Himself; No. 3. — Cousin Criticised; No. 4. — Cousin Criticised (concluded)]. *Monthly Magazine*, 3d ser., 4 (July, August, October, December 1840):1-14, 112-28, 331-38, 628-37.

— —. "Education." *Monthly Magazine*, 3d ser., 3 (April 1840):341-53.

Hicks, Granville. "A Conversation in Boston." *Sewanee Review* 39 (April-June 1931:129-43.

Higginson, Thomas Wentworth. *Cheerful Yesterdays*. Boston: Houghton, Mifflin, 1898.

— —. "Emerson." *Nation* 34 (4 May 1882):375-76.

— —. "James Elliot Cabot." *Proceedings of the American Academy of Arts and Sciences* 39 (1903-4):649-55.

— —. *Margaret Fuller Ossoli*. Boston: Houghton, Mifflin, 1884.

— —. "Memoir of James Elliot Cabot." *Proceedings of the Massachusetts Historical Society*, 2d ser., 20 (1906-7):526-33.

— —. "The Personality of Emerson." *Outlook* 74 (23 May 1903):221-27.

— —. "Report on the Parker Library." In *Thirty-First Annual Report of the Trustees of the [Boston] Public Library*, pp. 19-25. Boston: n. p., 1883.

— —. "Two 'Dial' Poets." *Literature*, 5 January 1889, pp. 178-82.

— —. "Walks with Ellergy Channing." *Atlantic Monthly* 90 (July 1902):27-34.

— —. "William Henry Channing." In *Heralds of a Liberal Faith*, edited by Samuel A. Eliot, 3:59-66. Boston: American Unitarian Association, 1910.

Hinsdale, B. A. "Notes on the History of Foreign Influence Upon Education in the United States." In *Annual Reports of the Department of the Interior for the Fiscal Year Ended June 30, 1898. Report of the Commissioner of Education*, 1:591-629. Washington, D.C.: Government Printing Office, 1899.

[Hoar, Elizabeth]. *Mrs. Samuel Ripley*. Philadelphia: J. B. Lippincott, 1877.

Hoar, George F. *Autobiography of Seventy Years*. 2 vols. New York: Scribners, 1903.

Hoeltje, Hubert H. *Sheltering Tree: A Story of the Friendship of Ralph Waldo Emerson and Amos Bronson Alcott*. Durham, N.C.: Duke University Press, 1943.

Holmes, Oliver Wendell. "Poetry; A Metrical Essay." In *Poems*, pp. 3-44. Boston: Otis, Broaders; New York: George Dearborn, 1836.

— —. *Ralph Waldo Emerson*. Boston: Houghton, Mifflin, 1884.

— —. "Terpsichore." *Graham's Magazine* 25 (January 1844):10-11.

[Hooper, Ellen Sturgis]. ["Poems" by Ellen Sturgis Hooper]. [Edited by Edward William Sturgis]. N. p.: n. p., [1872?].

Hounchell, Saul. "The Principal Literary Magazines of the Ohio Valley to 1840." Ph.D. dissertation, George Peabody College for Teachers, 1934.

Howard, Leon. *Victorian Knight-Errant: A Study of the Early Literary Career of James Russell Lowell*. Berkeley and Los Angeles, Calif.: University of California Press, 1952.

Howe, Julia Ward. *Reminiscences 1819-1899*. Boston: Houghton, Mifflin, 1899.

Howe, M. A. DeWolfe. *Memories of a Hostess: A Chronicle of Eminent Friendships Drawn Chiefly From the Diaries of Mrs. James T. Fields*. Boston: Atlantic Monthly Press, 1922.

Howe, Leonard & Co. *Catalogue of a Select Private Library. . . .* Boston: Alfred Mudge, 1846.

Hudson, Gertrude Reese, ed. *Browning to His American Friends: Letters Between the Brownings, the Storys and James Russell Lowell*. London: Bowes and Bowes, 1965.

Hudspeth, Robert N. *Ellery Channing*. New York: Twayne, 1973.

Hutchison, William R. *The Transcendentalist Ministers: Church Reform in the New England Renaissance*. New Haven, Conn.: Yale University Press, 1959.

"Introductory." *Western Messenger* 1 (June 1835):1-3.

James, Henry. *The Bostonians*. London: Macmillan, 1886.

— —. *The Letters of Henry James*. Edited by Percy Lubbock. 2 vols. New York: Scribners, 1920.

— —. *Notes of a Son and Brother*. New York: Scribners, 1914.

— —. *William Wetmore Story and His Friends*. 2 vols. Boston: Houghton, Mifflin, 1903.

Jones, Harry L. "The Very Madness: A New Manuscript." *CLA Journal* 10 (March 1967):196-200.

Jones, W. A. "Criticism in America." *United States Magazine, and Democratic Review* 15 (September 1844):241-49.

K[ennard]., J[ames]., Jr. "What is Transcendentalism? By a Thinking Man." *Knickerbocker* 23 (March 1844):205-11.

Kilgour, Raymond L. *Messrs. Roberts Brothers Publishers.* Ann Arbor, Mich.: University of Michigan Press, 1952.

[Kirby, Georgiana Bruce]. "Reminiscences of Brook Farm." *Old and New* 3 (April 1871): 425-38.

— —. *Years of Experience.* New York: Putnams, 1887.

Kunitz, Stanley J., and Haycraft, Howard, eds. *American Authors 1600-1900.* New York: H. W. Wilson, 1938.

Lane, Charles. "Being Good and Doing Good." *New Age, Concordium Gazette, and Temperance Advocate* 1 (1 August 1844):263.

— —. *The Law and Method in Spirit-Culture; an Interpretation of A. Bronson Alcott's Idea and Practice at the Masonic Temple, Boston.* Boston: James Munroe; London: J. Green, 1843.

— —. "Literature." *Union* 1 (1 November 1842):356-60.

— —. "On Sexual Communion." *New Age, Concordium Gazette, and Temperance Advocate* 1 (1 April 1844):201.

— —. "Practical Transcendentalism." *New Age, Concordium Gazette, and Temperance Advocate* 1 (1 July 1843):59.

— —. "Transatlantic Transcendentalism." *Union* 1 (1 August 1842):166-68.

"The Late Benjamin P. Hunt, of Philadelphia." *Twenty-Fifth Annual Report of the Trustees of the [Boston] Public Library,* pp. 119-23. Boston: n.p., 1877.

Lathrop, Rose Hawthorne. *Memories of Hawthorne.* Boston: Houghton, Mifflin, 1897.

Leland, Charles Godfrey. *Memoirs.* New York: D. Appleton, 1893.

Lesley, Susan I. *Recollections of My Mother: Mrs. Anne Jean Lyman. . . .* Boston: Houghton, Mifflin, 1899 [1875].

Lind, Sidney E. "Christopher Pearse Cranch's 'Gnosis': An Error in Title." *Modern Language Notes* 62 (November 1947):486-88.

"Literary Periodicals." *Boston Weekly Magazine* 3 (21 November 1840):78.

Long, O. W. *Frederic Henry Hedge: A Cosmopolitan Scholar.* Portland, Me.: Southworth-Anthoensen Press, 1940.

Longfellow, Fanny Appleton. *Mrs. Longfellow: Selected Letters and Journals of Fanny Appleton Longfellow (1817-1861).* Edited by Edward Wagenknecht. London: Peter Owen, 1959.

Longfellow, Henry Wadsworth. *The Letters of Henry Wadsworth Longfellow.* Edited by Andrew Hilen. 4 vols. to date. Cambridge, Mass.: Harvard University Press, 1966-.

Longfellow, Samuel. *Life of Henry Wadsworth Longfellow.* 2 vols. Boston: Ticknor, 1886.

Lowell, James Russell. *A Fable for Critics.* New York: G. P. Putnam, 1848.

— —. *Letters of James Russell Lowell.* Edited by Charles Eliot Norton. 2 vols. New York: Harpers, 1894.

— —. "Letters of James Russell Lowell, 1843-1854." *Bulletin of the New York Public Library* 4 (October 1900):339-45.

— —. *New Letters of James Russell Lowell.* Edited by M. A. DeWolfe Howe. New York: Harpers, 1932.

— —. [Review of H. W. Longfellow, *Poems on Slavery*]. *Pioneer* 1 (February 1843):92-93.

— —. [Review of H. D. Thoreau, *Letters to Various Persons*]. *North American Review* 101 (October 1865):597-608.

— —. "Some Letters of Walter Savage Landor." *Century Magazine* 35 (February 1888):511-21.

— —. "Studies for Two Heads." In *Poems, Second Series*, pp. 135-41. Cambridge, Mass.: George Nichols; New York: B. B. Mussey, 1848.

— —. *Uncollected Poems of James Russell Lowell*. Edited by Thelma M. Smith. Philadelphia: University of Pennsylvania Press, 1950.

— —. *A Year's Life*. Boston: Charles C. Little and James Brown, 1841.

McDonald, John Joseph. "Hawthorne at the Old Manse." Ph.D. dissertation, Princeton University, 1971.

McGill, Frederick T., Jr. *Channing of Concord: A Life of William Ellery Channing II*. New Brunswick, N.J.: Rutgers University Press, 1967.

[Magazine Literature]. *Newark Advertiser;* rpt., *Providence Daily Journal*, 29 October 1842, p. 2.

[Mann, Mary Peabody]. *Life of Horace Mann*. Boston: Walker, Fuller, 1865.

Marble, Annie Russell. "Margaret Fuller as Teacher." *Critic* 43 (October 1903):334-45.

Marshall, Helen E. "The Story of the Dial, 1840-1844." *New Mexico Quarterly* 1 (May 1931):147-65.

Marsh, James. *Coleridge's American Disciples: The Selected Correspondence of James Marsh*. Edited by John J. Duffy. Amherst, Mass.: University of Massachusetts Press, 1973.

Martineau, Harriet. *Society in America*. 2 vols. New York: Saunders and Otley, 1837.

Matthiessen, F. O. *The James Family*. New York: Alfred A. Knopf, 1947.

Maxfield-Miller, Elizabeth. "Elizabeth Hoar of Concord and Thoreau." *Thoreau Society Bulletin*, no. 106 (Winter 1969), pp. 1-3.

— —. "Emerson and Elizabeth of Concord." *Harvard Library Bulletin* 19 (July 1971):290-306.

Meltzer, Milton. *Tongue of Flame: The Life of Lydia Maria Child*. New York: Thomas Y. Crowell, 1965.

Melville, Herman. *Pierre*. Vol. 7 of *The Writings of Herman Melville*, edited by Harrison Hayford, Hershel Parker, and G. Thomas Tanselle, 5 vols. to date. Evanston, Ill.: Northwestern University Press, 1968-.

Miller, F. DeWolfe. *Christopher Pearse Cranch and His Caricatures of New England Transcendentalism*. Cambridge, Mass.: Harvard University Press, 1951.

— —. "Christopher Pearse Cranch: New England Transcendentalist." Ph.D. dissertation, University of Virginia, 1942.

Miller, Perry, ed. *The Transcendentalists: An Anthology*. Cambridge, Mass.: Harvard University Press, 1950.

Milne, Gordon. *George William Curtis & the Genteel Tradition*. Bloomington, Ind.: Indiana University Press, 1956.

"Monthly Record." *Western Messenger* 8 (October 1840):286-88.

Morley, John. "Emerson." In *Critical Miscellanies*, 1:293-347. London: Macmillan, 1886.

Morton, Doris. "Ralph Waldo Emerson and *The Dial*: A Study in Literary Criticism." *Emporia State Research Studies* 18 (December 1969):5-51.

Mott, Frank Luther. *A History of American Magazines 1741-1850*. Cambridge, Mass.: Harvard University Press, 1957 [1939].

Mueller, Roger Chester. "The Orient in American Transcendental Periodicals" (1835-1886)." Ph.D. dissertation, University of Minnesota, 1968.

Murdock, James. *Sketches of Modern Philosophy.* Hartford, Conn.: J. C. Wells, 1846.

Myerson, Joel. "An Annotated List of Contributions to the Boston *Dial.*" *Studies in Bibliography* 26 (1973):133-66.

——. "Bronson Alcott's 'Journal for 1836.' " In *Studies in the American Renaissance 1978.* Edited by Joel Myerson, pp. 17-104. Boston: Twayne, 1978.

——. "Bronson Alcott's 'Scripture for 1840.' " *ESQ: A Journal of the American Renaissance* 20 (IV Quarter 1974):236-59.

——. "A Calendar of Transcendental Club Meetings." *American Literature* 44 (May 1972):197-207.

——. "Caroline Dall's Reminiscences of Margaret Fuller." *Harvard Library Bulletin* 22 (October 1974):414-28.

——. "The Contemporary Reception of the Boston *Dial.*" *Resources for American Literary Study* 3 (Autumn 1973):203-20.

——. "Convers Francis and Emerson." *American Literature* 50 (March 1978):17-36.

——. "The Death of Charles Stearns Wheeler." *Concord Saunterer* 7 (September 1971):6-7.

——. "Eight Lowell Letters from Concord in 1838." *Illinois Quarterly* 38 (Winter 1975):20-42.

——. "Frederic Henry Hedge and the Failure of Transcendentalism." *Harvard Library Bulletin* 23 (October 1975):396-410.

——. "'In the Transcendental Emporium': Bronson Alcott's 'Orphic Sayings' in the *Dial.*" *English Language Notes* 10 (September 1972):31-38.

——. "Lowell on Emerson: A New Letter from Concord in 1838." *New England Quarterly* 44 (December 1971): 649-52.

——. "Margaret Fuller's 1842 Journal: At Concord with the Emersons." *Harvard Library Bulletin* 21 (July 1973):320-40.

——. "Sarah Clarke's Reminiscences of the Peabodys and Hawthorne." In *Nathaniel Hawthorne Journal 1973,* edited by C. E. frazer Clark, Jr., pp. 130-33. Englewood, Colo.: Microcard Editions, 1973.

——. "Thoreau and the *Dial*: A Survey of the Contemporary Press." *Thoreau Journal Quarterly* 3 (January 1973):4-7.

——. "Transcendentalism and Unitarianism in 1840: A New Letter by C. P. Cranch." *CLA Journal* 16 (March 1973):366-68.

——. "'A True & High Minded Person': Transcendentalist Sarah Clarke." *Southwest Review* 59 (Spring 1974): 163-72.

——. "Two Unpublished Reminiscences of Brook Farm." *New England Quarterly* 48 (June 1975):253-60.

——. "A Union List of the *Dial* and Some Information About Its Sales." *Papers of the Bibliographical Society of America* 67 (III Quarter 1973):322-28.

Newcomb, Charles King. *The Journals of Charles King Newcomb.* Edited by Judith Kennedy Johnson. Providence, R.I.: Brown University Press, 1946.

[Newell, D.]. "The Influence of Light Literature Upon the Family Circle." *Christian Family Magazine* 2 (January 1843):105-12.

Norton, Charles Eliot. *Letters of Charles Eliot Norton.* Edited by Sara Norton and M. A. DeWolfe Howe. 2 vols. Boston: Houghton Mifflin, 1913.

[Notice of Emerson's writings]. *New-York Weekly Tribune*, 2 April 1842, p. 3.

[Notice of the *Present*]. *Ladies' Companion* 20 (November 1843):52.

"Origin of Transcendentalism." *Salem Observer*, 17 April 1841.

Ossoli, Sarah Margaret (Fuller). *See* Fuller, Margaret.

"Our New Volume," *Western Messenger* 3 (June 1837):853-54.

Parke-Bernet Galleries. *The Library of Charles E. Feinberg*. 3 parts. New York: Parke-Bernet Galleries, 1968.

Parker, Theodore. *Experience as a Minister*. Boston: Rufus Leighton, 1859.

Peabody, Elizabeth Palmer. "Emerson as Preacher." In *The Genius and Character of Emerson*, edited by F. B. Sanborn, pp. 146-72. Boston: James R. Osgood, 1885.

— —. "Mr. Parker and the Unitarians." *Boston Quarterly Review* 5 (April 1842):198-220.

— —. *Reminiscences of Rev. Wm. Ellery Channing, D.D.* Boston: Roberts, 1880.

[Pennell, J. C.]. *Footprints: or, Fugitive Poems*. Philadelphia: John Penington, 1843.

Perkins, Norman C. "The Original 'Dial.'" *Dial* [Chicago] 1 (May 1880):9-11.

Perry, Bliss. *Park-Street Papers*. Boston: Houghton Mifflin, 1908.

Perry, Ralph Barton. *The Thought and Character of William James*. 2 vols. Boston: Little, Brown, 1935.

"Philosophy Run Mad." *New York Evening Post*, 11 January 1842, p. 2.

"A Plain Discussion with a Transcendentalist." *New Englander* 1 (October 1843):502-16.

"Plans and Prospects." *Western Messenger* 8 (June 1840):91-92.

Pochmann, Henry A. *German Culture in America: Philosphical and Literary Influences 1600-1900*. Madison, Wis.: University of Wisconsin Press, 1957.

Poe, Edgar Allan. "How to Write a Blackwood Article." *Broadway Journal* 2 (12 July 1845):1-4.

— —. *The Letters of Edgar Allan Poe*. Edited by John Ward Ostrom. 2 vols. Cambridge, Mass.: Harvard University Press, 1948.

— —. "The Literati of New York City. — No. III." *Godey's Lady's Book* 33 (July 1846):13-19.

— —. "Never Bet Your Head. A Moral Tale." *Graham's Magazine* 19 (September 1841):124-27.

— —. "Our Amateur Poets. No. III. — William Ellery Channing." *Graham's Magazine* 23 (August 1843):113-17.

— —. "Some Words with a Mummy." *American Whig Review* 1 (April 1845):363-70.

— —. "Tale-Writing — Nathaniel Hawthorne." *Godey's Lady's Book* 35 (November 1847):252-26.

"Poetry." *Boston Recorder*, 2 April 1841, p. 56.

Pollin, Burton R. "Emerson's Annotations in the British Museum Copy of the *Dial*." *Studies in Bibliography* 24 (1971):187-95.

Pommer, Henry F. *Emerson's First Marriage*. Carbondale, Ill.: Southern Illinois University Press, 1967.

Pope, Charles Henry, and Hooper, Thomas, comps. *Hooper Genealogy*. Boston: Charles H. Pope, 1908.

[Popular Literature]. *Literary Messenger* 1 (15 October 1841):62.

Porte, Joel. *Emerson and Thoreau: Transcendentalists in Conflict*. Middletown, Conn.: Wesleyan University Press, 1966.

Power, Edward John. "Orestes A. Brownson." *Records of the American Catholic Historical Society of Philadelphia* 62 (June 1951):72-94.

Presby, Joseph Waite. *William Presbrey of London, England, and Taunton, Mass., and His Descendants 1690-1918*. Rutland, Vt.: Tuttle, 1918.

"Prologomena." *New Englander* 1 (January 1843):4-8.

Raymond, Henrietta Dana. "Sophia Willard Dana Ripley, Co-Founder of Brook Farm." M. A. thesis, Columbia University, 1949.

Reid, T. Wemyss. *Life of the Right Honourable William Edward Forster*. 2 vols. London: Chapman and Hall, 1888.

"A Reprint of 'The Dial.'" *Journal of Speculative Philosophy* 16 (July 1882):329-31.

[Review of Francis Bowen, *Critical Essays*]. *Christian Examiner* 32 (July 1842):398.

[Review of C. P. Cranch, *Poems*]. *Southern Quarterly Review* 6 (July 1844):259-61.

[Review of R. W. Griswold, *Readings in American Poetry*]. *Pathfinder* 1 (29 April 1843):149.

[Review of *Lowell Offering*]. *Ladies' Repository* 4 (September 1844):286.

[Review of *North American Review*]. *New Orleans Daily Picayune*, 4 July 1840, p. 2.

[Review of *North American Review*]. *Knickerbocker* 15 (January 1840):81.

[Review of *The Prometheus and Agamemnon of Aeschylus*, trans. Henry William Herbert]. *Boston Semi-Weekly Advertiser*, 29 September 1849, p. 1.

Ricketson, Anna, and Ricketson, Walton, eds. *Daniel Ricketson and His Friends*. Boston: Houghton, Mifflin, 1902.

Riggs, Lisette. "George and Sophia Ripley." Ph.D. dissertation, University of Maryland, 1942.

Ripley, George. *The Claims of the Age on the Work of the Evangelist*. Boston: Weeks, Jordan, 1840.

— —. [Review of *Massachusetts Quarterly Review*]. *Harbinger* 7 (9 September 1848):150.

— — and Bradford, George P. "Philosophic Thought in Boston." In *The Memorial History of Boston*, edited by Justin Winsor, 4:295-330. Boston: James R. Osgood, 1882.

Roberts, Josephine E. "Elizabeth Peabody and the Temple School." *New England Quarterly* 15 (September 1942):497-508.

— —. "A New England Family: Elizabeth Palmer Peabody, 1808-1894; Mary Tyler Peabody (Mrs. Horace Mann), 1806-1887; Sophia Amelia Peabody (Mrs. Nathaniel Hawthorne), 1809-1871." Ph.D. dissertation, Western Reserve University, 1937.

Rocker, Rudolph. *Pioneers of American Freedom*. Los Angeles, Calif.: Rocker Publication Committee, 1949.

[Rogers, Nathaniel P.]. "Notice, from the Dial." *Herald of Freedom*, 10 May 1844, p. 46.

Rosa, Alfred Felix. "A Study of Transcendentalism in Salem with Special Reference to Nathaniel Hawthorne." Ph.D. dissertation, University of Massachusetts, 1971.

Rosebault, Charles S. *When Dana was "The Sun."* New York: Robert M. McBride, 1931.

Rosenthal, Bernard. "*The Dial*, Transcendentalism, and Margaret Fuller." *English Language Notes* 8 (September 1970):28-36.

Rusk, Ralph L. *The Life of Ralph Waldo Emerson*. New York: Scribners, 1949.

Salyer, Sandford. *Marmee: The Mother of Little Women*. Norman, Okla.: Univeristy of Oklahoma Press, 1949.

Sampson, Edward C. "Three Unpublished Letters by Hawthorne to Epes Sargent." *American Literature* 34 (March 1962):102-5.

Sanborn, F. B. "Biographical Introduction." In William Ellery Channing, *Poems of Sixty-Five Years*, pp. xiii-xlix. Philadelphia and Concord, Mass.: James H. Bentley, 1902.

— —. "A Concord Note-Book: Ellery Channing and his Table-Talk, Second Paper." *Critic* 47 (August 1905):121-28.

— —. "Cooke's Book on Emerson's Dial." *Springfield Sunday Republican*, 15 February 1903, p. 19.

— —. "The Dial: A Chapter for the Unwritten History of American Literature." *Harvard Magazine* 1 (April 1855):153-59.

— —. "The Friendships of Hawthorne." In *The Hawthorne Centenary Celebration at the Wayside*, [edited by Thomas Wentworth Higginson], pp. 158-98. Boston: Houghton, Mifflin, 1905.

— —. *Henry D. Thoreau*. Boston: Houghton, Mifflin, 1882.

— —. *The Life of Henry David Thoreau*. Boston: Houghton, Mifflin, 1917.

— —. "Manuscript Diary of Franklin B. Sanborn." Edited by Kenneth Walter Cameron. In *Transcendental Climate*, 1:205-43. Hartford, Conn.: Transcendental Books, 1963.

— —. *The Personality of Emerson*. Boston: Charles E. Goodspeed, 1903.

— —. *The Personality of Thoreau*. Boston: Charles E. Goodspeed, 1901.

— —. *Recollections of Seventy Years*. ° vols. Boston: Richard G. Badger, 1909.

— —. "Thoreau, Newcomb, Brook Farm." *Springfield Daily Republican*. 2 December 1896, p. 5.

— — and Harris, William T. *Bronson Alcott: His Life and Philosophy*. 2 vols. Boston: Roberts, 1893.

[Satire on Emerson and Transcendentalism]. *Boston Daily Evening Transcript*, 13 April 1843, p. 2.

Schlesinger, Arthur M., Jr. *Orestes A. Brownson: A Pilgrim's Progress*. Boston: Little, Brown, 1939.

Scott, Leonora Cranch. *The Life and Letters of Christopher Pearse Cranch*. Boston: Houghton Mifflin, 1917.

Scudder, Horace Elisha. *James Russell Lowell*. 2 vols. Boston: Houghton, Mifflin, 1901.

Sears, Clara Endicott. *Bronson Alcott's Fruitlands*. Boston: Houghton Mifflin, 1915.

Sedgwick, Ora Gannett. "A Girl of Sixteen at Brook Farm." *Atlantic Monthly* 85 (March 1900):394-404.

A Select Assembly of Notable Books and Manuscripts from the Allison-Shelley Collection of Anglica Americana Germanica. University Park, Pa.: Pennsylvania State University Library, 1972.

Sheldon, George. "History of Deerfield—No. 138." *Greenfield* [*Mass.*] *Gazette and Courier*, 1885; collected under the binder's title, *History of Deerfield*, The Newberry Library, F.844205.8.

Shepard, Odell. *Pedlar's Progress: The Life of Bronson Alcott*. Boston: Little, Brown, 1937.

Slater, Joseph. "George Ripley and Thomas Carlyle." *PMLA* 67 (June 1952):341-49.

Snodgrass, J. E. "Transcendentalism. A Miniature Essay." *Magnolia* 4 (April 1842):214-15.

Stearns, Bertha Monica. "Philadelphia Magazines for Ladies: 1830-1860." *Pennsylvania Magazine of History and Biography* 69 (July 1945):207-19.

Sterling, John. *A Correspondence Between John Sterling and Ralph Waldo Emerson*. Edited by Edward Waldo Emerson. Boston: Houghton, Mifflin, 1897.

Stern, Madeleine B. "Four Letters from George Keats." *PMLA* 56 (March 1941):207-18.

— —. *The Life of Margaret Fuller*. New York: E. P. Dutton, 1942.

— —. "Margaret Fuller and *The Dial*." *South Atlantic Quarterly* 40 (January 1941):11-21.

Stoller, Leo. "Christopher A. Greene: Rhode Island Transcendentalist." *Rhode Island History* 22 (October 1963):97-116.

S[tory]., W[illiam]. W[etmore]. [Review of J. R. Lowell, *A Year's Life*]. *Boston Daily Advertiser*, 1 January 1844, p. 2.

Straker, Robert L. "A Gloss Upon Glosses: Critical Comments on Two Books by Louise Hall Tharp, *The Peabody Sisters of Salem; Until Victory: Horace Mann and Mary Peabody*." Typescript, copies at Antioch College and the New York Public Library.

Strauch, Carl F. "Hatred's Swift Repulsions: Emerson, Margaret Fuller, and Others." *Studies in Romanticism* 7 (Winter 1968):65-103.

Strong, George Templeton. *The Diary of George Templeton Strong*. Edited by Allan Nevins and Milton Halsey Thomas. 4 vols. New York: Macmillan, 1952.

Sturgis, Roger Faxton, ed. *Edward Sturgis of Yarmouth, Massachusetts 1613-1695 and his Descendants*. Boston: Stanhope Press, 1914.

Swift, Lindsay. *Brook Farm: Its Members, Scholars, and Visitors*. New York: Macmillan, 1900.

Tarr, Rodger L. "Emerson's Transcendentalism in L. M. Child's Letter to Carlyle." *Emerson Society Quarterly*, no. 58 (I Quarter 1970), pp. 112-15.

Tharp, Louise Hall. *The Peabody Sisters of Salem*. Boston: Little, Brown, 1950.

Thomas, John Wesley. *James Freeman Clarke: Apostle of German Culture to America*. Boston: John W. Luce, 1949.

Thomas, Moses George. *A Rejected Article, in Reply to Parker's Review of "Hennell on the Origin of Christianity." Offered First to the Dial; then to the Christian Examiner*. Boston: Benjamin H. Greene, 1844.

Thoreau, Henry David. *Collected Poems of Henry Thoreau*. Edited by Carl Bode. Enlg. ed. Baltimore, Md.: The Johns Hopkins Press, 1964.

— —. *The Correspondence of Henry David Thoreau*. Edited by Walter Harding and Carl Bode. New York: New York University Press, 1958.

— —. *Early Essays and Miscellanies*. Edited by Joseph J. Moldenhauer and Edwin Moser. *The Writings of Henry D. Thoreau*, 5 vols. to date. Princeton, N.J.: Princeton University Press, 1975.

— —. *Familiar Letters of Henry David Thoreau*. Edited by F. B. Sanborn. Boston: Houghton, Mifflin, 1894.

— —. *Journal*. Edited by Bradford Torrey and Francis H. Allen. Vols. 7-20 of *The Writing of Henry David Thoreau*, The Walden Eidtion, 20 vols. Boston: Houghton Mifflin, 1906.

— —. *The Service*. Edited by F. B. Sanborn. Boston: Charles E. Goodspeed, 19012.

— —. *Walden*. Edited by J. Lyndon Shanley. *The Writings of Henry D. Thoreau*.

Princeton, N.J.: Princeton University Press, 1971.

Ticknor, Caroline. *Poe's Helen*. New York: Scribners, 1916.

Tiffany, Nina Moore, and Tiffany, Francis. *Harm Jan Huidekoper*. Cambridge, Mass.: Riverside Press, 1904.

"Transcendentalism." *Boston Daily Bee*, 11 April 1843, p. 2.

"Transcendentalism." *Boston Daily Times*, 21 January 1841, p. 2.

"Transcendentalism." *Christian Advocate and Journal* 16 (10 November 1841):52.

[Transcendentalism]. *Presbyterian*; rpt., *Boston Recorder*, 6 August 1841, p. 127.

Tuckerman, Bayard. *Notes on the Tuckerman Family of Massachusetts and Some Allied Families*. Boston: Privately printed [Riverside Press], 1914.

Tuomi, Martha Ilona. "Dr. Frederic Henry Hedge: His Life and Works to the End of His Bangor Pastorate." M. A. thesis, University of Maine, 1935.

V., W. "Opening of the Green-St. School." *Providence Daily Journal*, 17 June 1837, p. 2.

Vance, William Silas. "Carlyle and the American Transcendentalists." Ph.D. dissertation, University of Chicago, 1941.

Venable, W. H. *Beginnings of Literary Culture in the Ohio Valley*. Cincinnati, Ohio: Robert Clarke, 1891.

Vernon, Hope Jillson. *The Poems of Maria Lowell with Unpublished Letters and a Biography*. Providence, R.I.: Brown University Press, 1936.

Vincent, Howard. *The Trying-Out of "Moby-Dick."* Boston: Houghton Mifflin, 1949.

Vogel, Stanley M. *German Literary Influences on the American Transcendentalists*. New Haven, Conn.: Yale University Press, 1955.

W., M. F. "Popular Literature of the Day." *Evergreen* 1 (January 1844):17-18.

Wade, Mason. *Margaret Fuller: Whetstone of Genius*. New York: Viking, 1940.

Ward, Samuel Gray. *Ward Family Papers*. [Boston: Merrymount Press], 1900.

Warders, Donald F. "'The Progress of the Hour and the Day': A Critical Study of the *Dial*." Ph.D. dissertation, University of Kansas, 1973.

Ware, Ethel K. "Lydia Maria Child and Anti-Slavery." *Boston Public Library Quarterly* 3 (October 1951):251-275.

Warfel, Harry R. "Margaret Fuller and Ralph Waldo Emerson." *PMLA* 50 (June 1935):576-94.

Webster, Frank Martindale. "Transcendental Points of View: A Survey of the Criticism of Music, Art, and Letters in 'The Dial,' 1840-1844." *Washington University Studies* 7 (April 1920):187-203.

Weiss, John. *Discourse Occasioned by the Death of Convers Francis*. Cambridge, Mass.: Privately printed, 1863.

— —. *Life and Correspondence of Theodore Parker*. 2 vols. New York: D. Appleton, 1864.

Wells, Ronald Vale. *Three Christian Transcendentalists: James Marsh, Caleb Sprague Henry, Frederic Henry Hedge*. New York: Columbia University Press, 1943.

Wendt, Charles W. "Memoir." In Charles T. Brooks, *Poems, Original and Translated*, ed. W. P. Andrews, pp. 3-114. Boston: Roberts, 1885.

"Western Poetry. No. I." *Western Messenger* 1 (June 1835):60-68.

Wheeler, Charles Stearns. "Letters from Germany." *Pioneer* 1 (March 1843):143-44.

— —. [Review of J. R. Lowell, *A Year's Life*]. *Christian Examiner* 30 (March 1841):131-34.

[Whitaker, Daniel K.]. "Transcendentalism." *Southern Quarterly Review* 2 (October 1842):437-71.

White, William. "Emerson as Editor: A Letter to Benjamin F. Presbury." *American Notes & Queries* 12 (September 1973):59-61.

— —. "Three Unpublished Thoreau Letters." *New England Quarterly* 33 (September 1960):372-74.

— —. "Two Unpublished Emerson Letters." *American Literature* 31 (November 1959):334-36.

Whiting, Lilian. *Boston Days*. Boston: Little, Brown, 1911.

Whiting, Nathaniel. [Letter to the editors], [Providence] *Plain Speaker* 1 (April 1841):11.

Wilbur, Earl Morse. *A Historical Sketch of the Independent Congregational Church, Meadville, Pennsylvania 1825-1900*. Meadville, Pa.: n. p., 1902.

Wilde, Oscar. "Mr. Pater's Last Volume." *Speaker* 1 (22 March 1890):319-20.

Williams, Henry. *Memorials of the Class of 1837 of Harvard University*. Boston: Geo. H. Ellis, 1887.

Williams, Stanley T. "Unpublished Letters of Emerson." *Journal of English and Germanic Philology* 26 (October 1927):475-84.

Willis, Frederick L. H. *Alcott Memoirs*. Boston: Richard G. Badger, 1915.

Wilson, Carroll A. *Thirteen Author Collections of the Nineteenth Century*. . . . Edited by Jean C. S. Wilson and David A. Randall. 2 vols. New York: Scribner's, 1950.

Wilson, James Grant, and Fiske, John, eds. *Appleton's Cyclopædia of American Biography*. 6 vols. New York: D. Appleton, 1888-89.

Wilson, James Harrison. *The Life of Charles A. Dana*. New York: Harpers, 1907.

Wordsworth, William. *Wordsworth & Reed: The Poet's Correspondence with His American Editor: 1836-1850*. Edited by Leslie Nathan Broughton. Ithaca, N.Y.: Cornell University Press, 1933.

Index